Teaching Writing

Balancing Process and Product

Teaching Writing

Balancing Process and Product

FOURTH EDITION

Gail E. Tompkins

California State University, Fresno

PEARSON

Merrill
Prentice Hall

Upper Saddle River, New Jersey
Columbus, Ohio

Library of Congress Cataloging in Publication Data

Tompkins, Gail E.

    Teaching writing : balancing process and product / Gail E. Tompkins.—4th ed.
      p. cm.
    Includes bibliographical references and index.
    ISBN 0-13-112187-1
      1. English language—Composition and exercises—Study and teaching (Elementary) 2.
    Creative writing (Elementary education) I. Title.

LB1576.T66 2004
372.62'3—dc21

2002044896

Vice President and Executive Publisher: Jeffery W. Johnston
Senior Editor: Linda Ashe Montgomery
Editorial Assistant: Laura Weaver
Development Editor: Hope Madden
Production Editor: Mary M. Irvin
Production Coordination: Carlisle Publishers Services
Design Coordinator: Diane C. Lorenzo
Cover Designer: Ali Mohrman
Cover image: Mary O'Keefe Young
Production Manager: Pamela D. Bennett
Director of Marketing: Ann Castel Davis
Marketing Manager: Darcy Betts Prybella
Marketing Coordinator: Tyra Poole

This book was set in Korinna by Carlisle Communications, Ltd. It was printed and bound by R. R. Donnelley & Sons Company. The cover was printed by The Lehigh Press.

Pearson Education Ltd.
Pearson Education Singapore Pte. Ltd.
Pearson Education Canada, Ltd.
Pearson Education—Japan

Pearson Education Australia Pty. Limited
Pearson Education North Asia Ltd.
Pearson Educación de Mexico, S.A. de C.V.
Pearson Education Malaysia Pte. Ltd.

10 9 8 7 6 5 4 3
ISBN: 0-13-112187-1

To the teacher consultants in the San Joaquin Valley Writing Project.

I've learned from each of you, and I treasure your friendship.

Preface

Teaching Writing: Balancing Process and Product continues to be the definitive book on how to teach writing, as it is the only text with comprehensive coverage of both *process and product.* This is because I understand that teachers in kindergarten through eighth grade must balance the attention paid to both the process that children use as they write and the quality of their compositions.

Overview of the Fourth Edition

My new edition focuses on writing process, collaborative learning, reading and writing connections, writing genres, and writing across the curriculum. The text provides practical strategies for teaching and assessing writing—with step-by-step directions—presenting more than 100 student samples to illustrate the teaching strategies.

This edition is divided into two parts. The first part, "Process and Product," focuses on the writing process that children use as they write and on ways to assess children's writing.

Readers will learn about the stages in the writing process—involving prewriting, drafting, revising, editing, and publishing—and how to teach elementary students to use these stages as a recursive cycle when they write during writing workshop, literature focus units, and thematic units. Readers will also learn how to teach students to develop ideas, organize their writing, choose vocabulary, apply stylistic devices, and correct mechanical errors in order to create high-quality compositions.

The second part, "Writing Genres," includes chapters on eight writing forms: journal writing, letter writing, descriptive writing, biographical writing, expository writing, narrative writing, poetic writing, and persuasive writing. At the beginning of each chapter, I delineate an instructional sequence with goals and activities for teaching each genre in kindergarten through eighth grade.

I emphasize five levels of composition instruction that vary according to how much scaffolding the teacher provides: modeled writing, shared writing, interactive writing, guided writing, and independent writing. Through this sequence, teachers vary the amount of support they provide student writers, and students increasingly assume more responsibility for their own writing.

Special Features of the Fourth Edition

These features increase the effectiveness of this text and provide support for teachers as they teach writing, encourage students to assume more responsibility for using the writing process, and assess the quality of students' finished products.

NEW! *Teaching Notes: Supporting Struggling Writers* are regular features that help readers implement chapter content specifically for struggling students.

NEW! *Teaching Notes: Assisting English Language Learners* point out the best ways for teachers to support these student writers.

- *Vignettes* open every chapter to illustrate how real teachers have used the chapter content in their elementary classrooms.
- *Minilessons* in every chapter model skills and strategies instruction.

NEW! *Instructional Previews* help ground readers in chapter content, best addressing the question of what to teach and when.

- *Step-by-Step* features clearly illustrate instructional procedures.
- *Rubrics* throughout chapters address and clarify assessment issues.

NEW! *A Descriptive Writing chapter* addresses descriptive writing as a specific genre as well as an essential component of narrative writing, poetic writing, and other genres.

Acknowledgments

My heartfelt thanks go to the many people who have encouraged me and provided invaluable assistance as I wrote the first edition of *Teaching Writing: Balancing Process and Product* and revised it for subsequent editions. This text is a reflection of what the teachers and children with whom I have worked in California, Oklahoma, and across the United States have taught me. It is testimony to their excellence. The teachers featured in the vignettes at the beginning of each chapter deserve special recognition:

Chapter 1: Judy Reeves, Western Hills Elementary School
Chapter 2: Susan Zumwalt, Jackson Elementary School
Chapter 3: Eileen Boland, Tenaya Middle School
Chapter 4: Annette Jacks, Blanchard Elementary School
Chapter 5: Debbie Meyers, Cyril Elementary School
Chapter 6: Lynnda Wheatley, Briarwood Elementary School
Chapter 7: Whitney Donnelly, Pleasant Valley School
Chapter 8: Carol Ochs, Jackson Elementary School
Chapter 9: Betty Jordan, Western Hills Elementary School

Chapter 10: Tom Garcia, Washington Elementary School
Chapter 11: Deanie Dillen, Putnam City Elementary School
Chapter 12: Kimberly Clark, Aynesworth Elementary School
Chapter 13: Shirley Carson, Wayne Elementary School

Thank you all for welcoming me into your classrooms and permitting me to share stories of your teaching expertise.

I want to express my appreciation to the children whose writing samples appear in this text and to the teachers, administrators, and parents who shared writing samples with me: Kathy Bending, Highland Elementary School, Downers Grove, IL; Linda Besett, Sulphur Elementary School, Sulphur, OK; Gracie Branch, Eisenhower Elementary School, Norman, OK; Juli Carson, Jefferson Elementary School, Norman, OK; Pam Cottom and Jean Griffith, James Griffith Intermediate School, Choctaw, OK; Parthy Ford, Whittier Elementary School, Lawton, OK; Debbie Frankenberg, Purcell, OK; Chuckie Garner, Kennedy Elementary School, Norma, OK; Peggy Givens, Watonga Middle School, Watonga, OK; Teri Gray, James Griffith Intermediate School, Choctaw, OK; Debbie Hamilton, Irving Middle School, Norman, OK; Ernestine Hightower, Whittier Elementary School, Lawton, OK; Merry Kelly, Thomas Oleata School, Atwater, CA; Helen Lawson, Deer Creek School, Oklahoma City, OK; Diane Lewis, Irving Middle School, Norman, OK; Mark Mattingly, Central Junior High School, Lawton, OK; Tissie McClure, Nicoma Park Intermediate School, Nicoma Park, OK; Gina McCook, Whittier Middle School, Norman, OK; Joyce Mucher, Penryn Elementary School, Penryn, CA; Teresa Ossenkop, Eisenhower Elementary School, Norman, OK; Sandra Pabst, Monroe Elementary School, Norman, OK; Alice Rakitan, Highland Elementary School, Downers Grove, IL; Jelta Reneau, Lincoln Elementary School, Norman, OK; Becky Selle, Bethel School, Shawnee, OK; Linda Shanahan, Nicoma Park Intermediate School, Nicoma Park, OK; Jo Ann Steffen, Nicoma Park Junior High School, Nicoma Park, OK; Cecilia Uyeda, Eaton Elementary School, Fresno, CA; Gail Warmath, Longfellow Middle School, Norman, OK; Vera Willey, Lincoln Elementary School, Norman, OK.

I want to thank the reviewers of my manuscript for their comments and insights: Debbie East, Indiana University; Betty Goerss, Indiana University East; and Harold Nelson, Minot State University.

I want to express my sincere appreciation to my editors at Merrill. I offer very special thanks to my editors, Linda Montgomery and Hope Madden, for their creative inspiration and nurturing encouragement through this revision of *Teaching Writing*. Thanks, also, to Jeff Johnston, who originally provided the opportunity for me to pursue this project. I appreciate their continuing support of my work.

I also want to thank my production team. Melissa Gruzs has expertly put my manuscript into final form, and I am very grateful for her careful attention to detail. And thanks to Mary Irvin, my production editor, who successfully moved my manuscript through the maze of production details.

Gail E. Tompkins

Contents

Special Features Table of Contents

In addition to the featured Teaching Notes for English Language Learners and Struggling Readers, the following special features appear in this text.

Step by Step

Minilessons

About the Author

Gail E. Tompkins is a Professor at California State University, Fresno, in the Department of Literacy and Early Education, where she teaches courses in reading, language arts, and writing for preservice teachers and students in the reading/language arts master's degree program. She directs the San Joaquin Valley Writing Project and works regularly with teachers, both by teaching model lessons in classrooms and by leading staff development programs. Recently Dr. Tompkins was inducted into the California Reading Association's Reading Hall of Fame in recognition of her publications and other accomplishments in the field of reading. She has also been awarded the prestigious Provost's Award for Excellence in Teaching at California State University, Fresno.

Previously, Dr. Tompkins taught at Miami University in Ohio and at the University of Oklahoma in Norman where she received the prestigious Regents' Award for Superior Teaching. She was also an elementary teacher in Virginia for eight years.

Dr. Tompkins is the author of many books published by Merrill/Prentice Hall, among them: *Literacy for the 21st Century: A Balanced Approach,* 3rd ed. (2003), *50 Literacy Strategies* (2004), and *Language Arts: Content and Teaching Strategies,* 5th ed. (2002). She has written numerous articles related to reading and language arts that have appeared in *The Reading Teacher, Language Arts,* and other professional journals.

Educator Learning Center:
An Invaluable Online Resource

Merrill Education and the Association for Supervision and Curriculum Development (ASCD) invite you to take advantage of a new online resource, one that provides access to the top research and proven strategies associated with ASCD and Merrill—the Educator Learning Center. At **www.EducatorLearningCenter.com** you will find resources that will enhance your students' understanding of course topics and of current educational issues, in addition to being invaluable for further research.

How the Educator Learning Center will help your students become better teachers

With the combined resources of Merrill Education and ASCD, you and your students will find a wealth of tools and materials to better prepare them for the classroom.

Research

- More than 600 articles from the ASCD journal *Educational Leadership* discuss everyday issues faced by practicing teachers.
- A direct link on the site to Research Navigator™ gives students access to many of the leading education journals, as well as extensive content detailing the research process.
- Excerpts from Merrill Education texts give your students insights on important topics of instructional methods, diverse populations, assessment, classroom management, technology, and refining classroom practice.

Classroom Practice

- Hundreds of lesson plans and teaching strategies are categorized by content area and age range.
- Case studies and classroom video footage provide virtual field experience for student reflection.
- Computer simulations and other electronic tools keep your students abreast of today's classrooms and current technologies.

Look into the value of Educator Learning Center yourself

Preview the value of this educational environment by visiting **www.EducatorLearningCenter.com** and clicking on "Demo." For a free 4-month subscription to the Educator Learning Center in conjunction with this text, simply contact your Merrill/Prentice Hall sales representative.

Teaching Writing

Balancing Process and Product

Part One
PROCESS and PRODUCT

Both the process and the product are essential components in writing instruction.

The writing process is a multistep process based on how real writers write. This process is the foundation for teaching children to write. The product is the writing that children create. Their writing can take many forms or genres, ranging from stories and poems to letters and reports. Writing instruction also focuses on the conventions of written language that children learn to control in their writing, including paragraphing, spelling, and using capital letters and punctuation marks.

CHAPTER 1
Teaching Children to Write

Preview

 The writing process approach to writing instruction is based on how real writers write.

 The five stages in the writing process are prewriting, drafting, revising, editing, and publishing.

 Teachers support and scaffold children as they learn to write, gradually giving students more and more responsibility.

The five levels of support are modeled writing, shared writing, interactive writing, guided writing, and independent writing.

Writing About Weather

Mrs. Reeves's multiage primary class is learning about weather, and they use writing as a tool for learning. They begin the unit by making a K-W-L chart (Ogle, 1986). Mrs. Reeves divides the chart into three columns: "K: What We Know," "W: What We Wonder," and "L: What We Learned." Children begin by brainstorming things they already know about weather, and Mrs. Reeves writes them in the *K* column. The list includes "Weather is different in summer and winter," "Lightning is very dangerous," "You tell the temperature on a thermometer," and "Snow is frozen rain." Then a child asks, "How does it rain?" and Mrs. Reeves writes the question in the *W* column. Other questions about tornadoes and different types of clouds are asked, and she adds them to the *W* column. The discussion continues, and other information and questions are added to the *K* and *W* columns. During the unit, children continue to add questions to the *W* column, and as they learn more about weather, they write what they are learning in the *L* column to complete the chart.

Mrs. Reeves also talks with students about the kinds of activities they might pursue during the unit. The children want to keep daily weather calendars, interview a television weather forecaster, do weather experiments, and write an ABC book on weather, as they did on plants earlier in the school year. They also want to keep learning logs, read weather books, make posters about weather, and do self-selected projects. Writing will be an important tool in these activities. Mrs. Reeves uses the children's ideas together with the standards specified by her school district to plan the unit.

Mrs. Reeves prepares a large pocket chart for the "word wall"; children will write interesting and unfamiliar words about weather on cards and display them on the word wall during the unit. As they write and work on projects, children refer to the word wall. They suggest words, including *tornado, thermometer, hurricane, freezing,* and *thunderstorm,* to be added to the word wall. By the end of the 4-week unit, 50 or more words will have been collected on the word wall.

An assortment of weather books is displayed on a special rack in the classroom library. Mrs. Reeves gives a book talk about each, briefly mentioning something of interest about the book. Among the books she introduces are *Cloudy With a Chance of Meatballs* (Barrett, 1978), *The Cloud Book* (de Paola, 1975), *Snowballs* (Ehlert, 1995),

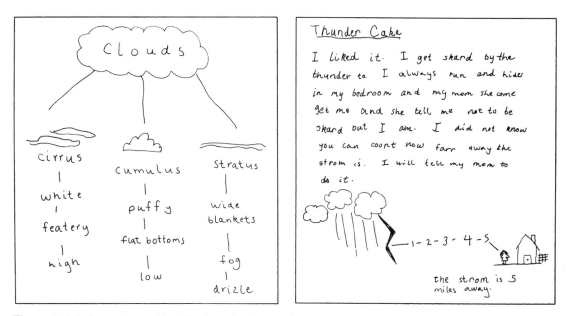

Figure 1–1 Independent writing: Two learning log entries

Weather Forecasting (Gibbons, 1987), and *Weather Report* (Yolen, 1993), a collection of poems. Children will read one book together as a class and read other books during reading workshop (independent reading of self-selected books).

Students write about what they read in learning logs. At the beginning of the theme, they make their own logs by compiling 20 sheets of notebook paper and construction paper covers, punching holes, and adding brads. During the unit, children decorate the covers with weather-related illustrations and diagrams. At the end of the unit, they number the pages and add a table of contents. In their logs, children write quickwrites (short informal writings), draw pictures, and add clusters (diagrams shaped like spider webs), charts, and other information. Two entries from children's learning logs are presented in Figure 1–1. The first entry is a cluster about clouds written after reading *The Cloud Book,* and the second is a quickwrite written after Mrs. Reeves read aloud Patricia Polacco's *Thunder Cake* (1990), a story about how a young girl overcame her fear of thunderstorms.

Mrs. Reeves's students use writing as a part of many science activities. One example is when the local television weather forecaster, Mr. Reed, visited the class for an interview. A group of children wrote a letter inviting Mr. Reed to visit the class and answer their questions. Next the class brainstormed a list of questions to ask him, and Mrs. Reeves listed the questions on a chart. Then each child chose a question to ask and wrote it on an index card. During Mr. Reed's visit, children took turns asking questions and taking notes about the answers on the backs of the cards. Afterwards, children discussed the weather forecaster's visit and decided to make a class book to share what they had learned. Mrs. Reeves demonstrated the procedure for making a page, and then children

Figure 1–2 Shared writing: A page from a class interview book

created their own pages. On each page, a child wrote the question he or she had asked Mr. Reed, along with his answer. They used the writing process to draft, revise, and edit their writing. Because the book was being published and would be shared with parents and other classes, it was important for the children to write in complete sentences and to spell all words correctly. A page from the class book is presented in Figure 1–2.

The children used the writing process again to write another class book on weather in an ABC format. They began by hanging a strip of paper beside the word wall and writing the alphabet on it. Then children identified words and phrases beginning with each letter on the first list and wrote them on the second list. For example, they wrote *forecasters, flurries,* and *fog* under *F* and *thermometers, temperature, thunder,* and *thunderstorms* under *T.* As a class, children decided on the page layout featuring the letter highlighted, an illustration, and accompanying text (a sentence or two), and Mrs. Reeves demonstrated how to lay out a page before the children began working on their pages. Then children, individually or in pairs, selected a letter to do. After creating rough drafts of their pages, they met in writing groups to share their drafts, get feedback on the accuracy of their illustrations and text, and get suggestions on additional information they might add. After they made revisions, Mrs. Reeves met with children in small groups for editing. She helped them proofread their sentences and correct spelling, capitalization, punctuation, and any factual errors. Then students made their final copies on special drawing paper and arranged the pages in alphabetical order. Several children worked together to make the title page and the cover. Mrs. Reeves punched holes in the pages and used ribbon to bind the book. The D page from the class ABC weather book is shown in Figure 1–3.

Figure 1–3 Guided writing: A page from a class ABC book

Children also chose individual projects to do that relate to weather. Their projects included

- drawing weather maps
- painting a mural about weather
- making weather safety posters
- performing a skit about weather forecasting
- constructing weather instruments
- retelling a favorite weather story such as *Cloudy With a Chance of Meatballs*
- making a weather can (a coffee can decorated with a picture and filled with five facts about a particular type of weather, such as tornadoes)
- writing a weather book

Mrs. Reeves set aside 45-minute chunks of time for children to work on these projects. They worked individually or in small groups, and Mrs. Reeves circulated around the classroom to supervise their work. She met with children briefly in conferences to keep track of their work and to solve problems as needed. After they completed their projects, children shared them with classmates during a special sharing time.

ELEMENTARY STUDENTS ARE WRITERS. Notions that children in the elementary grades cannot write, that they must learn to read before learning to write, and that they must learn to write letters, words, and sentences before writing longer texts are antiquated. Classroom teachers as well as writing researchers have discovered that even young children communicate through writing, and that they begin writing as they are learning to read or even before they read (Graves, 1983, 1994). During the elementary grades, writing serves three purposes:

1. *Children learn to write.* Through experiences with writing, children learn how to write. Informal writing activities, such as clustering and quickwriting, provide opportunities for children to acquire writing fluency. For more formal writing activities, such as stories, reports, and poems, children use the writing process. This is a multistage process through which children gather and organize ideas, write rough drafts, and refine and polish their writing before publishing it.

2. *Children learn about written language.* As children learn to write, they discover the uniqueness of written language and the ways in which it differs from oral language and drawing. They develop an appreciation for the interrelations of purpose, audience, and form in writing and learn to consider these three elements as they write. In addition, children learn about the mechanics of writing, including standard spelling and usage, capitalization, and formatting.

3. *Children learn through writing.* Writing is a valuable learning tool that has many applications across the curriculum. Children write informally to analyze and synthesize their learning, and they write formally and apply their knowledge when they write books and reports (Halliday, 1980).

Mrs. Reeves's second and third graders exemplified all three components as they used writing during their unit on weather. They learned to write by writing and practiced the writing process as they drafted, revised, and edited class books and individual projects. Mrs. Reeves's students learned about written language as they revised and edited their writing when it was to be published. They also used writing as a tool for learning about weather through both informal writing and more formal writing projects.

Frank Smith (1988) reflected that "the first time I explored in detail how children learn to write, I was tempted to conclude that it was, like the flight of bumblebees, a theoretical impossibility" (p. 17). The writing samples in the vignette about Mrs. Reeves's students show that just as bumblebees really do fly, elementary students really do write, even though it may seem improbable that children who are just becoming literate can be fluent and expressive writers.

In this chapter, you will read about the process and product dimensions of writing instruction. The key concepts are:

- The writing process approach to writing instruction is based on how real writers write.

- The five stages in the writing process are prewriting, drafting, revising, editing, and publishing.
- Teachers support and scaffold children as they learn to write, gradually giving students more and more responsibility.
- The five levels of support are modeled writing, shared writing, interactive writing, guided writing, and independent writing.

The Writing Process

The writing process is a way of looking at writing instruction in which the emphasis is shifted from students' finished products to what students think and do as they write. James Britton and Janet Emig were two of the first researchers to examine students' writing processes. In her study, Emig (1971) interviewed 12th graders as they wrote, and studied the writing processes that one teenager used in depth. Several years later, Britton and his colleagues (1975) examined 2,000 essays written by British high school students and found that students' writing processes differed according to the type of writing. At the same time, Donald Graves (1975) examined young children's writing and documented that 7-year-olds, like high school students, used a variety of strategies as they wrote.

These early researchers generally divided the writing process into three stages. Britton (1970b) labeled them as conception, incubation, and production. In the conception stage, writers choose topics and decide to write; in the incubation stage, they develop the topic by gathering information; and in the production stage, they write, revise, and edit the composition. Donald Graves (1975) described a similar process of prewriting, composing, and postwriting. In prewriting, writers choose topics and gather ideas for writing; in the composing stage, they write the composition; and in the postwriting stage, they share their writing.

Linda Flower and John Hayes (1977, 1981; Hayes & Flower, 1986) studied college students' writing and asked students to talk about their thought processes while they composed. They then analyzed students' talk to examine the strategies writers use and developed a model that describes writing as a complex problem-solving process. According to the model, the writing process involves three activities: planning, as writers set goals to guide the writing; translating, as writers put the plans into writing; and reviewing, as writers evaluate and revise the writing. These activities are not linear steps, according to Flower and Hayes, because writers continually monitor their writing and move back and forth among the activities. This monitoring might be considered a fourth component of the writing process. An important finding from their research is that writing is recursive: Using this monitoring mechanism, writers jump back and forth from one process to another as they write.

Some researchers have examined particular aspects of the writing process. Nancy Sommers (1982, 1994) described writing as a revision process in which writers develop their ideas, not polish their writing. Less experienced writers,

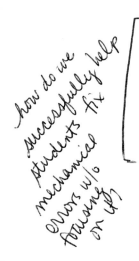

according to Sommers, focus on small, word-level changes and error hunting. This emphasis on mechanics rather than content may be due to teachers' behavior. Sondra Perl (1994) examined how the writing process is used in high school and college classrooms and concluded that teachers place excessive importance on mechanical errors. Flower and Hayes found that less successful writers have a limited repertoire of alternatives for solving problems as they write, and Bereiter and Scardamalia (1982) found that even though children participated in writing process activities, they were less capable of monitoring the need to move from one activity to another. Through both expert teaching and extensive writing practice, children can become better at self-monitoring by the time they reach middle school or high school levels.

The five-stage writing process presented in this chapter incorporates activities identified through research. The stages are prewriting, drafting, revising, editing, and publishing. The key features of each stage are presented in Figure 1–4. The numbering of the stages does not mean that this writing process is a linear series of discrete activities; research has shown that the process involves recurring cycles, and labeling is only an aid for identifying and discussing writing activities. In the classroom, the stages merge and recur as students write (Barnes, Morgan, & Weinhold, 1997). Moreover, students personalize the process to meet their own needs and vary the process according to the writing assignment.

Stage 1: Prewriting

Prewriting is the getting-ready-to-write stage. The traditional notion that writers have thought out their topic completely is ridiculous. If writers wait for the ideas to be fully developed, they may wait forever. Instead, writers begin tentatively by talking, reading, and writing to see what they know and in what direction they want to go. Pulitzer Prize–winning writer Donald Murray (1985, 1987) calls this stage the discovery of writing: You begin writing to explore what you know and to surprise yourself.

Prewriting has probably been the most neglected stage in the writing process; however, it is as crucial to writers as a warmup is to athletes. Donald Murray (1982) believes that 70% or more of writing time should be spent in prewriting. During the prewriting stage, the activities are

- choosing a topic
- considering purpose, audience, and form
- generating and organizing ideas for writing

Choosing a Topic.   Choosing topics for writing can be a stumbling block for students who have become dependent on teachers to supply their topics. In the traditional approach, teachers relieved students of the "burden" of topic selection by suggesting gimmicky story starters. Often, this tactic stymied students, who were forced to write on topics they knew little about or were not interested

Stage 1: Prewriting
Choose a topic.
Gather and organize ideas.
Consider the audience to whom students will write.
Identify the purpose of the writing activity.
Choose an appropriate genre for their compositions based on audience and
    purpose.

Stage 2: Drafting
Write a rough draft.
Craft leads to grab readers' attention.
Emphasize content rather than mechanics.

Stage 3: Revising
Share writing in writing groups.
Participate constructively in discussions about classmates' writing.
Make changes in compositions to reflect the reactions and comments of both
    teacher and classmates.
Make substantive rather than only minor changes between the first and final drafts.

Stage 4: Editing
Proofread compositions independently.
Help proofread classmates' compositions.
Increasingly identify and correct mechanical errors without assistance.

Stage 5: Publishing
Publish writing in an appropriate form.
Share finished writing with an appropriate audience.

Figure 1–4 Key features of the writing process

in. Donald Graves (1976) calls this traditional approach of supplying topics for students "writing welfare." Instead, children need to take responsibility for choosing their own topics for writing.

At first, dependent students will argue that they do not know what to write about; however, teachers can help them brainstorm a list of three, four, or five topics and then identify the one topic they are most interested in and know the most about. Children who feel they cannot generate any writing topics are often surprised that they have so many options available. Then, through prewriting activities, they talk, draw, read, and even write to develop information about their topics.

Asking children to choose their own topics for writing does not mean that teachers never give writing assignments. Rather, teachers provide general guidelines. Teachers may specify the writing form—journal, story, poem, report, and so on. At other times, they may establish the purpose—for example, to share what children have learned about life in ancient Egypt—while children choose the specific content and possibly the form of presentation. For instance, children can demonstrate what they have learned about life in ancient Egypt by writing a report about how people were mummified; by assuming the persona of someone who lived in ancient Egypt and writing a simulated journal; by writing a biography of Queen Nefertiti; by writing an acrostic poem on the word *pyramid;* or by writing a story set in ancient Egypt.

When teachers allow children to choose their own topics, the freedom of choice may lead to students' writing about topics that teachers find inappropriate, including violence, racism, homosexuality, religion, and sex. Sometimes teachers determine for themselves whether any topics are unacceptable in their classrooms, and sometimes school districts set guidelines about acceptable topics for writing. If any topics are "off-limits," children appreciate knowing ahead of time which topics to avoid. In a recent study, Schneider (2001) found that some teachers encourage children to express themselves even when the teachers themselves feel uncomfortable with the topic, and other teachers limit students' choices by assigning topics, prohibiting certain topics, or directing students toward other topics. How teachers handle the issue of taboo topics depends on their beliefs about the writing and the reasons why people write.

Considering Purpose.   As children prepare to write, they need to identify their purpose for writing. Are they writing to entertain? to inform? to persuade? This decision about purpose influences other decisions they make about audience and form. M. A. K. Halliday (1973, 1975) has identified seven language functions that apply to both oral and written language:

1. *Instrumental language.* Language to satisfy needs, such as in business letters.
2. *Regulatory language.* Language to control the behavior of others, such as in directions and rules.
3. *Interactional language.* Language to establish and maintain social relationships, such as in pen pal letters and dialogue journals.
4. *Personal language.* Language to express personal opinions, such as in learning logs and letters to the editor.
5. *Imaginative language.* Language to express imagination and creativity, such as in stories, poems, and scripts.
6. *Heuristic language.* Language to seek information and to find out about things, such as in learning logs and interviews.
7. *Informative language.* Language to convey information, such as in reports and biographies.

Children use writing for all of these purposes.

Considering Audience. Children may write primarily for themselves, to express and clarify their own ideas and feelings, or they may write for others. Possible audiences include classmates, younger children, parents, foster grandparents, children's authors, and pen pals. Other audiences are more distant and less well known. For example, children may write letters to businesses to request information, write articles to be published in the local newspaper, or submit stories and poems to be published in literary magazines.

Children's writing is influenced by their sense of audience. When students write for others, they adapt their writing to fit their audience, just as they vary their speech to fit the audience. Children must be aware of their audience while writing in order to choose the appropriate language. In contrast, when children write only to complete assignments, they lack a sense of audience.

Elementary students demonstrate their relationship with the audience in a variety of ways, often by adding parenthetical information or asides. For example, a seventh grader begins "George Mudlumpus and the Mystery of the Golden Spider," his sixth mystery featuring George Mudlumpus, "the detective with the outrageous rates," this way: "I had decided to take my vacation, as you already know from the last story I told you. So, I packed, got my airplane ticket, and got on a 747 jetliner. I was off to San Francisco!" This student feels a close relationship, that of a storyteller, with his unknown audience. He often includes asides in his stories, and George sometimes comments to his readers, "I know! You think I should have recognized that clue!"

When children write for others, teachers are the most common audience. Teachers can assume several roles, and how writers perceive these roles is crucial. Teachers can assume the role of trusted adult, a partner in dialogue, or judge (Britton et al., 1975). In writing to a trusted adult, children feel secure because they can rely on their reader to respond sympathetically. When writing a dialogue with a teacher, children are secure in the teacher's presence and assume that the teacher will be interested in the writing, responding to what has been written, not to how it has been written. Unfortunately, the teacher's most common role is that of judge, but this role is least conducive to good writing. When a teacher acts as a judge, children produce writing only to satisfy the teacher's requirement or to receive a grade.

Considering Form. One of the most important considerations is the form or genre the writing will take. A story? A letter? A poem? A journal entry? A writing project could be handled in any one of these ways. As part of a science theme on hermit crabs, for instance, children could write a story about a hermit crab, draw a picture of a hermit crab and label body parts, write an explanation of how hermit crabs obtain shells to live in, or keep a log of observations about hermit crabs living in the classroom. There is an almost endless variety of genres that children's writing may take, but too often the choices are limited to writing stories, poems, and reports. Instead, children need to experiment

Genre	Purpose	Activities
Descriptive Writing	Students become careful observers and choose precise language when they use description. They take notice of sensory details and learn to make comparisons (metaphors and similes) in order to make their writing more powerful.	Character sketches Comparisons Descriptive essays Descriptive paragraphs Descriptive sentences Five-senses poems Found poems Observations
Expository Writing	Students collect and synthesize information for expository writing. This writing is objective, and reports are the most common type of informative writing. Students use expository writing to give directions, sequence steps, compare one thing to another, explain causes and effects, or describe problems and solutions.	Alphabet books Autobiographies Biographies Brochures Cubes Data charts Dictionaries Directions Interviews Newspaper articles Posters Reports Simulated journals Summaries
Journals and Letters	Students write to themselves and to specific, known audiences in journals and letters. Their writing is personal and often less formal than other genres. They share news, explore new ideas, and record notes. Letters and envelopes require special formatting, and students learn these formats during the elementary grades.	Business letters Courtesy letters Double-entry journals E-mail messages Friendly letters Learning logs Personal journals Postcards Reading logs Simulated journals

Figure 1–5 Six Writing Genres

with a wide variety of writing genres and explore the purposes and formats of these forms. A list of six genres is presented in Figure 1-5. Through reading and writing, children develop a strong sense of these forms and how they are structured. Langer (1985) found that by third grade, children responded in different ways to story- and report-writing assignments. They organized compositions differently and varied the kinds of information and elaboration they used depending on the form. Similarly, Hidi and Hildyard (1983) found that elementary

Genre	Purpose	Activities
Narrative Writing	Students retell familiar stories, develop sequels for stories they have read, write stories called personal narratives about events in their own lives, and create original stories. They incorporate a beginning, middle, and end in the narratives they write. In the beginning, they introduce the characters, identify a problem, and interest readers in the story. In the middle, the problem becomes worse or additional roadblocks are set up to thwart the main character as he/she attempts to solve the problem. In the end, the problem is resolved.	Original short stories Personal narratives Retellings of stories Sequels to stories Scripts of stories
Persuasive Writing	Persuasion is winning someone to your viewpoint or cause. The three ways people are persuaded are by appeals to (1) logic, (2) moral character, and (3) emotion. Students present their position clearly and then support it with examples and evidence.	Advertisements Book and movie reviews Editorials Letters to the editor Persuasive essays Persuasive letters
Poetry Writing	Students create word pictures and play with rhyme and other stylistic devices as they create poems. As students experiment with poetry, they learn that poetic language is vivid and powerful but concise, and they learn that poems can be arranged in different ways on a page.	Acrostic poems Cinquin poems Color poems Diamante poems Five-senses poems Found poems Free verse Haiku "I am" poems "If I were . . ." poems "I wish . . ." poems Poems for two voices Preposition poems Riddles

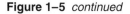

Figure 1–5 *continued*

students could differentiate between stories and persuasive essays. Because children are clarifying the distinctions between various writing genres during the elementary grades, it is very important that teachers use the correct terminology and not label all children's writing as "stories." Some second language learners, however, are not familiar with genres, and they benefit from explicit instruction so that they can "succeed in school and actively participate in the dominant community" (Gibbons 2002, p. 60).

Although most writing forms look like the text on this page does—block form written from left to right and from top to bottom—some linguistic forms require a special arrangement on a page or special structure. For example, scripts, recipes, poems, and letters are four writing forms that have very recognizable formats. Examples of writing forms that use special language patterns are a story that begins with "Once upon a time . . . " and letters that require "Dear . . . " and "Sincerely." As children are introduced to these writing forms and have opportunities to experiment with them, they will learn about the unique requirements of the formats.

Teaching children to make decisions about purpose, audience, and form is an important component of writing instruction. In each case, children need to know the range of options available to writers. Decisions about these aspects of writing have an impact on each other. For example, if the purpose is to entertain, a form such as a story, poem, or script might be selected. These three forms look very different on a piece of paper. Whereas a story is written in the traditional block format, scripts and poems have unique arrangements on the page. For example, in a script, the character's name appears first and is followed by a colon and then the dialogue. Action and dialogue, rather than description, carry the story line in a script. In contrast, poems have unique formatting considerations; words are used judiciously, and each word and phrase is chosen to convey a maximum amount of information.

Although decisions about purpose, audience, and form may change as children write and revise, writers must begin with at least a tentative understanding as they move into the drafting stage.

Gathering and Organizing Ideas.   Children gather and organize ideas for writing and the words and sentences to express these ideas by:

- drawing pictures
- talking with classmates and the teacher
- reading stories, informational books, and other texts
- dramatizing and retelling stories
- writing
- making graphic organizers

Graves (1983) calls these activities that children use to activate prior knowledge, gather and organize ideas, and collect words "rehearsal" activities.

Drawing is the way young children gather and organize ideas for writing. Kindergarten and first-grade teachers often notice that students draw before they write. When young children are asked to write before drawing, for example, they explain that they can't write yet because they don't know what to write until they see what they draw. As young children become writers, they use drawing and other symbol systems as they grapple with the uniqueness of writing (Dyson, 1993).

Children use a variety of writing activities to gather and organize ideas before beginning to draft their compositions (daSilva, 2001). They brainstorm words and images, sequence lists of events, cluster main ideas and details, make other charts or diagrams to record ideas, or quickwrite to discover what they know about a topic and what direction their writing might take. Outlining is another form of prewriting, but this traditional prewriting activity is less effective than clustering and not recommended for younger students.

Stage 2: Drafting

Children write and refine their compositions through a series of drafts. During the drafting stage, they focus on getting their ideas down on paper. Because writers do not begin writing with their compositions already fully formed in their minds, they begin with tentative ideas developed through prewriting activities. The drafting stage is the time to pour out ideas, with little concern about spelling, punctuation, and other mechanical errors. The activities in this stage are

- writing a rough draft
- writing leads

Writing a Rough Draft.   Children skip every other line as they write their rough drafts so as to leave adequate space for revising. They use arrows to move sections of text, cross-outs to delete sections, and scissors and tape to cut apart and rearrange text, just as adult writers do. Similarly, children write on only one side of a sheet of paper so that the paper can be cut apart or rearranged. Because word processors are increasingly available in elementary classrooms, revising, with all its shifting and deleting of text, is becoming much easier. However, for children who handwrite their compositions, the wide spacing of lines is crucial. Teachers often make small X's on every other line of young children's papers as a reminder to skip lines as they draft their compositions.

Children label their drafts by writing "Rough Draft" in ink at the top of their papers or by stamping the papers with a "Rough Draft" stamp. This label indicates to the writer, other students, parents, and administrators that the composition is a draft in which emphasis has been placed on content, not mechanics. It also explains why teachers have not graded the paper or marked mechanical errors. Also, if some children who are just learning the writing process plan to make the rough draft their final draft by writing carefully, the label "Rough Draft" at the top of the paper negates this idea and further emphasizes that writing involves more than one stage.

As children draft their compositions, they may need to modify their earlier decisions about purpose, audience, and, especially, the form their writing will take. For example, a composition that began as a story might be transformed into a report, letter, or poem: the new format may allow the child to communicate more effectively. This process of modifying earlier decisions also continues into the revising stage.

Teachers do not emphasize correct spelling and neatness at this stage. In fact, when teachers point out mechanical errors during the drafting stage, they send a false message to students that mechanical correctness is more important than content (Sommers, 1982). Later, during editing, children clean up mechanical errors and put their composition into a neat, final form.

Writing Leads.   A composition's lead, or opening sentences, is crucial. Think of the last time you went to a library to choose a book to read. Several titles or book jacket pictures may have caught your eye, but before making your selection, you opened each book and read the first paragraph or two. Which one did you choose? Probably the one that hooked you, or grabbed your attention. The same is true for children's writing: Students who consider audience as they write will want to grab the attention of the audience. Children may use a variety of techniques to appeal to their audience, such as questions, facts, dialogue, brief stories, and problems. Donald Graves (1983) and Lucy Calkins (1996) recommend that students create several leads and try them out on classmates before deciding on one. As students write these leads, they gain valuable knowledge about how to manipulate language and how to vary viewpoint or sequence in their writing.

Stage 3: Revising

Writers clarify and refine ideas in their compositions during the revising stage. Often novice writers terminate the writing process as soon as they complete a rough draft, believing that once their ideas are jotted down, the writing task is complete. In fact, they often see revision as punishment for not having gotten it right in the first place (Heard, 2002). Experienced writers, however, know that they must turn to others for reactions and revise on the basis of these comments. Revision is not just polishing writing; it is meeting the needs of readers by adding, substituting, deleting, and rearranging material. The word *revision* means "seeing again," and in this stage, writers see their compositions again with their classmates and the teacher helping them. The activities in the revising stage are

- rereading the rough draft
- sharing the rough draft in a writing group
- revising on the basis of feedback received from the writing group

Rereading the Rough Draft.   Writers are the first to revise their compositions. Some revision occurs during drafting when writers make choices and changes as they write. After finishing the rough draft, writers need to distance themselves from the draft for a day or two and then reread it from a fresh perspective, as a reader might. As they reread, children make changes—adding, substituting, deleting, and moving material—and place question marks by sections that need work. It is these trouble spots that children ask for help with in their writing group.

> **Teacher's Note: Supporting Struggling Writers**
>
> Struggling writers don't understand the writing process. They write single-draft compositions, thinking that they're done as soon as they put the words down on paper. Students need to appreciate the viewpoint of readers before they understand the importance of revising. One way to do this is to have students revise a composition that you've written. When they read a composition with incomplete ideas and confusing language, students are quick to make revision suggestions.

Writing Groups. Children meet in writing groups to share their compositions with small groups of classmates. Writing groups offer the writer choices; give the writers responses, feelings, and thoughts; show different possibilities in revising; and speed up revising (Mohr, 1984). These groups provide a scaffold, or supportive environment, in which teachers and classmates can talk about plans and strategies for writing and revising (Applebee & Langer, 1983; Calkins, 1983).

Writing groups can form spontaneously when several students have completed drafts and are ready to share their compositions, or they can be formal groupings with identified leaders. In some primary classrooms, for example, writing groups may form spontaneously; when students finish writing, they go to sit on an area rug or go to a special table. As soon as a child with writing to share arrives, others who are available to listen and respond to the writing come and join the group. When three or four children have arrived for the writing group, the writer reads the writing and the other children listen and respond to it, offering compliments and relating this piece of writing to their own experiences and writing. Sometimes the teacher joins the listeners on the rug to participate in the writing group; at other times, the children work independently. In other classrooms, writing groups are more formal: Writing groups meet when all children have completed a rough draft and are ready to share their writing with classmates and the teacher. The teacher participates in these groups, providing feedback along with the students. In some classrooms, writing groups may function independently: Four or five children are assigned to each group, and a list of the groups and their members is posted in the classroom. On the list, the teacher puts a star by one child's name, and that child serves as a group leader. Every quarter, the leader changes.

The steps in conducting a writing group are listed in the step-by-step feature on page 20.

Making Revisions. As they make revisions, children add words, substitute sentences, delete paragraphs, and move phrases. They cross out, draw arrows, and write in the space they left between the lines of writing when they double-spaced their rough drafts. Children move back and forth into prewriting to gather additional information, into drafting to write a new paragraph, and into revising to replace an often-repeated word. Messiness is inevitable, but despite the scribbles, children are usually able to decipher what they have written.

Writers make four kinds of changes as they revise: They add, substitute, delete, and move text from one place to another (Faigley & Witte, 1981). Sometimes their changes involve single words, phrases, sentences, or paragraphs. Children often focus at the word and phrase level and make more additions and substitutions than deletions and moves. Teachers and children can analyze the

Step by Step: Writing Groups

1. ***A writer reads.*** A group of four or five students take turns reading their compositions aloud. Everyone listens politely, thinking about compliments and suggestions for improvement they will make after the writer has finished reading. Typically, only the writer looks at the composition as it is read, because when classmates and the teacher look at it, they quickly notice and comment on mechanical errors even though the emphasis is on content during revising. Listening to the writing without looking at it keeps the focus on content.

2. ***Listeners offer compliments.*** Group members tell what they liked about the composition. These positive comments should be specific, focusing on strengths. Comments such as "I like the way you wrote 'Monika was as scared as a kindergartner on the first day of school.' That really makes me understand what she was feeling" are much more effective than general "I like it" or "It was good!" comments. Students usually focus on organization, leads, word choice, voice, sequence, dialogue, theme, or other elements of writing in their comments.

3. ***The writer asks questions.*** Writers ask their classmates for assistance on trouble spots or ask questions that reflect more general concerns about how well they are communicating. For example: "I don't have very much information in this part about Betsy Ross's childhood. It's short. What should I do?" Admitting that they need help from their classmates is a major step in learning to revise.

4. ***Listeners offer suggestions.*** Group members ask about things that are unclear and make revision suggestions. Students are careful to phrase their comments in helpful rather than hurtful ways. For example: "Here you tell why junk food is bad for you. Then you say 'Junk food is fun to eat.' Maybe you could move it to where you tell why junk food is good."

5. ***Repeat the process.*** Students take turns sharing their compositions and repeating the first four steps in the procedure. Each group member reads his or her composition aloud and receives feedback from classmates.

6. ***Writers plan for revision.*** Students each make a commitment about how they will revise their writing after considering their classmates' comments and suggestions. The final decision about what to revise rests with the writers themselves, but the suggestions that the group members make give the writers some good ideas to consider. Because children verbalize their revision plans, they are more likely to complete the revision stage.

types of revisions that children make by examining their revised rough drafts. The number and type of revisions are one gauge of children's growth as writers.

The minilesson feature on page 21 shows how one seventh-grade teacher drew his students' attention to the types of revisions they were making. For additional ideas for minilessons on revision, check Georgia Heard's *The Revision*

Four Types of Revisions

Mr. Ortiz's seventh-grade language arts students are writing persuasive essays, and because this is an important assignment, he wants them to revise more thoroughly than they sometimes do. The most common type of revision that his students make is single-word substitutions; they might change the word *suggest* to *recommend,* for example. It's easy for Mr. Ortiz to check his students' revisions because they code them in the margin of their papers using these letters: A (additions), S (substitutions), D (deletions), and M (moves). In today's minilesson, his students try other types of revisions using a sample student essay.

1. Introduce the topic

Mr. Ortiz asks his seventh graders to check their persuasive essays to see which types of revisions they are making. The students tally their revisions and report that most of the changes are single-word substitutions.

2. Share examples

Mr. Ortiz presents the first page of a student's three-page, double-spaced, typed essay written the previous year that needs a variety of revisions. He displays it on the overhead and reads it aloud. Together they revise it, and Mr. Ortiz encourages his students to think of revisions other than word substitutions. He points out a sentence in one paragraph that doesn't belong and another paragraph that is out of sequence. In all, they make 10 revisions.

3. Provide information

After they finish making revisions, Mr. Ortiz codes each revision in the margin and tallies each type. They made 5 additions, 2 substitutions, 3 deletions, and 1 move on the first page of the essay. Of the 10 revisions, 4 involved single words; the other 6 involved phrases, sentences, and paragraphs.

4. Guide practice

Mr. Ortiz passes out copies of the student's entire essay and asks students to work with partners to revise the rest of the essay. He encourages them to make all four types of revisions. Afterwards, students calculate the types of revisions they have marked and share some of them with the class.

5. Assess learning

Mr. Ortiz examines the types of revisions his students make on their persuasive essays. His students also write a reflection about the types of revisions they made and how they improved the quality of their writing through their revision choices.

Toolbox: Teaching Techniques That Work (2002) and Barry Lane's *Reviser's Toolbox* (1999).

Stage 4: Editing

Editing is putting the piece of writing into its final form. Until this stage, the focus has been primarily on developing the content of the composition. Here the focus changes to mechanics, and children "polish" their writing by correcting spelling and other mechanical errors (Parsons, 2001). The goal is to make the writing "optimally readable" (F. Smith, 1982). Writers who write for readers understand that if their compositions are not readable, they have written in vain because their ideas will never be read.

"Mechanics" refers to the commonly accepted conventions of written standard English. They include capitalization, punctuation, spelling, sentence structure, usage, and formatting considerations specific to poems, scripts, letters, and other writing forms. The use of these conventions is a courtesy to those who will read the composition. The most effective way to teach mechanical skills is during the editing stage of the writing process rather than through workbook exercises (Fearn & Farnan, 1998). When editing a composition that will be shared with a genuine audience, children are more interested in using mechanical skills correctly so they can communicate effectively. In a study of two third-grade classes, Calkins (1980) found that the children in the class who learned punctuation marks as a part of editing could define or explain more marks than the children in the other class, who were taught punctuation skills in a traditional manner with instruction and practice exercises on each punctuation mark. In other words, the results of this research as well as other studies (Weaver, 1996) suggest that a functional approach to teaching the mechanics of writing is more effective than practice exercises.

Children move through three activities in the editing stage:

- getting distance from the composition
- proofreading to locate errors
- correcting errors

Getting Distance. Children are more efficient editors when they set the composition aside for a few days before beginning to edit. After working so closely with the piece of writing during drafting and revising, they are too familiar with it to be able to locate many mechanical errors. After a few days, children are better able to approach editing with a fresh perspective and gather the enthusiasm necessary to finish the writing process by making the paper optimally readable.

Proofreading. Children proofread their compositions to locate and mark possible errors. Proofreading is a unique form of reading in which children read word-by-word and hunt for errors rather than read for meaning (King, 1985). Concentrating on mechanics is difficult because of our natural inclination to

Delete	ℒ	There were cots to sleep on and food to eat ~~or at~~ the shelter.
Insert	∧	Mrs. Kim's cat is the color ⌃of carrots.
Indent paragraph	⊓	⊓ Riots are bad. People can get hurt and buildings can get burned down but good things can happen too. People can learn to be friends.
Capitalize	≡	Daniel and his mom didn't like m̲rs. Kim or her cat.
Change to lowercase	/	People were /Rioting because they were angry.
Add period	⊙	I think Daniel's mom and Mrs. Kim will become friends ⊙
Add comma	⋀	People hurt other people⋀they steal things⋀and they burn down buildings in a riot.
Add apostrophe	⋁	Daniel⋁s cat was named Jasmine.

Figure 1–6 Proofreaders' marks

read for meaning. Even experienced proofreaders often find themselves reading for meaning and overlooking errors that do not inhibit meaning. It is important, therefore, to take time to explain proofreading and to demonstrate how it differs from regular reading.

To demonstrate proofreading, teachers take a piece of student writing and display it on an overhead projector. The teacher reads it several times, each time hunting for a particular type of error. During each reading, the composition is read slowly, with the teacher softly pronouncing each word and touching the word with a pencil or pen to focus attention on it. The teacher marks possible errors as they are located. Errors are marked or corrected with special proofreaders' marks. Children enjoy using these marks, the same ones that adult authors and editors use. A list of proofreaders' marks that elementary students can learn and use in editing their writing is presented in Figure 1–6.

Editing checklists also help children focus on particular categories of errors as they proofread their compositions. Teachers can develop these checklists with two to six items appropriate for the children's grade level. A first-grade checklist, for example, might have only two items, one about using a capital letter at the beginning of a sentence and another about using a period at the end of a sentence. In contrast, a middle-grade checklist might contain items on using

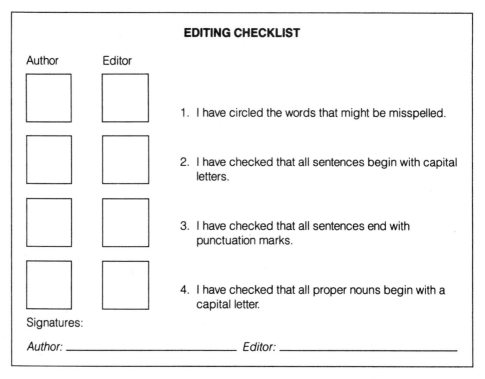

Figure 1–7 A third-grade editing checklist

commas in a series, indenting paragraphs, capitalizing proper nouns and adjectives, and spelling homonyms correctly. During the school year, teachers revise the checklist to focus attention on skills that have recently been taught. A sample third-grade editing checklist is presented in Figure 1–7. Using this checklist, two writers work together as partners to edit their compositions. First, children proofread their own compositions, searching for errors in each category listed on the checklist, and check off each item after proofreading. After completing the checklist, children sign their names and trade checklists and compositions. Now they become editors and complete each other's checklist. Having the writer and editor sign the checklist helps them to take the activity seriously.

Correcting Errors.   After children proofread their compositions and locate as many errors as possible, they correct these errors individually or with an editor's assistance. Some errors are easy to correct, some require using a dictionary or checking a word wall displayed in the classroom, and others involve instruction from the teacher. It is unrealistic to expect children to locate and correct every mechanical error in their compositions. Not even published books are error-free! Once in a while, children may even change a correct spelling or punctuation mark and make it incorrect, but overall, they correct far more errors than they create.

Editing can end after children and their editors correct as many mechanical errors as possible, or children may meet with the teacher in a conference for a final editing. When mechanical correctness is crucial, this conference is important. The teacher proofreads the composition with the child and assists in identifying and correcting the remaining errors, or the teacher makes check marks in the margin to note errors that the child corrects independently.

Stage 5: Publishing

In the final stage of the writing process, children publish their writing and share it with an appropriate audience. Publishing is the fun stage in the process; it motivates students to improve their writing because they will be sharing it with a real audience. In fact, Elbow (2002) believes that publishing is the single best way to encourage students to revise and edit their writing.

Children usually recopy a story or other piece of writing into a stapled booklet or hardcover book. These published books are added to the classroom or the school library. Sometimes children form a classroom publishing company and add the name of the publishing company and the year the book was made to the title page. In addition, children can add an "All About the Author" page with a photograph at the end of their books, similar to the author bio included on the jackets of books written by adult authors. A fifth grader's "All About the Author" page from a collection of poetry he wrote is presented in Figure 1–8. Notice that Brian used the third-person pronoun *he* in writing about himself, as in an adult biographical sketch.

One of the most popular ways for children to share their writing with others is by making and binding books. Simple booklets can be made by folding a sheet of paper into quarters like a greeting card. Children write the title on the front and have three sides remaining for their compositions. They can also construct booklets by stapling sheets of writing paper together and adding covers made out of construction paper. Sheets of wallpaper cut from old sample books also make good, sturdy covers. These stapled booklets can be cut into various shapes, too. Children can make more sophisticated hardcover books by covering cardboard covers with contact paper, wallpaper samples, or cloth. Pages are sewn or stapled together, and the first and last pages (endpapers) are glued to the cardboard covers to hold the book together. The directions for making one type of hardcover book are presented in Figure 1–9.

As they share their writing with real audiences of their classmates, other students, parents, and the community, children come to think of themselves as authors (Rubenstein, 1998). Donald Graves and Jane Hansen (1983) suggest that one way to help students develop the concept of author is to have a special chair in the classroom designated as the "author's chair." Whenever children read their own books aloud, they sit in that chair. Through sitting in the special author's chair to share their books, children gradually realize that they are authors. Graves and Hansen explain that children first understand that authors are the

All About the Author

Brian was born on August 22, 1994 in Woodward, Ok. He is going to be a USAF pilot and Army L.T., and a college graduate. He is also wanting to be a rockstar singer. He is going to write another book hopefully about the Air Force or Army. In his spare time he likes to run, ride his motorcycle, skateboard, and play with his dogs. He also wrote "How the Hyena Got His Laugh."

Figure 1–8 Independent writing: A child's "All About the Author" page

people who write books; next they realize that they, too, are authors; finally, children realize that authors make choices when they write, and this awareness grows after experimenting with various writing functions, forms, and audiences.

Children read their writing to classmates, or share it with larger audiences through hardcover books that are placed in the class or school library, class anthologies, letters, newspaper articles, plays, videotapes, or puppet shows. Ways to share children's writing include:

- Sit in an "author's chair" and read the writing aloud in class.
- Submit the piece to writing contests.
- Display the writing on a mobile.
- Contribute to a class anthology.
- Contribute to the local newspaper.
- Make a shape book.

1. Fold sheets of $8\frac{1}{2}$ x 11-in. writing paper in half and copy the composition on the paper. List the title and author's name on the first page.

2. Put an additional sheet of writing paper, construction paper, or other colorful paper on the outside of the folded sheets of writing paper to be the book's endpaper.

Add tape along fold.

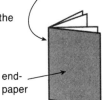

end-paper

3. Staple the folded papers together with two or three staples on the fold. Use a long-arm stapler to reach the fold more easily.

stapler

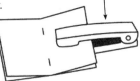

4. Cut a sheet of contact paper, 11 x 15 in., for the outside covering.

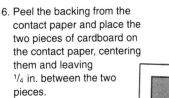

5. Cut two pieces of cardboard, 6 x 9 in., for the front and back covers.

6. Peel the backing from the contact paper and place the two pieces of cardboard on the contact paper, centering them and leaving $\frac{1}{4}$ in. between the two pieces.

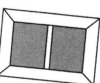

7. Cut off the four corners of the contact paper and place them on the adjacent corners of the cardboard pieces.

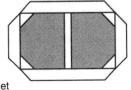

8. Fold the edges of contact paper back onto the cardboard pieces.

9. Set the stapled booklet inside the contact paper cover so that the stapled edge fits into the space between the two cardboard pieces.

10. Glue the outside of the endpaper to the cardboard pieces. First glue one side, making sure to keep the stapled edge in the space between the two cardboard pieces Then glue the other side of the paper to the second cardboard piece.

glue →

Figure 1–9 Directions for making hardcover books

- Record the writing on a cassette tape.
- Submit it to a literary magazine.
- Read it at a school assembly.
- Share at a read-around party.
- Share with parents and siblings.
- Produce a videotape of it.
- Display poetry on a "poet-tree."
- Send it to a pen pal.
- Make a hardbound book.
- Produce it as a roller movie.
- Display it on a bulletin board.
- Make a big book.
- Design a poster about the writing.
- Read it to foster grandparents.
- Share it as a puppet show.
- Display it at a public event.
- Read it to children in other classes.

Sharing writing is a social activity, and through sharing, children develop sensitivity to the audience and confidence in themselves as authors. Dyson (1993) advises that when children share writing, teachers consider the social interpretations—children's behavior, teacher's behavior, and interaction between children and the teacher—within the classroom context. Individual children will naturally interpret the sharing event differently. More than just providing the opportunity for children to share writing, teachers need to teach children how to respond to their classmates. Also, teachers themselves model how to respond to children's writing without dominating the sharing.

Supporting Children as They Learn to Write

Teachers support or scaffold children's writing as they demonstrate, guide, and teach, and they vary the amount of support they provide according to their instructional purpose and children's needs. Sometimes teachers model how experienced writers write, or they write along with students. At other times they carefully guide children as they develop ideas for their writing, record ideas on paper, and proofread to correct errors. Teachers also provide plenty of time for children to write independently, to experiment with writing, and to practice skills they have learned.

Teachers use five levels of support, moving from the highest level to the lowest level as students assume more and more of the responsibility for themselves

(Fountas & Pinnell, 1996). The five levels of support are modeled writing, shared writing, interactive writing, guided writing, and independent writing (see Figure 1–10). It is not that kindergartners and first graders always have the most support and older students the least; rather, teachers working with kindergartners through eighth graders use all five levels. For instance, when teachers introduce a new writing form or teach a writing strategy or skill, they use demonstrations or modeled writing. The purpose of the activity, not the activity itself, determines which level of support is used. The teacher is less actively involved in directing the writing activity in independent writing, but the quality of instruction that children have received is clearest in independent writing because they are applying what they are learning about writing when they write independently.

Gibbons (2002) also advocates a scaffolded approach for teaching English language learners. Teachers provide model compositions for students to examine, and then they work together in small groups to create collaborative compositions before writing their own pieces. Through this scaffolding, teachers demonstrate writing strategies, help students expand their knowledge about the craft of writing, and stretch students' linguistic capabilities.

Modeled Writing

Teachers demonstrate or model how expert writers write while children observe, and this is the level of the greatest support. Teachers usually decide what they will write and create the text themselves, although they do accept suggestions from students. Then teachers either write on chart paper or use an overhead projector so that all children can see what is being written. Teachers use modeled writing to demonstrate writing workshop procedures, such as how to make small books and how to do new writing forms and formats. Often teachers think aloud or reflect on their writing processes as they write to show students how experienced writers think as they are writing and the types of decisions they make and strategies they use.

Teachers use modeled writing for demonstrations to show how experienced writers write and solve problems as they write. Three purposes of modeled writing are:

1. To demonstrate how to do a new type of writing activity before having students do the writing activity independently or in small groups.
2. To demonstrate how to use writing strategies, such as proofreading, monitoring, sentence combining, and revising.
3. To demonstrate how writing conventions and other skills work.

In the vignette at the beginning of the chapter, Mrs. Reeves used modeled writing when she demonstrated how to write a page for the interview book and the ABC weather book. Her purpose in both of these examples was to demonstrate how to do a new type of writing activity.

	Modeled Writing	Shared Writing	Interactive Writing	Guided Writing	Independent Writing
What is it?	Teacher writes in front of students, creating the text, doing the writing, and thinking aloud about writing strategies and skills.	Teacher and students create the text together; then the teacher does the actual writing. Students may assist by spelling words.	Teacher and students create the text and share the pen to do the writing. Teacher and students talk about writing conventions.	Teacher presents a structured lesson and supervises as students write. Teacher also teaches a writing procedure, strategy, or skill.	Students use the writing process to write stories, informational books, and other compositions. Teacher monitors students' progress.
Who writes?	Teacher	Teacher	Teacher and students	Students	Students
How much support?	The most. The teacher does both the thinking and the writing.	The teacher and students do the thinking together but the teacher does the writing.	The teacher and student share the responsibility for doing the thinking and the writing.	The teacher provides the structure, but the students do the thinking and the writing.	The least. The students do both the thinking and the writing.
What size groups?	Whole class Small group	Whole class Small group Buddies Individuals	Whole class Small group Buddies Individuals	Small group Buddies Individuals	Buddies Individuals
Which activities?	Demonstrations	Language experience approach K-W-L charts	Predictions Daily news Innovations Letters	Class collaborations Class ABC books Formula poems	Writing centers Writing workshop Writing in journals Letters

Figure 1–10 A continuum of teacher support for student writers

Shared Writing

In shared writing, the teacher and children work together to compose a text, and the teacher serves as the scribe to record the text for children. As they write, teachers demonstrate how expert writers write while the children observe. They also draw children's attention to letters, words, and conventions of written language. Sometimes teachers write the texts on chart paper so that all children can see what is being written, or they write children's dictation beside drawings or in small books or have individual children each write small parts of the text to put together a class book. Three purposes for shared writing are:

1. To demonstrate how writing works.
2. To record students' ideas.
3. To create written texts for the classroom that children could not write independently.

The main way that shared writing differs from modeled writing is that the teacher writes the text with input from the students. In modeled writing, the teacher thinks of the text to write and does the actual writing.

Teachers at different grade levels use shared writing in a variety of ways. Primary-grade teachers often write students' dictation on paintings and brainstorm lists of words on the chalkboard, as is shown in the minilesson feature on page 33, whereas upper-grade teachers may take students' dictation when they make K-W-L charts, draw maps and clusters, and write class collaboration poems.

The language experience approach (LEA) is one type of shared writing. It is based on children's language and experiences (Ashton-Warner, 1965; Stauffer, 1970). Children dictate words and sentences about their experiences, and the teacher writes the dictation. As they write, teachers model how written language works. The text the class develops becomes the reading material because it has been written with conventional English spelling. Because the language comes from the children themselves and because the content is based on their experiences, they are usually able to read the text easily. The steps in the language experience approach are described in the step-by-step feature on page 32.

ELL **Teacher's Note: Assisting English Language Learners**

Too often, teachers think of interactive writing as an activity for young children, but ELL students at any grade level learn a great deal when they write with classmates and the teacher. Try working with a small group of students who write a sentence or paragraph together after reading a book or participating in a social studies or science lesson. Students make individual copies in journals as they write the group composition on chart paper.

The language experience approach is often used to create texts children can read and use as a resource for writing in a social studies or science unit. In the vignette at the beginning of the chapter, Mrs. Reeves used LEA to take children's dictation for the K-W-L chart, to list words on the word wall, and to write questions students wanted to ask the weather forecaster during the interview.

Interactive Writing

Teachers and children create a text and "share the pen" to write the text on chart paper (Button, Johnson, &

Step by Step: Language Experience Approach

1. *Provide an experience before writing.* The purpose of the experience is to provide the stimulus for the writing. For group writing, it can be an experience shared in school, a book read aloud, a field trip, or some other experience that students are familiar with. For individual writing, the stimulus can be any experience that is important for the particular child.

2. *Talk about the experience.* Children generate words as they talk and review the experience so that their dictation will be complete. Teachers often begin with an open-ended question, such as "What are we going to write about?" Through this talk, children clarify and organize ideas, use more specific vocabulary, and extend their understanding.

3. *Record the child's dictation.* Texts for individual students are written on sheets of writing paper or in small booklets, and group texts are written on chart paper. Teachers print neatly and spell words correctly, but they preserve children's language as much as possible. It is a great temptation to change the child's language to the teacher's own, in either word choice or grammar, but editing should be kept to a minimum so that children do not get the impression that their language is inferior or inadequate.

   For individual texts, teachers continue to take the child's dictation and write until the child finishes or hesitates. If the child hesitates, the teacher rereads what has been written and encourages the child to continue. For group texts, children take turns dictating sentences. After writing each sentence, the teacher rereads it.

4. *Read the text aloud, pointing to each word.* This reading reminds children of the content of the text and demonstrates how to read it aloud with appropriate intonation. Then students join in the reading. After reading group texts together, individual children can take turns rereading. Group texts can also be copied so that each child has a copy to read independently.

5. *Extend the writing and reading experience.* Children might draw illustrations to accompany the text, or they can add this text to a collection of their writings to read and reread. Teachers often put a sheet of plastic over class charts so children can circle key words or other familiar words in the text. When they write individual texts, children can also read them to classmates from the author's chair. Children can take their individual texts and copies of the class text home to share with family members.

6. *Prepare sentence cards.* Teachers rewrite the text on sentence strips or on small strips of tagboard, which children keep in envelopes. Children read and sequence the sentence strips, and after they can read the sentence strips smoothly, children can cut the strips into individual word cards. Then they can arrange the words into the familiar sentences and create new sentences with the word cards. Later the word cards can be added to children's word banks.

Dictating a Sentence

Mrs. Greene regularly writes her kindergartners' dictation on pictures they draw, and most of her students are able to dictate a sentence or two for her to write. However, a small group of students are still learning how to craft a sentence, remember it, and dictate it word-by-word. Today she reviews how to dictate a sentence with a group of five kindergartners.

1. Introduce the topic

"Today I have some photographs of Superman, our pet guinea pig," Mrs. Greene tells the children sitting with her at a kidney-shaped table. She spreads the photos out on the table and says, "Let's choose one to write about." The children choose a photo of their brown-and-white guinea pig munching on a carrot.

2. Share examples

Mrs. Greene and the children brainstorm words about the photo, including *carrot, Superman, guinea pig, eats, crunchy,* and *hungry.* Next she asks the children to suggest sentences including one or more of the words they brainstormed. For example, Tyrone suggests *Our guinea pig likes to eat a carrot,* and Cassie suggests *Superman eats healthy snacks.* Finally they decide on *Superman eats lots of carrots.*

3. Provide information

The kindergartners repeat the chosen sentence to themselves while Mrs. Greene picks up a pen. She reminds them to dictate the sentence word-by-word to her. The group recites the sentence, emphasizing each of the five words, and then Mrs. Greene writes the sentence as they dictate it again. Afterwards, the group reads the sentence aloud, and one child draws a line under each word and counts them.

4. Guide practice

Mrs. Greene glues the photo on the paper with their sentence and suggests that they make a book about Superman using the photos. Each child chooses a photo of Superman, glues it on a sheet of paper, crafts a sentence, and dictates it to Mrs. Greene. Finally, they compile the pages, make a cover, and bind the book. Later, they read the completed book to the class.

5. Assess learning

Mrs. Greene notes each child's ability to craft a sentence and dictate it word-by-word during the fourth step. Three of the children have difficulty remembering and dictating their sentences, so she plans to repeat this minilesson using some pictures she has cut from magazines.

Furgerson, 1996). The text is composed by the group, and the teacher guides the children as they write the text word-by-word on chart paper. Children take turns writing known letters and familiar words, adding punctuation marks, and marking spaces between words. The teacher helps children to spell all words correctly and use written language conventions so that the text can be read easily. All children participate in creating and writing the text on the chart paper, and they also write the text on small white boards. After writing, children read and reread the text using shared and independent reading.

Teachers use interactive writing to provide instruction and assistance to children as they are actually writing. It is much like shared writing except that the children are doing much of the actual writing. Four purposes of interactive writing are:

1. To demonstrate how to write words and sentences.
2. To teach how to use capital letters and punctuation marks.
3. To demonstrate how to use phonics and spelling patterns to spell words.
4. To create written texts for the classroom that children could not write independently.

When children begin interactive writing in kindergarten, they write letters to represent the beginning sounds in words and familiar words such as *the, a,* and *is.* The first letters that children write are often the letters in their own names, particularly the first letter. As children learn more about sound-symbol correspondences and spelling patterns, they do more of the writing. As they do interactive writing, children gain valuable experience applying the phonics skills and writing the high-frequency words they are learning. Figure 1–11 shows a first-grade class chart about insects. Many of the words have lines drawn under each letter; the teacher drew those lines as a spelling aid for children. The dotted letters represent letters that the teacher wrote, and the small squares represent correction tape used to cover mistakes.

Once children are writing words fluently, they can do interactive writing in small groups. Each student in the group uses a particular color pen and takes turns writing letters, letter clusters, and words. They also get used to using white correction tape to correct poorly formed letters and misspelled words. Children also sign their names in color on the page so that the teacher can track which children wrote which words.

Interactive writing can be used as part of literature focus units, in social studies and science thematic units, and for many other purposes, too. Some uses are:

- Write predictions before reading.
- Write responses after reading.
- Write letters and other messages.
- Make lists.

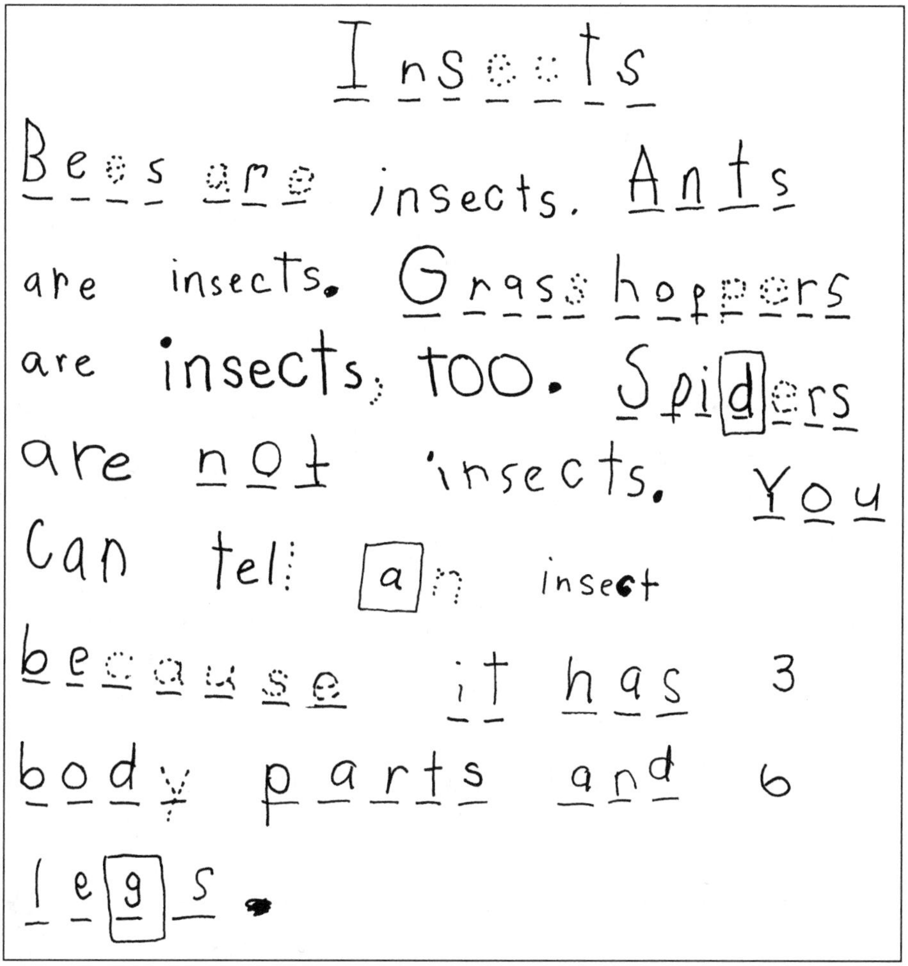

Figure 1–11 Interactive writing: A first-grade class writing about insects

- Write daily news.
- Rewrite a familiar story.
- Write information or facts.
- Write recipes.
- Make charts, maps, clusters, data charts, and other diagrams.
- Create innovations or new versions of a familiar text.
- Write class poems.

- Write words on a word wall.
- Make posters.

Moira McKenzie, a well-known British educator, is credited with developing interactive writing (Fountas & Pinnell, 1996). She developed the procedure based on Don Holdaway's work in shared reading. Interactive writing incorporates many of the features of LEA, but in interactive writing, children do much of the writing themselves. The steps in interactive writing are described in the step-by-step feature on page 37.

Guided Writing

Teachers scaffold or support children's writing during guided writing, but children do the actual writing themselves. Teachers plan structured writing activities and then supervise as children do the writing. For example, when children make pages for a class ABC book (as Mrs. Reeves's class did in the vignette at the beginning of the chapter) or when children write formula poems, they are doing guided writing because the teacher has set up the writing activity. Teachers also guide the writing when they conference with children as they write, participate in writing groups to help students revise their writing, and proofread with students. With novice writers, teachers use guided writing to help children choose what they want to write, organize their ideas into a sentence, and then transcribe each word onto paper.

Teachers use guided writing to provide instruction and assistance to children as they are actually writing. It is much like guided reading, in which teachers read with small groups of children and provide assistance as it is needed. Four purposes of guided writing are:

1. To scaffold a writing experience so that students can be successful.
2. To introduce different types of writing activities.
3. To teach children to use the writing process—in particular, how to revise and edit.
4. To teach procedures, concepts, strategies, and skills during minilessons.

Sometimes guided writing is equated with writing workshop, but students usually use a combination of independent writing and guided writing during writing workshop. The difference is the level of the teacher's support and guidance.

Independent Writing

In independent writing, children do the writing themselves and often use the writing process to write books. They practice the writing strategies and skills

Step by Step: Interactive Writing

1. ***Collect materials for interactive writing.*** Teachers use chart paper, colored marking pens, white correction tape, an alphabet chart, magnetic letters or letter cards, and a pointer for interactive writing. Also collect these materials for individual children's writing: small white boards, dry-erase pens, and erasers.

2. ***Provide a stimulus activity or set a purpose.*** Often teachers read or reread a trade book as a stimulus, but students can also write daily news, compose a letter, or brainstorm information they are learning in science.

3. ***Negotiate a text.*** Children create a text—often a sentence or two—to use for the writing activity. They repeat the sentence several times and segment the sentence into words. Children also count the number of words in the sentence. This practice helps children remember the sentence as it is written.

4. ***Pass out material for children to use.*** Children use individual white boards, dry-erase pens, and erasers to write the text individually as it is written together as a class on chart paper. Teachers periodically ask children to hold up their white boards so they can see what the children are writing.

5. ***Write the first sentence word-by-word.*** Before writing the first word, the teacher and children slowly pronounce the word, "pulling" it from their mouths or "stretching" it. Then children take turns writing the letters in the first word. The teacher chooses children to write the letters that represent each sound or spell the entire word, depending on children's knowledge of phonics and spelling. Teachers often have children use a pen of one color for the letters they write, and they use another color to write the parts of words that children don't know how to spell. In this way, teachers can keep track of how much writing children are able to do. Teachers keep a poster with the upper- and lowercase letters of the alphabet to refer to when children are unsure about how to form a letter, and they use white correction tape (sometimes called "boo-boo" tape) when students write a letter incorrectly or write the wrong letter. After writing each word, one child serves as the "spacer"; this child uses his or her hand to mark the space between words (and sentences). Teachers have children reread the sentence from the beginning each time a new word is completed. When appropriate, teachers call children's attention to capital letters, punctuation marks, and other conventions of print. They repeat this procedure to write additional sentences to complete the text. When teachers are using interactive writing to write a class collaboration book, this activity can take up to a week to complete.

6. ***Post the completed chart in the classroom.*** Children reread the completed chart using shared or independent reading. They often reread interactive writing charts when they "read the room." They may also want to add artwork to extend the chart. Also, children can use the words and sentences for other writing activities.

they are learning. Often children do independent writing in writing centers and during writing workshop, but they can also use independent writing when they write in reading logs, make posters, and do other types of writing activities. Teachers have students write independently for these six purposes:

1. To provide an authentic context for writing practice.
2. To give students opportunities to choose writing topics and forms.
3. To gain writing fluency and stamina.
4. As a tool for learning, such as when children write in reading logs and other types of journals.
5. To make and publish books.
6. To document learning in literature focus units and thematic units.

Children often write independently, whether they are writing in reading logs, making projects, or writing books during writing workshop. In the vignette at the beginning of the chapter, Mrs. Reeves's students were writing independently when they created projects. One child wrote a weather book called "Snowy Thoughts," which is presented in Figure 1–12. This child began by drawing the pictures on each page, and then he went back and wrote the text to accompany each illustration. After writing, he shared his book with Mrs. Reeves and a small group of classmates. He made a few revisions and then met with Mrs. Reeves again for an editing conference. He corrected several spelling and punctuation errors and then sat in the author's chair to share his book with classmates. Even though several spelling errors remain, he was very proud of his book!

ANSWERING TEACHERS' QUESTIONS ABOUT . . .

Teaching Children to Write

1. Is the writing process the same thing as writing workshop?

The writing process and writing workshop are related, but they are not the same thing. Writing workshop is one classroom application of the writing process, and it is discussed in Chapter 2, "Writing Workshop."

2. The writing process is just for older students, isn't it?

No, the writing process is for all students. Kindergartners and first graders participate in prewriting activities just as older students do, and they share their compositions in writing groups and use the author's chair. At first, young children may write only one draft, but they like hearing compliments about their writing, and before long a suggestion for improvement is intermingled with a series of compliments. For example, a child may say, "I really liked all the facts you told about gerbils, but you didn't say that they are mammals." And the writer responds, "Oh, I forgot. I think I can put it here. Thanks!" With the realization that readers provide worthwhile suggestions and that children need to revise their writing,

Figure 1–12 Independent writing: A child's weather book of "Snowy Thoughts"

these youngsters become full-fledged members of the writing process club.

3. How do you decide when to use modeled, shared, interactive, guided, or independent writing?

The type of support that teachers provide for a writing activity depends on their purpose for the activity. When teachers are introducing a new activity, they often use modeled or shared writing. When teachers want to focus on conventional spelling and other writing mechanics, they use interactive writing. When teachers want to provide individualized assistance or teach a strategy or skill, they might choose guided writing. And when teachers want children to practice skills they have learned, they have children write independently.

4. I don't feel comfortable with the writing process. Really, I'm afraid I'll lose control.

A writing process classroom is different from a traditional classroom. There is more noise as children work in groups and move around the classroom for different activities. This environment stimulates learning because children are actively involved in and are assuming responsibility for their own learning. To ensure that children are learning, teachers can move about the classroom, observing and talking with children as they write, talk, revise, and share their writing. If the noise or movement becomes too great, teachers can stop for a class meeting. At the meeting, they discuss the problem and consider ways to solve it.

To become more comfortable with the writing process approach, teachers might observe in a classroom that is already using the approach. They will observe a teacher who serves as a guide or a facilitator and children who know how to use the writing process and are actively involved in a writing project. In spite of the freedom to talk, move, and work independently, there is discipline and there are techniques for monitoring children's behavior and the work they complete.

5. Do children use the writing process every time they write?

Children's writing can be divided into formal writing and informal writing. Children use the writing process when they are doing formal writing—stories, reports, poems, and other pieces that they will publish and share with classmates and other audiences.

In contrast, children use informal writing as a tool for learning. When they write journal entries, K-W-L charts, clusters, and other types of informal writing, children do not usually use the writing process for these pieces. You will read more about informal writing in Chapter 6, "Journal Writing."

CHAPTER 2

Writing Workshop

Preview

 The components of writing workshop are writing, sharing, minilessons, and reading aloud to students.

 The purpose of writing workshop is to provide children with opportunities to use the writing process to create books and other compositions.

 Children can write about self-selected topics or write as part of a literature focus unit or thematic unit.

 Writing workshop and reading workshop are complementary activities.

Reading and Writing About Families

M rs. Zumwalt's third graders spend an hour and a half in the morning reading and talking about books that are about families, including *Ramona Quimby, Age 8* (Cleary, 1981), *Owl Moon* (Yolen, 1987), *When We Married Gary* (Hines, 1996), *The Relatives Came* (Rylant, 1985), *Grandpa Abe* (Russo, 1996), and *A Chair for My Mother* (Williams, 1982). They call this activity "reading workshop." Later in the day, they spend an hour and a half writing about their own families. They call this activity "writing workshop." Mrs. Zumwalt's schedule for writing workshop is

1:30–1:50	Class meeting
1:50–2:45	Writing
2:45–3:00	Sharing

Mrs. Zumwalt begins with a class meeting. She brings the class together for a variety of reasons: Sometimes they do shared writing and write a class composition together, sometimes she shares information about a favorite author of children's books, and at other times, she models how to write a poem or another writing form, or she teaches minilessons about writing skills and strategies, such as proofreading or writing leads. During the class meeting, Mrs. Zumwalt also does a "status of the class" to check on the progress each child is making. She calls each child by name, and the child responds by identifying the writing process stage at which he or she is working. This way she can check on how all 23 children are doing within 2 minutes, and she knows whom she needs to conference with once the class begins writing.

Next, students spend almost an hour writing independently and working on their compositions. Students are working at different stages of the writing process. Some are drawing pictures to illustrate their completed books, and others are meeting with Mrs. Zumwalt in a writing group to revise their compositions. Children's desks are arranged in five groups, and Mrs. Zumwalt briefly conferences with children in one group during each writing period and makes notes on a clipboard she carries. She describes the activities children are involved in and records her observations about their progress. An excerpt from a chart she uses for these notes is presented in Figure 2–1.

Connor	He finished proofing his book about learning to swim. He is doing a good job catching spelling errors. He says he likes using a red pen for editing. He's using quotation marks correctly for dialogue.
Belle	Belle should finish her book about her Mom and stepdad's wedding today or tomorrow. She included lots of details—a very memorable event! She is still capitalizing too many common nouns—needs a minilesson.
Anthony	He's still working on his rough draft about a trip to Yosemite. He's been working on it for almost two weeks. He says he wants to keep working on it, but I wonder. Does he like the topic? Does he know enough about the topic? Should he begin again on a new topic? Should I try shared writing? *Check him again tomorrow!*
Jason	Jason's revising page 3 of the book about his grandfather. There is too much information on this page. He's trying to reorganize it, but he is unwilling to cut any of it. He's very involved in his tribute to his grandfather. He has a photograph of him to put on the cover. His whole family is involved.
Marilynne	She is writing about a big family picnic last summer at her cousin's farm. In the rough draft she's writing only one sentence on each page so I encouraged her to expand the ideas with more sentences. I asked her to think of three sentences for each page and to say them to herself before she begins writing. *Check her again tomorrow!*

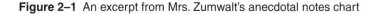

Figure 2–1 An excerpt from Mrs. Zumwalt's anecdotal notes chart

Children sign up on the chalkboard when they are ready to meet in revising groups. After four students have signed up, they form a group and meet at a table reserved for revising groups. Sometimes Mrs. Zumwalt joins the group, and at other times, the students meet by themselves. They take turns sharing their drafts and getting feedback on how well they are communicating. The students use the process that Mrs. Zumwalt has taught them.

Mrs. Zumwalt has another sign-up list for students who want to have a conference with her. She has found it easier than she expected to juggle the activities of students working at different writing process stages. Because her students are working independently on their own projects, some children are drafting or writing final copies when others need her assistance in writing groups or for proofreading.

Mrs. Zumwalt and her students use the last 15 minutes of writing workshop to meet as a class to share their completed compositions. Children sit in the author's chair, a place of honor, to read their published writings to the class. After reading, classmates clap and offer compliments. Sometimes a child offers a suggestion or asks for further information, but writers do not have to go back into their compositions to make further revisions.

As part of their study of families, the children are writing books about a family member. They began by brainstorming a list of questions about families, family histories, and memorable family events. Students interviewed their parents and sometimes their brothers, sisters, and other relatives. These are some of the questions they asked:

What family event do you remember best?
What things did we do when I was a baby?
What was one of your most embarrassing moments?
Did you have any arguments with your parents when you were a child?
Who taught you how to swim?
What do you remember about when you went to elementary school?
What pets did you have?

Students also brainstormed lists of their own memories. In a guided writing lesson, Mrs. Zumwalt showed a collection of objects including a dog biscuit, a sports trophy, a postcard, a teddy bear, a camera, a book, a slice of pizza, a bandage, and a package wrapped as a gift. As she shared each object, she asked students to jot down a phrase about a memory that the object brought to mind. She also asked students to list other memories that occurred to them.

Armed with this information, students sorted through their notes and selected memorable events to write about. They made a cluster about the event to collect and organize information before beginning to write. Some students drew pictures, and others chose a book about a family to use as a model. Other students had more developed ideas in mind and immediately began to write. Mrs. Zumwalt does not try to keep the students together, with everyone drafting or revising at the same time. Instead, they prewrite, draft, revise, edit, and publish independently, at their own speed. Some students write two compositions in the time it takes one child to complete one piece, and sometimes students decide to start over after spending a week or two on a topic. Although the students do not work at the same pace, they are all involved in the same type of assignment.

During the month they spend reading and writing about families, all students are expected to do the prewriting activities and complete at least one book, most likely a personal narrative about a memorable family event or a firsthand biography of a family member. Children can also experiment with other writing forms—a newspaper account of the event, a letter recounting the event, or a poem.

Here is Jason's book about his grandfather, entitled "The Railroad Man":

 My grandpap used to work on the railroad. His name was Bert Alan Simpson. He was an old man with white hair but he was nice to everybody. He used to always have gum in his pocket and he gave me some every time I saw him.

He was the engineer on freight trains from Fresno to Portland, and he worked on trains for 35 years. He just loves trains and he knows a lot about them.

When I was little he used to take me to the Fresno Train Station on Saturdays so we could look at the trains. We'd talk to his friends the engineers. I remember Hank and Bill they were his friends. They would let me get up on the engine and let me pretend that I was an engineer too. After we got off the train, we would look at the people getting on the trains and we would watch them pull out. Grandpap said he just loved the sound of trains. "Clackity-clack." He said it was music to his ears.

My Grandpap is dead now. He had a heart attack and he died but every time I see a train I think of him and remember the time we spent together. I have a red railroad handkerchief of his. I guess I love trains too.

Each paragraph represents one page in Jason's book.

Mrs. Zumwalt and her class developed a rubric for assessing the books they wrote about their families. As a class, they decided that the rubric should assess these points:

Describe the person you are writing about.
Tell about one or more experiences with lots of details.
Tell why the person is important to you.
Use complete sentences.
Use "good" spelling, capitalization, and punctuation.

Then the class decided to rate each item with 1, 2, or 3 (highest) points, and both Mrs. Zumwalt and the students would score their completed books. The score for the assignment would be the number circled most often. Jason's completed rubric for his book "The Railroad Man" is shown in Figure 2–2. Jason scored the rubric first, and he

Name ___Jason___ Date ___10-18___

Book ___The Railroad Man___

Rubric for Books About Our Families

Describe the person you are writing about. 1 ②③

Tell about one or more experiences with lots of details. 1 ②3

Tell why the person is important to you. 1 2 ③

Use complete sentences. 1 2 ③

Use "good" spelling, capitalization and punctuation. 1 ②③

Figure 2–2 Mrs. Zumwalt's class rubric

drew a triangle around the numbers to represent his score. Mrs. Zumwalt followed with circles around the numbers for her score.

Mrs. Zumwalt bases the grades that children receive for their work on the accumulated information they present in their writing folders. Students place in their folders their brainstormed lists of memorable events; notes from their interviews of family members; prewriting, drafting, and final copies of compositions; their self-assessment rubric for one book they wrote; and a reflective letter they have written to Mrs. Zumwalt at the end of the month about their writing and work habits.

TEACHERS IMPLEMENT THE WRITING PROCESS in their classrooms through writing workshop. Many teachers use writing workshop to provide an opportunity for students to write on self-selected topics and to work independently, employing the writing process as they work. Other teachers use writing workshop for their students to write stories, reports, poems, and other forms of writing as part of literature focus units and thematic units. In the vignette, Mrs. Zumwalt used writing workshop to provide opportunities for students to write on self-selected topics and to write as part of a unit on families. Her students worked independently on their writing projects during a regularly scheduled writing time. No matter which way teachers use writing workshop, its great benefit is that children become familiar with the ebb and flow of the writing process and experience the exhilaration that all authors feel as they publish their writing and share it with readers.

The writing workshop approach is an innovative way of implementing the writing process (Calkins, 1996; Fletcher & Portalupi, 2001; Graves, 1994). According to Lucy McCormick Calkins (1986), in this approach, students write about what is vital and real for them, and their writing becomes the curriculum. They assume ownership of their learning and choose what they write and how they will write. At the same time, the teacher's role changes from being a provider of knowledge and writing topics to serving as a facilitator and guide. The classroom becomes a community of writers who write and share their writing.

Self-selection, ownership, self-monitoring, feedback, and individualized instruction are the hallmarks of writing workshop (Atwell, 1998). Classrooms are social environments, and children are active participants as they choose the direction their writing will take, consciously monitor their writing processes, and turn to classmates and the teacher for feedback and guidance. These characteristics define the workshop environment, whether students are writing, reading, researching, or spelling (Barnes, Morgan, & Weinhold, 1997; Cohle & Towle, 2001; Opitz & Cooper, 1993; Rogovin, 2001).

In this chapter, you will learn how to set up writing workshop and teach the writing process, which was presented in Chapter 1. The key points about writing workshop are:

- The components of writing workshop are writing, sharing, minilessons, and reading aloud to students.
- The purpose of writing workshop is to provide children with opportunities to use the writing process to create books and other compositions.
- Children can write about self-selected topics or write as part of a literature focus unit or thematic unit.
- Writing workshop and reading workshop are complementary activities.

The Components of Writing Workshop

The heart of writing workshop is independent writing, and teachers provide 30 to 60 minutes or more each day for children to write independently during writing workshop. Teachers also add several other components. The four activities that are associated with writing workshop are:

1. *Writing.* Children spend 30 to 60 minutes working on writing projects. They use the writing process as they develop and refine their writing, and they conference with classmates and the teacher about their writing.
2. *Sharing.* The class gathers together to share their new publications, often during the last 5 to 15 minutes of writing workshop. Children take turns reading their writing aloud to classmates, who respond to the writing and offer compliments.
3. *Minilessons.* Teachers provide 15- to 30-minute lessons on writing workshop procedures, information about authors, literary concepts, and writing strategies and skills.
4. *Reading aloud to children.* Teachers read aloud picture books and chapter books to children to share examples of good writing and teach children about authors.

It is important to have a clear, simple structure for writing workshop so that children can anticipate the writing activities in which they will be involved. Mrs. Zumwalt had a predictable structure using three components, and other teachers organize their writing workshop in other ways. Figure 2–3 presents four schedules for writing workshop. Teachers decide which components to use according to the other language arts activities going on in the classroom and the time they have available. For example, if teachers read aloud to children every day after lunch, it may not be necessary to include that component in writing workshop. When teachers have only a short period of time available, they can alternate minilessons and sharing or include minilessons in their reading workshop.

Ms. Yang's First-Grade Schedule

During the first 90 minutes of the school day, Ms. Yang has students work at literacy centers while she conducts guided reading lessons in small groups. After a short recess, students move into writing workshop. Her schedule is:

10:00–10:15 Reading aloud to students
10:15–10:30 Guided writing activity
10:30–11:00 Independent writing
11:00–11:15 Sharing

During the guided writing activity, Ms. Yang and her students write a sentence together based on the book Ms. Yang read aloud. Ms. Yang emphasizes using conventional spelling, capitalization, and punctuation during guided writing.

Mr. Scott's Third- and Fourth-Grade Schedule

Mr. Scott's students spend the first hour of the school day working in reading and writing workshop. Students alternate between reading and writing projects during this time. His schedule is:

8:45–8:50 Status of the class
8:50–9:40 Independent reading or writing
9:40–9:45 Sharing

During the independent writing period, students move through the writing process, and Mr. Scott conferences with students as they work.

Mrs. Flores's Fifth-Grade Schedule

Mrs. Flores's fifth graders begin their literacy block with either literature circles, in which students read a book with a small group of classmates, or a literature focus unit, in which everyone in the class reads the same book. During writing workshop, the second half of the literacy block, students spend 75 minutes learning about authors, practicing writing skills, and writing independently. Mrs. Flores's schedule is:

10:30–10:50 Minilesson
10:50–10:55 Status of the class
10:55–11:55 Independent writing
11:55–12:05 Sharing

During the minilesson, Mrs. Flores alternates lessons on authors, spelling and mechanics, and sentence building using sentences from books students are reading.

Ms. Boland's Eighth-Grade Schedule

Ms. Boland teaches writing as part of a two-hour language arts and social studies block. She alternates reading and writing workshop, depending on the other activities in which students are involved. When they are working on writing projects, students often spend 60 minutes in writing workshop. Her schedule is:

1:05–1:10 Status of the class
1:10–1:55 Independent writing
1:55–2:05 Sharing

During the sharing period, Ms. Boland often asks all students to read aloud a powerful sentence they have written since no one has completed the project yet.

Figure 2–3 Four schedules for writing workshop

Writing

To write well, students need frequent and regular times to write. During the independent writing time, students spend 30 to 60 minutes working on writing projects. Graves (1994) emphasizes that children must write about things they know well so that they can be successful. Children are "experts" when they write about their hobbies, their family, or something they have learned during a social studies or science unit. They usually move through all five stages of the writing process—prewriting, drafting, revising, editing, and publishing—at their own pace as they write books and other compositions.

During prewriting, students choose topics to write about. They may refer to their writing notebooks where they have brainstormed lists of possible writing topics, drawn pictures, written snippets of conversation, and described settings and events. Students also draw pictures and reread favorite books when they are looking for a topic. They might also write a retelling of a favorite story, write out the verses of a familiar song or poem, or play with the sentence patterns from a favorite book.

Teachers help children learn to identify their own topics for writing. Instead of suggesting trivial story starters, teachers encourage children to "read the world" (Graves, 1994) by demonstrating how to develop topics using the ordinary events of daily life and school life. Teachers encourage children to talk about things that interest them, stories they have enjoyed, ideas they might want to share with classmates. Out of these conversations, topics emerge. Sometimes classmates can help students identify topics to write about. Graves (1983) explains that children come to school wanting to write, but too often teachers ignore children's urge to show what they know.

At other times, children have broad topics assigned to them, as Mrs. Zumwalt's students did. They were writing about families, but they chose the family member they wanted to write about and organized the information for their books as they wanted. Young children use drawings to organize their ideas, and older children use clusters and other graphic organizers to organize their ideas for writing.

Once students have gathered and organized their ideas, they begin to draft their compositions. Children work independently but often share their ideas with the teacher or classmates working nearby. They focus on the development of their piece rather than worrying about spelling each word correctly or making sure to capitalize and punctuate correctly. Students understand that in the drafting stage, writers pour out their ideas. They double-space their writing and mark their papers as "rough drafts" or "sloppy copies."

As they are writing, children stop to think of ideas, reread their piece, or ask a classmate a question. Sometimes they decide to make changes or start over if the piece is not working. The teacher walks around the classroom, stopping to say, "Tell me about your piece." Through brief conferences, teachers provide support for young writers and are available to help children when their writing is not going smoothly. Teachers and children must recognize that writing rarely goes smoothly; it develops with stops and starts, and with a few dead ends.

Children are constantly revising. They revise in their minds, even before they write a word, and they revise as they write, often stopping to reread what they have written, making changes and adding words, phrases, and sentences. After finishing their first draft, children reread it at least once to themselves and make some revisions. They may notice that some words were omitted as they wrote hastily or that too many sentences start with "It." They may think of a better way to express an idea, or discover that they need to check their facts. They make necessary changes before meeting with a writing group.

In the writing group, children share their rough drafts with a small group of classmates and get compliments and other comments from them. These comments give the writer ideas for revising. Sometimes the teacher meets with the group; at other times, children meet by themselves. It is crucial that children know how to conduct a writing group and how to give constructive suggestions to classmates. Many teachers have found that it is more effective for children to meet in a small group rather than with a partner because a group can provide more feedback than a single child can.

After sharing their compositions in a writing group, children make some revisions. They may choose to make revisions based on feedback they received from classmates in the writing group, or other ideas may come to mind. Some teachers have students use a blue pen to make revisions so that the changes will stand out. Rather than erasing the original, children cross out and make revisions so that the child and the teacher can track the child's use of revision strategies. Sometimes the revising stage leads to more prewriting and drafting; at other times, children move on to editing after they have made revisions.

During editing, children proofread their compositions to locate mechanical errors and then correct as many errors as they can. Many teachers have children use a red pen to make the corrections. Classmates help proofread each other's papers, and children often meet with the teacher for an editing conference to identify and correct any remaining errors.

After children's rough drafts have been edited, they make their final copies. Many times, children compile their final copies to make books during writing workshop, but sometimes they attach their writing to artwork, make posters, write letters that are mailed, or perform scripts as skits or puppet shows.

Sharing

For the last 5 to 15 minutes of writing workshop, the class gathers together so that students can share their new publications and make other related announcements. A child who has just finished writing a puppet show script and making puppets may ask for volunteers to help perform the puppet show, which could be presented several days later during sharing time. Younger children often sit in a circle or gather together on a rug for sharing time, and chil-

Writing Workshop Procedures

Writing rough drafts	Making and binding books
Participating in writing groups	Using word processing programs
Conferencing	Making revisions
Writing "All About the Author" pages	Choosing papers for portfolios
Using writing folders	Sharing published books
Writing reflections	Using the dictionary
Using writing process checklists	Making and using rubrics

Writers' Craft

Information about authors	Information about illustrators
Beginning-middle-end	Metaphors and similes
Plot	Personification
Characters	Onomatopoeia
Setting	Alliteration
Theme	Repetition
Point of view	Wordplay

Writing Skills and Strategies

Clustering	Adding details
Proofreading	Writing dialogue
Revising	Distinguishing between homophones
Monitoring	Sentence combining
Choosing titles	Capitalization
Making tables of contents	Punctuation

Figure 2–4 Topics for minilessons

dren take turns sitting in the author's chair to read their compositions. After reading, classmates clap and offer compliments. They may also make other comments and suggestions, but the focus is on celebrating completed writing projects, not on revising the composition to make it better.

Minilessons

Minilessons are brief discussions or demonstrations of writing workshop procedures, writers' craft, and writing strategies and skills (Atwell, 1998; Ray, 2002). A list of possible topics for minilessons is shown in Figure 2–4. The purpose of minilessons is to highlight the topic, provide information about the topic, and then give opportunities for guided practice. Worksheets are not used in minilessons; instead, students apply the lesson to their own writing. Minilessons can be conducted with the whole class, with small groups of students who have indicated that they need to learn more about a particular topic, and with individual students. Minilessons can be taught whenever teachers see a need as they observe children writing. Teachers can also plan minilessons on a regular basis to introduce and review topics.

The steps in teaching a minilesson are shown in the step-by-step feature on page 53. A description of a minilesson on revising for a small group of sixth graders is presented in the minilesson feature on page 54.

Reading Aloud to Children

Teachers read aloud stories, informational books, and poetry to children every day. Some teachers read aloud during writing workshop, and others schedule this activity during another part of the school day. As the teacher reads aloud, children have the opportunity to enjoy the literary experience and learn about authors and how they write. Teachers also share information about authors and sometimes read and compare several books written by the same author, so that children can examine how that author crafted his or her books or identify the stylistic devices he or she used. This activity also helps students to feel part of a community of writers.

> **ELL** **Teacher's Note: Assisting English Language Learners**
>
> The more your English language learners read and reread books at their level and listen to others read aloud, the better their writing becomes. Through reading, students learn about English sentence patterns and pick up new vocabulary words that they can incorporate in their writing. These students benefit from opportunities to talk and write about books they are reading; as they make reading-writing connections, their learning is enhanced.

Comparing Writing Workshop to Reading Workshop

Teachers often use writing workshop in conjunction with reading workshop, as Mrs. Zumwalt did in the vignette at the beginning of the chapter. In reading workshop, children have large chunks of time for reading and responding to literature and a choice about what they read (Atwell, 1998; Serafini, 2001). The components are similar to those of writing workshop, except that the focus is on reading, and students use many of the same reading and writing strategies and skills. The components of reading workshop often include the following:

1. *Reading.* Children spend 30 to 60 minutes reading and responding to books and other reading materials.

2. *Sharing.* The class gathers together to share books children have finished reading and projects they have created.

3. *Minilessons.* The teacher spends 15 to 30 minutes teaching brief lessons on reading workshop procedures, information about authors, literary concepts, and reading strategies and skills.

4. *Reading aloud to children.* The teacher reads aloud high-quality literature that children cannot read themselves to increase their understanding of literature and to provide children with a shared literature experience.

Step by Step: A Minilesson

1. *Introduce the topic.* Teachers identify the topic for the minilesson and often write the literary topic on chart paper or on the chalkboard; it may be a writing workshop procedure, a literary concept, or a writing strategy or skill. After identifying the topic, teachers briefly define the topic or mention the characteristics, and they write this information on the chart paper or on the chalkboard.

2. *Share examples.* Teachers provide examples of the procedure, concept, strategy, or skill using children's own writing or books written for children. Then they invite students to identify other examples. Children write some examples on the chart paper or on the chalkboard.

3. *Provide information.* Teachers provide additional information about the topic and how it is used in writing, or they review information presented in the first step. This is the step where teachers clarify misconceptions and contrast the topic with related topics. The teacher may model using the topic in a writing activity or have the students sort examples and nonexamples.

4. *Guide practice.* Children work in pairs or small groups to practice what they are learning. The teacher circulates around the classroom to provide assistance or review the information that has been presented.

5. *Assess learning.* Teachers ask children to reflect or speculate on how they can use this information as they write. These reflections can be oral or written. Teachers often ask children to commit to a particular course of action. They might ask: "How will you remember to _____?" "When will you _____?" "What will you say to yourself when you _____?" "What do you think the best way to _____ is?"

Just as writing workshop fosters independent writing for genuine purposes and authentic audiences, reading workshop fosters independent reading of self-selected stories, poems, and informational books. Teachers often connect the two, and students participate in many of the same types of activities.

Implementing Writing Workshop

Teachers begin writing workshop by introducing the writing process and modeling writing workshop procedures. They also create a writing workshop environment and arrange the classroom for workshop activities. And teachers continue modifying and refining writing workshop as their children grow as writers. Writing workshop is not easy to implement, but it is worth the effort. Many teachers and parents have reported the positive effects writing workshop has on children's development as writers (Atwell, 1998; Calkins, 1996; Rief, 1992; J. Wilde, 1993). One thing that makes writing workshop difficult to implement is that many teachers were not taught this way themselves, and

Vivid Verbs

Mrs. Hernandez is teaching a series of minilessons on vocabulary. She is concerned that her sixth graders use common, familiar words instead of more powerful and precise words that would energize their writing. She has introduced the thesaurus to her students and explained the importance of choosing words carefully. Today, she focuses on using vivid verbs.

1. Introduce the topic

"The focus of today's minilesson is on verbs because verbs are often the most powerful words in a sentence. They are the motor that drives the sentence," Mrs. Hernandez explains.

2. Share examples

The teacher passes out copies of two anonymous compositions (written by students the previous year) and asks the students to highlight the verbs as she reads the two compositions aloud. She accentuates each verb as she reads in order to assist students in identifying them. Then students read aloud the verbs they highlighted. Verbs in the first composition include *is, wanted,* and *thought*; *annoys, startled,* and *crackle* appear in the second composition. The sixth graders quickly notice that the verbs in the first composition are lackluster compared to those in the second composition.

3. Provide information

Mrs. Hernandez explains that during revision, students should look at the verbs they've used and make sure that they are powerful or vivid. Tami asks if they should highlight the verbs in their own writing, and the teacher agrees that it is a good way to check. Then, she continues, if students find that the verbs aren't vivid, they can substitute better words. Sometimes they can think of these more powerful words themselves, and sometimes they should use a thesaurus to find a better word.

4. Guide practice

Next, Mrs. Hernandez passes out copies of the thesaurus and asks the students to work in pairs to substitute more vivid verbs in the first composition to make the writing more powerful. As the students work, she circulates around the classroom, checking that the synonyms the students choose are appropriate ones.

5. Assess learning

As she ends the lesson, Mrs. Hernandez asks students to highlight at least 10 vivid verbs in their current compositions, and if they can't find that many, to revise so that they do.

they may not have seen other teachers use writing workshop effectively. Another difficulty is that both children and teachers assume new roles in writing workshop. Children assume more ownership of their work, apply strategies and writing skills, and self-assess their writing. Teachers spend a great deal of their time conferencing with students, working one-on-one or in small groups rather than directing the whole class. These new roles are different for both children and teachers, but with practice, they become comfortable, and most teachers and children could not imagine a school day without writing workshop!

Introducing the Writing Process

Regardless of whether you are teaching first graders or eighth graders, it is crucial to introduce them to the writing process and to help them learn the activities involved in each stage. Certainly students learn about the writing process as they write, but an introduction to the process and activities involved in each stage is in order. Teachers begin by explaining the process approach, describing and demonstrating each stage, and guiding students as they develop several brief compositions to experience the writing process. Guidelines for introducing the writing process are presented in Figure 2–5.

Students need to learn the procedures and activities involved in each stage of the writing process and the terminology associated with the writing process. In particular, they need to learn how to make clusters, participate in writing groups, revise, and proofread. Teachers use minilessons to demonstrate each procedure and then provide many opportunities for students to practice each procedure and activity through writing workshop and thematic projects.

Learning the writing process takes time. Students need to work through the entire process again and again using writing workshop and thematic projects until the stages and activities become automatic. Once students understand the writing process, they can manipulate the activities of each stage to meet the differing demands of particular writing projects and can modify the process to accommodate their personal writing styles.

It is often useful to hang charts outlining the writing process and related activities in the classroom. These charts should be developed with students rather than made in advance by the teacher. Five writing process charts are presented in Figure 2–6. Chart A, "We Use the Reading and Writing Processes," was developed in a first-grade classroom. Even though the two processes are briefly stated, the first graders recognize the similarities between them. Chart B, "The Writing Process," was developed by sixth graders and lists the five stages and activities involved in each one. Fourth graders developed "Your Jobs in a Writing Group" (chart C) to identify the responsibilities and duties of each person in a revising group. The same group of fourth graders also developed "Proofreading Reminders" (chart D) as part of a minilesson on proofreading. Chart E, "Things to Say in Writing Groups," is from a third-grade classroom; in the first

1. **Use the writing process terminology.** As teachers introduce the writing process, they should use the names of each stage and related terms. Students, even young children, learn to use *proofread, leads, compliments, cluster, writing groups,* and other terms quickly and easily.

2. **Develop charts listing the stages of the writing process.** Charts listing the stages of the writing process and activities involved at each stage should hang in classrooms. The chart is a useful reminder for students and emphasizes the importance of writing. Students should help make the charts. Teachers might begin by listing the five stages and then have students add information about the activities involved in each stage.

3. **Demonstrate the writing process.** Teachers demonstrate the writing process by writing a composition with the class. Teachers choose a topic related to a literature focus unit or a social studies or science thematic unit and work through the five stages of the writing process with the class to prewrite, draft, revise, edit, and publish the composition.

4. **Keep first writings short.** Students' first writings should be short pieces so that they can move through the writing process rather quickly. First graders might write a four-page "All About…" book with a sentence or two on each page; fourth graders might write a paragraph or two about an experience. A detailed, seven-page biography of a sports personality or a historical figure is not a good first-time project for students at any grade level because of the time and effort involved in gathering and organizing the information, writing the rough draft, sharing it in writing groups, revising the piece, locating and correcting mechanical errors, and recopying the final draft.

5. **Demonstrate revising and editing activities in minilessons.** Because revising and editing activities are unfamiliar to most students, teachers need to demonstrate the activities in minilessons. For a minilesson on revision, for example, teachers might read aloud a composition and invite students to take turns giving compliments, asking questions, and making suggestions for revising the piece. Then teachers make revisions and duplicate copies to share with the class during another minilesson. Students see how sections are crossed out and moved and how new sections are added. For a minilesson on editing, students proofread the revised composition to identify and correct mechanical errors.

6. **Use writing folders.** Students use writing folders to hold their prewriting, illustrations, rough drafts, writing group notes, and editing checklists. When the writing project is completed, all materials are organized, stapled together, and clipped to the final copy. The folder is used again for the next writing project.

Figure 2–5 Guidelines for introducing the writing process

part of the chart, students listed polite sentence stems for making comments, and in the second part, they identified important things to look for in a piece of writing. Students refer to this chart when they are thinking of comments to make in writing groups.

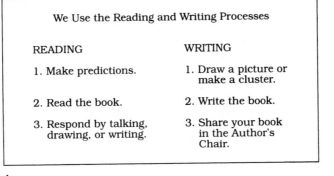

```
          We Use the Reading and Writing Processes

       READING                     WRITING

       1. Make predictions.        1. Draw a picture or
                                      make a cluster.

       2. Read the book.           2. Write the book.

       3. Respond by talking,      3. Share your book
          drawing, or writing.        in the Author's
                                      Chair.
```

A.

```
                    THE WRITING PROCESS

       1. PREWRITING:    Gather and organize ideas.

       2. DRAFTING:      Write a sloppy copy.

       3. REVISING:      Share your draft in a writing group.
                         Then make at least three changes.

       4. EDITING:       Proofread and correct errors.

       5. PUBLISHING:    Write the final copy and illustrate
                         it. Share with an audience.
```

B.

```
              YOUR JOBS IN A WRITING GROUP

   1. Bring your rough draft and blue revising pen.

   2. Share your rough draft.

   3. Talk about your rough draft and listen for compliments, questions, and
      suggestions.

   4. Take notes on your rough draft.

   5. Make a plan for revising your rough draft.

   6. Be a good listener when other people share their rough drafts.

   7. Give compliments, ask questions, and make suggestions about other
      people's rough drafts.
```

C.   *continues*

Figure 2–6 Five writing process charts

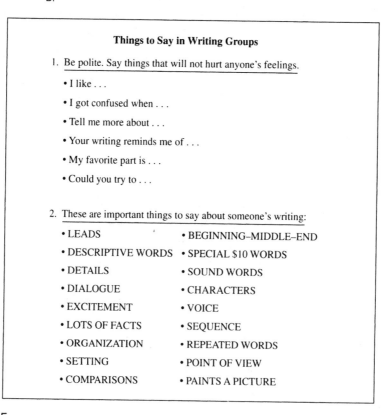

Proofreading Reminders

1. Say every word as you proofread.

2. Point with your pencil.

3. Proofread three times:
   a. for spelling errors
   b. for capitalization and punctuation
   c. for homonyms

4. Ask someone else to proofread your paper.

D.

Things to Say in Writing Groups

1. Be polite. Say things that will not hurt anyone's feelings.

   • I like . . .

   • I got confused when . . .

   • Tell me more about . . .

   • Your writing reminds me of . . .

   • My favorite part is . . .

   • Could you try to . . .

2. These are important things to say about someone's writing:

   • LEADS   • BEGINNING–MIDDLE–END

   • DESCRIPTIVE WORDS   • SPECIAL $10 WORDS

   • DETAILS   • SOUND WORDS

   • DIALOGUE   • CHARACTERS

   • EXCITEMENT   • VOICE

   • LOTS OF FACTS   • SEQUENCE

   • ORGANIZATION   • REPEATED WORDS

   • SETTING   • POINT OF VIEW

   • COMPARISONS   • PAINTS A PICTURE

E.

Figure 2–6 *continued*

Class Collaborations. One way to demonstrate the writing process is through a class collaboration. A class collaboration is shared writing in which children and the teacher write together, using all five stages of the writing process. Children practice the writing process within a supportive environment, and the teacher reviews concepts and clarifies misconceptions as the group piece is written. Children supply the ideas for writing and offer suggestions for how to tackle common writing problems.

The teacher begins by introducing the idea of writing a group composition and discussing the project. Almost any type of writing project can be written as a class collaboration, including poems, letters, stories, reports, and persuasive essays. What is most important is that all children are familiar with the topic and the writing form. For example, if children are writing an impassioned letter to the editor of the local newspaper about a community ecological problem, they should be knowledgeable about the problem and about how to write a persuasive letter. Or, if children are writing an innovation (a new version of a familiar text) of *Rosie's Walk* (Hutchins, 1968), they need to be familiar with the story.

Children write the composition together, moving through the prewriting, drafting, revising, editing, and publishing stages of the writing process. They prewrite to gather and organize ideas. The teacher records their ideas in a cluster or using another graphic organizer. Then children dictate a rough draft, which the teacher writes on chart paper or using an overhead projector, taking care to double-space the writing and label it "Rough Draft." Or children can take turns doing the writing. The teacher is alert for any misunderstandings children may have about writing or the writing process and, when necessary, reviews concepts and offers suggestions.

Then children and the teacher move on to the revising stage. The class becomes a writing group. The teacher or a child reads the rough draft aloud several times. Next, children comment on the strong points of the composition, ask questions, and make suggestions about how to fine-tune the draft. Some parts may be reworked; others may be deleted or moved. More specific words will be substituted for less specific ones, and redundant words and sentences will be deleted. Also, children may add new parts to the composition. After making the necessary content changes, children proofread the composition, identifying mechanical errors, checking paragraph breaks, and combining sentences as needed. They take turns making changes. The teacher clarifies any questions children have about mechanics, such as spelling homophones or using commas for a series of items.

Finally, the composition is published. The teacher or several students copy the completed composition on sheets of chart paper and compile them into a big or regular-size book or copy them on sheets of writing paper and duplicate copies of the composition for each student. Children add illustrations to a class book or personalize the individual copies they receive.

A first-grade class wrote this collaborative retelling of *Where the Wild Things Are* (Sendak, 1963):

Page 1:   Max got in trouble. He scared his dog and got sent to bed.
Page 2:   His room turned into a jungle. His room grew more and more.
Page 3:   A boat came for Max. It was his private boat.
Page 4:   He came to where the wild things lived. They made him king.
Page 5:   The wild things had a wild rumpus. They danced and hung on trees. Max sent them to bed without any supper.
Page 6:   Max waved good-bye and went back home.
Page 7:   His dinner was waiting for him. It was still hot from the microwave.

This version is very revealing: The children clearly understand the beginning, middle, and end of the story, and their explanation on page 7 of why Max's dinner was still hot is an interesting rationalization. The teacher was disappointed that the children chose not to include Sendak's vivid descriptions of the wild things "roaring their terrible roars" and "gnashing their terrible teeth"; their choices indicate a focus on the plot rather than literary language.

The children divided their retelling into pages, and they took turns copying the final version onto large sheets of chart paper, which were compiled in a big book. The first graders enjoyed the book so much that several days later, the teacher made smaller individual copies of the pages, which the children illustrated and bound into books. Children read and reread their versions, and many wrote other books about wild things and other adventures that might have happened to Max.

In "Marbles Lost, Marbles Found: Collaborative Production of Text," Esther Fine (1987) described how her middle-grade class of students with behavior disorders wrote a novel collaboratively. All of the students contributed to the writing, and learned through the experience that they could write and that they had valuable contributions to make. Fine summed up the experience this way: "Collaboration is learning to learn and to work together. . . . Collaboration is a great solution" (p. 487).

In another type of class collaboration, children divide the writing project into small segments, and each child or small group completes one part. If children are writing a report, for example, they divide into small groups, and each group writes one chapter. Or, if the class is writing a retelling of a favorite story, each child or pair of children writes and illustrates one page or chapter of the book. Often the class does the first page or chapter together to review the writing process and procedure for the particular writing project. Then children work independently on their own parts. Children come back together to revise and edit their writing and finally to compile and publish their writing as a book.

Figure 2–7 presents an excerpt from a class book, "California: The Golden State," written by fourth graders as the culmination of a year-long study of the state. Students brainstormed topics and divided into pairs and small groups to write the sections. This book is interesting because students wrote the chapters from the viewpoint of Californians in each setting; the chapter about the gold

---

A Tour of San Francisco

Clang! Clang! Clang! go the bells on the cable cars. The cable cars go up and down the hills of San Francisco. Let's take a ride. It's a good way to learn about this city. San Francisco is the third largest city in California and the population is 678,974. It is located on a peninsula next to the Pacific Ocean.

San Francisco is an old city. Spanish missionaries founded it in 1776. The city really began to grow in 1848 with the Gold Rush. It was an important mining supply center. People who made a lot of money came back to live in San Francisco, and they built beautiful homes on Nob Hill. Most of the homes are gone now because of the Great San Francisco Earthquake in 1906.

Our first stop is at Chinatown. There are many people from China that live in San Francisco. Some Chinese people came to America to work in the gold rush and some came to work on the First Transcontinental Railroad that was built in the 1860's. Now some of their great grandchildren live in one area that is called Chinatown. Look on the street signs. You see the names written in Chinese and in English. Do you hear people talking Chinese in the stores and on the street? We can stop and eat Chinese food and buy little gifts that come from China. Did you know there is a fortune cookie factory here, too?

Our second stop is at Fisherman's Wharf. Many, many fishing boats used to dock here. They caught fish in the ocean. Then they came here to sell the fish. Now there are only a few boats but there are good seafood restaurants here. We will walk over to two fun shopping centers. One shopping center is called the Cannery. It used to be a factory that made canned food. That's why it's called the Cannery. The other one is Ghirardelli Square, and it used to be a chocolate factory. You can eat Ghirardelli chocolates at a store there.

Now we will take a boat tour of San Francisco Bay and see the sights. Look straight ahead and you will see the Golden Gate Bridge. It is very tall and you can see the two towers and the cables that hang down to hold the bridge up. It is called a suspension bridge and it is 8,981 feet long. Many people drive across the bridge every day and you can even walk across it. There is a sidewalk. Over here you can see Alcatraz Island. It used to be a military fort and prison. The most dangerous criminals in America used to be put here, but it is closed now.

Thank you for taking this tour. I hope you have learned that San Francisco is a great and interesting city. There is much, much, much more to see and you can take more of our tours. I want you to leave your heart in San Francisco and come back soon. Good bye!

Figure 2–7 Shared writing: An excerpt from a fourth-grade class book, "California: The Golden State"

rush was written from a miner's viewpoint, and the chapter on Yosemite National Park was written from naturalist John Muir's viewpoint. The excerpt in Figure 2–7, "A Tour of San Francisco," was written from the viewpoint of a tour guide. This perspective makes the writing more interesting to read and allows students to add personal experiences to the information they present. There is no doubt that these students have visited San Francisco and have been on tours themselves. Students participated in all five stages of the writing process as they prepared the book. As the final step, the chapters were compiled and a cover, title page, dedication, and table of contents were added. Then copies were made for each student.

Collaborative compositions give children an opportunity to practice writing process activities and give teachers a chance to respond to children's questions and misconceptions. Teachers also use class collaborations when introducing writing forms or when children would have trouble doing the writing independently either because of the large size of the project or because of children's limited writing experience.

Writing Centers.   Teachers set up a writing center to provide a supportive environment for small groups of children as they write. A writing center is a designated area of the classroom, often a table where writing supplies, including paper, pens and pencils, art supplies, bookmaking materials, and staplers are stored. Dictionaries, thesauri, computerized spell checkers, and word books are also available at writing centers.

Children come to the writing center to work on writing projects. In kindergarten and first grade, they may write in journals or make books, and the teacher, another adult, or an upper-grade student is often at the center to provide additional guidance to children as they write. Young children work through an abbreviated version of the writing process, gathering and organizing ideas, often by drawing a picture, and then writing words using invented spelling. As the child writes, the teacher often guides the child, helping him or her connect words into sentences, and sounding out the spelling of some words and applying other strategies for spelling other words. After writing, children read their compositions to classmates at the writing center. At other times, children write notes to classmates at the writing center and then "mail" the notes to classmates in mailboxes or by tacking them to a "Message Center" board.

Older children participate in a variety of writing activities at writing centers. Often they write books on topics they have chosen using materials supplied at the writing center, but at other times, they may work on a particular writing project that is part of a literature focus unit or thematic unit. For example:

- Second graders make safety posters after reading *Officer Buckle and Gloria* (Rathmann, 1995).
- During a unit on the solar system, third graders write books about the planets.
- Fourth graders write sequels after reading *The Sign of the Beaver* (Speare, 1983).
- As part of a unit on Chris Van Allsburg, fifth graders create stories based on an illustration in *The Mysteries of Harris Burdick* (1984).

- Sixth graders make posters with information about an ancient god or goddess.
- As part of a unit on the middle ages, seventh graders write simulated journals modeled on *Catherine, Called Birdy* (Cushman, 1994).
- Eighth graders write found poems after reading *The Giver* (Lowry, 1993).

In each of these examples, children work side-by-side with classmates, talk with them to brainstorm ideas, get feedback, and share their writing.

Too often, teachers think of writing centers, as well as other types of centers, as a way to organize in primary classrooms, but writing centers can be used effectively at any grade level. One benefit is the support and guidance provided by the teacher, upper-grade student aide, or classmates. As children work in centers, they have support and guidance to move through the writing process and share writing. A second benefit is that children learn the routines of writing workshop as they work at a writing center. There are benefits for teachers, too. Sometimes teachers are overwhelmed with the idea of "turning their students loose" for writing workshop, and permitting a small group of children to work at a writing center while other students are involved in other literacy activities is the first step in implementing writing workshop.

Arranging the Classroom for Writing Workshop

No special classroom arrangement is necessary for writing workshop, but the classroom atmosphere should be free enough that children can converse quietly with classmates and move around the classroom to assist classmates or share ideas. Children often sit at desks or tables arranged in small groups as they write, and the teacher circulates around the classroom, conferencing with children. There is space for children to meet for writing groups, and often a sign-up sheet for writing groups is posted in the classroom. A table is available for the teacher to meet with individual children or small groups for conferences, writing groups, proofreading, and minilessons.

In a writing workshop classroom, children have writing folders in which they keep all papers related to the writing project they are working on. They also keep writing notebooks in which they jot down images, impressions, dialogue, and experiences that they can build on for writing projects (Calkins, 1991). Children have access to different kinds of paper, some lined and some unlined, and writing instruments, including pencils and red and blue pens. Art supplies for illustrating books and bookmaking supplies are also available in the classroom. Children also have access to a well-stocked classroom library. Many times, a child's writing project will grow out of a favorite book; for example, the child may write a sequel to a book or retell a story from a different point of view. Primary-grade students often use patterns from a book they have read to structure a book they are writing.

Adapting Writing Workshop for Emergent Writers

Kindergarten and first-grade teachers adapt writing workshop for use with their young students. The three most important steps in the writing process for emergent writers are prewriting, drafting, and publishing. The revising and editing stages can be added when students begin to see value in revising their writing to make it better, when they have moved from invented spelling toward more conventional spelling, and when they have been introduced to conventional capitalization and punctuation.

Kindergartners and first graders (and older students who are emerging writers) can either write single-draft books using invented spelling or write rough draft books that teachers transcribe for them. The choice depends on the purpose for writing and the time and resources that teachers have available.

Young children write single-draft books and spell words inventively according to the phonetic principles they know. They draw a series of pictures in a booklet and write the text to accompany the pictures. Children may be able to read their books, but classmates and the teacher may have difficulty deciphering the words or sentences, which may be strings of letters without any spaces between words. As children become more fluent writers, these books become easier to read.

An excerpt from a child's single-draft book about dinosaurs, which was written with invented spelling, is presented in Figure 2–8. On the page shown in the

Figure 2–8 Independent writing: An excerpt from a first grader's book about dinosaurs

figure, the child wrote "Baby dinosaurs hatch from eggs." The drawing and the spacing between words make it easier to decipher the child's writing. The emphasis in these books is on encouraging children to be independent writers. Students sit in an author's chair to share their books with classmates, but because students use idiosyncratic invented spelling strategies, the books are not widely read by classmates.

In transcribed books, young children write books that the teacher transcribes into conventional English for the final copy. They draw pictures and write the first draft using invented spelling. Then the teacher (or another adult) prints or types the final copy, changing the invented spelling to conventional spelling and adding appropriate capital letters and punctuation marks. Sometimes teachers type the final copy using a word processor and print out very professional-looking pages. Students bind the pages into a book and make new drawings for each page.

A first grader's transcribed book, "Lisa the Fish," is presented in Figure 2–9. The teacher transcribed the student's invented spelling for the final copy, and then the student added the illustrations. Two pages have been added to the back of the book. Next to the last page is a "Comments" page, where students and parents who read the book write compliments and other comments to the author. The last page is a list of the students in the class; after students read the book or take the book home to read with their parents, they cross off their name.

This approach is useful if students place the completed books in the class library for classmates to read or if the books are used as part of the reading program. Making transcribed books is more time-consuming for both children and teachers: Children have to draw the illustrations twice, and sometimes the second set of drawings is not as detailed as the first because children tire or lose interest in the project. Also, teachers spend a lot of time preparing the final copies of the books.

As students' writing becomes more fluent and their spelling approaches conventional forms, they make the transition to the five-stage writing process. Students show their readiness in several ways: If the teacher has been writing the final copy, children may express the desire to do all the writing on both the rough draft and the final copy themselves; or if they have been doing their own writing, they begin to squeeze revisions into their writing. Sometimes students mention how they might change part of a book and ask if they should start over. When students demonstrate an awareness of the need to refine the ideas in their writing and to correct mechanical errors, they are ready to move into the five-stage writing process. It is important that students see value in working through the process; otherwise, revision and editing will seem meaningless to them.

Incorporating Writing Workshop Into Units

Children also use writing workshop in literature focus units and social studies and science thematic units. Children make projects as they apply what they are learning, and many of these projects involve writing. Sometimes students

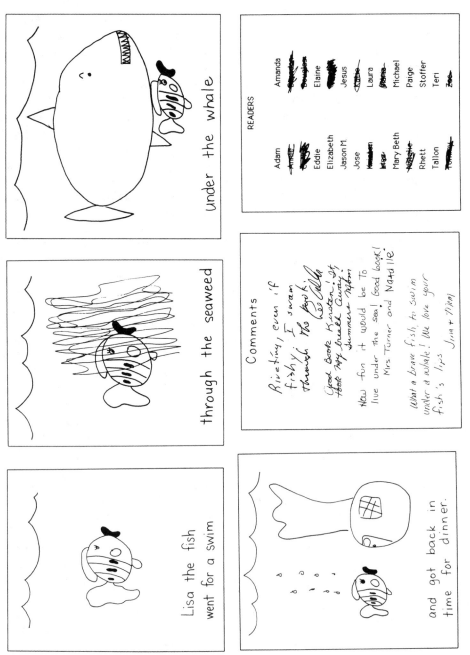

Figure 2–9 Independent writing: A first grader's transcribed book, "Lisa the Fish"

choose their own writing projects related to a particular unit, or they might work on a project chosen by the class. For example, during an author study on Eric Carle, first graders make marbleized paper and use it to illustrate books they are writing. Or, as part of a science unit on insects, fourth graders make models of insects and write an encyclopedia with an entry about each insect. In these two examples, teachers use a writing workshop format so that the children can use the writing process to develop and refine their compositions.

When children use writing workshop to create projects, teachers set aside a specific period of time for writing. After children read books or are introduced to concepts in social studies and science, they begin work on these writings. If children are working on self-selected projects, teachers usually set aside a period of time each day, perhaps 30 minutes to an hour, for them to create their projects. During this time, children move through the stages of the writing process. Teachers help children identify projects, keep track of their progress, and provide them with information on the various types of activities they have selected. For example, the teacher might explain or model how to write a description to accompany a diorama if a child is making a diorama, or how to format a letter if a child is writing a letter to a favorite author.

If the entire class is working on the same project, the writing proceeds in a more uniform fashion. The teacher works with the children to plan the writing project. Together they decide on the design of the project and the amount of time allowed for each stage of the writing process. The teacher keeps track of the children's progress and helps them follow the design and keep up with the time schedule. The teacher also guides children as they move from one stage to the next in the writing process.

Writing projects usually span a week or two in which children move through all five stages of the writing process. The projects usually begin partway through the unit, after children have read related books or learned some key concepts. The preceding activities that are related to the unit serve as prewriting for the project, and children work during the time allocated for the project to create a composition. Writing workshop activities, including sustained writing, sharing, and minilessons, are not delineated, but children and the teacher are involved in these activities nonetheless.

Students use writing to extend learning in literature focus units and social studies or science thematic units. They apply what they are learning by creating poems, reports, posters, and other projects. A list of projects is presented in Figure 2–10. Sometimes several students work together on a project, but at other times, every student in the class is working on a different project.

1. *A poem for two voices.* Create a poem for two voices on a topic related to a book or a thematic unit.
2. *Advertisements.* Design an advertisement related to a book, an author, or a thematic unit.
3. *"All About …" books.* Write an "All About …" book related to a thematic unit.
4. *Alphabet books.* Choose a letter of the alphabet and develop a page for a class alphabet book on a topic related to a book or a thematic unit.
5. *Biography.* Read a biography of a scientific, historical, or contemporary personality and share what you learn in a poem, a poster, a life line, or a report.
6. *Box or can.* Collect five items related to a book or a theme, put the items in a decorated shoebox or coffee can, and add an explanation of why each item was included.
7. *Business letters.* Write and mail a business letter to request information related to a social studies or science topic.
8. *Charts and diagrams.* Make a chart or a diagram to explain information related to a book or a thematic unit and add an explanation to accompany the visual.
9. *Color poems.* Write a color poem on a topic related to a book you have read.
10. *Comparison essay.* Write a comparison essay to compare two books or two topics related to a social studies or science thematic unit.
11. *Concrete poems.* Design a concrete poem in the shape of an object related to a book or a social studies or science theme.
12. *Cube.* Create a six-sided cube with different kinds of information about a book or a theme-related topic on each side.
13. *Data chart.* Make a data chart to categorize information related to a series of books or a social studies- or science-related topic.
14. *Descriptive sentence or paragraph.* Write a descriptive sentence or paragraph to illustrate a book or a thematic unit topic.
15. *Dialogue between characters.* Write a dialogue between two book characters or two historical personalities.
16. *Double-entry journals.* Write a double-entry journal with predictions and summaries, questions and answers, or quotes and reflections in the two columns.
17. *Five senses poem.* Write a poem on a topic related to a book or a thematic unit that has one line or stanza focusing on each of the senses.
18. *Found poems.* Write a found poem using words and phrases from a book.
19. *Friendly letters.* Write and mail a friendly letter to a pen pal telling about a book you are reading or what you are learning in a thematic unit.
20. *Haiku poems.* Write a haiku poem related to a book you are reading or to a thematic unit.
21. *"I Am" poems.* Choose a book character or a historical personality and write an "I Am" poem from that person's viewpoint.
22. *Interviews.* Interview someone with special knowledge about the thematic unit and share what you learn in a report, a newspaper article, a video, or a poster.
23. *I-search paper.* Design a research question, research to find the answer, and then share your answer in an essay or report.
24. *Letters to authors.* Write and mail a friendly letter to a favorite author.

Figure 2–10 50 Writing Projects for Kindergarten Through Eighth Grade Students

25. *Life boxes.* Decorate a shoebox and fill it with items that describe you, a character, or a historical personality.
26. *Life line.* Create a life line (similar to a time line) to document events in a person's life.
27. *Maps.* Make a map about a book's setting or a thematic unit topic and write an explanation of the map and its purpose.
28. *Multigenre projects.* Develop a multigenre project to explore a repetend or theme related to a book or a thematic unit by writing several compositions using different genres and visuals; then display them on a project board.
29. *Mural.* Make a mural about some aspect of a book or a thematic unit and add captions.
30. *Newspapers.* Create a newspaper with articles and illustrations about events related to a book or a thematic unit.
31. *Patterned books.* Write an original story patterned on the structure of the book that was read.
32. *Persuasive essay or letter.* Write an essay or a letter to persuade someone to your viewpoint on a topic related to a book you have read or to a thematic unit.
33. *Point-of-view stories.* Rewrite a familiar story or an episode of a longer story from one character's viewpoint.
34. *Postcards.* Create a postcard to celebrate a book or a thematic unit and send it to a friend or a family member.
35. *Posters.* Make a poster to share information you have learned.
36. *PowerPoint presentations.* Create and give a PowerPoint presentation on a book you have read, an author or illustrator, or a topic related to a theme cycle.
37. *Prequels and sequels.* Write a prequel (a story set earlier) or a sequel (a story that follows) the book you have read.
38. *Quilts.* Create a paper or fabric quilt about a book character or a thematic unit.
39. *Quotes poster.* Identify several powerful quotes from a book and copy them on a poster; then explain why you chose each quote.
40. *Rap.* Write and perform a rap about a book you have read or a thematic unit topic.
41. *Research reports.* Choose a topic, design research questions, conduct research using books and the Internet, compile the information, and develop a report.
42. *Riddles.* Write a book of riddles related to a book or a thematic unit.
43. *Scripts.* Change a story into a script for readers theatre, a puppet show, or a play.
44. *Simulated journals.* Write several simulated journal entries as a book character or a historical personality.
45. *Simulated letters.* Write a simulated letter to a book character or a historical personality to persuade him or her to take a particular action.
46. *Speech.* Write a speech that a book character or a historical personality might give.
47. *Stories.* Write a story set during a historical period or a story that applies concepts learned during a thematic unit or a literature focus unit.
48. *Time line.* Create a time line to document historical events.
49. *Websites.* Create a website and post information on it about a book you have read or information you have learned in a thematic unit.
50. *Word walls.* Create an alphabetized word wall with words and pictures related to a book or a social studies or science unit.

Figure 2–10 *continued*

Students in a sixth-grade class chose different projects to pursue after reading *Tuck Everlasting* (Babbitt, 1975). One boy decided to put together a story box. He brought a shoebox from home and decorated it with the title, scenes, and characters from the book. Then he collected four items related to the story and placed them in the box: a small bottle of water, Winnie's tombstone made from construction paper, a picture of a Ferris wheel, and a small music box. He wrote a paragraph-length composition explaining the book and the items in his box, and glued the final copy of the explanation into the inside of the box top. Here is his explanation:

> *Tuck Everlasting* is an awesome book. The story is about life and how life is like a wheel. The wheel is supposed to keep turning from birth to death. But what happens if the wheel stops? It could if you drank magic water and you stopped getting any older. You would keep on living the same old way year after year after year. You would keep going back to the same old places while the rest of the world lived and died. You would finally learn that the lucky ones are the people who live and love and then grow old and die.

This project demonstrates the depth of understanding that students can develop and display through writing projects. Writing is a powerful way of learning.

In an eighth-grade science class, students each wrote picture books about scientific concepts and planned to donate the books to an elementary school. To develop these picture books, students used the writing process and worked through each of the five stages. Because they were publishing their books as picture books, students had an additional step: They had to break their revised and edited compositions into pages and design illustrations to accompany each page. They kept their audience in mind as they planned their books, and were careful to explain concepts simply and to draw easily interpreted illustrations. Figure 2–11 presents an excerpt from one student's picture book about solstices and equinoxes.

Monitoring Children's Progress

Monitoring is an essential component of writing workshop because students are working on different projects and moving through the writing process at different speeds. When teachers don't monitor students' learning, they often feel as though they are not in control, and students often feel that same loss of control. Teachers use three management strategies to monitor students' work. The first strategy is status of the class (Atwell, 1998). Before students begin to write, the teacher or a student calls roll and students each respond with a word or phrase about their progress on their writing project, such as "Making my final copy," "Clustering," "Ready for a writing group," or "I'm still drafting." The person calling roll writes a word or code number by each student's name on a

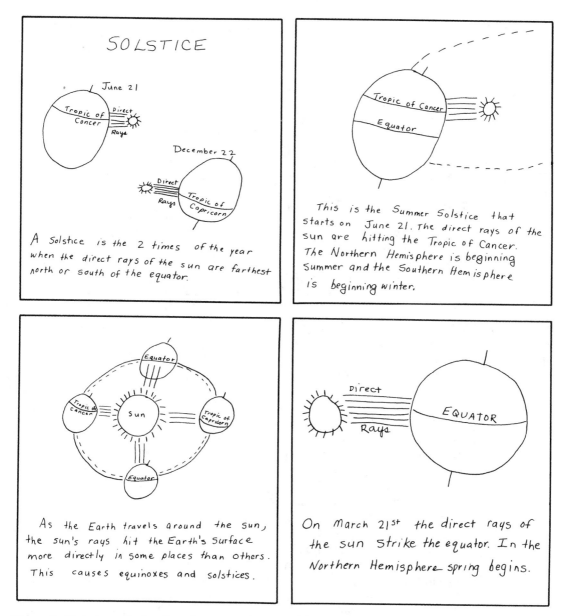

Figure 2–11 Independent writing: An excerpt from an eighth grader's picture book on solstices and equinoxes

	Writing Workshop Chart							
Names	Dates 3/18	3/19	3/20	3/21	3/22	3/25	3/26	3/27
Antonio	4	S	S	S	S	1	1	1 2
Bella	2	2	2 3	2	2	4	S	S
Charles	3	3 1	1	2	2 3	4	S	S
Dina	4 S	S	S	1	1	1	1	2 3
Dustin	3	3	4	4	4	S	S 1	1
Eddie	2 3	2	2 4	S	S	1	1 2	2 3
Elizabeth	2	3	3	4	4	4 S	S	1 2
Elsa	1 2	3 4	4 S	S	S	1	2	2
Code: 1 = Prewriting 2 = Drafting 3 = Revising 4 = Editing 5 = Publishing								

Figure 2–12 A status of the class chart

chart. Many teachers use numbers representing the five stages of the writing process on their status of the class charts, as shown in Figure 2–12. Some teachers write status of the class charts on transparencies that they display using an overhead projector, and other teachers make paper charts that they post in the classroom.

Other teachers use variations of the status of the class chart. Some use pocket charts, with a pocket for each of the five stages of the writing process, and students place popsicle sticks with their names printed on them in the pocket for the stage showing their progress. Others have students clip clothespins with their names printed on them onto writing stage coat hangers or onto large circle charts made from pizza cardboards.

The second way that teachers monitor students' progress during writing workshop is by conferencing with students and making anecdotal notes, as Mrs. Zumwalt did in the vignette at the beginning of the chapter. Many teachers use clipboards with a page for each child, index cards with a card for each child, or charts with boxes for each child. Teachers observe students, read their writing, and talk with them about their progress. They also help students make plans for their work over the next few days and set goals for new writing projects. This conference usually takes 5 minutes or less, and then teachers write notes before moving on to the next student.

Students also keep project checklists listing the stages in the writing process that they mark as they move through the stages. They keep this checklist in their writing folders along with clusters, drawings, lists, drafts, and other materials related to their project. They compile all of these materials when they finish a project and turn them in to the teacher along with the final copy of their project; these materials document students' use of the writing process.

Ultimately, learning the writing process is far more important than the quality of a student's project. The writing process is a tool that students can use for any project, and learning that process is the most important goal of writing workshop.

ANSWERING TEACHERS' QUESTIONS ABOUT . . .

Writing Workshop

1. My students just aren't mature enough to work independently during writing workshop. What should I do?

Some teachers complain that their students are uninterested in writing, inattentive in writing groups, or irresponsible about completing assignments. The best way to help these students become interested in and feel responsible for their writing is to use writing workshop. When students make decisions about their writing, choose topics that are important to them, and share their writing with classmates, their behavior changes.

2. My students keep writing about the same tired topics during writing workshop. How can I get them to move on?

Do your students generate lists of possible writing topics? If they don't, they should start lists. Then you can encourage them to choose a new topic from the lists for their next compositions. Or, you might conference with those students who stick to safe and familiar topics and ask them to think of a new topic, and then stay with them while they get started in order to provide support that they might need. They may need to talk the idea

out with you or need help in brainstorming words about the topic to get started.

3. Is it better to have students write about anything they want during writing workshop, or to coordinate writing workshop with my thematic units?

Neither way is better than the other. They are both effective ways to teach writing, but they serve different purposes. When students choose their own topics during writing workshop, the focus is on helping them to become fluent writers and to have a chance to write about their own lives, experiences, and interests. Through thematic projects, students use writing to learn and to apply what they are learning. It is important that teachers understand the purpose of each approach and plan activities to fit their goals.

4. I teach fifth grade. Do you mean that I should set up a writing center?

Sure, you should have several centers in your classroom and provide opportunities for students to work at the centers on a regular basis. Possibilities include a library center, a word work center (with spelling and vocabulary activities), a computer center, a listening center, and, of course, a writing center. Include writing folders, a variety of paper, pens, a dictionary and a thesaurus, and bookmaking supplies in the center. Arrange materials in each center area and hang signs to label the areas. Explain the centers to students, and then provide time in your daily schedule for students to work at each center as part of their daily assignments, not as busywork for after they finish their regular assignments.

5. I just don't have time in my daily schedule for writing workshop. What can I do?

Teachers never have enough time in their schedules. What you find a way to include are the subjects you value; those that you don't include are not as important to you. Write out your schedule and look for possible time. What can you combine? What might you alternate with writing workshop? Some teachers alternate reading and writing workshop. Other teachers use writing workshop as part of their social studies and science period. Others use writing workshop as the first or last activity of the day. If you really want to include writing workshop, you'll find 30, 45, or even 60 minutes to squeeze it in. And, of course, you should value it. Using the writing process on a daily basis provides lots of writing opportunities and translates into improved learning in reading, writing, and spelling.

CHAPTER 3
Writing Strategies and Skills

Preview

 Strategies are problem-solving behaviors that writers use thoughtfully and consciously.

 Skills are information-processing techniques that writers use automatically and unconsciously.

 Teachers use minilessons to provide direct instruction about strategies and skills.

 Teachers model skill and strategy use and take advantage of teachable moments to explain their use.

Working With Novice Writers

Ms. Boland is concerned about a group of seventh graders in her third-period class. During the first month of school, she notices that they avoid writing whenever possible. When they should be writing, several students talk to their neighbors and joke about each other's compositions. One day during writing workshop, she sees Julian look over at Ruben's writing and ask, "What are you writing about?" He picks up Ruben's paper and reads the first sentence. Then he says, "Oh, that's so stupid, man!" Ruben angrily wads up his paper and tosses it in the trash can. He gets out another sheet of paper but doesn't begin to write, and Julian turns around and repeats the procedure with Alyce.

Ms. Boland notices Houa and Mai at another table. After they write several lines on their papers, they put their pencils down, stretch their arms across the table, and slouch down in their chairs with chins on their chests. They sit quietly like that for 5 minutes or more as Ms. Boland observes them. They seem to be waiting for class to be over. Ms. Boland approaches Houa and Mai to talk to them about their writing in hopes of getting them back on track. She pulls up her stool and settles onto it. "What are you writing?" she asks. Mai says, "I don't know," and Houa says, "Nothing." Ms. Boland notices that they don't have their writing folders out, and she asks them to get them out. The folders should have various rough drafts and clusters, lists of writing topics, editing checklists, self-assessment charts, and other information sheets, but Houa's and Mai's folders have only a couple of pages, and these are either incomplete or blank! Ms. Boland realizes that she has her work cut out for herself.

The following week, Ms. Boland interrupts writing workshop for her students to participate in the All-School Writing Assessment. All language arts teachers at the school have their students write in response to a prompt at the beginning and again at the end of the school year. This year's topic is "a memorable moment in your life." Students have 60 minutes to write their compositions without any input from their teacher, but they are encouraged to use the writing process to draft and refine their papers. Ms. Boland uses this opportunity to observe her students as they deal with the demands of the assignment. As she expects, this writing assignment is difficult for a small group of her students, including Julian, Ruben, Alyce, Houa, and Mai.

Even though the topic is broad and is something that the teachers hope all students can relate to, this group of students finds it difficult. They begin to write without brainstorming or thinking about how to organize their thoughts. They write hesitantly and stare into space, but they don't reread what they have written to get a running start before beginning to write again. Their writing is short and not broken into paragraphs. They write four, five, and up to eight sentences, and do not revise or edit their writing even though they are writing in pencil and both erasers and correction fluid are available. They write single drafts even though Ms. Boland knows that their teachers in elementary school have emphasized the writing process.

These students write about doing something with their best friend, going to a nearby lake with their family, going to the mall with friends, playing soccer, talking on the telephone, or hanging around the apartment complex. As she reads these students' papers, Ms. Boland notices that they write about everyday activities, not more memorable moments.

Mai wrote this composition about talking on the telephone:

> You call Pam at 8:30 and we stay on the phone a long time. You like to talk and she like to talk so you can talk. You talk and your brother say to hang up the phone! And you keep to talking and your brother say hang up! I like to talk to Pam so you talk and talk. Your brother he get real mad and you talk and talk.

It is very interesting that Mai writes in the second person even though memories are typically written in the first person. Also, Mai writes about a habitual activity rather than a specific memory of one special telephone call.

Ruben writes about playing soccer:

> I play soccer on Saturday and I play at Calwa Field. My team has won many trophies. I play forward and I scored many goals. We play weekend tournaments. It is fun and this is my fifth year to play soccer. My brother plays too and he's a striker.

Ruben also writes about a habitual activity, but he does write from the first-person viewpoint. Both Mai's and Ruben's writings are very general, lack details about a specific memory, and use simplistic vocabulary and sentence structure.

Ms. Boland and her colleagues score the papers using an eight-point rubric, and two teachers read and score each paper. If there is a span of more than one point between the two scores, a third teacher also reads and scores the paper. Although most of her students score five or six, and some score higher, Mai's paper scores a one and Ruben's paper a two.

Ms. Boland decides to interview these five students to learn more about them as writers. She decides to talk to them individually and ask some questions from an interview list that she often has students complete in writing. These questions explore students' understanding of what writers do and what makes good writing.

She asks a number of questions about the writing process. She asks Julian, for example, "What do you do when you start writing?" and he responds, "It's like getting an idea and then it runs down my nerves from my head to my fingers of my hand and then to the pen and onto the paper." "What about your ideas? How do you get them?" Ms. Boland probes. "I don't know. They just come to me," he replies. Julian's answers, like the others', show a lack of organizational skills and no use of writing strategies.

"When you finish writing the first draft of your paper, what do you do?" she asks Alyce. "You mean after I'm done? Well, I turn it in," she replies. "Do you reread it? Do you check it or ask someone in the class to read it for you and give you some ideas?" Ms. Boland explores. "No, when I'm done, well, I'm done," Alyce answers. The other students' responses are similar. They write single-draft papers, they write in isolation from classmates, and they cannot articulate any writing strategies that they use.

These students make it very clear that they don't like to write. "No, I don't like to write very much. It's boring and it's hard work" is the universal response to her questions, "Do you like to write? Why or why not?" They talk about how their hands hurt when they write, so Ms. Boland asks if they would prefer writing on the computer so that the handwriting demands would be less. They all want to try that, even though they have had little previous computer experience.

"What do you think makes writing good?" Ms. Boland asks Mai, and she answers, "It is long and the writing is pretty. That's what makes it good." Ms. Boland then asks, "What about the ideas? Are they important?" "Yes, they are important," Mai responds, but she doesn't seem sure. Then Ms. Boland asks, "So, what's the most important—how the paper looks, or having good ideas?" "Your paper, it should be pretty to be a good paper," Mai responds. Mai and the other students focus on the surface features of writing.

Ms. Boland asks other questions about topics, forms, and audiences for writing. "What topics do you like to write about?" she asks. "I don't know. I just write about stuff," answers Houa. "There are lots of different types of writing, like writing stories, letters, charts, reports, poems, and journals. What kinds do you like best?" she asks next. "I don't know" is the universal response. She also asks, "When you write, who reads your writing?" Ruben looks surprised at her question and says, "You do. You read what I write because you are the teacher. I will put it in a box on your desk and you will read it and give me a grade." "What about other people? Aren't there some other people who read your writing?" Ms. Boland asks. Ruben seems confused and responds, "No. I don't think so." Ms. Boland concludes that the students don't have a repertoire of topics about which to write, that they aren't aware of choices they can make about the form their writing would take, and that the only audience they are aware of is the teacher.

Reflecting on what she has learned about these novice writers, Ms. Boland sets four instructional priorities. Her first priority is to engage them in writing about topics that are important to them. She begins by having them write about their slang and what the words mean, and next they write about their favorite music and compare it to their parents' music. She encourages these students to write at the computer and use the spell checker. Her second priority is teaching the students about writing. She does modeled and shared writing lessons and thinks aloud about what writers do as they write collaborative pieces. The students learn the writing process, including how to revise and edit. Her third priority is reading lots of literature to and with these students. They focus on sentences in the books they read and learn to identify examples of figurative language. They manipulate these sentences and write imitation sentences following the structure of the sentence taken from literature. Providing lots of writing opportunities is her fourth goal. Ms. Boland plans lessons using modeled, shared, interactive, guided, and independent writing. She structures their writing so that they apply what they are learning about writing and what writers do as they write.

Ms. Boland collects writing samples each month and finds significant improvements in all five students' writing. First she notices that their sentence length increases and they use more specific and descriptive words. They make clusters before writing and break their writing into paragraphs according to the sections on their clusters. They become more confident in themselves as writers and add wordplay to their writing. They also become more aware of their audience because they now volunteer to read a sentence or two aloud in their small group each week. They begin to engage readers by asking questions or adding parenthetical comments directed to the reader, such as "So, do you see what I mean?" By the end of the first semester, these five students are writing first drafts and revising and editing them. They are learning writing strategies and can talk about what they do as writers. They consider options when they write instead of writing whatever comes to mind.

At the end of the school year, Ms. Boland's students participate in the All-School Writing Assessment and write again about a memorable moment. Most students write on different topics, but Ruben writes again about playing soccer. In the fall assessment, he began his paper, "I play soccer on Saturday." Eight months later, he begins his paper this way: "It's easy for me to wake up on Saturday morning! Do you want to know why? It's because Saturday is when I play soccer. Last Saturday we had a great game and I will tell you about it."

Ms. BOLAND'S SEVENTH GRADERS ARE NOVICE WRITERS. Much like younger, beginning writers, they lack knowledge about the writing process and have few strategies available to use while they are writing. Researchers have compared novice and more capable writers, and they have documented these characteristics of capable writers:

- Capable writers vary how they write depending on their purpose for writing and the audience who will read the composition.
- Capable writers use the writing process flexibly.
- Capable writers focus on developing ideas and communicating effectively.
- Capable writers turn to classmates for feedback on how they are communicating.
- Capable writers monitor how well they are communicating in the piece of writing.

- Capable writers use formats and structures for stories, poems, letters, and other texts.
- Capable writers use a variety of strategies and monitor their strategy use.
- Capable writers postpone attention to mechanical correctness until the end of the writing process.
- Capable writers assess writing according to how well they communicate with their audience.

Perhaps the most remarkable difference between capable and less capable writers is that those who are less successful are not strategic. They seem reluctant to use unfamiliar strategies or those that require much effort. They do not seem to be motivated or to expect that they will be successful. These writers don't understand or use all stages of the writing process effectively. They do not monitor their writing (Garner, 1987). Or, if they do use strategies, they remain dependent on primitive ones. Novice writers move through the writing process in a lockstep, linear approach. They use a limited number of strategies, most often a "knowledge-telling" strategy in which they list everything they know about a topic with little thought to choosing information to meet the needs of their readers or to organizing the information to put related ideas together (Dudley-Marling, 1996; Faigley, Cherry, Jolliffe, & Skinner, 1985; Scardamalia & Bereiter, 1986).

In contrast, capable writers understand the recursive nature of the writing process and turn to classmates for feedback about how well they are communicating. They are more responsive to the needs of the audience that will read their papers, and they work to organize their paper in a cohesive manner. Figure 3–1 compares capable and novice writers. You will notice that Ms. Boland's students exemplified many of the characteristics of novice writers.

In this chapter, you will learn about strategic writers and ways to teach students to use strategies and skills effectively. The key points are:

- Strategies are problem-solving behaviors that writers use thoughtfully and consciously.
- Skills are information-processing techniques that writers use automatically and unconsciously.
- Teachers use minilessons to provide direct instruction about strategies and skills.
- Teachers model skill and strategy use and take advantage of teachable moments to explain their use.

Strategies and Skills

We all have skills that we use automatically, as well as self-regulated strategies for things that we do well—driving defensively, playing volleyball, training a new pet, or maintaining classroom discipline. We apply skills we have learned un-

Characteristics	Capable Writers	Novice Writers
Audience, purpose, and form	Capable writers vary how they write depending on their purpose for writing and the audience who will read the composition.	Novice writers are unaware of audience, purpose, and form demands.
The writing process	Capable writers use the writing process flexibly.	Novice writers move through the writing process in a lockstep, linear approach.
Goal of writing	Capable writers focus on developing ideas and communicating effectively.	Novice writers view writing as putting words on paper.
Peer response	Capable writers turn to classmates for feedback on how they are communicating.	Novice writers are unable to collaborate with classmates.
Self-assessment	Capable writers monitor how well they are communicating in the piece of writing.	Novice writers are unable to assess their own writing.
Genres	Capable writers use formats and structures for stories, poems, letters, and other texts.	Novice writers don't vary how they format or structure writing according to the assignment.
Strategies	Capable writers use a variety of strategies and monitor their strategy use.	Novice writers use few strategies, most often a knowledge-telling strategy.
Editing concerns	Capable writers postpone attention to mechanical correctness until the end of the writing process.	Novice writers are more concerned with mechanics than ideas.
Judging quality	Capable writers assess the quality of their writing according to how well they communicate with their audience.	Novice writers assume that longer is better and neater is better.

Figure 3–1 A comparison of capable and novice writers
Adapted from Faigley, Cherry, Jolliffe, & Skinner (1985).

consciously and solve problems as we think strategically. The strategies we use in these activities are problem-solving mechanisms that involve complex thinking processes. When we are just learning how to drive a car, for example, we learn both skills and strategies. Some of the first skills we learn are how to start the engine, make left turns, and parallel park. With practice, these skills become automatic. Some of the strategies we learn are how to pass another car and how to stay a safe distance behind the car ahead of us. These are strategies, not skills, because drivers must think about speed, visibility, road condition, and other variables in using the strategies. At first, we have only a small repertoire of strategies, and we don't always use them effectively. That's one reason why we take lessons from experienced drivers and practice with their guidance and supervision. These seasoned drivers teach us defensive driving strategies. We learn strategies for driving on interstate highways, on slippery roads, and at night. With practice, we become more successful drivers, able to anticipate driving problems and take defensive actions.

Writing Strategies

Students learn and use strategies for writing, too. Writing strategies are "deliberate thinking procedures writers use to solve problems that they encounter while writing" (Collins, 1998, p. vii). Strategic writers take conscious and deliberate control of the writing process. They select and use appropriate strategies, organize ideas for writing, monitor the development of their compositions, and revise their meaning as they refine their writing (Lewin, 1992; Paris & Jacobs, 1984; Schmitt, 1990). Ten strategies that writers use are:

Teacher's Note: Supporting Struggling Writers

How do you turn struggling writers into capable writers? The most important thing you can do is to teach them to be strategic. Elementary students should learn to use all 10 writing strategies described in this section. Explain, model, and practice these writing strategies until your students can use them independently. Tapping prior knowledge is a good strategy to begin with, but teachers can introduce the strategies in any order.

---

1. *Tap prior knowledge.* Students think about what they already know about the topics as they prepare to write. This knowledge includes information and vocabulary about the topics as well as information about authors and literary genres. Students' knowledge is stored in schemata (or categories) and is linked to other knowledge through a complex network of interrelationships. As students learn, they add new information to their schemata. Students brainstorm ideas, draw pictures, reread books and notes they have written, and talk with classmates as they tap prior knowledge.

2. *Organize ideas.* Students make clusters, data charts, and outlines to organize ideas and to group ideas and words before writing, and they often refer to their organizational plans as they write. The way students organize ideas varies depending on whether they are writing stories, informational books, letters, or poetry. Each type of text has unique organizational patterns. When students write stories, for example, they often organize the events into the beginning, middle, and end. When they write informational books, they often use sequence, comparison, or cause-and-effect structures. When they write poetry, students use various poetic forms, including haiku and "I Am" poems.

3. *Visualize.* Students write description and sensory details to make their writing more vivid and bring it to life for the people who will read it. Sometimes teachers have students brainstorm lists of words related to each of the five senses and then incorporate some of the sensory words into their writing.

Adding dialogue is another way that students make their characters more vivid. Teachers also teach minilessons on figurative language, including metaphors, similes, personification, alliteration, and onomatopoeia, and encourage students to use figurative language to strengthen their writing.

4. *Summarize.* Students pick out the main ideas and write a condensed version when they summarize. When they take notes, use the note-taking/note-making activity, or write summaries in journal entries, students are using summarizing as a learning tool. They also summarize when they write reports, letters, or other formal pieces of writing.

5. *Make connections.* Students make three kinds of connections as they write: They make "personal" connections to their background knowledge and previous writing experiences; they make "world knowledge" connections to what they have learned about the writing process, genres, and audiences; and they make "literary" connections to books they have read and other compositions they have written. Children use personal connections during prewriting, for example, as they think about what they know about a topic and the vocabulary they can use to express their ideas. They use "world knowledge" connections as they choose a lead for their compositions that will interest their readers. They make "literary" connections as they pattern or model their writing after a book they have read or try out the voice of a favorite author.

The connections students make to books they have read previously are called "intertextuality" (de Beaugrande, 1980). Cairney (1990, 1992) identified five characteristics of intertextuality:

- *Individual and unique.* Students' literary experiences and the connections they make among them are different.
- *Dependent on literary experiences.* Intertextuality is dependent on the types of books students have read, their purpose for and interest in reading and writing, and the literary communities to which students belong.
- *Metacognitive awareness.* Most students are aware of intertextuality and consciously make connections among texts.
- *Links to concept of story.* Students' connections among stories are linked to their knowledge about literature.
- *Reading-writing connections.* Students make connections between stories they read and stories they write.

Students use intertextuality as they incorporate ideas and structures from the stories they have read into the composition they are writing.

6. *Revise meaning.* Writing is a process of making meaning, and as students write, they are continually revising the compositions they are creating. As they reread their compositions, they ask themselves if what they are writing fits their purpose and meets the needs of their audience. Students participate in writing groups for classmates to read and react to their rough drafts so that

writers can revise their writing and make it stronger. Writers revise on the basis of the feedback they get from classmates. As they revise, students add words and sentences, make substitutions and deletions, and move text around to communicate more effectively. They also add titles and illustrations to clarify meaning.

7. *Monitor.* Students coordinate all writing-related activities and check on how well they are communicating as they monitor their writing. When they realize that understanding has broken down, they ask themselves questions and take action by turning to a classmate for help or by doing more prewriting.

8. *Play with language.* Students incorporate figurative and novel uses of language in their writing. They use metaphors and similes; write idioms, alliterations, and personification; add jokes, riddles, and rhymes; and invent new words.

9. *Generalize.* Students draw out main ideas and details and use the main ideas to make inferences to direct readers through the text. Students identify main ideas as they make clusters, write topic sentences to organize paragraphs, and write conclusions.

10. *Evaluate.* Students make judgments about, reflect on, and value their writing. They use self-assessments, rubrics, and checklists to ask themselves whether their writing says what they want it to say—in other words, whether or not it is effective. They think about what they have experimented with in a particular piece of writing and reflect on the writing processes that they use. As a strategy, evaluation is not the teacher's judgment handed down to students, but rather students' own thinking about their goals and accomplishments.

These strategies are summarized in Figure 3–2, and a checklist to use in monitoring students' knowledge about strategies and their ability to apply them in their writing is shown in Figure 3–3. The research on capable and less capable writers has focused on differences in how students use strategies. It is noteworthy that all research comparing writers focuses on differences in strategy use, not differences in students' use of skills.

There are many reasons why it is so important that all students become strategic writers. Let's consider five of the most important ones. First, strategies allow students to generate, organize, and elaborate meaning more expertly than they could otherwise. Being strategic is an important characteristic of learning. Second, children learn all sorts of cognitive strategies, including reading, mathematical, and scientific investigation strategies, during the elementary grades, and the acquisition of writing strategies coincides with this cognitive development. As students learn to reflect on their learning, for example, they learn to reflect on themselves as writers; and as they learn to monitor their learning, they learn to monitor their writing. Many of the cognitive strategies that students learn have direct application to writing. In this way, children's growing awareness about thinking and their writing are mutually supportive.

Third, strategies are cognitive tools that students can use selectively and flexibly. For students to become independent writers, they need to be able to

Strategy	Explanation	Sample Activities
Tap prior knowledge	Students think about what they already know about the topic of their composition.	Brainstorm ideas Draw pictures Talk with classmates
Organize ideas	Students group and sequence ideas before writing.	Cluster ideas Make data charts Make an outline
Visualize	Students use description and sensory details to make their writing more vivid.	Add sensory words Write dialogue Use metaphors and similes
Summarize	Students write the main ideas or events in a text they have read or written.	Take notes Take notes/Make notes Write journal entries
Make connections	Students make "personal," "world knowledge," and "literary" connections to the composition they are writing.	Brainstorm ideas and words Consider the needs of readers Apply genre or format guidelines Write pattern books
Revise meaning	Students add words and sentences, make substitutions and deletions, and move text around to communicate more effectively.	Reread Participate in a writing group Make revisions
Monitor	Students coordinate all writing-related activities, check on how well they are communicating, and ask self-questions.	Reread Ask self-questions
Play with language	Students incorporate figurative and novel uses of language in their writing.	Use metaphors and similes Use idioms Write alliterations Create invented words
Generalize	Students draw out main ideas and details and use main ideas to direct readers through the compositions.	Cluster ideas Write topic sentences Write conclusions
Evaluate	Students make judgments about, reflect on, and value their writing.	Self-assess the writing Use rubrics Write reflections

Figure 3–2 Strategies that writers use

apply these thinking tools. Fourth, writing is a tool for learning across the curriculum, and strategic writing enhances learning in math, social studies, science, and other content areas. Children's competence in writing affects all areas of the curriculum. Fifth, teachers can teach students how to apply

Writing Strategies

Name _____

Strategy	Introduced	Practiced	Reflected on Strategy Use	Applied Independently
1. Tap prior knowledge				
2. Organize ideas				
3. Visualize				
4. Summarize				
5. Make connections				
6. Revise meaning				
7. Monitor				
8. Play with language				
9. Generalize				
10. Evaluate				

Figure 3–3 A writing strategies checklist for upper grades

writing strategies (Paris, Wasik, & Turner, 1991). Just as driving instructors teach novice drivers about defensive driving, teachers demonstrate and explain strategic writing and provide students with opportunities for guided practice.

The Reading-Writing Connection. Even though these strategies are called "writing strategies," they are the same strategies that students use when they read and use the other language arts (Tompkins, 2003). Let's consider one strategy—organizing. Just as students organize ideas before writing, which facilitates readers' understanding of what students have written, readers organize ideas as they read, and this organization facilitates their comprehension. When students are reading stories, for example, they organize ideas into the beginning, middle, and end, and they understand the roles of foreshadowing, plot development, setting, point of view, and theme. They expect stories to be structured in specific ways, and they use this organization when they retell stories or create new versions.

Students also use the organization of other types of texts to aid in comprehension. When students read informational books, they use expository text structures, and when they read poetry, they recognize and use poetic structures. Students use the organizing strategy when they listen, talk, view, and visually represent. When they view videos, for instance, students organize ideas in much the same way as when they read. When students talk and visually represent, they use the strategy much like they do in writing. As they plan their projects, they use the organizing strategy to structure the information they will present.

The Role of Motivation. Motivation is intrinsic and internal—a driving force within us. Often students' motivation for becoming more capable writers diminishes as they reach the upper grades. Oldfather (1995) conducted a 4-year study to examine the factors influencing students' motivation and found that when students had opportunities for authentic self-expression as part of literacy activities, they were more highly motivated. Students she interviewed reported that they were more highly motivated when they had ownership of the learning activities. Specific activities they mentioned included opportunities to express their own ideas and opinions, choose topics for writing, share their writing with classmates, and pursue "authentic" writing activities, not worksheets.

Some students are not motivated to learn to write, and they adopt strategies for avoiding failure rather than strategies for making meaning; these strategies are defensive tactics (Dweck, 1986; Paris et al., 1991). Unmotivated writers give up or remain passive, uninvolved in writing, as two of Ms. Boland's students did in the vignette at the beginning of the chapter. Others don't think writing is important, and they choose to focus on other curricular areas—math or sports, for instance. Some students complain about feeling ill or that other students are bothering them. They place the blame on anything other than themselves.

There are other students who avoid writing entirely. They just don't do it. Another group of students writes short pieces so that they don't have to exert much effort. Even though these strategies are self-serving, students use them because they lead to short-term success. The long-term result, however, is devastating because these students fail to learn to write. Because it takes quite a bit of effort to write strategically, it is especially important that students experience personal ownership of the literacy activities going on in their classrooms and that they know how to manage their own writing behaviors.

Teachers can use a recently developed assessment instrument, the Writer Self-Perception Scale (Bottomley, Henk, & Melnick, 1998/1999), to evaluate children's views of themselves as writers and the classroom writing climate. The items on the assessment focus on both general writing ability and specific dimensions of writing, including organization and style. The assessment presents 38 statements that children read and then rate according to how much they agree or disagree with the statement using a 5-level Likert scale. It can be administered to children individually or in whole-class groups.

Writing Skills

Skills are information-processing techniques that writers use automatically and unconsciously as they construct meaning. Many writing skills focus on words and parts of words, but some require writers to attend to larger chunks of text. For example, writers employ word-level skills such as forming contractions, choosing the appropriate homophone, and capitalizing people's names, and they use sentence-level skills when they punctuate sentences, combine sentences, and write alliterative sentences. Other skills focus on paragraphs, as when students craft topic sentences, indent paragraphs, and keep to a single topic in a paragraph.

During the elementary grades, students learn to use five types of writing skills:

1. Structuring skills
2. Spelling, punctuation, and capitalization skills
3. Language skills
4. Reference skills
5. Handwriting and word processing skills

Figure 3–4 lists examples of each type of skill. Students use some of these skills, such as spelling skills, almost every time they pick up a pencil to write, but they use other skills only for one type of writing or another. When they write in reading logs, for example, students underline titles of books and sequence events. In contrast, when students write letters, they write dates and use commas after the greeting and the closing. Even though students don't use every skill listed for any particular writing task, capable writers are familiar with most of these skills and can use them automatically whenever they are needed.

Structuring Skills.   Students use structuring skills as they craft sentences, group sentences into paragraphs, and organize the entire composition. By the time children come to school, they have developed a sophisticated system of syntactic rules—in fact, kindergartners and first graders use most of the sentence structures that adults use (O'Donnell, Griffin, & Norris, 1967). They have developed a concept of story and can distinguish between stories and informational books (Pappas, 1993). During the elementary grades, students learn additional written-language structures through reading and writing (Weaver, 1996, 1998). Opportunities to learn these structures are especially important for second-language learners (Elley & Mangubhai, 1983), and Krashen (1989) found that through reading, second-language learners learn complex grammatical structures that they have never been explicitly taught.

Children learn that a sentence expresses a complete thought and that the four types of sentences are simple, compound, complex, and compound-complex. They learn to make their sentences more sophisticated through both reading and writing. Don Killgallon (1997, 1998) suggests that teachers have students work with sentences taken from books they are reading. He suggests four types of sentence work:

1. *Sentence unscrambling.* The teacher selects a sentence from a book children are reading and breaks it apart into phrases and clauses. Then students rearrange the parts to make a sentence and compare the sentence they craft with the original sentence.

Structuring Skills

Use simple, compound, and complex
  sentences
Imitate, combine, and expand sentences
Avoid sentence fragments
Combine sentences into paragraphs
Use topic sentences in paragraphs
Sequence ideas
Categorize information
Identify cause and effect
Compare and contrast ideas
Use organizational patterns of poetry, plays,
  business and friendly letters, stories, essays,
  and reports
Use genre characteristics in writing folktales,
  tall tales, myths, science fiction, informational
  books, ABC books, biography, autobiography,
  and poetry

**Spelling, Punctuation,
and Capitalization Skills**

Sound out words
Apply spelling rules
Divide words into syllables
Recognize root words
Add affixes
Choose among homophones
Proofread
Consult a dictionary
Use abbreviations
Punctuate the ends of sentences with periods,
  question marks, and exclamation points
Use quotation marks to mark dialogue
Use commas and semicolons within sentences
Use commas in dates and letters
Use apostrophes in possessives and
  contractions

Capitalize the word I
Capitalize words at beginning of sentences
Capitalize proper nouns and adjectives

Language Skills

Use similes and metaphors
Use alliteration
Use idioms and slang appropriately
Play with rhyme and other poetic devices
Choose synonyms and antonyms

Reference Skills

Sort in alphabetical order
Use a dictionary
Locate information in an encyclopedia, atlas,
  almanac, or other reference book
Locate synonyms in a thesaurus
Read and create tables of contents
Read and create indexes
Read and create graphs, tables, and diagrams
Read and create time lines and life lines
Read newspapers and magazines
Use bibliographic forms

Handwriting and Word Processing Skills

Form manuscript letters legibly and fluently
Form and connect cursive letters legibly and
  fluently
Space appropriately between letters, words,
  sentences, and paragraphs
Do keyboarding
Format on the computer
Import illustrations
Use spell checkers

Figure 3–4 Skills that writers use

2. *Sentence imitating.* Students write a new sentence that imitates the structure of a sentence taken from a book they are reading.

3. *Sentence combining.* The teacher chooses a sentence from a book children are reading and breaks it into several simple sentences. Then students combine the short sentences to make a

more sophisticated sentence. They also compare the sentence they craft with the original sentence.

4. *Sentence expanding.* The teacher selects a sophisticated sentence from a book children are reading and has students expand the nucleus of the sentence into a longer sentence in the author's style. Then students compare their sentence with the original sentence.

Figure 3–5 reviews Killgallon's four types of sentence composing with sample sentences from E. B. White's *Charlotte's Web* (1980). Through these activities, students create more sophisticated sentences than they might write otherwise, and as a bonus, they learn more about authors' writing styles and use of figurative language.

Paragraphing is an important structuring skill. Children in the elementary grades learn that a paragraph is a group of sentences that tells about one idea, and that the first sentence is indented 5 spaces or 1 tab from the left margin. They examine paragraphs to learn that each sentence in the paragraph contributes to the development of the idea, and that the sentences must be in a logical order so that readers understand the information. They also learn about these parts of a paragraph:

1. *Topic sentence.* A paragraph begins with a topic sentence that tells readers what the paragraph is about. A topic sentence has two main parts—a specific subject and a focus. The subject has to be small enough to explain in one paragraph. A focus is usually a feeling or attitude about the subject. For example:

   In *The Ballad of Lucy Whipple,* Lucy [subject] was a reluctant pioneer during the Gold Rush [focus].
   Sea otters [subject] are one of the very few animals that use tools [focus].
   I [subject] love spending Friday night every week at my Grandma's house because we make chocolate chip cookies and we watch videos [focus].

2. *The body.* The middle of the paragraph is the body. It contains sentences between the topic sentence and the closing sentence. These sentences give readers all the information needed to understand the topic.

3. *The closing sentence.* The paragraph ends with a closing sentence that sums up the information in the paragraph or tells what the information means.

Of course, not all paragraphs follow this basic structure, but many do, and this structure is a useful one for young writers.

Writers vary the information they put into paragraphs, particularly the body of the paragraph, according to their purpose for writing. When students are writing

1. Sentence Unscrambling

Students reassemble the parts of a sentence to examine how professional writers structure their sentences. They may duplicate the author's sentence or create an original sentence they like better. The original sentence from E. B. White's *Charlotte's Web* is "A minute later Fern was seated on the floor in the middle of the kitchen with an infant between her knees, teaching it to suck from the bottle" (pp. 6–7). The parts are:

in the middle of the kitchen
teaching it to suck from the bottle
a minute later
with an infant between her knees
Fern was seated on the floor

2. Sentence Imitating

Students create sentences that imitate the structure of a model sentence. The original sentence from *Charlotte's Web* is "Avery noticed the spider web, and coming closer, he saw Charlotte" (p. 71). One group's imitation sentence was "The police officer noticed the car parked at the side of Highway 99, and coming closer, he saw a woman running away from the car and a man racing after her." Another model sentence is "His medal still hung from his neck; by looking out of the corner of his eye he could still see it" (p. 163).

3. Sentence Combining

Students combine sentences, examine possible combinations, and compare their results with the original sentence. The original sentence from *Charlotte's Web* is "No one had ever had such a friend—so affectionate, so loyal, and so skillful" (p. 173). The shorter sentences that students combine are:

No one ever had such a friend.
The friend was so affectionate.
The friend was so loyal.
The friend was so skillful.

A more complex sentence that students might practice combining is "For several days and several nights they crawled here and there, up and down, around and about, waving at Wilbur, trailing tiny draglines behind them, and exploring their home" (p. 178).

4. Sentence Expanding

Students expand an abridged version of a sentence so that the text students add blends in with the rest of the professional writer's sentence. The original sentence from *Charlotte's Web* is "There is no place like home, Wilbur thought, as he placed Charlotte's 514 unborn children carefully in a safe corner" (p. 172). From this original sentence, students expand "There is no place like home . . ." One sixth grader wrote, "There is no place like home, like his home in the barn, cozy and warm straw to sleep on, the delicious smell of manure in the air, Charlotte's egg sac to guard, and his friends Templeton, the goose, and the sheep." The student's sentence differs from the original, but it retains the character of E. B. White's writing style.

Figure 3–5 Killgallon's four types of sentence composing

a descriptive paragraph, for example, they include sensory and figurative information, as this "snapshot of life" paragraph written by one of Ms. Boland's students shows:

> The baby loves to eat strained squash. He smiles as he sits in the high-chair, watching Mom heat the jar of squash in the microwave. It's his favorite food! He claps his little fists together like he is applauding when Mom takes the baby spoon to scoop up his first mouthful of stuff that looks like orange mashed potatoes. And it smells worse. Mom lifts the spoon. He opens his mouth. In goes the first spoonful of squash. Then another and another. Now and then the baby spits some out. There are morsels of orange everywhere—even on the tip of his nose.

In contrast, when students write a persuasive paragraph, they state their viewpoint and try to sway readers to their point of view. For narrative paragraphs, students write events to tell a story. And for expository paragraphs, students provide information using sequence, comparison, or other text structures. Figure 3–6 summarizes information about four types of paragraphs.

Type	Description	Applications
Descriptive	A descriptive paragraph describes a person, place, thing, or idea. Writers use the five senses and figurative language, including personification, onomatopoeia, and comparisons, so that readers will feel as though they are right there with the author.	Observe scene and write a description Describe photographs and pictures Observe plants and animals and write descriptions
Narrative	A narrative paragraph tells a story by sharing the details of an experience, including the beginning, middle, and end. Writers answer the five W's (who, what, when, where, and why) and include colorful details.	Narrate historical events Rewrite familiar stories Observe event and write a narration
Persuasive	A persuasive paragraph gives the writer's opinion on a topic. Writers present facts and examples to support their opinions.	Write letter to the editor of local newspaper Write persuasive letter to parents Write book or movie review
Expository	An expository paragraph presents information about a topic. It may explain ideas, give directions, or show how to do something. Writers often use cue words (e.g., first, second, third, in contrast, therefore).	Write steps in life cycle of an animal Write directions for making something Compare book and video versions of a story Write scientific cause and effect Write historical problem and solution

Figure 3–6 Types of paragraphs

Students use hierarchical structures to organize their writing, and these structures vary depending on the genre of their composition. Students use story structures such as beginning, middle, and end when they write stories, and expository structures such as sequencing, comparison, and cause and effect for ABC books, reports, and informational books. They also use poetic structures when they write poems. In upcoming chapters, you will learn more about narrative, expository, and poetic structures.

Spelling, Punctuation, and Capitalization Skills.   Spelling, punctuation, and capitalization are the traditional "mechanics" of writing. Students apply spelling patterns, add affixes to root words, use abbreviations, and check spellings in the dictionary as they write words and when they proofread. Students focus on these skills during the editing stage of the writing process.

During the elementary grades, students learn that capital letters divide sentences and signal important words within sentences (Fearn & Farnan, 1998). Consider how the use of capital letters affects the meaning of these three sentences:

They were going to the white house for dinner.
They were going to the White house for dinner.
They were going to the White House for dinner. (S. Wilde, 1992, p. 18)

Capital letters also express loudness of speech or intensity of emotion because they stand out visually.

Children often begin writing during the preschool years using only capital letters; during kindergarten and first grade, they learn the lowercase forms of letters. They learn to capitalize *I,* the first word in a sentence, and names and other proper nouns and adjectives. By the upper elementary grades, the most common problem is overcapitalization, or capitalizing too many words in a sentence, as in this example: *I think Hermit Crabs are very interesting because they change Houses every time they grow Bigger.* This problem tends to persist into adolescence and even into adulthood because students have trouble differentiating between common and proper nouns (Shaughnessy, 1977). Too often, students assume that "important" words in the sentence should be capitalized.

It's a common assumption that punctuation marks signal pauses in speech, but punctuation plays a greater role than that, as Sandra Wilde (1992) explains. Punctuation marks both signal grammatical boundaries and express meaning. Some punctuation marks indicate sentence boundaries; periods, question marks, and exclamation points mark sentence boundaries and indicate whether a sentence makes a statement, asks a question, or expresses an exclamation. In contrast, commas, semicolons, and colons mark grammatical units within sentences.

Quotation marks and apostrophes express meaning within sentences. Quotation marks are used most often to indicate what someone is saying in dialogue, but a more sophisticated use is to express irony, as in *My son "loves" to wash the dishes.* Apostrophes are used in contractions to join two words and in possessive nouns to show relationships. Consider the different meanings of these phrases:

> The monkey's howling (and it's running around the cage).
> The monkey's howling (annoyed us; we wanted to kill it).
> The monkeys' howling (annoyed us; we wanted to kill them).
> (We listened all night to) the monkeys howling. (S. Wilde, 1992, p. 18)

Researchers have documented that learning to use punctuation, like spelling and capitalization, is a developmental process. Beginning in the preschool years, children notice punctuation marks and learn to discriminate them from letters (Clay, 1975, 1991; Ferreiro & Teberosky, 1982). In kindergarten and first grade, children are formally introduced to the end-of-sentence punctuation marks and learn to use them conventionally about half the time (Cordeiro, Giacobbe, & Cazden, 1983). Many beginning writers use punctuation marks in more idiosyncratic ways, such as between words and at the end of each line of writing, but over time, children's usage becomes more conventional. Edelsky (1983) looked at first- through third-grade bilingual writers and found similar developmental patterns for second-language learners.

Language Skills.   Writing involves choosing precise and imaginative language, and during the elementary grades, children learn language skills to make their writing more interesting. They learn about synonyms and how to use a thesaurus to choose exactly the right word. For example, children learn more precise words for *said,* such as *cried* and *mentioned,* and more descriptive words for *noise,* such as *racket* and *uproar.* They also learn to use these five types of figurative language:

1. *Alliteration.* Writers use several words that begin with the same sound side by side in a sentence. Third graders wrote silly sentences such as *The king sat in the kitchen with a kangaroo, tying a key on a kite* and included two or three words beginning with the same sound in more serious sentences, such as *The fox with orange fluffy fur trotted out of sight behind the barn.*

2. *Onomatopoeia.* Writers use sound words rather than descriptions of sounds to enliven their writing. A fifth grader, for example, wrote *The truck burped and then the engine died.*

3. *Personification.* Writers attribute human characteristics to inanimate objects, and then use words that normally refer to people to describe the inanimate objects. Eighth graders wrote *The pigeon tiptoed across the telephone wire* and *The moon winked and then a cloud covered it.*

4. *Similes.* Writers create comparisons using *like* or *as* to compare two things. In this example written by a seventh grader, *The jet was as sleek as a porpoise,* the student compares an airplane to an aerodynamic animal.

5. *Metaphors.* Writers create comparisons, and these comparisons are stronger because *like* or *as* is not used. Compare these two versions of the same idea: *The ballerina was as graceful as a swan* (simile) and *The ballerina was a graceful swan* (metaphor). The metaphor is more powerful than the simile, don't you think? Most students write similes more easily than metaphors, but they can be helped to turn their similes into metaphors during the revising stage of the writing process.

Reference Skills.   Writers use a variety of reference tools, and elementary students learn about the useful information in dictionaries, thesauri, and other reference books, as well as how to use these resources. Figure 3–7 lists a variety of dictionaries and thesauri that have been published specifically for elementary students. Students also learn to use atlases and almanacs, and the Internet is becoming increasingly useful as a reference tool. Students enjoy using computers to conduct research; they can locate all sorts of information on-line.

Students also learn reference skills to locate and read information in informational books. The index is probably the most common reference tool, but students also learn to locate information in photos and their captions, charts, figures, maps, and other diagrams.

Handwriting and Word Processing Skills.   Students develop effective manuscript and cursive handwriting skills so that they can write legibly and fluently. They learn how to form upper- and lowercase forms of the letters and how to join cursive letters. Students develop preferences for using manuscript or cursive writing, and they learn to vary how neat their writing is, depending on whether their purpose is public or private.

The goal is for students in the elementary grades to develop legible and fluent handwriting. Their handwriting must be legible so that readers can understand what they have written, and fluent so that their writing is not laborious and slow. There are six elements of legible and fluent handwriting:

1. *Letter formation.* Letters are formed with specific strokes. Letters in manuscript handwriting are composed of vertical, horizontal, and slanted lines plus circles or parts of circles. Cursive letters are composed of slanted lines, loops, and curved lines. An additional component in cursive handwriting is the connecting stroke used to join letters.

2. *Size and proportion.* During the elementary grades, students' handwriting becomes smaller, and the proportional size of uppercase to lowercase letters increases from 2:1 to 3:1.

3. *Spacing.* Students leave adequate space between letters in words and between words in sentences.

Dictionaries

The American Heritage children's dictionary.
(1998). Boston: Houghton Mifflin. (M) This
appealing hardcover dictionary contains
14,000 entries and more than 600 color
photos and illustrations. Word history, language detective, synonym, and vocabulary-
builder boxes provide additional interesting
information. A 10-page phonics guide and
6-page thesaurus are also included in this
reference book. This dictionary is also
available on CD-ROM.

The American Heritage first dictionary.
(1998). Boston: Houghton Mifflin. (P) More
than 1,800 entries and 650 color photographs and graphics are included in this
attractive reference book. A clearly stated
definition and easy-to-read sentence are
provided for each entry.

The American Heritage student dictionary.
(1998). Boston: Houghton Mifflin. (U) This
comprehensive dictionary for middle
school students presents 65,000 detailed
entries with sentence examples and etymologies and more than 2,000 photographs. New
computer and Internet terms have been
included, and synonym lists, word-history
boxes, and word-building features are
highlighted in the text. Charts on the periodic table, geological eras, and weights and
measures add to the book's usefulness.

DK Merriam-Webster children's dictionary.
(2000). London: Dorling Kindersley. (M–U)
This stunning volume pairs the 32,000
entries from *Merriam-Webster's Elementary
Dictionary* with the striking design and
color illustrations that DK is famous for.
This visually appealing book includes more
than 3,000 photos and charts.

Franklin MWD-400 *Pocket Merriam-Webster
Dictionary.* (U) This hand-held electronic
dictionary contains 80,000 words and a
four-line display. Students can learn a new
word every time they turn the unit on, and
in addition to checking the meaning and
spelling of words, they can use the electronic dictionary for vocabulary and
spelling games and puzzles.

Levey, J. S. (1998). *Scholastic first
dictionary.* New York: Scholastic. (P) More
than 1,500 entries are in this visually
appealing dictionary for beginning readers.
Each entry word is highlighted, defined,
and used in a sentence.

Merriam-Webster's elementary dictionary.
(2000). Springfield, MA: Merriam-Webster.
(M–U) This paperback dictionary contains
32,000 entries and 600 black-and-white
illustrations. Entries are easy to read.
Synonym boxes and word-history boxes
provide additional useful information. In
comparison to other dictionaries, this book
lacks visual appeal.

Figure 3–7 Reference Books for Elementary Students
P = Grades K–2; M = Grades 3–5; U = Grades 6–8.

4. *Slant.* Letters should be consistently parallel. Letters in manuscript
handwriting are vertical, and letters in the cursive form slant slightly
to the right, or vertical or slightly to the left for left-handed writers.

5. *Alignment.* For proper alignment in both manuscript and cursive
handwriting, all letters should be uniform in size and consistently
touch the baseline.

6. *Line quality.* Students should write at a consistent speed and hold
their writing instruments correctly and in a relaxed manner to
make steady, unwavering lines of even thickness.

Scholastic children's dictionary. (1996). New York: Scholastic. (M) More than 30,000 entries are presented with color illustrations and bright page decorations. Attractively designed boxes with information about synonyms, affixes, and word histories are featured throughout the book.

Swanson, M. (1998). *The American Heritage picture dictionary.* Boston: Houghton Mifflin. (P) The 900 common words in this book designed for kindergartners are listed alphabetically and illustrated with lively color drawings. Nine thematic illustrations featuring related vocabulary are included at the back of the book.

Thesauri

Beal, G. (1996). *The Kingfisher illustrated pocket thesaurus.* New York: Kingfisher. (U) In this pocket-size paperback book, over 5,000 entries with sample sentences are presented. Antonyms are marked with a star, which is somewhat confusing.

Bollard, J. K. (1998). *Scholastic children's thesaurus.* New York: Scholastic. (M) This attractive reference book for middle-grade students contains 500 entries and 2,500 synonyms grouped under the entries. All synonyms are defined and used in sample sentences. Antonyms are not listed.

Hellweg, P. (1997). *The American Heritage children's thesaurus.* Boston: Houghton Mifflin. (M–U) This well-designed and attractive reference book contains more than 4,000 entries and 36,000 synonyms. For each entry, synonyms are listed with the best matches first and each is used in a sentence to clarify its meaning. Antonym and word-group boxes provide additional information and extend the book's usefulness.

Wittels, H., & Greisman, J. (1985). *A first thesaurus.* Racine, WI: Western Publishing Company. (P–M) More than 2,000 entries are listed, with the main words printed in bold type. Synonyms are printed in regular type and antonyms in red. Some black-and-white illustrations are also included.

Wittels, H., & Greisman, J. (1999). *The clear and simple thesaurus dictionary.* New York: Grosset & Dunlap. (M) This easy-to-use thesaurus lists 2,500 words in alphabetical order in a dictionary format. Each entry is followed by its synonyms printed in black and antonyms printed in red.

Figure 3–7 *continued*

Children learn a number of computer skills during the elementary grades. Developing strong keyboarding skills is undoubtedly of primary importance so that students can type text quickly and efficiently. Even though very young children use one or two fingers and the hunt-and-peck approach to type on the computer, beginning in third grade, children should learn how to keyboard with both hands. Children also learn how to use word processing programs to format text, spell-checker programs to identify and correct misspelled words, and graphics programs to create illustrations. By the time they enter high school, students should be proficient computer users who can use word processing and other writing-related computer programs.

Teaching Strategies and Skills

Teachers use both direct and indirect instruction to teach writing strategies and skills. When teachers teach minilessons and other lessons, they directly and explicitly provide information and guide students as they explore skills and strategies. Also, as part of direct instruction, students apply concepts they are learning in their own writing. In contrast, through indirect instruction, teachers model skills and strategies or implicitly or informally explain skills and strategies.

All five types of writing provide opportunities for instruction; sometimes the instruction is direct, but at other times it is indirect. When teachers do a modeled writing lesson to write a found poem, for example, they demonstrate writing strategies and skills for students, and when they teach a guided writing lesson to create an innovation on a book, students practice using writing strategies and skills with teacher guidance. Even when students are doing independent writing, they are applying strategies and skills they are learning. When students confer with the teacher during independent writing, teachers use teachable moments created when students make comments and ask questions to teach brief lessons.

Through both direct and indirect instruction, students learn information about strategies and skills, and then they learn when and how to use them during writing (Duffy & Roehler, 1991; Duffy et al., 1987). The purpose of instruction is to enhance students' awareness of strategic writing so that they can plan, evaluate, and regulate their own thinking. Rather than teaching isolated skills with fragmented bits of language, stripped of meaning, teachers scaffold and support students' developing writing strategies and skills through interaction with authentic and meaningful texts. As Kucer (1991) explains, "The ability to link classroom-based literacy lessons with real-world, authentic reading and writing experiences is critical if our instruction is to promote literacy development in the children we teach" (p. 532). Guidelines for teaching writing strategies and skills are presented in Figure 3–8.

Ineffective instruction often focuses on isolated skills followed by lots of practice on worksheets. In contrast, effective instruction orients students to the task of constructing meaning from texts and provides a variety of tactics to use during the writing process. In a study of two third-grade classes, Calkins (1980) found that the students in the class who learned punctuation marks as a part of editing conferences during writing workshop could define or explain more marks than the students in the other class who were taught punctuation marks in a more traditional manner, with instruction and practice exercises on each punctuation mark. Calkins concluded that a functional approach to the teaching of

---

ELL | Teacher's Note: Assisting
English Language Learners

Do the grammatical and spelling errors in your English language learners' compositions jump out at you as you read their writing? If so, you're probably frustrated because as your students learn more about English, they make more errors. It's important to remember that errors are signs of growth. Consider your students' stage of second-language acquisition as you decide which errors to correct and which to explain in minilessons.

1. Teach Minilessons

Teachers present minilessons to introduce and review writing skills and strategies. While teachers sometimes use minilessons to teach concepts listed in grade-level competencies or standards documents, the best time to teach a minilesson is when students ask questions, demonstrate the need for instruction, or are developmentally ready to learn a skill or strategy. Teachers who carefully observe and listen to their students recognize when students are ready for minilessons on particular skills and strategies.

2. Differentiate Between Strategies and Skills

Teachers understand that strategies are problem-solving tactics, while skills are automatic behaviors that writers use, and they differentiate between strategies and skills as they teach minilessons and demonstrate writing. They are also careful to use the terms *strategies* and *skills* correctly when talking to students.

3. Provide Step-by-Step Explanations

Teachers describe the skill or strategy step-by-step so that it is sensible and meaningful to students. For skills, teachers demonstrate how experienced writers use skills in modeled and shared writing. For strategies, they use think-aloud procedures to show how experienced writers solve problems and monitor their writing. Teachers also explain to students why they should learn the strategy or skill, and how using it will make writing easier.

4. Model How to Use Strategies

Teachers model using strategies in the context of authentic writing activities, rather than in isolation, and students are also encouraged to model using strategies for classmates.

5. Provide Practice Opportunities

Students have opportunities to practice the strategy or skill in meaningful, authentic writing activities. Teachers need to ensure that all students are successful using the strategy or skill so that they will be motivated to use it independently.

6. Apply Strategies and Skills Across the Curriculum

Teachers provide opportunities for students to use the strategy or skill in writing activities related to social studies and science. The more opportunities students have to use the strategy or skill, the more likely they are to learn it.

7. Teach Students to Reflect

Teachers teach students how to reflect on their strategy and skill use. Then, as part of publishing, students reflect on and assess their strategy and skill use in the writing project.

8. Post Charts About Strategies and Skills

Teachers hang lists of skills and strategies students are learning in the classroom and encourage students to refer to them when writing. Separate charts should be used for strategies and skills so that students remember which are which.

Figure 3–8 Guidelines for strategy and skill instruction
Adapted from Pressley & Harris, 1990; Winograd & Hare, 1988.

the mechanics of writing is more effective than practice exercises. This research documents that children's knowledge of how to use punctuation marks, like other skills, develops from an early awareness through exploration and gradual refinement to increasingly conventional use during the elementary grades (S. Wilde, 1992).

Minilessons

Minilessons (Atwell, 1998) are 15- to 30-minute direct-instruction lessons designed to help students learn writing skills and become more strategic writers. Sometimes the strategies and skills are taught in a single session, and at other times, the lessons are extended and take place over several days. In minilessons, students and the teacher focus on a single goal; students are aware of why it is important to learn the strategy or skill, and they are explicitly taught how to use a particular strategy or skill through modeling, explanation, and practice. Then independent application takes place using authentic literacy materials. The steps in a minilesson are shown in the feature on page 101. In this five-step minilesson, there is scaffolding and a transfer of responsibility from teacher to students as they apply what they have learned in authentic writing activities (Bergman, 1992; Duffy & Roehler, 1987; Pearson & Gallagher, 1983).

This minilesson procedure can be adapted to fit whatever strategy or skill is being taught. Teachers often teach minilessons during writing workshop, but they can teach them during other types of writing activities as well. The minilesson on page 102 shows how Ms. Boland uses this five-step procedure to teach her seventh graders about similes. Dudley-Marling (1996), Freppon and Headings (1996), McIntyre (1996), and other researchers have emphasized that direct instruction is important for all students, and especially beneficial for students who are likely to have difficulty becoming capable writers.

Demonstrations and Other Teachable Moments

Teachers demonstrate writing skills and strategies through modeled, shared, and interactive writing. These demonstrations are an important component of writing instruction because students need to watch experienced writers as they write and solve problems during writing. They see teachers organize their writing into paragraphs, stop and reread their writing, check spellings in the dictionary, make revisions, add punctuation marks, and consider alternative ways of crafting a sentence. Guided writing offers other opportunities for informal instruction. As teachers provide structured writing experiences, they observe students as they write and encourage students to use particular writing strategies.

Teachers often give impromptu lessons during writing conferences. Teachers answer students' questions, model how to use strategies and skills, provide brief explanations, and encourage students to talk about the strategies they

Step by Step: Strategy and Skill Minilessons

1. *Introduce the strategy or skill.* The teacher names the strategy or skill and explains why it is useful. The teacher also shares examples of how and when the strategy or skill is used.

2. *Demonstrate the strategy or skill.* The teacher explains the steps and models how to use the strategy or skill in a writing activity.

3. *Provide guided practice using the strategy or skill.* Students practice the strategy or skill that the teacher demonstrated, with the teacher's guidance and support. The teacher provides feedback to students about how well they are doing. Students make notes about the strategy or skill in their writing notebooks or on a poster to be displayed in the classroom.

4. *Review the strategy or skill.* Students reflect on what they have learned and how they can use their strategy or skill in writing activities. Teachers also often explain how the strategy or skill is used in reading and writing.

5. *Apply the strategy or skill.* Students use the newly learned strategy or skill in new and authentic writing activities. The teacher serves as a coach as students use the strategy or skill in guided writing and independent writing activities.

use. For example, during a conference with one of her students, Ms. Boland notices that the student's writing is not divided into paragraphs. She asks the student about paragraphs, and she responds that she really doesn't understand about them. Ms. Boland explains that a paragraph is like a sandwich, and on a piece of scratch paper she draws a picture of two pieces of bread for the top and bottom of the sandwich and luncheon meat, cheese, and lettuce in between the pieces of bread. She explains that the top piece of bread is the topic sentence; the cheese, meat, and lettuce are the body; and the bottom piece of bread is the closing sentence. Ms. Boland's drawing is shown in Figure 3–9. Then Ms. Boland and the student break the student's writing into paragraphs and add topic sentences and closing sentences. The student keeps the picture of the paragraph sandwich, and Ms. Boland notices that she continues to refer to it when she is writing paragraphs several days later.

Ms. Boland's lesson was informal because it was unplanned and occurred in response to a student's question. She explained a concept, made a graphic to represent the concept, and then applied the concept to the student's own writing.

Why Teach Strategies and Skills?

Some teachers argue about whether or not to teach strategies and skills—and, if they are taught, whether students should learn them inductively or whether teachers should teach explicitly. The position in this book is that teachers have

Similes

Ms. Boland is teaching her seventh graders a series of minilessons on ways to make their writing more powerful during writing workshop, and today her topic is similes. After the minilesson, she encourages the students to apply what they are learning in their writing.

1. Introduce the topic

"Writers often compare one thing to something else," Ms. Boland explains. "If they want to say that an old man is very quiet, for example, they might say that 'the old man is a quiet as a *clam*.'" The students laugh because they don't know that saying, and she explains the meaning. Then she continues, "Or, we might write 'the old man is as quiet as *fog*' because we know how quiet it becomes when the fog rolls in." She writes both sentences on the chalkboard and underlines the similes. She identifies the similes in each sentence and explains that they are called similes. Then she steps back and rereads the two sentences and announces that she prefers the "fog" comparison because it's fresher and more clever.

2. Share examples

The students brainstorm a list of other things that are quiet: death, sleep, a mouse, an angry parent, night, a whisper, and a telephone when you don't have any friends. Ms. Boland asks students to try each comparison in "the old man was as quiet as _____ ," and they decide that *sleep* is the most appropriate comparison.

3. Provide information

Ms. Boland and her students make a list of the steps in creating a simile, and the students write them in their writing notebooks.

4. Guide practice

Ms. Boland passes out magazines and asks students to select a picture to use in writing a comparison. Students create similes, making sure to use *like* or *as* in the comparison, and they write them on cards that they attach to the pictures. Then students post their pictures on the classroom wall and take a gallery walk to read each other's work.

5. Assess learning

Several days later during writing workshop, Ms. Boland asks students to examine their writing and share similes they have written. Five students haven't written any similes, so Ms. Boland meets with them as a group for more practice.

Figure 3–9 Ms. Boland's graphic of a paragraph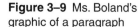

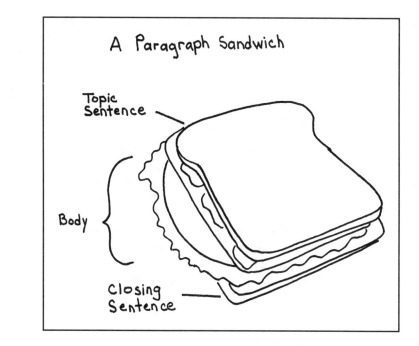

the responsibility to teach students how to write, and part of that responsibility is teaching students the strategies and skills that capable writers use. Although it is true that students learn many things inductively through meaningful literacy experiences, instruction is important. Effective teachers do teach strategies and skills. The question is not whether to teach strategies and skills, but how and when to teach them (Dudley-Marling & Dippo, 1991; McIntyre & Pressley, 1996).

Researchers have compared classrooms in which teachers focused on teaching skills with other programs in which strategies and skills were taught inductively or using a whole-part-whole instructional sequence, and they concluded that the transitional skills programs were no more effective according to students' performance on standardized tests. Moreover, researchers suggest that traditional skills programs may be less effective when you take into account that students who read and write for authentic purposes also think of themselves as readers and writers and have more knowledge about written language.

Freppon (1991) compared the reading achievement of first graders in traditional and literature-based classrooms and found that the literature group was more successful. Similarly, Reutzel and Hollingsworth (1991) compared students who were taught skills with students who spent an equal amount of time reading books and found that neither group performed better on skill tests. This research suggests that students who do not already know skills and strategies can benefit from instruction, but the instruction must stress application to authentic reading and writing activities.

Carefully planned instruction, however, may be especially important for minority students. Lisa Delpit (1987) cautions that many students who grew up outside the dominant culture are at a disadvantage when certain knowledge, strategies, and skills expected by teachers are not made explicit in their classrooms. Explicitness is crucial because people from different cultures have different sets of understandings. When they teach children from other cultures, teachers often find it difficult to get their meaning across unless they are very explicit (Delpit, 1991). Too often, teachers assume that children make the connection between the strategies and skills they are teaching and the future use of those strategies and skills in writing.

On the other hand, several studies suggest that mainstream and nonmainstream students benefit from the same types of instruction. Lesley Morrow (1992) examined the impact of a literature-based reading program on minority students' reading achievement, and she found that both minority and mainstream children performed better in literature-based reading programs than in traditional classrooms on all measures of reading and writing development except on standardized tests, where there were no differences. Similarly, Karin Dahl and Penny Freppon (1995) found that minority students in literature-based classrooms do as well as students in skill-based classrooms, plus they develop a greater sense of the purposes of literacy and see themselves as readers and writers.

ANSWERING TEACHERS' QUESTIONS ABOUT . . .

Writing Strategies and Skills

1. I think skills are more important than strategies. Don't you think so?

It's true that both skills and strategies are important. Spelling errors, unsophisticated sentence structure, lack of paragraphing, and handwriting problems stand out on some students' papers, and we want to fix these problems. We know how to fix them; we know how to teach these skills. In contrast, other writing problems—disorganization, single-draft compositions, lack of audience awareness—are less obvious when we first look at a paper. These are strategy problems, and they are much harder to fix, but it is crucial that we teach students about organization, revising, editing, audience awareness, and other writing strategies. Good writers use both strategies and skills effectively.

2. I teach second grade, and my students are too young to learn strategies. I think I should focus on skills instead.

Your students already know and use some strategies. For example, they activate background knowledge when they draw pictures or make clusters before writing, and they make predictions when they read. Activating background knowledge and making predictions are strategies that readers and writers use. Teachers at every grade level are responsible for teaching both strategies and skills. You demonstrate strategies as well as skills when you do modeled and shared writing, and you support your second graders' use of strategies and skills during interactive and guided writing.

3. What's the best way to teach strategies and skills?

There is no single best way to teach strategies and skills. Depending on the topic and students' background knowledge, teachers may choose to teach a minilesson or a series of lessons; to demonstrate the strategy or skill through modeled, shared, or interactive writing; to provide practice opportunities through guided and independent writing; or to take advantage of teachable moments. Effective teachers use all of these teaching approaches because students need multiple opportunities to learn strategies and skills.

4. I need help teaching students how to write paragraphs. What should I do?

Teaching students to write paragraphs takes time. You could begin with a series of minilessons on paragraphs. The students could examine paragraphs from books they are reading, learn about the three parts of a paragraph, and then unscramble the sentences from paragraphs they had examined. Next, you could model creating topic sentences and writing paragraphs, and then use shared writing to craft paragraphs. Then students could work with partners and small groups to write paragraphs using guided writing. Finally, students could examine the paragraphs they have written using samples in their writing folders and then write paragraphs independently.

5. How do I know when to teach formal minilessons and when to take advantage of "teachable moments"?

You're asking about instructional strategies, and as with other types of strategy use, there are several factors to consider. Is the skill or strategy a grade-level expectation? How many students need the instruction? Does it fit into your instructional plan? Would it be more effective to teach a formal lesson or to take a minute and explain the skill or strategy now? There is no hard-and-fast rule. You must consider various factors and decide what to do. If you decide to take advantage of a teachable moment and students need more practice, then teach a more formal minilesson later. Or, if you teach a lesson and several students need more support, teach another minilesson or use teachable moments. It's fortunate that teachers have more than one opportunity to teach skills and strategies.

CHAPTER 4
Writers' Tools

Preview

 Children move through five stages of spelling development as they learn to spell.

 Teachers assess children's spelling development by analyzing their invented spellings and provide appropriate instruction according to children's stage of spelling development.

 Spelling words correctly is a courtesy to readers. Conventional spelling is important when the writing will be made public but of less concern when the writing is private, for the writer alone.

 Children need to develop legible and fluent handwriting so that their compositions can be written and read easily.

 Computers are mechanical tools, and as computers become familiar tools in elementary classrooms, children will find that writing, revising, and editing are simplified through word processing software.

Writing Pen Pal Letters

Mrs. Jacks's fourth graders are pen pals with students in Ms. Mitchell's fourth-grade class located about 75 miles away. Mrs. Jacks and Ms. Mitchell met several years ago during a summer course at the local university, and their students have been writing back and forth every year since. They exchange letters, postcards, and photos at least six times during the year and then meet each other in May during a field trip to the state capitol. This year, they've begun writing e-mail messages, too, because both classrooms are equipped with computers that are Internet accessible.

During the first week of the school year, Mrs. Jacks and her students write a class collaboration e-mail message introducing themselves to Ms. Mitchell's class. They brainstorm a list of topics for their first e-mail message, and decide to tell the students about their classroom and the things they like to do. Using the language experience approach, Mrs. Jacks records their dictation on chart paper and helps the children revise and edit the message. Then several students work together to type the message on the computer, and Mrs. Jacks proofreads the e-mail message and corrects several spelling and spacing errors. Then each child types in his or her name at the bottom of the message, and before sending it, one student prints out a copy of the message for each child. Then, the class watches as one child clicks on the "send" button to send their message to Ms. Mitchell's classroom. Here is the class's e-mail message:

Hi!

We are the new fourth graders in Mrs. Jacks's class at Pioneer Middle School. There are 28 of us in room 17. Our classroom is a portable but it is very nice. We have tables instead of desks, and our bulletin boards go from the floor to the ceiling. Mrs. Jacks is always tacking papers, posters, and lots of other stuff on the bulletin boards. We have a science center that has three aquariums. One has fish, one has frogs, and one has a snake named Mr. Slicker. What is your classroom like?

We have a big classroom library because we love to read. Mrs. Jacks reads to us for 30 minutes after lunch, and she does it every single day. Our first book that she is reading is *Tales of a Fourth Grade Nothing* by

Judy Blume. It is a very funny book. Does your teacher read to you? What book is she reading?

We are eager for an e-mail message from you. Then we can get your names and write letters to you. We promise to be good and faithful writers.
Your friends and pen pals,
Mrs. Jacks's Fourth Grade Class

Mrs. Jacks passes out pen pal folders for each student. They place their copy of the e-mail message in their folders, and during the year, they add the correspondence and photos they have received and letters they are writing. They also include notes from the minilessons that Mrs. Jacks teaches about writing e-mail messages, letters, and postcards to their folders.

The next day, Ms. Mitchell's class sends a return e-mail message, and Mrs. Jacks's students eagerly read their message. Choosing pen pals is easy because Ms. Mitchell's students have written their names next to the names of Mrs. Jacks's students. After a minilesson on the format of letters, the students are ready to write their first pen pal letters.

As the fourth graders work on their first letters, Mrs. Jacks takes a digital photo of each student holding a favorite object brought from home and a favorite book, and she prints two copies of each photo, one for the child to keep and one to send to the pen pal. The students tell about the objects and books in their letters and share other information about themselves, too. They use the writing process to draft, revise, and edit their writing. They work hard on their letters because they care about their pen pals and want them to like their letters. The students work in pairs to edit their writing and correct spelling, capitalization, and punctuation errors. Then Mrs. Jacks proofreads the letters before children make their final copies. Some children word process their letters and others handwrite theirs. The children put their letters in envelopes and address them to pen pals, and Mrs. Jacks collects the envelopes and sends them to Ms. Mitchell's school. Mrs. Jacks has finished reading *Tales of a Fourth Grade Nothing* (Blume, 1972) to the class, so they suggest that she send the book to Ms. Mitchell so that she can read it to her students. Mrs. Jacks agrees, and the two teachers begin exchanging books as well as letters. The students in both classrooms are eager to listen to the books their pen pals have enjoyed.

The two classes continue to write and send letters to each other along with Halloween treats in October, small holiday gifts—bookmarks they have made and Mrs. Jacks has laminated—in December, and Valentine's Day poems they have written in February. As the school year progresses, the pen pals become friends, and with each letter exchange, the students become more and more interested in editing because they want their pen pals to be able to read their letters easily.

Mrs. Jacks teaches a series of minilessons on how to proofread a pen pal letter. She explains that proofreading is not like regular reading because the students must look at every letter in every word, think about when to use capital letters, and notice whether or not punctuation marks are used correctly. In fact, she explains that children working with partners must proofread their letters several times, each time

EDITING CHECKLIST	Author	Editor
1. I have circled misspelled words.	☐	☐
2. I have checked for these spelling monsters:	☐	☐

☐ friend
    ☐ school
    ☐ their-there-they're
    ☐ a lot		

3. I have checked that proper nouns and adjectives begin with capital letters.	☐	☐
Pioneer Intermediate School American flag		
4. I have added commas to separate items in a series.	☐	☐
5. I have checked for the friendly letter format:	☐	☐

☐ return address
    ☐ date
    ☐ greeting
    ☐ closing		

Signatures: _____   _____
               Author   Editor

Figure 4–1 An editing checklist for a pen pal letter

checking for something different. She models the proofreading procedure and demonstrates how to use an editing checklist. A copy of Mrs. Jacks's editing checklist is shown in Figure 4–1. She passes out copies of the editing checklist and asks students to use it to proofread their next pen pal letters.

Stephanie and Danielle work together to proofread their pen pal letters as Mrs. Jacks walks around the classroom, conferencing with some students and watching as others use the editing checklist. Stephanie pulls her chair over to Danielle's desk, and they trade rough drafts of their pen pal letters. A copy of Stephanie's letter with the spelling errors corrected appears in Figure 4–2. Each girl reads through the draft, checking for spelling errors. They point at each word with a green pen and pronounce the word softly, using pronunciation as an aid to spelling whenever they can. Danielle circles the word *anser* (answer) on Stephanie's letter because she thinks it might be misspelled. She mumbles that it just doesn't look right. Then they continue reading.

When they finish reading their two-page letters, each girl has circled 5 to 10 words. They share their findings with each other, agree or disagree about misspellings, and write correct spellings that they know above circled spelling words. Then they ask

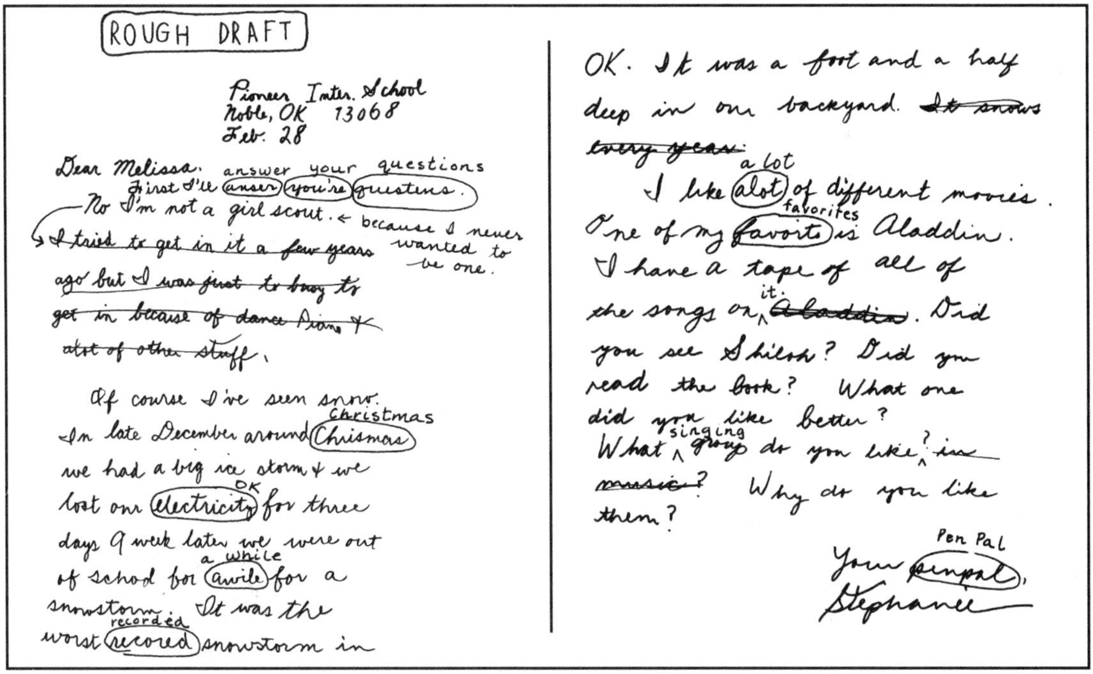
ROUGH DRAFT

Pioneer Inter. School
Noble, OK 73068
Feb. 28

Dear Melissa.
answer your questions
First I'll anser you're qustens.
No I'm not a girl scout. ← because I never wanted to be one.
~~I tried to get in it a few years ago but I was just to busy to get in because of dance Piano & alot of other stuff.~~

Of course I've seen snow.
Christmas
In late December around Chrismas
we had a big ice storm & we
OK
lost our electricity for three
days A week later we were out
a while
of school for awile for a
snowstorm. It was the
recorded
worst recored snowstorm in

OK. It was a foot and a half
deep in our backyard. ~~It snows every year.~~
a lot
I like alot of different movies.
favorites
One of my favorits is Aladdin.
I have a tape of all of
it.
the songs on ~~Aladdin~~. Did
you see Shiloh? Did you
read the book? What one
did you like better?
singing
What ~~group~~ do you like? ~~in music?~~ Why do you like
them?

Pen Pal
Your ~~penpal~~,
Stephanie

Figure 4–2 Independent writing: The rough draft of a fourth grader's pen pal letter

Katrina, who happens to walk by Danielle's desk, for advice about spelling several remaining words. She can't help with these words, but she does note one other misspelled word on Danielle's paper. Finally, they resort to the dictionary to locate the correct spelling for *colet* (collect), *awile* (awhile), *Chrismas* (Christmas), *achemet* (achievement), and *favorit* (favorite), words that neither girl is sure how to spell. Then they add a check mark to the spelling box in the editor's column on their editing checklists.

Then the girls reread the pen pal letters again, checking specifically for words that Mrs. Jacks has noticed were used and frequently misspelled in their previous pen pal letters. Her students check specifically for these words and correct them if they are misspelled: *friend, school, their–there–they're,* and *a lot.* They find *a lot* spelled as one word in Stephanie's letter, and they make the correction. None of these words are misspelled in Danielle's letter.

The next day, the girls finish checking for punctuation, capitalization, and friendly letter format errors, which are the remaining three categories on the editing checklist. Next they meet with Mrs. Jacks for a final editing, and she approves their work. They are ready to make the final copies of their letters and send them to their pen pals.

For their next pen pal exchange, Mrs. Jacks's students make postcards to share what they have learned in a science unit on sound. Earlier in the school year, students wrote postcards about stories they were reading, but this is their first science postcard experience. Mrs. Jacks teaches a minilesson to remind students about drawing illustrations, writing messages, and addressing postcards; next, students brainstorm information they could share. The students use 4-x-6-inch blank, white index cards for the postcards. They draw and color an illustration on one side of the card, write an explanation about the illustration on half of the other side, and write their pen pal's name and address on the other half.

After several more pen pal exchanges, the students in both classes make plans for their get-together at the state capitol. After touring the capitol building, the two classes have lunch together at a park across the street. They sit and talk with their pen pals, and the children in each class sing songs and perform a skit for the other class. Back in their classrooms, the students write a final letter to each other, reflecting on their year of corresponding.

EVERYONE KNOWS THAT mechanics, plumbers, carpenters, and electricians have tool boxes filled with the equipment they need to perform their jobs. Writing is a craft, and writers also need tools, but they don't use hammers, wrenches, or wire cutters. The most common writer's tool is a pencil or a pen, but computers with word processing and other writing-related programs have become popular writing tools in elementary classrooms. You probably would consider dictionaries and thesauri as writers' tools as well; they are pieces of equipment that writers use. In addition to concrete objects such as pens, computers, and dictionaries, writers' knowledge and writing strategies might be considered tools, too.

Mrs. Jacks's students used both kinds of writers' tools when they wrote pen pal letters: They used pens and computers to write their letters, and they used their knowledge of the writing process and the friendly letter genre to write effectively. They used writing strategies, too: They applied what they had learned about engaging an audience as they chose topics to write about, and they used proofreading to identify and correct spelling errors because they understood that using conventional spelling is a courtesy to readers.

This chapter focuses on three tools that writers use: spelling, handwriting, and computers. They key concepts are:

- Children move through five stages of spelling development as they learn to spell.
- Teachers assess children's spelling development by analyzing their invented spellings and provide appropriate instruction according to children's stage of spelling development.

- Spelling words correctly is a courtesy to readers. Conventional spelling is important when the writing will be made public but of less concern when the writing is private, for the writer alone.
- Children need to develop legible and fluent handwriting so that their compositions can be written and read easily.
- Computers are mechanical tools, and as computers become familiar tools in elementary classrooms, children will find that writing, revising, and editing are simplified through word processing software.

Spelling

The alphabetic principle suggests that there should be a one-to-one correspondence between graphemes (the letters) and phonemes (the sounds) such that each letter consistently represents one sound. English does not have this correspondence: Twenty-six letters, used singly or in combination, represent approximately 44 phonemes. Moreover, three letters—c, q, and x—are superfluous because they do not represent unique phonemes. The letter c, for instance, can be used to represent either /k/ as in cat or /s/ as in decide. The letter c can also be combined with h to represent the digraph /ch/. To further complicate the situation, there are more than 500 spellings (and perhaps as many as 2,000) to represent these 44 phonemes. For example, the long e, according to Ernest Horn (1957), is spelled 14 ways in English words! This situation is known as a "lack of fit."

The reasons for this lack of fit can be found by examining events in the history of the English language (Tompkins & Yaden, 1986). Approximately 75% of English words have been borrowed from other languages, and many of these words, especially the more recently acquired words (e.g., cul-de-sac, which was borrowed from French in the early 1700s and literally means "bottom of a sack"), have retained their native spellings. The spellings of other words have been tinkered with by linguists. More than 400 years ago, for instance, in an effort to relate the word island to its supposed French or Latin origin, the unnecessary and unpronounced s was added. However, island (spelled ilond in the Middle Ages) is a native English word, and the current spelling sends a false message about the word's etymology.

The controversy over whether English is a phonetic language has been waged for years, and will not likely be settled soon. Yet the fact remains that spelling is a problem for many children. Because of the lack of fit between phonemes and graphemes, it is unlikely that children will learn to spell simply by sounding out words, even though that is the strategy they are often advised to use by well-meaning teachers and parents. Instead, it is necessary to examine how children actually learn to spell and how their spelling development relates to writing.

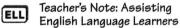

Teacher's Note: Assisting English Language Learners

Have you noticed that English language learners' invented spellings often reflect their pronunciation errors? It's important to show these children how to pronounce words correctly and, if their spellings continue to reflect their pronunciations, to encourage them to develop a visual memory for words so that they can recognize when their spellings don't look right.

Invented Spelling

Charles Read (1975, 1986) studied preschoolers' efforts to spell words and found that they used their knowledge of the alphabet and the English spelling system to invent spellings for words. These children used letter names to spell words, such as *U (you), B (be),* and *R (are),* and they used consonant sounds rather consistently: *GRL (girl), TIGR (tiger),* and *NIT (night).* The preschoolers used several unusual but phonetically based spelling patterns to represent affricates: They spelled *tr* with *chr* (e.g., *CHRIBLES* for *troubles*), spelled *dr* with *jr* (e.g., *JRAGIN* for *dragon*) and substituted *d* for *t* (e.g., *PREDE* for *pretty*). Words with long vowels were spelled using letter names: *MI (my), LADE (lady),* and *FEL (feel).* The children used several ingenious strategies to spell words with short vowels. These 3-, 4-, and 5-year-olds rather consistently selected letters to represent short vowels on the basis of place of articulation in the mouth: Short *i* was represented with *e* as in *FES (fish),* short *e* with *a* as in *LAFFT (left),* and short *o* with *i* as in *CLIK (clock).* Although these spellings may seem odd to adults, they are based on phonetic relationships. The children often omitted nasals within words (e.g., *ED* for *end*) and substituted *-eg* or *-ig* for *-ing* (e.g., *CUMIG* for *coming* and *GOWEG* for *going*). Also they often ignored the vowel in unaccented syllables, as illustrated in *AFTR (after)* and *MUTHR (mother).*

These children developed strategies for their spellings based on their knowledge of phonology, their knowledge of letter names, their judgments of phonetic similarities and differences, and their ability to abstract phonetic information from letter names. Read suggested that from among the many components in the phonological system, children abstract out certain phonetic details and preserve other phonetic details in their invented spellings.

Stages of Spelling Development

Based on observations of children's spellings, researchers have identified five stages that children move through on their way to becoming conventional spellers. At each stage, they use different types of strategies and focus on different aspects of spelling. The stages are emergent spelling, letter-name spelling, within-word pattern spelling, syllables and affixes spelling, and derivational relations spelling (Bear, Invernizzi, Templeton, & Johnston, 2003). The characteristics of the five stages of spelling development are summarized in Figure 4–3.

Stage I: Emergent Spelling.   Children string scribbles, letters, and letterlike forms together, but they do not associate the marks they make with any specific

Stage 1: Emergent Spelling

Children string scribbles, letters, and letterlike forms together, but they do not associate the marks they make with any specific phonemes. This stage is typical of 3- to 5-year-olds. Children learn:

- the distinction between drawing and writing
- how to make letters
- the direction of writing on a page
- some letter-sound matches

Stage 2: Letter-Name Spelling

Children learn to represent phonemes in words with letters. At first, their spellings are quite abbreviated, but they learn to use consonant blends and digraphs and short-vowel patterns to spell many short-vowel words. Spellers are 5- to 7-year-olds. Children learn:

- the alphabetic principle
- consonant sounds
- short-vowel sounds
- consonant blends and digraphs

Stage 3: Within-Word Pattern Spelling

Students learn long-vowel patterns and *r*-controlled vowels, but they may confuse spelling patterns and spell *meet* as *mete*, and they reverse the order of letters, such as *form* for *from* and *gril* for *girl*. Spellers are 7- to 9-year-olds, and they learn these concepts:

- long-vowel spelling patterns
- *r*-controlled vowels
- more complex consonant patterns
- diphthongs and other less common vowel patterns

Stage 4: Syllables and Affixes Spelling

Students apply what they have learned about one-syllable words to spell longer, multisyllabic words, and they learn to break words into syllables. They also learn to add inflectional endings (e.g., *-es, -ed, -ing*) and to differentiate between homophones, such as *your–you're*. Spellers are often 9- to 11-year-olds, and they learn these concepts:

- inflectional endings
- rules for adding inflectional endings
- syllabication
- homophones

Stage 5: Derivational Relations Spelling

Students explore the relationship between spelling and meaning and learn that words with related meanings are often related in spelling despite changes in sound (e.g., *wise–wisdom, sign–signal, nation–national*). They also learn about Latin and Greek root words and derivational affixes (e.g., *amphi-, pre-, -able, -tion*). Spellers are 11- to 14-year-olds. Students learn these concepts:

- consonant alternations
- vowel alternations
- Latin affixes and root words
- Greek affixes and root words
- etymologies

Figure 4–3 Stages of spelling development
Adapted from Bear, Invernizzi, Templeton, & Johnston, 2003.

phonemes. Spelling at this stage represents a natural, early expression of the alphabet and other concepts about writing. Children may write from left to right, right to left, top to bottom, or randomly across the page, but by the end of the stage, they have an understanding of directionality. Some emergent spellers have a large repertoire of letter forms to use in writing, whereas others repeat a small number of letters over and over. They use both upper- and lowercase letters, but they show a distinct preference for uppercase letters. Toward the end of this stage, children are beginning to discover how spelling works and that letters represent sounds in words. This stage is typical of 3- to 5-year-olds. During the emergent stage, children learn:

- the distinction between drawing and writing
- how to make letters
- the direction of writing on a page
- some letter-sound matches

Stage 2: Letter-Name Spelling. Children learn to represent phonemes in words with letters. They develop an understanding of the alphabetic principle, that a link exists between letters and sounds. At first, the spellings are quite abbreviated and represent only the most prominent features in words. Children use only several letters of the alphabet to represent an entire word. Examples of early Stage 2 spelling are D (*dog*) and KE (*cookie*), and children may still be writing mainly with capital letters. Children pronounce slowly the words they want to spell, listening for familiar letter names and sounds.

In the middle of the letter-name stage, students use most beginning and ending consonants and often include a vowel in most syllables; they spell *like* as *lik* and *bed* as *bad*. By the end of the stage, students use consonant blends and digraphs and short-vowel patterns to spell *hat, get,* and *win,* but some students still spell *ship* as *sep*. They can also spell some CVCe words such as *name* correctly. Spellers at this stage are usually 5- to 7-year-olds. During the letter-name stage, students learn:

- the alphabetic principle
- consonant sounds
- short-vowel sounds
- consonant blends and digraphs

Stage 3: Within-Word Pattern Spelling. Students begin the within-word pattern stage when they can spell most one-syllable short-vowel words, and during this stage, they learn to spell long-vowel patterns and *r*-controlled vowels (Henderson, 1990). They experiment with long-vowel patterns and learn that words such as *come* and *bread* are exceptions that do not fit the vowel patterns. Students may confuse spelling patterns and spell *meet* as *mete,* and they reverse the order of letters, such as *form* for *from* and *gril* for *girl.* Students also learn about complex consonant sounds, including -*tch* (*match*) and -*dge* (*judge*) and less frequent vowel patterns, such as *oi/oy* (*boy*), *au* (*caught*), *aw* (*saw*), *ew* (*sew, few*), *ou* (*house*), and *ow* (*cow*). Students also become aware of homophones and compare long- and short-vowel combinations (*hope–hop*) as they experiment with vowel patterns. Spellers at this stage are 7- to 9-year-olds, and they learn these spelling concepts:

- long-vowel spelling patterns
- *r*-controlled vowels
- more complex consonant patterns
- diphthongs and other less common vowel patterns

> **Teacher's Note: Assisting English Language Learners**
>
> Many second-language learners omit inflectional endings—the -*ed* on *wanted* or the -*s* on *boys*, for example—when they talk. It probably won't surprise you that these students are likely to do the same thing when they write. When ELL students reach the fourth stage of spelling development, they benefit from minilessons that draw their attention to this linguistic feature.

Stage 4: Syllables and Affixes Spelling. The focus is on syllables in this stage. Students apply what they have learned about one-syllable words to longer, multisyllabic words, and they learn to break words into syllables. They learn about inflectional endings (-*s*, -*es*, -*ed*, and -*ing*) and rules about consonant doubling, changing the final *y* to *i*, or dropping the final *e* before adding an inflectional suffix. They also learn about homophones and compound words and are introduced to some of the more common prefixes and suffixes. Spellers in this stage are generally 9- to 11-year-olds. Students learn these concepts during the syllables and affixes stage of spelling development:

- inflectional endings (-*s*, -*es*, -*ed*, -*ing*)
- rules for adding inflectional endings
- syllabication
- homophones

Stage 5: Derivational Relations Spelling. Students explore the relationship between spelling and meaning during the derivational relations stage, and they learn that words with related meanings are often related in spelling despite changes in vowel and consonant sounds (e.g., *wise–wisdom, sign–signal, nation–national*) (Templeton, 1983). The focus in this stage is on morphemes, and students learn about Greek and Latin root words and affixes. They also begin to examine etymologies and the role of history in shaping how words are spelled. They learn about eponyms (words from people's names), such as *maverick* and *sandwich*. Spellers at this stage are 11- to 14-year-olds. Students learn these concepts at this stage of spelling development:

- consonant alternations (e.g., *soft–soften, magic—magician*)
- vowel alternations (e.g., *please–pleasant, define–definition, explain–explanation*)

- Greek and Latin affixes and root words
- etymologies

Teachers do many things to scaffold children's spelling development as they move through the stages of spelling development, and the kind of support they provide depends on students' stage of development. As young children scribble, for example, teachers encourage them to use pencils, not crayons, for writing, to differentiate between drawing and writing. Letter-name spellers notice words in their environment, and teachers help them use these familiar words to choose letters to represent sounds in the words they are writing. As students enter the syllables and affixes stage, teachers teach syllabication rules, and in the derivational relations stage, they teach students about root words, and the variety of words created from a single Latin or Greek root word. For example, from the Latin root word -*ann* or -*enn,* meaning "year," students can learn these words: *annual, centennial, biannual, millennium, anniversary, perennial,* and *sesquicentennial.* Figure 4–4 presents a list of guidelines for supporting children's spelling development.

Analyzing Children's Spelling Development

Teachers can analyze spelling errors in children's compositions by classifying the errors according to the five stages of spelling development. This analysis will provide information about the child's current level of spelling development and the kinds of errors the child makes. Knowing the stage of a student's spelling development helps teachers suggest the appropriate type of instruction. Minilessons and spelling activities that are appropriate to a student's stage of development, such as learning visual and morphological strategies for a transitional speller, are the most beneficial.

A personal journal entry written by Marc, a first grader, is presented in Figure 4–5. He reverses *b* and *s,* and these two reversals make his writing difficult to decipher. Here is a translation of Marc's composition:

> Today a person at home called us and said that a bomb was in our school and made us go outside and made us wait a half of an hour and it made us waste our time on learning. The end.

Marc was writing about a traumatic event, and it was appropriate for him to use invented spelling in his journal entry. Primary-grade students should write using invented spelling, but correct spelling is appropriate when the composition will "go public." Prematurely differentiating between "kid" and "adult" spelling interferes with children's natural spelling development and makes them dependent on adults to supply the adult spelling.

Spelling can be categorized using a chart, also shown in Figure 4–5, to gauge students' spelling development and to anticipate upcoming changes in their spelling strategies. Teachers write the stages of spelling development across the

Stage 1: Emergent Spelling
Allow the child to experiment with making and placing marks on the paper.
Suggest that the child write with a pencil and draw with a crayon.
Model how adults write.
Point out the direction of print in books.
Encourage the child to notice letters in names and environmental print.
Ask the child to talk about what he or she has written.

Stage 2: Letter-Name Spelling
Sing the alphabet song and name letters of the alphabet with children.
Show the child how to form letters in names and other common words.
Demonstrate how to say a word slowly, stretch it out, and isolate beginning, middle, and ending sounds in the word.
Use Elkonin boxes to segment words into beginning, middle, and ending sounds in the word.
Post high-frequency words on a word wall.
Teach lessons on consonants, consonant digraphs, and short vowels.
Write sentences using interactive writing.

Stage 3: Within-Word Pattern Spelling
Teach lessons on long-vowel spelling rules, vowel digraphs, and *r*-controlled vowels.
Encourage students to develop visualization skills in order to recognize whether a word "looks" right.
Teach students to spell irregular high-frequency words.
Focus on silent letters in words (e.g., *k*now, li*gh*t).
Have students sort words according to spelling patterns.
Have students make words using word cards.
Introduce proofreading so students can identify and correct misspelled words in compositions.
Write sentences using interactive writing.

Stage 4: Syllables and Affixes Spelling
Teach students to divide words into syllables and the rules for additional inflectional endings.
Teach schwa sound and spelling patterns (e.g., *handle*).
Teach homophones, contractions, compound words, and possessives.
Sort two-syllable words and homophones.
Have students make words using word cards.
Teach proofreading skills and encourage students to proofread all writings.

Stage 5: Derivational Relations
Teach root words and derivational affixes.
Make clusters with a root word in the center and related words on the rays.
Teach students to identify words with English, Latin, and Greek spellings.
Sort words according to roots or language of origin.
Have students check the etymologies of words in a dictionary.

Figure 4–4 Ways to support children's spelling at each stage of development

> To bay a perezun at home kob
> uz anb seb that a bome wuz in
> on skuwl anb mab uz go at sib
> anb makbe uz wat a haf uf
> a awr anb it mab uz wazt on
> time on loren ee ing.
>
> THE eNb

Emergent	Letter Name	Within-Words	Syllables and Affixes	Derivational Relations
	KOB/called	BOME/bomb	TO BAY/today	
	SEB/said	OR/our	PEREZUN/person	
	WUZ/was	SKUWL/school	MAKBE/maked	
	MAB/made	AT SIB/outside		
	WAT/wait	UF/of		
	HAF/half	AWR/hour		
	MAB/made	OR/our		
	WAZT/waste	LORENEEING/learning		

Data Analysis		Conclusions
Emergent	0	Marc's spelling is at the Letter Name and Within-Word stages. From his misspellings, he is ready for the following instruction:
Letter Name	8	
Within Word	8	• high-frequency words
Syllables and Affixes	3	• CVCe spellings
Derivational Relations	0	• r-controlled vowels
Correctly spelled words	22	• compound words
Total words in sample	41	He also reverses b/d and s/z.

Figure 4–5 An analysis of a first grader's spelling

top of the chart and list each word in the student's composition under one of the categories, ignoring proper nouns. When teachers are scoring young children's spellings, they often ignore capitalization errors and poorly formed or reversed letters, but when scoring older students' spellings, these errors are considered.

Perhaps the most interesting thing about Marc's writing is that he spelled half the words correctly even though at first reading it might seem that he spelled very few words correctly. Marc wrote this paper in January of his first-grade year, and his spellings are typical of first graders. Of his misspellings, eight were categorized as letter-name spelling, and another eight were within-word spellings. This score suggests that he is moving into the within-word stage.

Marc is clearly using a sounding-out strategy, which is best typified by his spelling of the word *learning*. His errors suggest that he is ready to learn CVCe and other long-vowel spelling patterns and *r*-controlled vowels. Marc spells some high-frequency words phonetically, so he would benefit from more exposure to high-frequency words, such as *was* and *of*. Marc also spelled *today* and *outside* as separate words, so he is ready to learn about compound words.

Marc pronounced the word MAKBE as "maked" and the DE is a reversal of letters, a common characteristic of within-word spelling. Based on this categorization of Marc's spelling errors, he would benefit from instruction on high-frequency words, the CVCe long-vowel spelling pattern, *r*-controlled vowels, and compound words. His teacher should also monitor his *b/d* and *s/z* reversal problem to see if it disappears with more writing practice. It is important, of course, to base instructional recommendations on more than one writing sample. Teachers should look at three or more samples to be sure the recommendations are valid.

Older students' spelling can also be analyzed the same way. Fifth-grader Eugenio wrote the "Why My Mom Is Special" essay shown in Figure 4–6. Eugenio is Hispanic; his native language is Spanish, but he is now fully proficient in English. His writing is more sophisticated than Marc's, and the spelling errors he makes reflect both his use of longer, more complex words and his pronunciation of English sounds.

All but one of Eugenio's spelling errors are classified at either the within-word stage or the syllables and affixes stage. His other error, classified at the letter-name stage, is probably an accident because when he was asked, he could spell the word correctly.

Eugenio's within-word stage errors involve more complex consonant and vowel spelling patterns. Eugenio has moved beyond spelling *because* as BECUZ, but he still must learn to replace the *u* with *au* and the *z* with *s*. His spelling of *shoes* as SHOSE is interesting because he has reversed the last two letters. He doesn't recognize that, however, when he is questioned. Instead, his focus is on representing the /sh/ and the /oo/ sounds correctly. His spelling of both *school* and *career* seem to be influenced by his pronunciation. The /sh/ sound is difficult for him, as it is for many children whose first language is Spanish, and he doesn't recognize that *school* begins with /sk/, not /sh/. Eugenio pronounces

My mom is specil to me. She gave me everething when I was small. When she gets some mony she byes me pizza. My mom is specil to me beauze she taks me anywhere I want to get some nike shose. She byes me some.

My mom changed my life. She is so nice and loveble. She cares what I am doing in shool. She cares about my grades. I will do anything for mom. I would get a ceriar. Maybe I could be a polisman. That is why I think she is so nice.

Emergent	Letter Name	Within-Words	Syllables and Affixes	Derivational Relations
	TAKS/takes	BECUZE/because	SPECIL/special	
		SHOSE/shoes	EVERETHING/everything	
		SHOOL/school	MONY/money	
		CERIAR/career	BYES/buys	
		POLISMAN/policeman	SPECIL/special	
			BYES/buys	
			LOVEBLE/loveable	

Data Analysis		Conclusions
Emergent	0	Eugenio's spelling is at the syllables and affixes stage. Based on this sample, this instruction is suggested:
Letter Name	1	• dividing words into syllables
Within Word	5	• compound words
Syllables and Affixes	7	• using *y* at the end of 1- and 2-syllable words
Derivational Relations	0	• homophones
Correctly spelled words	82	• suffixes
Total words in sample	95	

Figure 4–6 An analysis of a fifth grader's spelling

the first syllable of *career* as he spelled it, and he explains that it was a hard word but it looks right to him. These comments suggest that Eugenio understands that spelling has both phonetic and visual properties. In the word *policeman,* Eugenio used *s* rather than *ce* to represent the /s/. Even though it is a compound word, this word is classified at this level because the error has to do with spelling a complex consonant sound.

The largest number of Eugenio's spelling errors fall in the syllables and affixes stage. Most of his errors at this stage deal with spelling multisyllabic words. In SPECIL, Eugenio has misspelled the schwa sound, the vowel sound in unaccented syllables of multisyllabic words. In *everything,* Eugenio wrote *e* instead of *y* at the end of *every.* What he did not understand is that the long *e* sound at the end of a two-syllable word is usually represented by *y.* Eugenio spelled *money* as MONY. It's interesting that he used *y* to represent the long *e* sound here but in this case *ey* is needed. BYES for *buys* is a homophone error, and all homophone errors are classified as this stage even though they are one-syllable words. Eugenio's other spelling error at this stage is LOVEBLE. Here he added the suffix -*able* but misspelled it. He wasn't aware that he added a suffix. When he was asked about it, he explained that he sounded it out and wrote the sounds that he heard. It is likely that he also knows about the -*ble* end-of-word spelling pattern because if he had spelled the suffix phonetically, he probably would have written LOVEBUL.

Even though Eugenio has a number of errors at both the within-word and the syllables and affixes stages, his spelling can be classified at the syllables and affixes stage because most of his errors are at that stage. Based on this one writing sample, it appears that he would benefit from instruction on dividing words into syllables, compound words, using *y* at the end of one- and two-syllable words, homophones, and suffixes. These instructional recommendations should not be based on only one writing sample, of course; they should be validated by examining several other writing samples.

The steps in analyzing a student's stage of spelling development are reviewed in the step-by-step feature on page 124.

Teaching Children to Spell Conventionally

Conventional spelling is important. By the time children enter fourth grade, they should spell approximately 85% to 90% of the words they write correctly. In order to spell words correctly, children learn to spell high-frequency words such as *how* and *should,* apply phonics and spelling patterns, build multisyllabic words using root words and affixes, and use a dictionary to check unfamiliar spellings. Children also learn that conventional spelling is a courtesy to readers. Through a process approach to writing, students who are planning to make their compositions public, as Stephanie and Danielle in the vignette at the beginning of the chapter will with their pen pal letters, use the editing stage of the writing process to identify and correct misspelled words.

Step by Step: Analyzing a Student's Stage of Spelling Development

1. **Choose writing samples.** Teachers choose one or more writing samples written by a single student to analyze. In the primary grades, the samples should total at least 50 words; in the middle grades, at least 100 words; and in the upper grades, at least 200 words. Teachers must be able to decipher most words in the sample in order to analyze it.

2. **Identify misspelled words.** Teachers read the writing samples and identify the misspelled words and the words the student was trying to spell. When necessary, teachers check with the student who wrote the composition to determine the intended word.

3. **Make a spelling analysis chart.** Teachers draw a chart with five columns, one for each of the stages of spelling development, at the bottom of the student's writing sample or on another sheet of paper.

4. **Categorize the student's misspelled words.** Teachers classify the student's spelling errors according to the stage of development. They list each spelling error in one of the stages, ignoring proper nouns, capitalization errors, and grammar errors. Teachers often ignore poorly formed letters or reversed letter forms in kindergarten and first grade, but these are significant errors when they are made by older students. They write the student's spelling followed by the correct spelling in parentheses to make the analysis easier.

5. **Tally the errors.** Teachers count the number of errors in each column to determine the stage with the most errors. The stage with the most errors is the student's current stage of spelling development.

6. **Identify topics for instruction.** Teachers examine the misspelled words to identify spelling concepts for instruction, such as vowel patterns, possessives, homophones, syllabication, and cursive handwriting skills.

Teachers support children's spelling development in a variety of ways. Figure 4–7 offers suggestions for supporting children's development through the stages of spelling development. Spelling instruction begins the first time a child watches an adult write or picks up a pencil to write. As teachers model writing; present lessons on phonics, spelling patterns, and high-frequency words; and do shared and interactive writing, they are teaching spelling. Ten ways to teach spelling are described in the following sections.

1. *Provide daily reading and writing opportunities.* Spelling is a writer's tool, and daily writing opportunities are an essential component of spelling

A	B	C	D	E
a and about are after around all as am at an	back be because but by	came can could	day did didn't do don't down	
F for from	**G** get got	**H** had his have home he house her how him	**I** I into if is in it	**J** just
K know	**L** like little	**M** man me mother my	**N** no not now	**O** of our on out one over or
P people put	**Q**	**R**	**S** said saw school see she so some	**T** that think the this them time then to there too they two things
U up us	**V** very	**W** was when we who well will went with were would what	**X** **Y** you your	**Z**

Figure 4–7 The 100 most frequently used words

instruction (S. Wilde, 1992). Students who write daily and are encouraged in kindergarten and first grade to use invented spellings will move quickly toward correct spelling. When they write, children guess at spellings using their developing knowledge of sound-symbol correspondences and spelling patterns. Most of the informal writing students do each day doesn't need to be graded, and spelling errors should not be marked. Learning to spell is a lot like learning to play the piano. These daily writing opportunities are the practice sessions, not the lesson with the teacher.

When students use the writing process to develop and polish their writing, emphasis on conventional spelling belongs in the editing stage. Through the process approach, children learn to recognize spelling for what it is—a courtesy to readers. As they write, revise, edit, and share their writing with genuine audiences, students understand that they need to spell conventionally so that their audience can read their compositions.

Reading plays an enormous role in spelling development, too. Good readers are often good spellers. As children read, they store the visual shapes of words, and the ability to recall how words look helps children decide when a spelling they are writing is correct. When students decide that a word doesn't look right, they rewrite the word several ways using their knowledge of spelling patterns. Or they can ask the teacher or a classmate who knows the spelling, or check the spelling in a dictionary.

2. *Post word walls.* Teachers use word walls to direct children's attention to high-frequency words, important words in books they are reading, or important words related to content-area units. Children and the teacher choose words to write on word walls displayed in the classroom. Word walls can be made from large sheets of butcher paper or pocket charts. Words are written directly on the butcher paper in alphabetical order or on index cards or sentence strips and then grouped and displayed in alphabetical order in the pocket chart so that children can refer to these word walls when they are writing or for word work activities.

The 100 most common words are very useful because they represent more than 50% of all the words that children and adults write (Horn, 1926)! Researchers suggest that in the primary grades, these words be displayed on a classroom word wall in alphabetical order so that students can refer to them as they write (Cunningham, 1995; Martinelli, 1996). These 100 high-frequency words are listed in Figure 4–7. Because so many of the words cannot be sounded out, it is important that they be presented visually. Teachers begin by making a blank word wall with a section for each letter of the alphabet. Then they introduce two or three words each week, and as they are introduced, teachers write them on the word wall in large enough print that children can see the words. For older students, the entire list can be typed up and attached to tagboard cards that students keep at their desks.

Older children who continue to misspell many common words also benefit from having a word wall with high-frequency words posted in the classroom. The words posted on the word wall may be the same words as listed in Figure 4–7, or they may be more difficult common words, such as *watch, experience,* and *because.* A list of 100 high-frequency words that are appropriate for upper-grade students is presented in Figure 4-8.

Teachers post other word walls for literature focus units and content-area units. It is important that separate word walls be used to help students categorize the words they are learning; the words related to a novel children are reading should

A	B	C	D	E
a lot	beautiful	caught	decided	etc.
about	because	close–clothes	desert–dessert	either
again	beginning	coming	difference	embarrassed
all right	believe	complete	different	enough
aloud–allowed	beneath		doesn't	especially
already	between			everything
although	board–bored			everywhere
always	breathe			excellent
another	brought			experience
around	buy–by–bye			

F	G	H	I	J
familiar		heard–herd	immediately	
favorite		hear–here	independent	
field		height	interesting	
finally		hole–whole	it's–its	
foreign		house		
friends		humorous		
frighten		hungry		

K	L	M	N	O
knew–new	lying	maybe	necessary	of–off
knowledge			neighbor	often
know–no				once
				our–hour
				ourselves

P	Q	R	S	T
peace–piece	quiet–quite	really	safety	their–there–they're
people		receive	school	themselves
possible		recommend	separate	though
probably		remember	serious	thought
		restaurant	since	together
			something	to–too–two
			special	through–threw
			success	

U	V	W	X–Y	Z
until		weight	your–you're	
		were		
		where–wear		
		whether		
		world		

Figure 4–8 100 high-frequency words for students in grades 4–8

not be mixed with the words related to a social studies or science unit. Teachers post blank word walls with boxes for each letter of the alphabet and then ask students to identify "important" words related to the unit. Teachers often begin word walls on the first day of a unit and then continue to add words during the unit, day by day. Children, in turn, use the words for vocabulary activities and refer to the word walls to check the spelling when they are writing.

3. *Use interactive writing.* Teachers and children create a text together and "share the pen" to write the sentences on chart paper as children write them on small white boards. The teacher guides the children as they take turns writing letters and words on the chart, and the teacher helps children to correct any misspelled words as they write (Button, Johnson, & Furgerson, 1996). As children participate in interactive writing activities, they practice spelling high-frequency words and review phonics concepts and spelling patterns. Many primary teachers include short interactive writing lessons in their daily schedules, and children often write about daily news, books they are reading, and information they are learning in social studies or science units. (For more information about interactive writing, see Chapter 1, "Teaching Children to Write.")

4. *Teach children to proofread.* Proofreading is a special kind of reading that children use to locate misspelled words and other mechanical errors in their rough drafts. As students learn about the writing process, they are introduced to proofreading. In the editing stage, they receive more in-depth instruction about how to use proofreading to locate spelling errors and then correct these misspelled words (S. Wilde, 1996). Through a series of minilessons, children can proofread sample student papers and mark misspelled words. Then, working in pairs, they can correct their misspellings.

Proofreading should be introduced in the primary grades. Young children and their teachers proofread class collaboration and dictated stories together, and children can be encouraged to read over their own compositions and mark necessary corrections soon after they begin writing. This way children accept proofreading as a natural part of both spelling and writing. Proofreading activities are more valuable for teaching spelling than dictation activities in which teachers dictate sentences for students to write and correctly capitalize and punctuate; few people use dictation in their daily lives, but children use proofreading skills every time they polish a piece of writing.

5. *Teach spelling strategies.* Students learn spelling strategies for figuring out the spelling of unfamiliar words. As students move through the stages of spelling development, they become increasingly more sophisticated in their use of phonological, semantic, and historical knowledge to spell words; that is, they become more strategic. Important spelling strategies include:

- segmenting the word and spelling each sound
- predicting the spelling of a word by generating possible spellings and choosing the best alternative

- breaking the word into syllables and spelling each syllable
- applying affixes to root words
- spelling unknown words by analogy to known words
- writing a letter or two as a placeholder for a word they do not know how to spell when they are writing rough drafts
- locating words on word walls and other charts
- proofreading to locate spelling errors in a rough draft
- locating the spelling of unfamiliar words in a dictionary

Instead of giving the traditional "sound it out" advice when children ask how to spell an unfamiliar word, teachers should help them use a more strategic approach. That is, once children move into the transitional stage of spelling development, teachers can encourage them to "think it out" when they want to know how to spell a word. When children think out the spelling of a word, they spell as much of the word as they can phonetically. Then they see if the word "looks" right. Next they think about spelling patterns, root words and affixes, and syllabication rules and make any necessary changes. Finally, if children still think the word might be misspelled, they consult a classmate, the teacher, or a dictionary or other reference book. This advice reminds children that spelling involves more than phonological information and suggests a more strategic approach.

Teachers teach children about spelling skills and strategies during minilessons using the minilesson format discussed in Chapter 3, "Writing Strategies and Skills." Rather than simply assigning practice activities, it is crucial that teachers demonstrate how to use strategies and skills, make connections to children's own writing, and provide supervised practice activities using students' own reading and writing.

6. *Learn to use a dictionary.* Although it is relatively easy to find a known word in the dictionary, it is much harder to locate an unfamiliar word, and students need to learn what to do when they do not know how to spell a word. They should consider spelling options and predict possible spellings for unknown words and then check their predicted spellings by consulting a dictionary. This strategy involves six steps:

a. Identify root words and affixes.
b. Consider related words (e.g., *medicine/medical*).
c. Determine the sounds in the word.
d. Generate a list of spelling options for each sound.
e. Select the most likely alternative.
f. Consult a dictionary to check the correct spelling.

The fourth step in the strategy is undoubtedly the most difficult one: Using their knowledge of both phonology and morphology, students develop a list of possible spellings. For some words, phoneme-grapheme relationships may rate primary consideration in generating spelling options, but for others, root words and affixes or related words may be more important in determining how the word is spelled.

Students should be encouraged to verify the spellings of words in a dictionary as well as to use dictionaries to check multiple meanings of a word or the etymology of the word. Too often, students view consulting a dictionary as punishment; teachers must work to change this view of dictionary use. One way to do this is to appoint some students in the classroom as dictionary checkers. These students keep dictionaries on their desks, and they are consulted whenever questions about spelling, word meaning, and word usage arise.

7. *Keep a spelling log.* One strategy for helping upper-grade students deal with their spelling errors is a spelling log (Van DeWeghe, 1982). Students keep a personal spelling notebook in which they list their misspellings and the correct spellings. They also consider why the spelling confuses them and design a mnemonic device to remember the correct spelling of the word. A sample spelling log is presented in Figure 4–9.

This strategy is important because researchers have found that words rarely have only one possible misspelling. Instead, many words have a number of trouble spots, and what is a trouble spot for one student may not be for another. Therefore, students must analyze their own spelling errors and design their own mnemonic devices. Although this is a strategy that many good spellers use intuitively, formalizing the strategy will help less strongly motivated students.

8. *Provide opportunities for children to sort words.* Teachers create packs of word or picture cards for children to sort into two or more categories to practice spelling skills (Bear, Invernizzi, Templeton, & Johnston, 2000). For example,

My Spelling Log			
Correct Spelling	My Misspelling	Why the Word Confuses Me	Helps to Remember the Correct Spelling
demonstrate	demestrate	I use *e* instead of *o*.	A dem*o* is used to demonstrate.
coarse	course	I get it mixed up with course as a class.	a = co*a*rse is hard.
meant	ment	I spell it like I think it sounds.	It's the past of *mean*.

Figure 4–9 Excerpt from an upper-grade student's spelling log

From "Spelling and Grammar Logs," by R. Van DeWeghe, in *Nonnative and Nonstandard Dialect Students: Classroom Practices in Teaching English* (p. 102), ed. C. Carter, 1982, Urbana, IL: National Council of Teachers of English. Reprinted with permission.

children can sort words according to consonant digraphs (e.g., *wash, chain, these, whale, bath*), according to long and short vowels (e.g., *bike, cup, feet, cry*), according to number of syllables (e.g., *refrigerator, classroom, beginning*), or according to root words and affixes (e.g., *vis, -ing, pre-, -tion*). There are two types of sorts: When teachers provide the categories for the sort, it is a closed sort, and when children identify the categories, it is an open sort.

9. *Provide opportunities for children to make words.* Children arrange and rearrange a group of letter cards to build words in word-making activities (Cunningham & Cunningham, 1992; Cunningham & Hall, 1994). Primary-grade students can use the letters *s, p, i, d, e,* and *r* to make *is, red, dip, rip, sip, side, ride,* and *ripe.* With the letters *t, e, m, p, e r, a t, u, r,* and *e,* a class of fifth graders built these words:

> 1-letter words: *a*
> 2-letter words: *at, up*
> 3-letter words: *pet, are, rat, eat, ate, tap, pat*
> 4-letter words: *ramp, rate, pare, pear, meat, meet, team, tree*
> 5-letter words: *treat*
> 6-letter words: *temper, tamper, mature, repeat, turret*
> 7-letter words: *trumpet, rapture*
> 8-letter words: *repeater*
> 9-letter words: *temperate, trumpeter*

Teachers pass out packs of letter cards that will spell a particular word when arranged in a certain order. Children work in small groups and begin sorting the letter cards to spell one-letter words. Then they build two-letter words and progressively longer words by arranging and rearranging letter cards. Children record the words they build on a chart, in columns according to the length of the word. Teachers often introduce these activities as a whole-class lesson and then set the cards and the word list in a center for children to use again independently or in small groups. Teachers can use almost any words for word-building activities, but words related to literature focus units and thematic units work well. The words *spider* and *temperature* were selected from science themes.

10. *Teach spelling options.* In English, there are alternate spellings for a number of sounds because so many words that have been borrowed from other languages retain their native spellings. There are many more options for vowel sounds than for consonants. Even so, there are four spelling options for /f/ (*f, ff, ph, gh*). Spelling options sometimes vary according to the letter's position in the word. For example, *ff* is found in the middle and at the end of words but not at the beginning (e.g., *muffin, cuff*), and *gh* represents /f/ only at the end of a syllable or word (e.g., *cough, laughter*). Common spelling options for phonemes are listed in Figure 4–10.

Teachers point out spelling options as they write words on word walls and when students ask about the spelling of a word. They also can use a series of

Sound	Spellings	Examples	Sound	Spellings	Examples
long a	a-e	date	short oo	oo	book
	a	angel		u	put
	ai	aid		ou	could
	ay	day		o	woman
ch	ch	church	ou	ou	out
	t(u)	picture		ow	cow
	tch	watch	s	s	sick
	ti	question		ce	office
long e	ea	each		c	city
	ee	feel		ss	class
	e	evil		se	else
	e-e	these	sh	ti	attention
	ea-e	breathe		sh	she
short e	e	end		ci	ancient
	ea	head		ssi	admission
f	f	feel	t	t	teacher
	ff	sheriff		te	definite
	ph	photograph		ed	furnished
j	ge	strange		tt	attend
	g	general	long u	u	union
	j	job		u-e	use
	dge	bridge		ue	value
k	c	call		ew	few
	k	keep	short u	u	ugly
	ck	black		o	company
l	l	last		ou	country
	ll	allow	y	u	union
	le	automobile		u-e	use
m	m	man		y	yes
	me	come		i	onion
	mm	comment		ue	value
n	n	no		ew	few
	ne	done	z	s	present
long o	o	go		se	applause
	o-e	note		ze	gauze
	ow	own	syllabic l	le	able
	oa	load		al	animal
short o	o	office		el	cancel
	a	all		il	civil
	au	author	syllabic n	en	written
	aw	saw		on	lesson
oi	oi	oil		an	important
	oy	boy		in	cousin
long oo	u	cruel	contractions		didn't
	oo	noon		ain	certain
	u-e	rule	r-controlled	er	her
	o-e	lose		ur	church
	ue	blue		ir	first
	o	to		or	world
	ou	group		ear	heard
				our	courage

Figure 4–10 Common spelling options

Spelling	Word	Location		
		Initial	Medial	Final
o	oh, obedient	x		
	go, no, so			x
o-e	home, pole		x	
ow	own	x		
	known		x	
	blow, elbow, yellow			x
oa	oaf, oak, oat	x		
	boat, groan		x	
ew	sew			x
ol	yolk, folk		x	
oe	toe			x
ough	though			x
eau	beau			x
ou	bouquet		x	

Figure 4–11 Spelling options chart for long *o*

minilessons to teach upper-grade students about these options. During each lesson, students can focus on one phoneme, such as /f/ or /ar/, and as a class or small group, they can develop a list of the various ways the sound is spelled in English, giving examples of each spelling. A sixth-grade chart on long *o* is presented in Figure 4–11.

Spelling involves more than just learning to spell specific words, whether they are drawn from children's writing or from words listed in spelling text-books. Robert Hillerich (1977) believes that children need to develop a spelling conscience, or a positive attitude toward spelling, and a concern for using conventional spelling. He lists two dimensions of a spelling conscience: understanding that conventional spelling is a courtesy to readers, and developing the ability to proofread to spot and correct misspellings.

Students in the middle and upper grades need to learn that it is unrealistic to expect readers to decipher numerous misspelled words as they read a piece of writing. This first dimension, understanding that conventional spelling is a courtesy to readers, develops as children write frequently and for genuine audiences. By writing for real audiences, children acquire a concept of audience and realize that there are readers to read their writing. As children move from writing for themselves to writing that communicates, they internalize this concept. Teachers help children to recognize the purpose of conventional spelling by providing meaningful writing activities directed to a variety of genuine audiences.

Handwriting

Like spelling, handwriting is a functional tool for writers. Donald Graves (1983) explains: "Children win prizes for fine script, parents and teachers nod approval for a crisp, well-crafted page, a good impression is made on a job application blank . . . all important elements, but they pale next to the substance they carry" (p. 171). It is important to distinguish between writing and handwriting. Writing is the content of a composition, whereas handwriting is the formation of alphabetic symbols on paper.

The Goal of Handwriting

Too often, teachers insist that students demonstrate their best handwriting every time they pick up a pencil or a pen. This requirement is very unrealistic; certainly there are times when handwriting is important, but sometimes speed or other considerations outweigh neatness. Even though a few students take great pleasure in flawless handwriting skills, most students feel that excessive attention to handwriting is boring and unnecessary. Instead, the goal should be for students to develop and use legible handwriting to communicate effectively through writing.

Students need to develop a legible and fluent style of handwriting to fully participate in all writing activities. Legibility means that the writing can be easily and quickly read. Fluency means the writing can be easily and quickly written. When students are writing for public display, legibility is more important than when they are doing private writing, but fluency is always important. Whether students are writing for themselves or for others, they need to be able to write quickly and easily.

The best way to help students develop fluency and legibility is to use handwriting for genuine and functional public writing activities. A letter sent to a favorite author that is returned by the post office because the address on the envelope is not decipherable, or a child's published, hardcover book that sits unread on the library shelf because the handwriting is illegible makes clear the importance of legibility. Illegible writing means a failure to communicate—a harsh lesson for a writer!

Teaching Handwriting Through Writing

Handwriting instruction can be taught either through direct instruction or incidentally (Farris, 1991). As first-grade teachers introduce manuscript handwriting and third-grade teachers introduce cursive handwriting forms, they use

Teacher's Note: Supporting Struggling Writers

Many struggling writers' handwriting is almost illegible. It's as though they don't want teachers to be able to read what they have written! These students often need to talk out what they plan to write before beginning to write. When they are confident that they have something worthwhile to say, students care more about writing legibly. In fact, struggling writers' handwriting often improves as their writing does.

direct instruction, and teachers at other grade levels also use direct instruction to review these handwriting forms (Tompkins, 2002). As a part of teaching writing, however, teachers often teach handwriting incidentally. This approach supplements the formal instructional program in the primary grades when students are learning the correct formation of each letter in manuscript and cursive forms. In the middle and upper grades, this approach is more efficient because it is individualized. As teachers observe students writing, they identify letters that are formed incorrectly or other handwriting problems that they can work with students to remedy.

Elements of Fluency and Legibility.   The goal of handwriting instruction is for students to develop fluent and legible handwriting. To reach this goal, students must first understand what qualities constitute fluency and legibility and then analyze their own handwriting according to these qualities and work to solve problems. There are six characteristics of fluent and legible handwriting according to the Zaner-Bloser handwriting program (Barbe, Wasylyk, Hackney, & Braun, 1984):

1. *Letter formation.* Each letter is formed with specific strokes. In manuscript handwriting, letters are composed of vertical, horizontal, and slanted lines plus circles or parts of circles. Cursive letters are composed of slanted lines, loops, and curved lines.

2. *Size and proportion.* The size of students' handwriting decreases during the elementary grades, and uppercase letters become proportionately larger than lowercase letters.

3. *Spacing.* Students leave adequate space between letters in words and between words and sentences so their handwriting can be read easily.

4. *Slant.* Letters are consistently parallel. In the manuscript form, letters are vertical. In cursive handwriting, letters slant slightly to the right for right-handed students and are vertical to 45 degrees to the left of vertical for left-handed students.

5. *Alignment.* For proper alignment in both handwriting forms, all letters are uniform in size and consistently touch the baseline.

6. *Line quality.* Students write at a consistent speed and hold their writing instruments correctly and in a relaxed manner to make steady, unwavering lines of even thickness.

Teachers teach fluency by making sure that students write easily and quickly without excessive muscular discomfort. Some children stop writing periodically, put down their pens or pencils, and shake their arms to relax their muscles. Others complain that their arms hurt when they write. Often these students squeeze their pens or pencils too tightly, causing unnecessary tension. Teachers can talk to students about the problem and ask them to monitor themselves, periodically stopping and removing their writing instruments from their hands. Students should hold the pencil or pen loosely enough that they can easily pull it out of their hands. Also, students who haven't written very much will benefit from daily journal writing or quickwriting to exercise their arm muscles.

Correct letter formation and spacing receive the major focus in handwriting instruction during the elementary grades. Although the other four elements usually receive less attention, they, too, are important in developing legible and fluent handwriting.

Assessing Handwriting Skills.   Students can use the characteristics of the six elements of fluency and legibility in assessing their handwriting skills. Primary-grade students, for example, can check to see if they have formed a particular letter correctly, if the round parts of letters are joined neatly, or if slanted letters are joined in sharp points. Older students can examine a piece of handwriting and check to see if their letters are consistently parallel or if the letters touch the baseline consistently.

Checklists for students to use in assessing their own handwriting on final copies of their compositions can be developed from the characteristics of the six elements of legibility and fluency. A sample checklist for assessing manuscript handwriting is presented in Figure 4–12. Checklists can also be developed for cursive handwriting. It is important to involve students in developing the checklists so they can appreciate the need to make their handwriting more legible and fluent.

Handwriting Minilessons.   Handwriting can be tied to writing through minilessons in which the teacher introduces or reviews a specific handwriting skill. Students practice the skill immediately in a short teacher-supervised writing activity and later in their own writing projects. Then one item on the evaluation checklist for the writing project is whether or not the specific handwriting skill is used correctly on the final copy. For example, to review the formation of lowercase cursive *b* and how to connect it to the following letter, the teacher might demonstrate on the chalkboard, as part of the minilesson, how to form the letter and connect it to other letters, such as *r, a, l,* and *o.* Then students apply what the teacher presented and practice the letter by working in small groups to create a tongue twister composed of *b* words, which they each recopy in their best handwriting.

The minilesson feature on page 139 shows how Mrs. Matkowski taught a minilesson on diagnosing and correcting handwriting problems to her sixth-grade class.

HANDWRITING CHECKLIST

Name _____

	Never	Sometimes	Always
1. Do I form my letters correctly?	☐	☐	☐
☐ Do I start my line letters at the top?			
☐ Do I start my circle letters at 1:00?			
☐ Do I join the round parts of letters neatly?			
☐ Do I join the slanted strokes in sharp points?			
2. Do my lines touch the midline or top line neatly?	☐	☐	☐
3. Do I space evenly between letters?	☐	☐	☐
4. Do I leave enough space between words?	☐	☐	☐
5. Do I make my letters straight up and down?	☐	☐	☐
6. Do I make all my letters sit on the baseline?	☐	☐	☐

Figure 4–12 A checklist for assessing manuscript handwriting

Left-Handed Writers.   Left-handed students have unique handwriting problems, and special adaptations of procedures used for teaching right-handed students are necessary (Howell, 1978). In fact, many of the problems that left-handed students have can be made worse by using the procedures designed for right-handed writers (Harrison, 1981). These special adjustments are necessary to allow left-handed students to write legibly, fluently, and with less fatigue.

The basic difference between right- and left-handed writers is physical orientation: Right-handed students pull their hand and arm away from the body, but as left-handed students write, they move their left hand across what has just been written, often covering it. Many children adopt a "hook" position with their wrists to avoid covering and smudging what they have just written.

Because of this different physical orientation, left-handed writers need to make three major adjustments (Howell, 1978). First, they should hold pencils or pens an inch or more farther back from the tip than right-handed writers do. This change will help them to see what they have just written and to avoid smearing their writing. Left-handed writers need to work to avoid hooking their wrists. They should keep their wrists straight and elbows close to their bodies to avoid the awkward hooked position.

Second, left-handed students should tilt their writing papers slightly to the right (in contrast to right-handed students, who tilt their papers to the left) to more comfortably form letters without twisting their wrists. Sometimes it is helpful to place a piece of masking tape on the student's desk to indicate the proper amount of tilt.

Third, left-handed students should slant their letters in a way that allows them to write comfortably. Students and their teachers should accept that left-handed students often write cursive letters vertically or even slightly backward, in contrast to right-handed students, who slant cursive letters to the right. Some handwriting programs recommend that left-handed writers slant cursive letters slightly to the right, as right-handed students do, but others advise teachers to permit any slant between vertical and 45 degrees to the left of vertical.

The Handwriting-Writing Connection

Most students use handwriting to record their ideas, which makes an undeniable connection between handwriting and writing, although this may change as computers with word processing programs become standard equipment in homes and elementary classrooms. This connection raises a number of questions about handwriting and writing: Should young children who have not learned to form the letters of the alphabet be permitted to write? Should students use manuscript or cursive handwriting for writing? Which writing instruments and paper are best? Does handwriting influence teachers' assessment of students' writing?

Young Children's Handwriting.   Preschoolers begin writing before they have been taught how to form the letters, and they often develop their own unique ways to form letters in much the same way adults might if they were trying to figure out how to form Chinese or Japanese characters. Fluency is important, and children should not be stopped from using letters they don't form correctly. Instead, they should be allowed to experiment with writing and to gain confidence with using marks on paper to express meaning. Parents and preschool teachers can demonstrate "simpler" ways to form letters when children inhibit their fluency by making letter formation more difficult than it needs to be. It is adequate to simply demonstrate the formation of the letter for the child; handwriting practice sheets are unnecessary. Through experience with writing and by modeling adults' writing, children will learn to form most of the letters. Any problematic letters can be taught in kindergarten or first grade.

Young children's writing often reveals reversed letters, such as *d* for *b* and *z* for *s*. These reversals are quite common for children who are learning the alphabet. In fact, it is amazing that more reversals are not made. Also, most

Diagnosing and Correcting Handwriting Problems

Many of the sixth graders in Mrs. Matkowski's class have developed trademark handwriting styles with unique letterforms and flourishes. Mrs. Matkowski is concerned that her students' handwriting can be difficult to decipher and that some students use illegible handwriting to mask spelling problems. To draw the sixth graders' attention to the problem, Mrs. Matkowski teaches this minilesson on diagnosing and correcting handwriting problems.

1. Introduce the topic

Mrs. Matkowski shares a composition written by an anonymous student from the previous year with poor handwriting. The students complain that the nearly illegible handwriting makes the paper difficult to read. Several students point out specific handwriting problems that make the writing hard to read, including problems that are similar to those that they have.

2. Share examples

The students divide into five groups, and Mrs. Matkowski gives each group an anonymous composition written with poor handwriting to read and analyze. The students identify specific problems—incorrect letter formation, poor connections between letters, mixing manuscript and cursive handwriting, reversed letters, and extremely small handwriting—in the compositions. She also shares several other papers with good handwriting for students to use as a comparison.

3. Provide information

Mrs. Matkowski demonstrates on lined chart paper how to avoid or solve the handwriting problems the students identified in the previous step, and they practice their handwriting on white boards using dry-erase pens. Afterward, Marcie, Connor, and Bradley describe their own handwriting problems and ask how to solve them. Mrs. Matkowski asks the students to demonstrate the problems, and then she shows how to solve each one.

4. Guide practice

On the second day, students bring in two samples of their own writing to analyze. Mrs. Matkowski asks them to work in pairs to identify handwriting problems and to work with their partners to solve the problems. They use highlighters to mark problem areas on their compositions. The teacher circulates, demonstrating how to form and connect letters and providing other assistance as needed.

5. Assess learning

At the end of the minilesson, Mrs. Matkowski asks her students to recopy in their best handwriting a 100-word excerpt from one of the compositions they analyzed for her to assess.

reversals are left-right reversals, not top-bottom reversals. Most reversals take care of themselves by the end of first grade, especially if children are not continually reminded of their errors.

Manuscript Versus Cursive Handwriting.   Upper-grade students are often faced with a decision when they write: whether to use manuscript or cursive writing. Teachers may require students to use either manuscript or cursive handwriting when they are teaching or reviewing the form, but in general, students should write in whatever form they find more comfortable. Handwriting should not interfere with getting ideas down on paper during the drafting stage or with preparing a legible final copy to share.

Writing Instruments and Paper.   Students use all sorts of writing instruments on both lined and unlined paper. Special pencils and handwriting paper are often provided for writing activities in the primary grades. Kindergartners and first graders commonly use fat beginner pencils, 13/32 inch in diameter, because it has been assumed that these pencils are easier for young children to hold. However, most children prefer to use the regular-size, 10/32-inch pencils that older students and adults use. Moreover, regular pencils have erasers! Research has indicated that beginner pencils are not better than regular-size pencils for young children (Lamme & Ayris, 1983). Likewise, there is no evidence that specially shaped pencils and little writing aids that slip onto pencils to improve children's grip are effective.

Many types of paper, both lined and unlined, are used in elementary classrooms. The few research studies that have examined the value of lined paper in general, and paper lined at specific intervals for particular grade levels, offer conflicting results. One study suggests that young children's handwriting is more legible using unlined paper, whereas older children's handwriting is better using lined paper (Lindsay & McLennan, 1983). Most teachers seem to prefer that students use lined paper for most writing activities, but students easily adjust to whichever type of writing paper is available. Students often use rulers to line their paper when they are given unlined paper, and they may ignore the lines on lined paper if the lines interfere with their drawing or writing.

Impact of Handwriting on Writing.   The quality of students' handwriting has been found to influence how teachers assess and grade compositions. Markham (1976) found that both student teachers and experienced elementary classroom teachers consistently graded papers with better handwriting higher than papers with poor handwriting, regardless of the quality of the content. Students in the elementary grades are not too young to learn that poor quality or illegible handwriting may lead to lower grades, and teachers must recognize that it is likely they also have this bias.

Computers

Computers are a valuable tool for student writers, and word processing is one of the most important classroom applications. Teachers and researchers have found that when students compose on computers, they write more and both the quality of their writing and their attitude toward writing improve (Bangert-Drowns, 1993). Several reasons for these improvements seem obvious. First of all, it is fun to use a computer. Students can experiment with writing and easily correct errors, thus encouraging risk taking and problem solving. Next, computers allow students to revise and refine their writing without the chore of having to recopy the final draft. In addition, writing looks professional after it is printed out on a printer, and graphics can be added. However, researchers have also learned that students compose the same way on the computer that they compose with pen and paper; simply using a computer won't change the way writers write. In other words, students who normally write single-draft papers or who limit revisions to making minor changes are likely to continue to do so. This finding reinforces the idea that the computer is only a tool, and that good teaching is required for students to learn to write well (Cochran-Smith, 1991).

> **Teacher's Note: Supporting Struggling Writers**
>
> It's important that struggling writers have plenty of opportunities to use computers in the classroom. Too often they're the students who never get the chance to learn keyboarding skills because they haven't finished other assignments, or they don't finish their rough drafts so they don't get to type their final copies on the computer. Students who don't do well with paper-and-pencil tasks may be more successful with a computer.

Word Processing and Other Computer Programs for Writers

Word processing programs are tools for writing. They support writers as they work through the writing process, because they simplify revising, editing, and publishing text. Numerous word processing programs are currently available. Many of these writing programs were developed for adults but can be used by elementary students. Others have been developed specifically for children. A list of some of these programs is presented in Figure 4–13. Auxiliary computer programs include keyboarding programs, graphics programs, desktop publishing, digital cameras, hypermedia programs, and more. Students use these programs in conjunction with computer writing projects; sample programs are also listed in Figure 4–13.

Word processing is a useful tool, no matter whether teachers are modeling writing, children are writing collaboratively with the teacher during shared and interactive writing, or children are writing themselves during guided or independent writing. When teachers have a large-screen monitor available, they display the writing to the class. When a bank of computers is available, children can write and revise as the teacher circulates, providing assistance as needed.

Word processing programs support all five stages of the writing process. In the process approach, children write by developing and refining their compositions, and when children write on a computer, they realize that writing is a "fluid and

Type of Program	Title	Publisher
Integrated packages	Claris Works	Claris
	Microsoft Works	Microsoft
	The Writing Center	The Learning Company
Word processing programs	Bank Street Writer	Scholastic
	Kid Works II	Davidson
	Kidwriter Gold	Spinnaker
	Mac Write Pro	Claris
	Microsoft Word	Microsoft
	Magic Slate	Sunburst
	Talking Text Writer	Scholastic
	Writer's Helper	CONDUIT
Desktop publishing programs	Big Book Maker	Pelican/Toucan
	The Children's Writing and Publishing Center	The Learning Company
	Newspaper Maker	Scholastic
	Newsroom	Springboard
	PageMaker	Adobe
	Print Shop	Broderbund
	Publish It!	Microsoft
	Ready, Set, Go!	Manhattan Graphics
	Super Print	Scholastic
	Toucan Press	Pelican/Toucan
Graphics packages	Bannermania	Broderbund
	PrintShop Deluxe	Broderbund
	SuperPrint	Scholastic
Drawing and painting programs	DazzleDraw	Broderbund
	Freehand	Macromedia
	Kid Pix Studio Deluxe	Broderbund
Presentation software	Kid Pix SlideShow	Broderbund
Digital cameras	QuickTake	Apple
	XapShot	Canon
Hypermedia programs	HyperCard	Apple
	HyperStudio	Roger Wagner
	Multimedia Workshop	Davidson
Keyboarding programs	Kids on Keys	Spinnaker
	Microtype: The Wonderful World of Paws	South-Western
	Type to Learn	Sunburst

Figure 4–13 Computer programs for children and programs that children can use

ever-changing" process (Strickland, 1997, p. 10). In prewriting, children use word processing to take notes, to quickwrite, to brainstorm, and for other rehearsal activities. As they pour out and shape their ideas in the drafting stage, the computer is a more efficient tool than pencil and paper. Children who have good typing skills can input text or make changes more quickly than they can write by hand. Even children who have not learned to type very well may prefer to write using the word processor.

In the revising stage, children print out copies of their rough drafts to use in conferences. After reading and discussing their compositions during a conference, children return to the computer to make substantive revisions that reflect the reactions and suggestions received in the conference. Word processing allows children to revise easily, without cutting and pasting changes in their rough drafts. In fact, children are more willing to revise without the recopying penalty (Moore, 1989).

Computers are especially useful during editing when children correct mechanical errors in their compositions. Children have "clean" texts to proofread, whether they read them on the screen or as a printed copy. After proofreading and editing, children return again to the computer to make their corrections quickly and easily.

After children have completed all corrections, they decide how to format their compositions (e.g., margins, typefaces, spacing, numbering) and then print out the final copy to share with an audience. Word processing relieves children from the tedium of recopying their final copies by hand. The professional-looking final copies often boost children's feeling of accomplishment, especially for children with poor handwriting skills.

Typically, two or three children work together in a buddy system and take turns using the computer. Although this system is often necessitated by the small number of computers available, there is an added benefit: social interaction. Children working together are more inclined to collaborate with each other, providing support, assistance, and feedback as they compose (De-Groff, 1990).

Over a 2-year period, Cochran-Smith and her colleagues (1988) researched the methods used to introduce word processing to students in kindergarten through fourth grade. They found that children had conceptual "bugs" about word processing and that these misconceptions caused problems as they were learning to use word processing programs. One problem was equating keyboard-and-screen with paper-and-pencil: Children did not recognize and appreciate the unique capabilities of a computer for formatting, revising, and editing text. A second problem was their inexperience with keyboarding and locating letters on the keyboard. Despite these problems, however, teachers report again and again that young children are very eager to write on computers and are capable of using word processing programs effectively, especially when they work collaboratively (Butler & Cox, 1992).

Spell Checkers. Spell checkers are built into many word processing programs and may also be purchased separately. After students have completed a piece of writing, a spell-check program is used to search through the composition for misspelled words. A dictionary included in the computer program usually holds 50,000 words or more, and the program compares the words in the student's composition against the words in the dictionary. The two greatest drawbacks of spell checkers are that they do not recognize inflectional endings of words or homonym errors. For instance, students may write *their* and spell it correctly, but if the word should be *there,* a spell checker will not catch the error. Most spell checkers allow users to add other words to the dictionary, such as classmates' names, content-area vocabulary, and slang.

Betza (1987) offers five suggestions for selecting and using a spell checker with elementary students:

1. Find the best spell checker available for your computer, and have students experiment with it and add words to make it better.
2. Use spell checkers to involve students with editing.
3. Keep records of students' spelling progress.
4. Use spell checkers selectively.
5. Reserve the spell checker for the final draft.

Thesaurus and grammar programs are also available that allow students to highlight specific problems in their compositions and ask the computer to supply options. Many teachers, however, feel that the usefulness of these programs is quite limited.

Keyboarding Tutorials. Keyboarding is an essential computer skill, and children need to learn keyboarding skills in order to use computers to their fullest potential. Tutorial programs are designed to teach typing skills to children so they can use word processing more effectively. Comprehensive and game format are two types of tutorials. Comprehensive tutorials teach the home keys and correct fingering on the keyboard. They include these features:

- Students learn the home row of keys first.
- Students use the space bar and shift key.
- Students practice the keys using meaningful letter and word combinations.
- Students receive feedback about accuracy and speed.
- Students correct errors while typing.

One of the best-known comprehensive keyboarding tutorials is Microtype: The Wonderful World of Paws (South-Western Publishing). Other tutorials are presented in a game format, such as Kids on Keys (Spinnaker). These drill programs are better suited for increasing children's typing speed than for introducing them to keyboarding.

When students begin to use the computer for word processing, the question of keyboarding arises because familiarity with the location of letters on the keyboard allows students to enter words more easily and faster. Students who don't know the locations of keys on the keyboard use the hunt-and-peck technique to arduously produce their compositions. This ties up the computer longer than necessary, and children learn bad keyboarding habits that are hard to break later. The fact is that word processing is already a standard method of writing, and keyboarding is becoming a basic literacy skill.

Many educators recommend teaching students basic keyboarding skills as soon as they begin to use computers, whereas others suggest postponing keyboarding instruction until third or fourth grade, after students have learned manuscript and cursive handwriting skills (Hoot & Silvern, 1988; Roblyer, Edwards, & Havriluk, 1997). However, even first graders can learn the positions of the keys on the keyboard. Kahn and Freyd (1990) recommend that young children become familiar with the location of keys and typing conventions as soon as they begin to use word processing programs. They suggest several weeks of brief, whole-class minilessons during which children practice keyboarding using photocopied laminated printouts of the keyboard. Whether or not they have learned the correct fingering on the keyboard, children should not be discouraged from using a computer.

Other Computer Programs.   Numerous other computer programs are available to expand the multimedia options for student writers. Students use text and graphics programs such as Newsroom (Springboard), Newspaper Maker (Scholastic), and Print Shop (Broderbund) to create class newspapers, literary magazines, signs, and greeting cards. These programs allow students to publish their writing in very professional-looking publications. They use HyperCard to create reports and other databases with text and graphics, and use desktop publishing programs to produce books and other projects. Digital cameras are also available so that students can add photos to multimedia projects they are creating. Jamie Smith (1991) and other teachers and researchers report success in using these multimedia programs with elementary students, and Daiute (1992) reported that multimedia composing is especially effective with children who have difficulties learning to write.

Using the Internet

The Internet is a "network of networks" that connects computers around the world into a global communications system (Ryder & Hughes, 1997), and classroom computers can be connected to the Internet using a modem and an Internet service provider. Students can use the Internet to send and receive messages using e-mail, and they can use the World Wide Web to locate and retrieve information about authors, books, and topics related to social studies and science themes.

Electronic Mail.   One use of the Internet is for electronic mail (or e-mail). Students use e-mail to send notes and letters to classmates, pen pals, the teacher, and the wider community at little cost. (In the vignette at the beginning of the chapter, Mrs. Jacks's students sent e-mail messages to their pen pals.) They write messages on the computer and transmit them electronically to another computer. Teachers can also write messages back and forth to students and send announcements and reminders to students through electronic mail (Newman, 1986, 1989). A real advantage of this communication system is that students develop an increased sense of audience (Bruce, Michaels, & Watson-Gegeo, 1985), and when students write back and forth to classmates or pen pals about the books they are reading, they share initial reactions and create deeper interpretations (Moore, 1991).

The World Wide Web.   The World Wide Web (WWW or Web) uses a point-and-click hypertext format to link information together. Students use the Internet to browse the Web, an almost limitless source of information. Students can gain access to text, graphics, audio, and digital video clips on thousands of topics on the WWW. As part of prewriting activities, students research topics and download text and graphics to use in their writing projects. Students are fascinated by on-line searching and may spend a great deal of time on the WWW without accomplishing much writing. Teachers should find productive ways to use the Web. For example, teachers might locate useful resources in advance and list the addresses on a "favorites" list or as "bookmarks" so that students can easily locate the websites (Newby, Stepich, Lehman, & Russell, 1996). Teachers should also be aware that the Internet is unregulated and that unsuitable materials are easily accessible to elementary students.

ANSWERING TEACHERS' QUESTIONS ABOUT . . .

Writers' Tools

1. I'm concerned that if my students misspell words on rough drafts, they will learn to spell them incorrectly.

In a single composition—and sometimes in a single sentence—children may spell an unfamiliar word several ways as they problem-solve for the "best" spelling. Research studies have shown that allowing children to use invented spelling leads to increased, rather than decreased, achievement in spelling. Because learning to spell a word involves much more than simply writing it once or twice, there is little chance that children will internalize the incorrect spelling.

Seeing misspelled words on a composition bothers many teachers. Actually, children's misspellings are a teacher problem, not a student problem. One way to solve the problem is not to look too closely while students are writing rough drafts and sharing them in writing groups. Instead of reading the drafts yourself, ask students to read their rough drafts to you. An overemphasis on correct spelling during writing distracts students from their real purpose in writing—communicating! The time to express concern about student's spelling is during editing.

2. My students' parents have complained when their children misspell words on work I've sent home. What should I do?

It is crucial that parents understand the role of spelling in the writing process and the emphasis you will place on spelling in your classroom. It is helpful to have a rubber stamp marked "Rough Draft" for students to stamp on their papers to identify papers in which content counts more than mechanics. Also, even with careful editing, it is likely that children will continue to misspell a few words on their final copies. Spelling is a writer's tool, and it needs to be put in proper perspective.

3. I don't want my students to learn bad habits, so I always expect them to use their best handwriting skills. Are you suggesting that it is all right for them to be messy?

No one uses his or her best handwriting all the time. Think about the last time you scribbled a grocery list or wrote a letter to a friend. Was your handwriting more important on the grocery list or on the letter? There are two purposes for handwriting. When people write for themselves, their writing is private and handwriting is not very important; however, when people write for others, legibility is more important. Students are aware of these differences, and they should be encour-

aged to think about their purpose and write more legibly when their writing will be shared with others.

4. I have only one computer in my classroom. How can I use it to teach writing?

Although an ideal situation would be to have a computer available on each student's desk, it is, unfortunately, not yet a reality. When you have only one or two computers in the classroom, students will probably prewrite and write rough drafts with paper and pencil, and then type their compositions on the word processor before revising them. A schedule is needed so that all students can have access to the computer. Expect students to volunteer to collaborate on compositions so they can have more time on the computer. This collaboration will also benefit their writing.

5. I don't know enough about computers to teach my students how to use word processing and other computer tools. What can I do?

It isn't necessary for you or your students to know much about computers or word processing programs. These programs are user-friendly, and you and your students can learn to use them with several hours of practice and a few basic commands. The programs designed for elementary students are even easier to use than programs for adults. Also, in almost every class, one or two children will be familiar with computers and word processing programs, and they will quickly become the resident computer experts.

CHAPTER 5

Assessing Students' Writing

Preview

 Teachers regularly use informal monitoring or daily observation to keep track of children's progress.

 Process and product assessment are more formal measures and are appropriate when children use the process approach to writing.

 In process assessment, teachers monitor the process children use as they write, and product assessment deals with the quality of children's finished compositions.

 The goal of all types of assessment is to help children become better writers.

Teachers should report children's progress and find ways to involve parents in their writing programs.

Using Portfolios

In Mrs. Meyers's third-grade classroom, children keep reading and writing workshop folders in their desks. They place all the materials they are working on, checklists, and other records in their folders as they work. (They have math folders and theme folders in their desks, too.) After they complete a theme study or at the end of a grading period, children organize the materials in these folders, self-evaluate their work, and choose materials from their works-in-progress folders to put into their portfolios.

Portfolios are more than collections of children's work; they are a tool for systematically documenting children's growth as learners. Mrs. Meyers's children assume an important role in keeping track of what they are learning. Each student's portfolio is an accordion file subdivided into three sections: language arts, math, and theme studies. In each section, children place samples of their completed and graded work, including writings that have been revised and edited, and informal writings, such as journal entries, quickwrites, clusters, charts, and diagrams.

During the last week of the fall semester, Tiffany reviews the work in her portfolio. She selects the following writings for the second grading period:

- a photocopy of the final version of her autobiography along with her rough drafts, prewriting clusters, and life line
- a simulated journal about Eleanor Roosevelt written after reading a biography about the famous First Lady
- a collection of Christmas poems
- her literature log with entries written to classmates about books she read during reading workshop
- story problems written in math as part of a money unit
- a math log for a unit on fractions, with quickwrites and drawings
- a report about games the Plains Indians played written as part of a theme on Native Americans, with rough drafts and other preliminary writings
- a learning log from the theme study, including maps, clusters, and quickwrites

Mrs. Meyers has already read and graded these writings. Some assignments, such as the math log, were scored using a point system for daily work, and other assignments, such as the autobiography and report, were graded using a rubric.

As she adds each item to her portfolio, Tiffany writes a reflection, or self-assessment, pointing out her accomplishments and explaining why she selected each item for her portfolio. She considers the grades received on each writing, but the grade is not her primary reason for choosing a piece for her portfolio. She clips a reflection to the top of each item. Figure 5–1 presents two of these reflections. The first one is about her autobiography, and her comments reflect her pride in this book.

My autoboigraphy is my very best book I have ever writen. It is my story. It has a table of contets a 3 chapters. I put 3 photos in it. My mom and dad cryed when they read it.

my Reflection

Hi! This is my best lit log. 15 entires. I wrote to difrent kids like Crystal and Jason. I rembered to ask questions and to tell about the plot and charcters in my book.

my Reflection

Figure 5–1 A third grader's reflections on two of her writings

Her parents value it greatly, and Tiffany points out some of her accomplishments, including the table of contents, three chapters, and photo illustrations. The second reflection is about her literature log, which is a series of letters sent back and forth to classmates in which she remarks about the books she is reading. Previously, Tiffany limited her comments to the title and a sentence describing the book. After a conference with Mrs. Meyers, Tiffany is trying to write longer, more interesting letters. She is writing to a more varied audience and including a question to spur the classmate to respond.

Mrs. Meyers keeps two crates holding children's portfolios on a counter in the classroom; it is accessible to the children at any time. She encourages them to review their own portfolios and look for ways their writing and their knowledge about written language has developed.

By the end of the year, children's portfolios will be thick with papers that document the activities they have been involved in and each student's learning during third grade. During the last week of the school year, children will review their portfolios and remove three-quarters of the materials. The other quarter will be passed on to the fourth-grade teacher. Children make a take-home portfolio for the materials they remove to document their third-grade year. Mrs. Meyers adds a cover letter for these take-home portfolios, in which she comments on the portfolios, reflects on the class and their year together, and invites parents to celebrate their children's successes as learners as they review the portfolio.

PORTFOLIO ASSESSMENT IS AN INNOVATIVE WAY to document children's learning that shifts assessment from a test or a grade to complete pieces of writing that represent a student's achievements (Farr & Tone, 1994; Graves & Sunstein, 1992). Portfolios contain a collection of writings selected by children, along with their self-assessments of their writings. The writing portfolio is similar to an artist's portfolio, a collection of exemplary work gathered over time to document the talents and achievements of the artist (D'Aoust, 1992). The goal of portfolio assessment is to learn how children develop and perform as writers. It is a more authentic form of assessment because entire student papers (usually with rough drafts and prewriting clusters), not just grades, are used to document student learning.

A portfolio is not just a manila folder with a collection of student writing; it is a way of learning about children and how they write, and it gives evidence of both the products children create and the process they use (de Fina, 1992; Farr & Tone, 1994; Lucas, 1992). The difference between a writing folder and a portfolio is reflection (D'Aoust, 1992). Reflection requires children to pause and become aware of themselves as writers. Indeed, reflection is part of the writing process itself. Children write, pause, reflect, write some more, reflect, and so on. Many children initially lack the vocabulary to be reflective; they do not know what to say or how to apply writing concepts to themselves as writers.

There are three types of portfolios: showcase, collaborative, and benchmark (Jenkins, 1996). The three types differ according to whether the student, the teacher, or the student and teacher together assume responsibility for the child's learning. The portfolios that Mrs. Meyers's children developed are showcase portfolios: The children self-assessed their writing and assumed responsibility for choosing pieces to include (Hansen, 1994). In contrast, teachers select writing samples for benchmark portfolios: The pieces they select demonstrate "benchmarks" of children's writing development (Cambourne & Turbill, 1994). Somewhere in between showcase and benchmark portfolios are collaborative portfolios, in which children and the teacher work together to collect pieces for their portfolios (Tierney, Carter, & Desal, 1991).

Writing assessment, however, involves more than having children place some of their writing into portfolios. In fact, portfolios are the last step in the assessment process. Assessment involves monitoring, responding, evaluating, self-reflecting, and grading, although not all components are necessarily used for any one writing project (Tchudi, 1997). Teachers monitor children as they write and move through the writing process, and they evaluate and grade children's finished compositions. Teachers also respond to student writing, providing feedback as well as a quality assessment. And children self-assess their writing and reflect on themselves as writers.

This chapter focuses on three ways to assess children's writing: informal activities, process measures, and product measures. As you read this chapter, you will learn:

- Teachers regularly use informal monitoring or daily observation to keep track of children's progress.

- Process and product assessment are more formal measures and are appropriate when children use the process approach to writing.

- In process assessment, teachers monitor the process children use as they write, and product assessment deals with the quality of children's finished compositions.

- The goal of all types of assessment is to help children become better writers.

- Teachers should report children's progress and find ways to involve parents in their writing programs.

Informal Monitoring of Student Writing

Keeping track of children's progress in each curricular area is one of the more complex responsibilities facing elementary teachers, and this ongoing assessment is more difficult in writing than in other areas. Writing is multidimensional and not adequately measured simply by counting the number or quality of compositions a student has written. Three procedures for daily monitoring of children's progress in writing are observing, conferencing, and collecting writing in folders. These informal procedures allow teachers to interact daily with children and to document the progress children make in writing.

Observing

Careful, focused observation of children as they write (and keeping detailed notes of these observations) is part of good teaching as well as part of assessment in writing classrooms. Teachers watch children as they write, participate in writing groups, revise and proofread their writing, and share their finished compositions with genuine audiences. Teachers observe to learn about children's attitudes toward writing, the writing strategies that children use, how children interact with classmates during writing, and whether classmates seek out particular children for assistance or sharing writing.

While observing, teachers may ask questions (e.g., "Are you having a problem?" "What are you planning to do next?") to clarify what they have observed. Observing is not necessarily time-consuming. Even though teachers watch and interact with children throughout their reading and writing projects, these observations take only a few minutes, and for experienced teachers who know their children well, a single glance may provide the needed information about a student's progress.

One of the richest sources of information is observing children as they read and write. Graves (1994) suggests that teachers should observe the class as a whole during writing as well as spend a few minutes observing each individual student. This observation involves sitting next to or across from children as they write. Graves recommends that teachers tell children why they are observing. For example, teachers might say, "I'm going to watch as you write so I can help you become a better writer. Pretend I'm not here, and just continue with what you're doing." Teachers can observe individual children once a month or so as children write for varied purposes and audiences.

Conferencing

As children write, teachers often hold short, informal conferences to talk with them about their writing or to help them solve a problem related to their writing. These conferences can be held at children's desks as the teacher moves around the classroom, at the teacher's desk, or at a special writing conference table. Some occasions for these conferences include the following:

1. *On-the-spot conferences.* Teachers visit briefly with children at their desks to monitor some aspect of the writing assignment or to see how the student is

progressing. These conferences are brief, with the teacher often spending less than a minute at a student's desk before moving on.

2. *Prewriting conferences.* The teacher and student make plans for writing in a prewriting conference. They may discuss possible writing topics, how to narrow a broad topic, or how to gather and organize information before writing.

3. *Drafting conferences.* At these conferences, children bring their rough drafts and talk with the teacher about specific trouble spots in their writing. Together the teacher and the student discuss the problem and brainstorm ideas for solving it.

4. *Revising conferences.* A small group of children and the teacher meet in a revising conference to get specific suggestions about how to revise their compositions. These conferences offer student writers an audience to provide feedback on how well they have communicated.

5. *Editing conferences.* In these individual or small-group conferences, the teacher reviews children's proofread compositions and helps them correct spelling, punctuation, capitalization, and other mechanical errors.

6. *Instructional minilesson conferences.* In these conferences, teachers meet with individual children or small groups to provide special instruction on a strategy or skill (e.g., writing a lead, using commas in a series) that is particularly troublesome for children.

7. *Assessment conferences.* In assessment conferences, teachers meet with children after they complete their compositions to talk with them about their growth as writers and their plans for future writing. Teachers ask children to reflect on their writing competencies and to set goals for their next writing assignment.

8. *Portfolio conferences.* The teacher meets individually with children to review the writing samples and other materials they have placed in their portfolios. Children might explain why they chose to include particular writing samples in the portfolio, or the teacher might read and respond to the self-evaluations attached to each writing sample. As with assessment conferences, teachers and children can use portfolio conferences for setting goals and reflecting on children's growth as writers.

At these conferences, the teacher's role is to be a listener and a guide. Teachers can learn a great deal about children and their writing if they listen as children talk about their writing. When children explain a problem they are having, teachers are often able to help them decide on a way to work through it. A list of questions that teachers can use in conferences to encourage children to talk about their writing is presented in Figure 5–2. Graves (1983) suggests that teachers balance the amount of their talk with the child's talk during the conference, and at the end reflect on what the child told them, what responsibilities the child can take, and whether the child understands what to do next.

As students begin to write:
What are you going to write about?
How did you choose (or narrow) your topic?
What prewriting activities are you doing?
How are you gathering ideas for writing?
How will you organize your writing?
How will you start writing your rough draft?
What form will your writing take?
Who will be your audience?
What problems do you think you might have?
What do you plan to do next?

As students are drafting:
How is your writing going?
Are you having any problems?
What do you plan to do next?

As students revise their writing:
What questions do you have for your writing group?
What help do you want from your writing group?
What compliments did your writing group give you?

What suggestions did your writing group give you?
How do you plan to revise your writing?
What kinds of revisions did you make?
What do you plan to do next?

As students edit their writing:
What kinds of mechanical errors have you located?
How has your editor helped you proofread?
How can I help you identify (or correct) mechanical errors?
What do you plan to do next?
Are you ready to make your final copy?

After students have completed their compositions:
What audience will you share your writing with?
What did your audience say about your writing?
What do you like best about your writing?
If you were writing the composition again, what changes would you make?
How did you use the writing process in writing this composition?

Figure 5–2 Questions teachers ask in writing conferences

Collecting Writing Samples

Children keep their current writing in their desks in manila writing folders. These folders contain works-in-progress, including stories, poems, reports, and other pieces being developed and refined using the writing process. All prewriting activities and drafts should be kept together to document the process that children use. Children also keep their informal writing, including learning logs, quickwrites, diagrams, and clusters in literature focus unit, literature circle, or theme folders.

Children select their best pieces of writing to place in their portfolios. Writing should be dated, and all pieces related to one project should be clipped together. Many pieces of writing in a student's portfolio should illustrate all stages of the writing process so that the student's progress can be tracked month by month. Many aspects of the writing process can be documented through the samples in a student's portfolio, including topics and themes, writing genres, types of revisions, proofreading skills, spelling, and handwriting.

Writing portfolios can also be used for parent conferences and as part of the assessment at the end of each grading period. Parents may need help in understanding what the pieces of writing demonstrate. Rynkofs (1988) recommends that parents and teachers examine portfolios together for what they show children know and apply rather than what they don't know. Also, when portfolios are sent home for parents to examine at the end of a grading period, Rynkofs suggests preparing a cover sheet that describes the types of writing parents will see in the portfolio, the competencies the student demonstrated in the writings, and goals for the upcoming grading period. After viewing the portfolio, parents may make comments or ask questions on the cover sheet and return it to school.

Portfolios can also be passed from teacher to teacher to provide a developmental perspective on children's growth as writers, and the summary sheets written at the end of each grading period will provide useful information for teachers as well as parents. Bingham (1988) explains that writing portfolios are useful because they provide accountability by documenting the writing program and individual children's progress.

In a writing process classroom, children rarely throw away a piece of writing or take it home to stay because part of the record of the child's writing development is lost. Also, these pieces of writing may be used in the classroom for minilessons on specific writing skills and strategies.

Keeping Records

Teachers need to document the data collected through observations and conferences. Simply recording a grade in a grade book does not provide an adequate record of a student's writing progress; instead, teachers should keep a variety of records to document children's writing progress. These records may include copies of children's writing, rubrics, anecdotal notes from observations and conferences, checklists of strategies and skills taught in minilessons, strategies and skills applied in children's writing, and writing process activities that children participate in while writing.

Anecdotal Notes. Teachers make brief anecdotal notes as they observe children writing informally—making clusters or writing in journals—and doing writing projects using the writing process. Anecdotal notes provide teachers with rich details about children's writing and their knowledge of written language. These notes are a powerful tool for ongoing literacy assessment (Rhodes & Nathenson-Mejia, 1992). As teachers take notes, they describe the specific event and report what they have observed, without evaluating or interpreting the information. Teachers also connect the student's writing behavior with other information about the student. A year-long collection of these notes provides a comprehensive picture of a student's development as a writer. Instead of recording random samples, teachers should choose events that are character-istic of each student's writing.

Several organizational schemes are possible, and teachers should use the format that is most comfortable for them. Some teachers make a card file with dividers for each child and write anecdotes on note cards. They feel com-fortable jotting notes on these small note cards or even carrying around a set of cards in their pockets. Other teachers divide a spiral-bound notebook into sections for each child and write the anecdotes in the notebook, which they keep on their desks. A third scheme is to write anecdotes on sheets of paper and clip these sheets to the children's writing portfolios. Another possibility is to use self-sticking notes that can be attached to note cards or in note-books. Like note cards, little pads of these notes are small enough to fit into a pocket.

Teachers need a routine for making anecdotal notes. Some teachers identify five children to observe each day, and others concentrate on one small group of children each day. Whatever the arrangement, teachers use note cards, a notebook, or little pads of paper to take notes. Later they transfer the notes to a more permanent file. Periodically, teachers review and analyze the notes they have collected. Rhodes and Nathenson-Mejia (1992) recommend that teach-ers identify patterns that emerge over time (including similarities and differ-ences), identify strengths and weaknesses, and make inferences about children's writing development. It is important that teachers make time to both record and analyze anecdotal notes.

An excerpt from an anecdotal record documenting a fifth grader's progress in writing is presented in Figure 5–3. In this excerpt, the teacher has dated each entry, used writing terminology such as "cluster" and "drafting," and offered compliments. Each entry provides information about the skills and strategies the child has demonstrated.

Checklists.   Teachers can develop a variety of checklists to use in assessing children's progress in writing. Some of the possible checklists include inven-tories of

> writing forms
> writing strategies
> punctuation marks and other mechanical skills
> writing topics or themes
> writing process activities
> misspelled words by category
> types of revisions
> writing competencies

Two sample checklists are presented in Figure 5–4. Teachers add check marks, dates, comments, or other information to complete these checklists. The forms can be clipped inside children's writing portfolios.

NAME: ___Matthew_____   GRADE: ___5_____

American Revolution Theme

March 5   Matthew selected Ben Franklin as historical figure for American
               Revolution projects.

March 11   Matthew fascinated with information he has found about B. F. Brought
               several sources from home. Is completing B. F.'s life line with many
               details.

March 18   Simulated journal. Four entries in four days! Interesting how he picked
               up language style of the period in his journal. Volunteers to share daily.
               I think he enjoys the oral sharing more than the writing.

March 25   Nine simulated journal entries, all illustrated. High level of enthusiasm.

March 29   Conferenced about cluster for B. F. biography. Well developed with five
               rays, many details. Matthew will work on "contributions" ray. He
               recognized it as the least-developed one.

April 2   Three chapters of biography drafted. Talked about "working titles" for
               chapters and choosing more interesting titles after writing that reflect
               the content of the chapters.

April 7   Drafting conference. Matthew has completed all five chapters. He and
               Dustin are competitive, both writing on B. F. They are reading each
               other's chapters and checking the accuracy of information.

April 12   Writing group. Matthew confused Declaration of Independence with
               the Constitution. Chapters longer and more complete since drafting
               conference. Compared with autobiography project, writing is more
               sophisticated. Longer, too. Reading is influencing writing style, e.g.,
               "Luckily for Ben." He is still somewhat defensive about accepting
               suggestions except from me. He will make 3 revisions—agreed in
               writing group.

April 15   Revisions: (1) eliminated "he" (substitute), (2) resequenced Chapter 3
               (move), and (3) added sentences in Chapter 5 (add).

April 19   Proofread with Dustin. Working hard.

April 23   Editing conference—no major problems. Discussed use of commas
               within sentences, capitalizing proper nouns. Matthew and Dustin more
               task-oriented on this project; I see more motivation and commitment.

April 29   Final copy of biography completed and shared with class.

Figure 5–3 Excerpts from an anecdotal writing record

Process Measures

Until recently, the formal assessment of student writing has focused on the quality of children's finished compositions; however, the writing process and its emphasis on what children actually do as they write has spawned a different

Punctuation Mark Skills Checklist

Name: _____ Grading Period 1 2 3 4

	Period		Comma
	at the end of a sentence		to separate words in a series
	after abbreviations		between day and year
	after numbers in a list		between city and state
	after an initial		after greeting in a friendly letter
	Question Mark		after closing of a letter
	at the end of a question		after an initial *yes* or *no*
	Exclamation Mark		after a noun of direct address
	after words or sentences showing excitement or strong feeling		to separate a quote from the speaker
	Quotation Marks		before the conjunction in a compound sentence
	before and after direct quotations		
	around title of a poem, short story, song, or TV program		after a dependent clause at the beginning of a sentence
	Apostrophe		**Parentheses**
	in contractions		to enclose nonessential information
	to show possession		to enclose stage directions in a script
	Colon		**Hyphen**
	before a list		between parts of a compound number
	in writing time		to divide a word at the end of a line
	after the greeting of a business letter		between parts of some compound words

Figure 5–4 Checklists for monitoring students' writing

approach to writing assessment. Process assessment is designed to probe how children write, the decisions they make as they write, and the strategies they use rather than the quality of their finished products. Three measures for process assessment are writing process checklists, student-teacher assessment conferences, and self-assessment by children. Information from these three measures, together with the product assessment measures, provides a more complete assessment picture.

Writing Forms Checklist	
Name: _____	Grading Period 1 2 3 4
ABC book	learning log
ad/commercial	letter—business
autobiography	letter—friendly
biography	letter—simulated
book/film review	life line/time line
brainstormed list	map
comic strip	myth/legend
chart/diagram/poster	newspaper
cluster	newspaper—simulated
comparison	persuasive essay
cubing	poem
directions	puzzle
fable	research report
greeting card	script
interview	story
journal—dialogue	other
journal—personal	
journal—simulated	

Figure 5–4 *continued*

Writing Process Checklists

As teachers observe children while they are writing, they can note how children move through the writing process stages: gathering and organizing ideas during prewriting; pouring out and shaping ideas during drafting; meeting in writing groups to get feedback about their writing and then making substantive changes during revising; proofreading and correcting mechanical errors during editing; and publishing and sharing their writing (L. McKenzie & Tompkins, 1984). The checklist presented in Figure 5–5 lists several characteristic activities for each stage of the writing process. Teachers observe children as they write and participate in other writing process activities, and place check marks

Name _____ Date _____

Title _____

Prewriting
  1. Student considers purpose, audience, and form for   _____
     writing.
  2. Student gathers and organizes ideas before writing.   _____

Drafting
  3. Student writes one or more rough drafts   _____
  4. Student labels paper as a "draft" and double-   _____
     spaces text.
  5. Student places a greater emphasis on content   _____
     than on mechanics.

Revising
  6. Student meets in a writing group to share   _____
     his/her writing.
  7. Student makes changes to reflect suggestions   _____
     made by classmates and the teacher.

Editing
  8. Student proofreads writing to identify mechanical   _____
     errors.
  9. Student meets with teacher to identify and correct   _____
     errors.

Publishing
 10. Student makes a final copy.   _____
 11. Student shares writing with an appropriate audience.   _____

Figure 5–5 A writing process checklist
Note. From "Assessing the Processes Students Use as Writers," by G. E. Tompkins, 1992, *Journal of Reading, 36,* p. 245. Copyright © 1992. Reprinted with permission.

and add comments as necessary for each observed activity. Children can also use the checklist for self-assessment to help them become aware of the activities involved in the writing process. Temple, Nathan, Burris, and Temple (1988) advocate periodic process assessments to determine whether children are using the writing process.

The writing process checklist can also be adapted for various types of writing projects. For example, if children are writing autobiographies, items can be added in the prewriting stage about developing a life line and clustering ideas for each chapter topic. In the publishing stage, items focusing on adding a table of contents, providing an illustration for each chapter, and sharing the completed autobiography with at least two other people can be included.

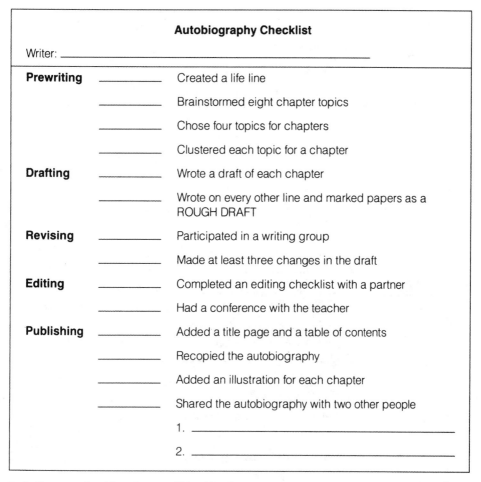

Autobiography Checklist

Writer: _____

Prewriting	_____	Created a life line
	_____	Brainstormed eight chapter topics
	_____	Chose four topics for chapters
	_____	Clustered each topic for a chapter
Drafting	_____	Wrote a draft of each chapter
	_____	Wrote on every other line and marked papers as a ROUGH DRAFT
Revising	_____	Participated in a writing group
	_____	Made at least three changes in the draft
Editing	_____	Completed an editing checklist with a partner
	_____	Had a conference with the teacher
Publishing	_____	Added a title page and a table of contents
	_____	Recopied the autobiography
	_____	Added an illustration for each chapter
	_____	Shared the autobiography with two other people

1. _____

2. _____

Figure 5–6 Process checklists for specific writing forms   *continues*

Checklists for an autobiography project and for a project on fables are presented in Figure 5–6 to show how the basic writing process checklist can be adapted for two types of writing.

Writing process checklists can also be used in conjunction with product assessment. Teachers can base a percentage of children's grades on how well they used the writing process and the remaining percentage on the quality of the writing.

Assessment Conferences

Through assessment conferences, teachers meet with individual children, and together they discuss the student's writing, examine papers from the writing portfolio,

	Fables Project Checklist	Student	Teacher
	Writer: _____		
Prewriting	Read 5 fables and took notes in your reading log.	☐	☐
	Drew a story cluster of one fable.	☐	☐
	Copied the list of characteristics of fables that we developed together.	☐	☐
	Listed morals from 10 fables.	☐	☐
	Planned a fable and drew a story cluster.	☐	☐
Drafting	Wrote a rough draft from your story cluster.	☐	☐
Revising	Participated in a writing group and compared your fable with the list of characteristics of fables.	☐	☐
	Made at least one revision.	☐	☐
Editing	Proofread with a partner and corrected spelling and other errors.	☐	☐
	Had a conference with the teacher.	☐	☐
Publishing	Wrote the final copy in your best handwriting.	☐	☐
	Added an illustration.	☐	☐
	Shared with classmates from the author's chair.	☐	☐

Figure 5–6 *continued*

and decide on a grade based on their goals for the writing project or grading period. These discussions may focus on any aspect of the writing process, including topic selection, prewriting activities, word choice, writing group activities, types of revisions, consistency in editing, and degree of effort and involvement in the writing project. These questions encourage children to reflect on their writing:

What was easy (or difficult) about writing this paper?
What did you do well on this writing assignment?
What did you do to gather and organize ideas before writing?

What kinds of help did you get from your writing group?
What kind of revisions did you make?
How do you proofread your papers?
What mechanical errors are easy (or difficult) to locate?
What is your favorite part? Why?

Through the judicious use of these questions, teachers help children probe their understanding of the writing process and their own competencies. Atwell (1987) keeps these conferences brief, spending only 10 minutes with each student, and at the end of the meeting, she and the student develop a set of goals for the following writing project or grading period. This list of goals can be added to the student's writing folder and used to begin the next assessment conference. An upper-grade student's list of goals might include the following:

I will have my rough drafts ready for my writing group on time.
I will write five poems during the next grading period.
I will locate 75% of my spelling errors when I proofread.
I will explain the purpose in the first two paragraphs of the essays I write.

Self-Assessment

Temple and his colleagues (1988) recommend that we teach children to assess their own writing and writing processes. In self-assessment, children assume responsibility for assessing their own writing and for deciding which pieces of writing they will share with the teacher and classmates and place in their portfolios. This ability to reflect on one's own writing promotes organizational skills, self-reliance, independence, and creativity. Furthermore, self-evaluation is a natural part of writing (Stires, 1991).

Children assess their writing throughout the writing process. They assess their rough drafts as well as their finished compositions. Before sharing their writing with classmates in a writing group, for example, children examine their rough drafts and make some preliminary assessments. This self-assessment may deal with the quality of writing—that is, whether or not the writing communicates effectively and how adequately the writing incorporates the requirements for the composition as stipulated by the teacher. For example, third graders can check to see that their animal reports answer these questions:

Where does the animal live?
What does the animal eat?
What does the animal look like?
How does the animal protect itself?

> **Teacher's Note: Supporting Struggling Writers**
>
> Struggling writers often feel powerless. They often don't remember much about the writing assignment even though it was explained clearly, and they aren't sure how to develop the piece of writing. Having them complete a self-assessment checklist several times during the writing process reinforces the assignment and helps them to examine their own writing. After each self-assessment, you can work with them on one of the assessment points.

Name: _____ State: _____

After you have written the rough draft of your state report, complete this checklist to make sure that you have included all the necessary information.

Yes   No
☐   ☐   Have you written information about the **geography** of the state?

☐   ☐   Have you drawn a **map** of the state?

☐   ☐   Have you written information about the **history** of the state?

☐   ☐   Have you made a **time line** of the state?

☐   ☐   Have you written information about the **economy** of the state?

☐   ☐   Have you written information about **places to visit** in the state?

☐   ☐   Have you written **something special** about the state?

☐   ☐   Have you included maps and other information that the **state tourist department** sent to you?

Figure 5–7 Self-assessment checklist for a report on a state

Fifth graders who are writing reports on states can verify that they have included geographic, historical, and economic information as well as other information that the teacher has specified. Teachers can guide children as they assess their writing by listing questions on the chalkboard or developing a checklist for children to complete as they consider their writing. A sample checklist for fifth graders who are writing state reports is presented in Figure 5–7.

After children meet in a writing group, they use self-assessment again as they decide which revisions to make. This assessment is often difficult for children because they struggle to deal with their own egocentricity as well as with the sometimes laborious suggestions made by others. They also consider the teacher's revision suggestions, but in the end, they often choose to make a revision suggested by a classmate instead.

Teachers can develop a self-assessment questionnaire for children to complete after sharing their writing. Some questions should deal with the writing process and others with the composition. A self-assessment questionnaire for eighth graders is presented in Figure 5–8. As children gain experience with self-assessment, they can write more sophisticated reflections. Completing the self-assessment questionnaire, sharing their reflections, can be considered as one of the steps in the publishing stage of the writing process.

Children use self-assessment as they select pieces of writing to place in their portfolios. They choose favorite compositions as well as those that demonstrate new competencies or experimentation with new techniques. During evaluation conferences, teachers help children make selections and talk about how

Name _____ Date _____

Title _____

As you publish your writing, reflect on your writing processes and this piece of writing. Please respond briefly to at least three questions in each section.

Part 1: Your Writing Processes

What part of the writing process was most successful for you?

What writing strategies did you use?

What part of the writing process was least successful for you?

What do you need help with?

Part 2: This Piece of Writing

What pleases you most about this piece of writing?

Are you comfortable with this topic and genre?

How did you organize your writing?

Does your lead grab your readers' attention?

Which type of mechanical errors cause you the most trouble?

Figure 5–8 A self-assessment questionnaire

Note. From "Assessing the Process Students Use as Writers," by G. E. Tompkins, 1992, *Journal of Reading, 36,* p. 246. Copyright © 1992. Reprinted with permission.

the writing demonstrates the student's growth as a writer. Children also write self-assessments or reflections to attach to compositions that are placed in portfolios, as Mrs. Meyers's student did in the vignette at the beginning of this chapter. In their reflections, children comment on their reasons for selecting a particular piece of writing.

Self-assessment can also be used for an assessment at the end of the school year. Coughlan (1988) asked his seventh graders to "show me what you have learned about writing this year" and "explain how you have grown as a written language user, comparing what you knew in September to what you know now" (p. 375). These upper-grade children used a process approach to develop and refine their compositions, and they submitted all drafts with their final copies. Coughlan examined both the content of their compositions and the strategies they used in thinking through the assignment and writing their responses. He found this "test" to be a very worthwhile project because it "forced the children to look within themselves . . . to realize just how much they had learned" (p. 378). Moreover, the children's compositions verified what they had learned about writing and that they could articulate that learning.

Product Measures

Even though assessment of the process children use when writing may be of greater importance in assisting children to improve their writing, it is the finished composition, the product, that parents, teachers, and employers use to judge writing. Product assessment focuses on the quality of children's compositions and often is equated with assigning a grade.

Assessing the quality of student writing is one of the most laborious and time-consuming responsibilities of teaching, so much so that some teachers assign very few writing projects in order to avoid assessment. Teachers can decrease the time spent assessing children's writing in two ways. First, they teach children to use a process approach to writing. When children use the writing process, assessment is not as difficult because children write better compositions. Second, teachers identify the requirements of the writing project for children as it is assigned; when children understand the requirements of the project before they write, the finished compositions are easier to grade because they more closely meet the requirements of the project.

When teachers assess children's writing, they should have specific criteria in mind. These criteria vary according to the writing project and the purpose of the assessment, but they should get to the heart of writing and not focus just on mechanical errors. No matter what type of assessment measure is used, the goal of assessment is to help children improve as writers and feel successful.

The most common way to assess student papers is for teachers to mark mechanical errors, make a few comments, assign a grade, and return the composition to the student. However, writing is a complex cognitive activity, and measuring only one or two dimensions of a student's work, as in this common procedure, is inadequate. Four product measures that provide a broader assessment of writing and address its multiple dimensions are holistic scoring, primary trait scoring, analytic scoring, and error analysis. The following sections discuss each type of measure.

Holistic Scoring

In holistic scoring, teachers read children's writing for a general or whole impression, and according to this general impression, they sort compositions into three, four, five, or six piles from strongest to weakest. Then the compositions in each pile can be awarded a numerical score or letter grade. Every aspect of the composition, both content and mechanical considerations, affects the teacher's response, but none of them are specifically identified or directly addressed using a checklist. Instead, the focus is on overall writing performance.

Holistic scoring is often used for large-scale school district or national writing assessments, and readers are carefully trained for these assessments. Compositions are typically rated on 4- or 8-point numerical scales. Even-number scales are favored so there is no middle number for average compositions. Before the scoring begins, trainers review a small group of compositions to iden-tify anchor papers representative of each point on the scale. All compositions are read by at least two readers, and numerical scores are either averaged or added together for a cumulative score.

The holistic approach is rapid and efficient and is used to judge overall writ-ing performance without emphasis on any particular writing skill. However, it is not an appropriate measure to use when teachers want to assess how well children have used a particular writing form or applied specific writing skills in a composition. The major drawback of this approach in elementary classrooms is that teachers may unintentionally place too much emphasis on mechanical correctness—particularly spelling, grammar/usage, and handwriting—and therefore bias their assessment (Rafoth & Rubin, 1984; Searle & Dillon, 1980).

Primary Trait Scoring

The focus in primary trait scoring is on whether or not children have incorpo-rated specific traits or qualities in their compositions. These primary, or most important, traits vary depending on the writing genre and the audience. For ex-ample, the primary traits that teachers want to assess in friendly letters written to pen pals differ from those in business letters written to state departments of tourism. Similarly, the primary traits assessed for tall tales that children write are different from those for myths.

Primary trait assessment is based on two ideas: first, that compositions are written using specific genres for specific purposes and audiences; and second, that writing should be judged according to situation-specific criteria. Because the criteria are specific, primary traits differ from one writing project to another, depending on the nature of the assignment. Strong compositions exemplify the primary traits, and weak compositions do not, even though they might be in-teresting, well organized, or free of mechanical errors.

The first step in primary trait scoring is to determine which traits are essen-tial to a specific writing project; these are the traits that will be scored. The next step is to develop a scoring guide with a list of the primary traits to use in as-signing scores. Teachers distribute the scoring guide to children before they be-gin writing so that they know the criteria the teacher will use to assess their finished compositions.

As with holistic scoring, this measure was first used for large-scale writing assessments, but teachers use it when they specify what children are to include in the writing project. For example, if children are writing a research report and they are directed to include the answers to at least three research questions and a bibliography, these are primary traits, and children's compositions can be as-sessed as to whether each component was included. In large writing assess-ments, if children include one item, they receive a score of 1, a 2 for two items, and so on. Usually a 4-point system is used, but the number of points depends on the number of traits being assessed.

Reading Log Scoring Guide

Name: _____   Book: _____

Part 1: Required Criteria

_____   Bibliographic information about the book

_____   A list of 20 interesting or new words found in the book

_____   At least 8 entries

_____   A cover with title and illustration

Part 2: Grading Criteria (1 for C; 2 for B; 3 or 4 for A)

_____   Entries include opinions and feelings

_____   Entries include 2 interesting words from the book

_____   Entries make comparisons with other books

_____   Entries make comparisons between the book and the reader's life

---

Figure 5–9 A primary trait scoring guide

A primary trait scoring guide for reading logs written by fifth graders is presented in Figure 5–9. The criteria are divided into two parts. The reading log must meet the basic criteria presented in the first part before the quality of the entries can be assessed using the criteria in the second part. The criteria in the second part are listed in order of increasing difficulty. For children to receive the highest grade, the entries must exhibit almost all of the criteria.

Analytic Scoring

In analytic scoring, teachers score compositions against a range of writing skills. This traditional form of assessment is most appropriate when teachers want to compare children's writing to a standard of excellence. Paul Diederich (1974) developed an analytic scoring system for high school and college students that divided writing performance into two main categories, general merit and mechanics, and he identified several specific traits related to each category. The specific traits for general merit are ideas, organization, wording, and style. The specific traits related to mechanics are usage and sentence structure, punctuation and capitalization, spelling, and handwriting and neatness. Diederich's two categories, general merit

 Teacher's Note: Assisting English Language Learners

Are you overwhelmed by the number of errors in your English language learners' writing? Try categorizing their errors, analyzing the categories, and using this information to make instructional decisions. You may find, for example, that most of a student's errors involve inflectional endings, so you can review the topic in a minilesson and ask the student to proofread and correct this one type of error.

Student _____ Date _____ Title _____	1	2	3	4
Ideas				
1. Ideas are creative.				
2. Ideas are well developed.				
3. Audience and purpose are considered.				
Organization				
1. An organizational pattern is used.				
2. Ideas are presented in logical order.				
3. Topic sentences are clear.				
Style				
1. Good choice of words.				
2. Use of figurative language.				
3. Variety of sentence patterns.				
Mechanics				
1. Most words are spelled correctly.				
2. Punctuation and capitalization are used correctly.				
3. Standard language is used.				
Comments:				

Figure 5–10 An analytic scoring rubric

and mechanics, are comparable to the two categories discussed in this book, content and mechanics. Perhaps the most significant drawback of this system is that equivalent weight is given to the two categories even though writing educators recommend that greater emphasis be given to content.

One analytic scoring rubric, adapted from Diederich's scale, that can be used to assess the quality of elementary children's compositions is presented in Figure 5–10. In this rubric, the traits of good writing are divided into four categories: ideas, organization, style, and mechanics. This arrangement emphasizes mechanics less than do some other analytic scoring systems, such as Diederich's. Percentage values can also be assigned to each category to determine a grade. Some teachers may assign 25% to each of the four categories, whereas others may assign 30% to each of the first three categories and 10% to mechanics.

This factor analysis of writing is more time-consuming than other assessment measures, and it has been criticized for several reasons. Edward White (1985, p. 124) characterizes this approach as "pedagogically destructive and theoretically bankrupt" even though it is the most commonly used measure in schools today. Analytic scoring is subjective, and the categories may not be appropriate for some writing forms or may not reflect what children are learning about writing, as a primary trait scoring system would. Also, children who are rated high on one trait tend to be rated high on other traits; this is known as the "halo" effect.

Rubrics

Rubrics are scoring guides that teachers and students can use to assess students' achievement on particular writing assignments (Bratcher, 1994; Farr & Tone, 1994). Although commercially prepared rubrics are available, teachers and students should develop their own rubrics because teachers have the opportunity to teach students valuable lessons about what makes a good composition as they develop a rubric together. Rubrics combine elements of primary trait scoring and analytic scoring to simplify the assessment and grading of student writing. Teachers use rubrics to assess student writing, and rubrics are often used to determine scores in districtwide and statewide writing assessments because they make the assessment process more reliable and consistent.

Rubrics can have three, four, five, or six levels, with descriptors related to ideas, organization, language, and mechanics at each level. Primary-grade teachers sometimes develop rubrics with three levels, but in the middle and upper grades, teachers usually prepare rubrics with four, five, or six levels. Researchers recommend either four or six levels on a rubric so that there is no "middle" score—each level is either above or below the middle—but teachers often prefer rubrics with five levels so that the levels can be equated to the letter grades, A–F. Teachers find it challenging to develop rubrics with six or more levels because it is difficult to divide requirements or writing qualities into so many levels; nonetheless, students are more likely to show growth during a school year when the rubrics used to assess their writing have more levels. It seems obvious, for example, that students' writing could improve from a 3 to a 4 more easily when a rubric has six levels instead of four.

Some rubrics are general and appropriate for almost any writing assignment at a specific grade level, and others are designed for specific types of writing assignments. Two general writing rubrics are shown in Figure 5–11 on pp 173–176; one is a four-level kindergarten writing rubric, and the other is a five-level rubric

Kindergarten Writing Rubric
4 Exceptional Writer
• Writes several complete sentences or one more-sophisticated sentence. • Spaces between words and sentences consistently. • Spells some high-frequency words correctly. • Spells some CVC words correctly. • Uses capital letters to begin some sentences. • Uses periods and other punctuation marks to end some sentences.
3 Developing Writer
• Writes a complete sentence. • Spaces between some words. • Spells one or more high-frequency words correctly. • Spells beginning and ending sounds in most words. • Uses both upper- and lowercase letters.
2 Beginning Writer
• Writes from left to right and top to bottom. • Writes one or more words using one or more letters that represent beginning or other sounds in the word. • Can reread the writing with one-to-one matching of words.
1 Emergent Writer
• Uses random letters that do not correspond to sounds. • Uses scribbles to represent writing. • Draws a picture instead of writing. • Dictates words or sentences.

Figure 5–11 Two general writing rubrics

continues

for assessing fifth graders' writing. The same qualities of writing are described at each level on a rubric. For example, the first bulleted item on the fifth-grade writing rubric focuses on ideas, the second on organization, the third on vocabulary, the fourth on sentences, and the fifth on mechanics. Notice that the bulleted qualities at each level are scaled from weak to strong. The fourth bulleted quality in each level on the fifth-grade rubric in Figure 5–11 deals with sentences, and the qualities range from "sentence fragments" at level 1 to "sophisticated sentences" at level 5. Each level between the weakest and the strongest represents improvement in students' application of that quality of writing.

Figure 5–12 presents two more rubrics, and they are designed to assess a genre or a specific writing assignment. One is a five-level, second-grade rubric designed for assessing stories, and the other is a four-level rubric for assessing sixth graders' reports on ancient Egypt. In contrast to a general rubric, the story rubric includes story elements, and the report rubric identifies specific

Fifth-Grade Writing Rubric
5   Exceptional Achievement
• Creative and original • Clear organization • Precise word choice and figurative language • Sophisticated sentences • Essentially free of mechanical errors
4   Good Achievement
• Some creativity, but more predictable than an exceptional paper • Definite organization • Good word choice but no figurative language • Varied sentences • Only a few mechanical errors
3   Adequate Achievement
• Predictable paper • Some organization • Adequate word choice • Little variety of sentences and some run-on sentences • Some mechanical errors
2   Limited Achievement
• Brief and superficial • Lacks organization • Imprecise language • Incomplete and run-on sentences • Many mechanical errors
1   Minimal Achievement
• No ideas communicated • No organization • Inadequate word choice • Sentence fragments • Overwhelming mechanical errors

Figure 5–11 *continued*

components that students were to include in their reports. Both types of rubrics are useful; teachers choose which type of rubric to use, depending on the writing assignment and the students' experience with that type of writing. When

Second-Grade Rubric for Stories
5 **Writing has an original title.** Story shows originality, sense of humor, or cleverness. Writer uses paragraphs to organize ideas. Writing contains few spelling, capitalization or punctuation errors. Writer varies sentence structure and word choice. Writer shows a sense of audience.
4 **Writing has an appropriate title.** Beginning, middle, and end of the story are well developed. A problem or goal is identified in the story. Writing includes details that support plot, characters, and setting. Writing is organized into paragraphs. Writing contains few capitalization and punctuation errors. Writer spells most high-frequency words correctly and spells unfamiliar words phonetically.
3 **Writing may have a title.** Writing has at least two of the three parts of a story (beginning, middle, and end). Writing shows a sequence of events. Writing is not organized into paragraphs. Spelling, grammar, capitalization, or punctuation errors may interfere with meaning.
2 **Writing has at least one of the three parts of a story (beginning, middle, and end).** Writing may show a partial sequence of events. Writing is brief and underdeveloped. Writing has spelling, grammar, capitalization, and punctuation errors that interfere with meaning.
1 **Writing lacks a sense of story.** An illustration may suggest a story. Writing is brief and may support the illustration. Some words may be recognizable, but the writing is difficult to read.

Figure 5–12 Two specific writing rubrics   *continues*

students are learning about a genre or doing a writing project for the first time, a more specific rubric is helpful.

The two most important ideas about developing and using rubrics are that teachers develop the rubrics with students, and that rubrics are developed before students begin to write, not afterwards. When students participate in making the rubric, they become more aware of the characteristics of good writing, and they understand the assignment better. They are more likely to meet the

Sixth-Grade Rubric for Reports on Ancient Egypt

4 Excellent Report
_____ Three or more chapters with titles
_____ Main ideas clearly developed in each chapter
_____ Three or more illustrations
_____ Effective use of Egypt-related words in text and illustrations
_____ Very interesting to read
_____ Very few mechanical errors
_____ Table of contents

3 Good Report
_____ Three chapters with titles
_____ Main idea somewhat developed in each chapter
_____ Three illustrations
_____ Some Egypt-related words used
_____ Interesting to read
_____ A few mechanical errors
_____ Table of contents

2 Average Report
_____ Three chapters
_____ Main idea identified in each chapter
_____ One or two illustrations
_____ A few Egypt-related words used
_____ Some mechanical errors
_____ Sort of interesting to read
_____ Table of contents

1 Poor Report
_____ One or two chapters
_____ Information in each chapter rambles
_____ No illustrations
_____ Very few Egypt-related words used
_____ Many mechanical errors
_____ Hard to read and understand
_____ No table of contents

Figure 5–12 _continued_

teachers' expectations, too, when they more clearly understand the assignment and how it will be graded. The step-by-step feature on page 177 lists the steps in developing and using rubrics in elementary classrooms.

Step by Step: Rubrics

1. ***Prepare a rubric chart.*** Teachers determine the number of levels in the rubric; identify the word, numbers, or letters to describe each level; and prepare a rubric chart on a transparency or on chart paper, leaving blank spaces to add the requirements for each level.

2. ***Complete the rubric.*** Students and the teacher work together to identify the requirements or qualities for a strong composition, determine the scaled requirements for each level, and write the requirements in the spaces on the rubric chart.

3. ***Distribute copies of the rubric.*** Teachers make copies of the rubric for students before beginning the writing assignment so that they can use it to guide their writing.

4. ***Have students use the rubric to self-assess their writing.*** Students use the rubric to self-assess their writing as part of the revising stage of the writing process or after completing the assignment. Students highlight phrases in the rubric or check off items that best describe the composition. Then they determine the overall level of the composition by determining the level with the most highlighted words or check marks and highlight it on the rubric.

5. ***Assess students' compositions.*** Teachers assess students' compositions by highlighting phrases in the rubric or checking off items that best describe the composition. Then they determine the overall level of the composition by determining the level with the most highlighted words or check marks and highlight it on the rubric.

Responding to Student Writing

When teachers assess children's compositions, they often feel compelled to respond to the writing with comments. Searle and Dillon (1980) examined the comments middle- and upper-grade teachers made on writing and found that four categories of comments accounted for more than 86% of all written responses made by the teachers in the study: grades for content and mechanics; correction of most mechanical errors; comments about sentence, paragraph, and other structural errors; and comments such as "good work" to encourage children. This overwhelming attention to error led the researchers to conclude that the message children receive from these comments is that correctness of form is more important than audience, purpose, and content.

Other researchers have suggested that teachers should not write comments on student writing after it has been completed (Gee, 1971). Donald Graves

(1983) and Eileen Tway (1980a, 1980b) recommend that comments about writing be shared with children orally in writing groups and conferences. Tway also recommends that teachers find and encourage the "nuggets" of possibility in children's writing as a way to foster growth in writing. She lists these nuggets:

Original comparisons
Interesting observations
Elaborations
Unusual treatment or twist to an usual idea or expression
Creative spin-off from traditional or popular stories
Wordplay
Contrived spelling for effect
Spoof on vagaries of life
Vivid impressions
Surprise ending (1980a, p. 304)

Tway suggests a variety of ways that teachers foster these nuggets, including encouraging children as they write, using questions to probe children's thinking, demonstrating how to support general statements with details, helping children to expand the nucleus of an idea, using literature as a model, and enjoying writing and the empowerment of language with children.

Assigning Grades

Researchers have concluded again and again that grading is not helpful and can be harmful to young writers, but the practice of grading continues because of school district or parental demands (Glasser, 1968; O'Hagan, 1997). "Grading is a fact of life," according to Donald Graves (1983, p. 93), but he adds that teachers should use grades to encourage children as they write, not to hinder their achievement. Teachers gather information to use in grading children's progress in writing from a variety of sources, including observations, checklists, conferences, and the writing in portfolios. An adequate assessment of children's writing should include informal monitoring of student writing and process measures as well as product measures.

When children's writing is graded using product measures, only compositions that children have revised and edited should be graded, and only those papers that children identify as their best papers from all the writing they have done during a grading period should be graded. It is unfair to grade all writing and then average the grades, according to Graves, because "dry periods, slumps, high peaks are the pattern for writers of all abilities" (1983, p. 93). Further, Tom Romano (1987) explains that grades don't teach nearly as much as teachers think, but they do have far-reaching effects on children's attitudes toward writing and on their willingness to write.

Suzanne Bratcher (1994) urges teachers to make grading serve instruction by "choosing a grading tool that supports the teaching purpose of the writing assignment" (p. 113). Teachers do this by deciding how they will grade the writing at the same time they plan the assignment, and by developing the grading criteria with children or at least making the criteria clear to them when the writing project is begun. Teachers can use checklists with point values attached or rubrics in which the grading criteria have been spelled out to evaluate and grade writing projects, and children can use these same checklists and rubrics to self-assess their writing.

Reporting to Parents

Reporting to parents is crucial in a process-oriented writing program because this approach to language learning is different from what parents experienced in school. It is only natural that they question the rough draft papers that children bring home with unmarked errors, or that if they visit the classroom, they are surprised by the movement around the classroom and the accompanying noise as children work in writing workshop. Nonetheless, parental participation in schooling is a key factor in children's academic achievement (Morrow, 1995).

Gill Potter (1989) argues that parents should be participants, not just interested parties, in their children's schooling. He points out that there is a subtle difference between *involvement* and *participation,* with the latter term indicating a more in-depth relationship. Educators have articulated hierarchical models of parent participation in schools (Wood, 1974) to describe how parents move from attendance at parent-teacher meetings to participation in curriculum planning. At the most basic level, parents monitor school activities by chatting informally with the teacher before and after school or by exchanging informal notes. At the next level, teachers strive to inform parents about the instructional program and their child's achievement through hallway displays, parent-teacher conferences, report cards, and other printed materials distributed by the school. At the third level, parents participate in the instructional program by volunteering in the classroom and providing special expertise for content-area instruction. At the highest, most formal level, parents develop the curriculum through participation in curriculum planning committees and textbook selection committees.

Explaining the Rationale

When any new educational program is being implemented, parents will be curious about it, and to the extent that it differs from what they recall from their elementary school experience, they will be more concerned about it. Often parents expect their children to be educated as they were educated.

Writing workshop and the process approach to writing are predicated on a new view of language learning, and introducing parents to a new writing program begins with an overview of how children learn to write using authentic and meaningful writing activities, as well as an explanation of the role of teachers in supporting children's writing. Parents' understanding of the rationale for the program, the contribution of writing to literacy, and how writing relates to higher-level thinking skills and learning across the curriculum is important if they are to accept the new writing program.

Parents will also be interested in some of the specifics of the program. They will want to know about the process approach to writing and the five stages of the writing process, the types of writing activities involved, how the program will be implemented, and, in particular, how this new emphasis on writing will benefit their children.

Teachers also talk to parents about how they can encourage writing at home. Just as children need to see their parents reading for enjoyment and for genuine communicative purposes, they need to see them writing in order to appreciate writing as a genuine, functional communicative tool rather than only as something teachers make them do in school. Teachers can order copies of the brochure "How to Help Your Child Become a Better Writer" from the National Council of Teachers of English (1111 W. Kenyon Road, Urbana, IL 61801; also available on-line at www.ncte.org/positions/how-to-help.shtml) for use in a workshop for parents. Knowledge about the writing program their children are involved in and ways they can support that learning empower parents so that they can participate meaningfully in their children's education.

Parents may feel uncomfortable about the amount of responsibility children assume in writing process classrooms or the fact that skills are not taught in a definite sequence using a workbook. However, teachers' taking time to explain the rationale, describe the program, and invite parents to observe the program in action will help to allay their fears.

Demonstrating the Program

Having parents visit in classrooms and observe as children work in writing workshop is the best way to demonstrate the program. Children are enthusiastic and committed to their writing, and as they talk about their writing, they use terms such as "clustering," "rough draft," "bibliography," and "proofreading"; their behavior provides additional evidence of the value of the program. Parents who visit classrooms see their children assuming more responsibility, working cooperatively, and taking risks as they extend their knowledge. Eleanor Baker (1994) was a volunteer-aide in her son's first-grade writing workshop classroom, and she described her experiences and the literacy growth she saw in her son and his classmates in an interesting article published in *The Reading Teacher.*

When it is not possible for parents to view a classroom during the school day, children can demonstrate a writing group or a class collaboration activity for parents at an evening meeting. Also, writing activities in classrooms can be videotaped and then shown to parents at a later date. A teacher or a student can narrate the videotape and explain what parents are seeing and why the activities are useful.

Teachers can also set up an evening or Saturday writing program for children and their parents. Children and their parents participate in writing workshop activities to write books of family stories, and parents learn firsthand how their children use reading and writing in the classroom. Like many other teachers working in multicultural and multilingual communities, Susan Akroyd (1995) set up a student-parent writing class in which parents learned and used the same writing workshop procedures that their children use. Not only did parents learn about the instructional program in their children's classrooms, but they also had the opportunity to share experiences and write books, either in English or in their native languages. Parents and the teacher opened new lines of communication, and parents came to view the school as a community center.

Displaying the Results

The results of a process-oriented writing program can be displayed in many ways. During parent-teacher conferences, parents can examine children's portfolios and the many pieces of writing they contain. Class newspapers and anthologies are two ways to publish student writing and, at the same time, communicate with parents. Also, in class newspapers, children can explain writing projects in progress and enlist parental support. Writing should also be displayed in the hallways and as bound books in the school library. When children write scripts for skits, plays, puppet shows, or commercials, they should be performed for parents. Inviting parents to view the presentations offers a convincing way to display the results of writing.

After a thorough orientation to the writing process approach, parents will understand why their children don't bring work home every day, why they may need to go to the public library to do research or to check out a book to read, why misspelled words have not been corrected on rough drafts, and the important difference between revising and editing. A list of ways to encourage parents' participation in a school writing program is presented in Figure 5–13.

Communicating Through Report Cards

Report cards remain a part of school life, and they are probably the most obvious form of communicating with or reporting to parents. Even though teachers change how they teach children when they implement the process approach to writing, the report cards often remain the same, with space for a single letter or number grade in language arts or writing. What does change, however, is the way teachers determine these grades. Teachers use informal monitoring procedures, process measures, and product measures to determine grades. Many teachers also insert a sheet describing the informal and formal writing projects children were involved in during the grading period or the specific writing skills that children demonstrated through these projects. Children may also take their writing portfolios home for their parents to review and then return them to school.

1. **Open houses.** Invite parents to attend open houses to view recently completed writing projects.
2. **Portfolios.** Send portfolios home for parents to review at the end of each grading period.
3. **Videotapes.** Plan viewings of videotapes (either those that are commercially available or made locally) to show the writing process in action.
4. **Professional library.** Lend books about writing from a professional library established in the school.
5. **Newsletters.** Prepare weekly or monthly newsletters for parents that describe the writing program and explain new terminology and activities.
6. **Displays.** Display student writing in school hallways, the public library and other community buildings, and shopping malls.
7. **School assemblies.** Celebrate writing in weekly assemblies that all students in the school attend and participate in.
8. **Interviews with community persons.** Interview community people with special expertise in various content areas as a part of writing projects.
9. **Anthologies.** Publish an annual anthology of student writing that contains entries written by each student in the school.
10. **Volunteers.** Invite parents to serve as volunteers in the classroom to assist with writing projects.

Figure 5–13 Ten ways to encourage parents' participation in a school writing program

ANSWERING TEACHERS' QUESTIONS ABOUT . . .

Assessing Students' Writing

1. Don't I have to grade every paper my students write?

No. In a writing process classroom, children write many more papers than teachers can read and critique. As often as possible, children should write for themselves, their classmates, and other genuine audiences rather than for the teacher. Teachers need to ask themselves whether assessing each piece of writing will make their students better writers, and most teachers will admit that such a rigorous critique will not. More likely, grading every composition will clear teachers' conscience about whether they are good teachers; it will not do much, however, to improve children's writing. Teachers should use the informal monitoring procedures and process assessment measures discussed in this chapter as well as

grades. Donald Graves (1983) recommends that teachers grade only the compositions that children identify as their best ones.

2. There are so many ways to assess writing, I don't know which one to use.

How you assess a piece of writing depends on the writing project and on your reason for assessing it. Informal monitoring of student writing provides one measure that children are writing and completing assignments. Using process measures can help assess children's use of the writing process and various writing strategies. Process assessment should be used when teachers want to measure how well children are using the writing process. Most teachers are more familiar with product assessment and more inclined to use a product-oriented measure. If the goal of the assessment is to determine the relative merits of one composition over another, then a product measure is appropriate. Over the grading period, teachers should use a variety of assessment measures to have a more complete picture or portfolio of children as writers.

3. If I don't correct children's errors, how will they learn not to make the errors?

You do help children correct many, many errors during the editing stage of the writing process, but always focusing on error correction does not ensure that children become capable writers. Writing researchers have documented that children with differing amounts of writing experience make different kinds of writing errors, and that the errors of inexperienced writers are less sophisticated than those made by more experienced writers. Teachers can make a far more important contribution to children's learning by structuring worthwhile writing experiences, providing instruction in writing as it relates to the writing projects that children are involved in, and providing opportunities for children to share their writing with classmates than by correcting children's errors after the writing has been completed.

4. I just don't agree with you. The mechanics are important—they are the mark of a good writer—and they should count the most in grading a student's writing.

It's true that using correct spelling, grammar, and other mechanics is one indication of a good writer, and when the conventions of written English are followed, the writing is easier to read. However, literary prizes are not awarded for technically correct writing; they are awarded for writing that exhibits unique content. Writing that is clever, creative, and well organized that makes the reader laugh or cry, even if it has some mechanical errors, is preferable to a bland, error-free composition. Think for a moment about book reviews. Are books

ever recommended because they don't have mechanical errors, or are they recommended because of their memorable characters or vivid language? The mechanics of writing are important, but they are better dealt with in the editing stage, after children have drafted and revised their writing, than in the early stages of the writing process, when children are concerned with gathering and organizing ideas and finding the words to express those ideas.

5. We've tried keeping portfolios at our school, but they are just too much work. And what are we supposed to do with all the stuff we collect? Upper-grade teachers don't have space in their classrooms for thick portfolios with collections for 5 years' worth of papers. What do you suggest?

Teachers can find many reasons for not using portfolios, and portfolios can be a great deal of work. Nonetheless, portfolios are an essential component of a writing process classroom, whether or not they are passed on to the next teacher. Children's writing changes substantially when they reflect on their writing and collect it in portfolios. When teachers don't use portfolios, children often view their writing simply as work to be completed for a grade. Teachers can begin by having children put all of their completed projects into their portfolios; at the end of each grading period, they sort what they have placed in their portfolios, select several pieces to keep, and take the rest home. Having children sort through their own writing helps them to set purposes for themselves as writers, and the end of a grading period is an appropriate time for self-reflection. If the other teachers at your school aren't interested in implementing a school-wide portfolio program, then children can take their portfolios home at the end of the school year. However, portfolios can be manageable if only four writing projects are passed on each year. That way, portfolios moving to sixth grade would contain 24 compositions with attached information from the teacher and student self-assessments.

Part Two
Writing Genres

Children vary the way they write according to purpose, audience, and form.

When they write to entertain, for example, children write differently than when they write to inform or persuade. Audience is the second important consideration: A letter written to a parent or grandparent is more informal than one written to a local business or to the President. And writing forms vary, too: Scripts and poems look different from stories and reports. As students learn about the writing domains, they learn how the forms vary.

CHAPTER 6
Journal Writing

Preview

Purpose   Students use journals to record personal experiences, explore reactions and interpretations to books they read and videos they view, and record and analyze information about literature, writing, and social studies and science topics.

Audience   The audience is usually very limited. Sometimes the writer is the only audience, and when writers share journal entries with others, these readers are typically well known and trusted.

Forms   Journal forms include personal journals, dialogue journals, reading logs, learning logs, double-entry journals, and simulated journals. Students often write personal and dialogue journal entries in spiral-bound notebooks, and use small stapled booklets for other types of journal entries.

Instructional Preview: Journal Writing

Grades	Goals and Activities
Kindergarten–Grade 2	**Goal 1:** Write personal journals • Students use a combination of drawing and writing in entries. • Students use a dialogue format and write back and forth to the teacher. • Students brainstorm ideas for writing topics.
	Goal 2: Respond to stories in reading logs • Students write responses that summarize the beginning, middle, and end of stories. • Students write responses that make connections to self, world, and other texts. • Students write responses that evaluate the story.
Grades 3–5	**Goal 1:** Keep learning logs during thematic units • Students brainstorm lists of words or ideas. • Students make clusters and other diagrams in the logs. • Students write quickwrites in the logs. • Students create data charts to organize information.
	Goal 2: Continue to respond to books in reading logs • Students write entries using prompts. • Students write entries without prompts.
Grades 6–8	**Goal 1:** Assume another point of view and create simulated journals • Students choose a book character and write a journal from that character's viewpoint. • As part of a history unit or while reading a biography, students choose a historical figure and write a journal from that person's viewpoint. • Students use the writing process to draft, revise, and edit the simulated journal.
	Goal 2: Write double-entry journals • Students choose a quote while reading and respond to it. • Students use the double-entry format to compare characters or for other purposes.

Responding in a Reading Log

To begin a literature focus unit on Natalie Babbitt's *Tuck Everlasting* (1975), the story of a family who unknowingly drank from a magic spring that stopped them from growing any older (a condition they found to have some surprising disadvantages), Mrs. Wheatley asks her sixth-grade class, "Would you like to live forever?" After a lively discussion of the advantages and disadvantages of immortality, she becomes more specific and asks students to write their answers to this question: "If I offered you a drink of water from a magic spring that would allow you to stay the same age you are right now forever, would you drink it?"

Students quickwrite their answers on the first page of their reading logs. Veronica answers:

> I think I would save the water until I finish college and started my career. Then I would drink it because I would like to know how the world would be in about 200 years, and if I lived forever I could become a very important person.

After Veronica and her classmates share their writings, Mrs. Wheatley introduces the book. They read the Prologue together and talk about the author's comparison of August to the top of a huge Ferris wheel. Mrs. Wheatley explains that *Tuck Everlasting* is a "think-about" story. Like their impromptu writing about immortality, their other writings in this log will be informal and personal, written for and about themselves rather than for the teacher. They will be thinking on paper, she explains, because by writing about the story, they will comprehend it better.

Each day, Mrs. Wheatley and her students read a chapter or two, and afterwards they talk about the story in small groups or together as a class. Then students spend approximately 10 minutes writing entries in their reading logs. The discussions serve as prewriting, and in their entries, students often comment on topics they discussed. Rather than having them simply summarize the chapter, Mrs. Wheatley emphasizes that students should relate the story to their own lives and gives them this list of possible writing topics:

Who is your favorite or least favorite character?
Does one character remind you of a friend or family member?

Does one character remind you of yourself?

Do any of the events in this story remind you of your own life?

What event would you have handled differently if you were the character?

Does anything puzzle you about the story? If so, explain.

Does the setting remind you of somewhere you have been?

What do you like best or least about the story?

How does this story make you feel?

What other stories that you have read does this story remind you of?

What would you change about this story, if you could?

After writing, some students will eagerly share their entries with the class, whereas others will keep their entries private. Here are excerpts from Veronica's reading log:

Chapter 1:   I found the book quite boring although the author did use a lot of imagination in making the animals seem like real people.

Chapter 4:   At this point of the story I am beginning to like it a lot. My favorite character right now is Winnie. She seems like quite a little girl and the elf music I think is coming from Mae's music box. Winnie's grandmother seems pretty funny also.

Chapter 6:   Winnie has been kidnapped by the Tucks and you can tell she has a big imagination when you think about how she imagined the kidnappers. In a way I think she kind of enjoys this but as they go farther she begins to become more scared. Mae started playing the music box and the music was the same music her grandmother had told her was elf music.

Chapter 8:   Indomitable—unstoppable; eddies of dust—small whirlpools or swirls; mirage—illusion, trick of eyes. I did notice the food they ate is rarely eaten today. I never really thought about chewing but now that I do think about it, it is kind of a personal thing. I don't really like people watching me chew.

Chapter 18:   Right now in the story I like Jesse the best because he has big dreams and seems intent on making them come true. He's always looking at the bright side of things.

Chapter 22:   Winnie is feeling really guilty about Mae so she is going to help them get her out of jail. If I was Winnie I think I might run away with them because they are really nice people and she has grown to love them. She would probably miss her family a lot but if she drank the water, they wouldn't have to worry about her getting hurt.

Chapter 24:   I wish I was more like Winnie in a way. She is a very brave person and would do anything to help someone. "Stone

> walls do not a prison make" means there are other kinds of prisons besides rock walls and you can put yourself in a prison by shutting out others and not helping other people.
>
> *Epilogue:* I think Tuck is happy that Winnie died and didn't have to live forever. I think it was neat that they saw the toad that lived forever. I liked the way the story ended but I kind of wanted Winnie to find Jesse and the Tucks and to drink the water and live forever.

Veronica's use of the first-person pronoun "I" in this log demonstrates that she wrote about what she thought, what she liked, and what was meaningful to her. She didn't try to second-guess what author Natalie Babbitt intended or what Mrs. Wheatley thought. She wrote for herself. Also, Veronica used the log to note unfamiliar words and phrases (e.g., "eddies of dust" in Chapter 8) and sayings (e.g., "Stone walls do not a prison make" in Chapter 24).

After finishing the story, Mrs. Wheatley asks the students to respond again to the question, "If I offered you a drink of water from a magic spring that would allow you to stay the same age you are right now forever, would you drink it?" This time Veronica writes:

> If someone offered me some magic water that would let me live forever, I wouldn't take it because I believe if the Lord wanted us to live forever he would let us. And I wouldn't want to because forever is an awful long time.

The about-face in Veronica's second response demonstrates the power of a reading log to stimulate thinking and verifies Toby Fulwiler's statement that "when people write about something they learn it better" (1987, p. 9). Having thought about immortality, Veronica has become less egocentric and more perceptive in her response.

ALL SORTS OF PEOPLE—artists, scientists, dancers, politicians, writers, assassins, and children—keep journals. In most of these journals, people record the everyday events of their lives and the issues that concern them. Typically written in notebook form, these journals are personal records, not intended for public display. In other journals, which might be termed "working journals," writers record observations and other information that they will use for another purpose. For example, farmers might record weather or crop data, or gardeners might note the blooming cycle of their plants.

The journals of some well-known public figures have survived for hundreds of years and provide a fascinating glimpse of their authors and the times in which they lived. For example, the Renaissance genius Leonardo da Vinci recorded his daily activities, dreams, and plans for his painting and engineering projects in more than 40 notebooks. In the 1700s, Puritan theologian Jonathan Edwards documented his spiritual life in his journal. In the late 1700s, American explorers Meriwether Lewis and George Rogers Clark kept a journal of their travels across the North American continent, more for geographical than personal use. In the 19th century, the American writer Henry David Thoreau filled 39 notebooks with his essays. French author Victor Hugo carried a pocket notebook to record ideas as they came to him, even at inopportune moments while talking with friends. American author F. Scott Fitzgerald filled his notebooks with snippets of conversation that he overheard, many of which he later used in *The Great Gatsby* and other novels. Anne Frank, who wrote while hiding from the Nazis during World War II, is the best-known child diarist.

In this chapter, you will learn about the types of journals that elementary students can use effectively and how to teach students to write in journals. The key points presented about journal writing are:

- Students use different types of journals for different purposes.
- Even young children can use different types of journals.
- Teachers need to teach students how to use each type of journal.
- Students use quickwriting, clustering, and other techniques in writing journal entries.
- Teachers assess students' journal writing differently from other types of writing.

Types of Journals

Elementary students use journals for a variety of purposes, just as adults do. Six types of journals are described in Figure 6–1. In each type of journal, the focus is on the writer, and the writing is personal and private. Students' journal writing is spontaneous, is loosely organized, and often contains more mechanical errors than other types of writing because students are focusing on thinking, not on spelling, capitalization, and punctuation, and the writer has not moved through the writing process. James Britton and his colleagues (1975) compare this type of writing to a written conversation, and that conversation may be with oneself or with trusted readers who are interested in the writer. Some of the purposes of a journal are to

record experiences
stimulate interest in a topic
explore thinking
personalize learning

Personal Journals
Students write about events in their own lives and other topics of special interest in personal journals. These journals are the most private type. Teachers respond as interested readers, often asking questions and offering comments about their own lives.

Dialogue Journals
Dialogue journals are similar to personal journals except that they are written to be shared with the teacher or a classmate. The person who receives the journal reads the entry and responds to it. These journals are like a written conversation.

Reading Logs
Students respond to stories, poems, and informational books they are reading in reading logs. They write and draw entries after reading, record key vocabulary words, make charts and other diagrams, and write memorable quotes.

Learning Logs
Students write in learning logs as part of social studies and science theme cycles and math units. They write quickwrites, draw diagrams, take notes, and write vocabulary words.

Double-Entry Journals
Students divide each page of their journals into two columns and write different types of information in each column. Sometimes they write quotes from a story in one column and add reactions to the quotes in the other, or write predictions in one column and what actually happened in the story in the other.

Simulated Journals
Students assume the role of a book character or a historical personality and write journal entries from that person's viewpoint. Students include details from the story or historical period in their entries.

Figure 6–1 Six types of journals

develop interpretations
wonder, predict, and hypothesize
engage the imagination
ask questions
activate prior knowledge
assume the role of another person
share experiences with trusted readers

Veronica and the other students in Mrs. Wheatley's sixth-grade class wrote for many of these purposes in their reading logs. Students wrote to activate prior knowledge when they wrote in response to Mrs. Wheatley's question about immortality before reading *Tuck Everlasting*; they wrote to record experiences, explore thinking, and develop comprehension as they were reading; and they wrote to personalize their learning as they related the experiences in *Tuck Everlasting* to their own lives.

Personal Journals

Students can keep personal journals in which they recount the events in their lives and write about topics that they choose themselves. These third graders' entries show the variety of topics students may choose. Kerry reviews the events of a school day:

> I came to school and cleaned out my desk and got my work all done and put a layer on a pumpkin and went to lunch. On recess me, Rex, Ray and Tray got chased and then we came in and worked.

Andrea tells about Thanksgiving vacation:

> Yesterday was the end of Thanksgiving break. I went to the church crafts fair and they served soup. I got a gingerbread cookie and it was about 6 inches long. We had for Thanksgiving dinner: mashed potatoes, turkey, stuffing, sweet potatoes, pumpkin pie, Dutch apple pie, oregano beans, and water. We put up our Christmas tree. So far it has almost drunk a gallon of water and we have some presents.

Micah describes a grandparent's death:

> My PaPa had a heart attack by sitting down and he could not get up. My Grandma called the ambulance and I saw the people in the ambulance help. And he died.

Michael shares a problem:

> Today I made a friend an enemy, and I am glad of it, too. It all started about the beginning of the year. My brother and somebody else and me started a club, so the person that I am mad at was jealous. He started hanging around us and we didn't like it so we didn't pay attention to him. So yesterday he started a club. Today I talked some of his people in his club into being in my club. That's why he is mad at me and I am mad at him.

Micah writes about his plans for the future:

> I am going to be a golfer when I grow up. Now I can hit a golf ball almost 80 yards. My dad can hit a golf ball almost 300 yards. I go golfing almost every 2 months. And I might be a baseball player or a basketball player.

And Jenna writes about a disappointment:

My class all got pen pals. My pen pal's name is Eric. He is 8 1/2 years old and lives in Washington. See I wanted a girl but when I went up to Mrs. Carson she was fresh out of girls.

Many teachers develop a list of possible journal-writing topics with students. This list is then displayed in the classroom or duplicated for students to clip inside their journals so that they can refer to it when they have trouble thinking of something to write about. A first- and second-grade class brainstormed these possible topics: pets, jokes, holidays, my family, basketball, playing jumprope, things to do, Disneyland, and friends. Referring students to the list or asking them to brainstorm a list of topics encourages them to become more independent writers and discourages them from depending too much on teachers for writing topics.

Privacy is an important issue as students grow older. Most primary-grade students are very willing to share what they have written, but by third or fourth grade, some students become reluctant to share their writing with classmates. Usually they are willing to share their personal journal entries with a trusted teacher, so teachers must be scrupulous about protecting students' privacy and not insist that students share their writing. It is also important to require students to respect each other's privacy and not read each other's journals. To protect students' privacy, many teachers keep personal journals on a shelf out of the way when they are not being used.

When students share personal information with teachers through their journals, a second issue also arises: Sometimes teachers learn details about students' problems and family life that they may not know how to deal with. Entries about child abuse, suicide, or drug use may be the child's way of asking for help. Although teachers are not counselors, they have a legal obligation to protect their students and report possible problems to appropriate school personnel. Occasionally a student may invent a personal problem in a journal entry as an attention-getting tactic. However, asking the student about the entry or having a school counselor do so will help to ensure that the student's safety is being fully considered.

Dialogue Journals

Students converse in writing with the teacher or a classmate through dialogue journals (Bode, 1989; Gambrell, 1985; Staton, 1980). These journals are interactive, conversational in tone. Most important, they are an authentic writing activity and provide the opportunity for real communication between students or between a student and the teacher, something that is too often missing in elementary classrooms (Shuy, 1987). Each day, students write informally to the teacher about something of interest or a concern, and the teacher responds. Students choose their own topics for writing and usually control the direction that the writing takes. Staton (1987) offers these suggestions for responding to students' writing and continuing the dialogue:

1. Acknowledge students' ideas and encourage them to continue to write about their interests.
2. Support students by complimenting their behavior and schoolwork.
3. Provide new information about topics so that students will want to read your responses.
4. Write less than the students do.
5. Avoid nonspecific comments such as "good idea" and "very interesting."
6. Ask few questions; instead, encourage students to ask you questions.

Teachers' responses do not need to be lengthy; a sentence or two is often enough. Even so, it is very time-consuming for teachers to respond to 20, 25, 30, or more journal entries every day. Often teachers read and respond to students' journal entries on a rotating basis; for example, they might respond to one group of students' writing one week and another group the next week.

In this fifth grader's dialogue journal, Daniel shares the events and problems in his life with his teacher, and she responds sympathetically. Daniel writes:

 Over spring break I went down to my grandma's house and played basketball in their backyard and while we were there we went to see some of my uncles who are all Indians. Out of my whole family down there they are all Indians except Grandpa Russell.

And Daniel's teacher responds:

 What a fun spring break! That is so interesting to have Indians in your family. I think I might have some Indian ancestors too. Do you still plan to go to Padre Island for the summer?

The next day Daniel writes:

 My family and I plan to go to Padre Island in June and I imagine we will stay there for quite a while. I think the funnest part will probably be swimming or camping or something like that. When we get there my mom says we will probably stay in a nice motel.

Daniel's teacher responds:

 That really sounds like a fun vacation. I think swimming is the most fun, too. Who will go with you?

Daniel continues to talk about his family, now focusing on the problems he and his family are facing:

> Well, my mom and dad are divorced so that is why I am going to court to testify on Tuesday but my mom, me, and my sister, and brother are all going and that kind of makes me sad because a couple of years ago when my mom and dad were together we used to go a lot of places like camping and hiking but now after what happened we hardly go anywhere.

His teacher responds:

> I am so sorry your family is having problems. It sounds as if your mom and dad are having problems with each other, but they both love you and want to be with you. Be sure to keep talking to them about how you feel.

Daniel replies:

> I wish my mom and dad did not have problems because I would have a lot more fun and get to go and do a lot more things together, but since my mom and dad are divorced I have to take turns spending time with both of them.

His teacher offers a suggestion:

> I'm sure that is hard. Trevor and Carla have parents who are divorced, too. Maybe you could talk to them. It might help.

Teacher's Note: Supporting Struggling Writers

Struggling writers are often more successful with journal writing when they write back and forth to the teacher using the dialogue journal format. Having an immediate audience works better for students who are reluctant to write. It may be necessary to have students read their entries aloud to you at first, if their writing is difficult to decipher. With practice, students' handwriting usually improves.

This journal is not a series of teacher questions and student answers. Instead, Daniel and his teacher are having a dialogue or conversation, and their interchange is built on mutual trust and respect.

Dialogue journals are especially effective in promoting the writing development of students learning English as a second language. Researchers have found that these students are more successful writers when they choose their own topics for writing and when their teachers contribute to the dialogue with requests for a reply, statements, and other comments (Peyton & Seyoum, 1989; Reyes, 1991). Not surprisingly, students wrote more in response to teachers' requests for a reply than when teachers made comments that did not require a response. Peyton and Seyoum found that when a student was particularly interested in a topic, it was less important what the teacher did, and when the teacher and student were both interested in a topic, the topic seemed to take over as they shared and built on each other's writing. Reyes also found that bilingual students were much more successful in writing dialogue journal entries than in writing in response to books they had read.

Yesterday I went to the Fair with my brother-in-law and my brother, sister my sister tell me to use the three doller to get that big miorrow so I use the three doller but I only got one dart to throw at the balloon then I hit the balloon and I got a big miorrow for my sister my brother-in-law tell me to get one for my brother-in-law so I got a biger one then I give to my sister and I got my self some tiket to ride I went on the super sidle and I got scard then I was sitting and I jump up hight when I was going down.

You must have good aim to be able to throw a dart and hit a balloon. I'm glad you won some mirrors. Was this your first trip to the Fair?

Figure 6–2 Shared writing: An excerpt from a fourth grader's dialogue journal

Figure 6–2 presents an excerpt from a fourth grader's dialogue journal. This student is a native speaker of Lao and is learning English as a second language. In this entry, the fourth grader writes fluently about a trip to a county fair, recounting his activities there, and his teacher responds briefly to the account.

Students can use dialogue journals to write to classmates or the teacher about books they are reading (Atwell, 1987; Barone, 1990; Dekker, 1991).

In these journal entries, students write about the books they are reading, compare the books to others by the same author or others they have read, and offer opinions about the book and whether a classmate or the teacher might enjoy reading it. This approach is especially effective for reading workshop when students are reading different books. Students are often paired, and they write back-and-forth to their reading buddies; this activity provides the socialization that independent reading does not. Depending on whether they are reading relatively short picture books or longer chapter books, students write dialogue journal entries every day or two or once a week, and then classmates write back. Here is an entry that a fourth grader wrote to a classmate:

Dear Adam,

I'm reading the coolest book. It's about snakes and it's called *A Snake's Body* [Cole, 1981]. Look at the pictures on pages 34, 35, 36, 37, 38, 39, 40, 41, and 42 to see how a python strangles and eats a chick. It's awesome.

Your Friend, Todd

And here is Adam's response:

Dear Todd,

Awesome! I saw that on TV and it was just like in the book. I am reading *Shiloh* [Naylor, 1991]. It's about a boy and the dog he wants bad. Do you want it? You can have it on Friday.

From Adam

Reading Logs

Students write in reading logs about the stories and other books they are reading during literature focus units and reading workshop (Barone, 1990; Hancock, 1992, 1993). As students read or listen to books read aloud, they respond to the book or relate it to events in their own lives, as Veronica did in the *Tuck Everlasting* reading log described in the vignette at the beginning of the chapter. Students can also list unfamiliar words, jot down quotable quotes, and take notes about characters, plot, or other elements of the story, but the primary purpose of these journals is for students to think about the book, connect literature to their lives, and develop their own interpretations. These journals go by a variety of names, including literature response journals (Hancock, 1992), literature journals (Five, 1986), and reading journals (Wollman-Bonilla, 1989), but no matter what they are called, their purpose remains the same.

Researchers have examined students' responses and noticed patterns in their reading log entries. Hancock (1992, 1993) identified these eight categories:

1. *Monitoring understanding.* Students get to know the characters and explain how the story is making sense to them. These responses usually occur at the beginning of a book.

2. *Making inferences.* Students share their insights into the feelings and motives of a character. They often begin their comments with "I think."

3. *Making, validating, or invalidating predictions.* Students speculate about what will happen later in the story and also confirm or deny predictions they made previously.

4. *Expressing wonder or confusion.* Students reflect on the way the story is developing. They ask "I wonder why" questions and write about confusions.

5. *Character interaction.* Students show that they are personally involved with a character, sometimes writing "If I were _____, I would . . . ." They also express empathy and share related experiences from their own lives. Also, they may give advice to the character.

6. *Character assessment.* Students judge a character's actions and often use evaluative terms such as "nice" and "dumb."

7. *Story involvement.* Students reveal their involvement in the story as they express satisfaction with how the story is developing. They may comment on their desire to continue reading or use terms such as "disgusting," "weird," or "awesome" to react to sensory aspects of the story.

8. *Literary criticism.* Students offer "I liked/I didn't like" opinions and praise or condemn an author's style. Sometimes students compare the book with others they have read or compare the author with other authors with whom they are familiar.

The first four categories are personal meaning-making options in which students make inferences about characters, offer predictions, ask questions, or discuss confusions. The next three categories focus on character and plot development; students become involved with the story, and they offer reactions to the characters and events of the story. The last category is literary evaluation, in which students evaluate books and reflect on their own literary tastes.

These categories can extend the possibilities of response by introducing teachers and students to a wide variety of response options. Hancock (1992, 1993) recommends that teachers begin by assessing the kinds of responses students are currently making. They can read students' reading logs, categorize the types of responses, tally the categories, and make an assessment. Often students use only a few types of responses, not the wide range that is available. Teachers can teach minilessons and model types of responses that students aren't using, and they can ask questions when they read journals to prompt students to think in new ways about the story they are reading.

For example, a third grader wrote this reading log entry during an author study of Eve Bunting; the focus is literary criticism:

> I just read *Fly Away Home* [Bunting, 1991] and it is the best book that Eve Bunting ever wrote. The boy was like the bird and I know he made it out of the airport.

A sixth grader wrote this entry after reading the third chapter of *Summer of the Swans* (Byars, 1970); the focus is on character interaction:

> I think looks are not the most important thing because the way you act is. When some people look good and still act good—that's when people are really lucky, but I just think you should go ahead and appreciate the way you look.

The next two entries were written by seventh graders after finishing *The Giver* (Lowry, 1993). Even though they reach different conclusions about the book, their focus is story involvement:

> I can't believe it ended this way. They froze to death. I think they died but I wish they found freedom and happiness. It is very sad.

> The ending is cool. Jonas and Gabe come back to the community but now it is changed. There are colors and the people have feelings. They believe in God and it is Christmas.

Learning Logs

Students use learning logs to record or react to what they are learning in social studies, science, or math. Students write in these journals to reflect on their learning, to discover gaps in their knowledge, and to explore relationships between what they are learning and their past experiences.

Students often keep learning logs as a part of thematic units in social studies. In their logs, students write in response to informational books, write vocabulary related to the theme, create time lines, and draw diagrams and maps. For example, as part of a study of the Pilgrims, middle-grade students might include the following in their learning logs:

- Informal quickwrites about Pilgrims
- A list of words related to the theme
- A chart comparing the Pilgrims of 1620 to modern-day pilgrims
- A time line showing when groups of Pilgrims came to America

- A brainstormed list of questions to ask parents about how each student's family came to America
- Answers to these questions
- A map showing how the student's family came to America
- A picture of the Statue of Liberty with labels for the various parts
- Notes from interviewing a recent immigrant to America
- A response to *Molly's Pilgrim* (Cohen, 1983)

Through these learning log activities, students explore concepts they are learning and record information they want to remember about the Pilgrims.

Science-related learning logs can take several forms. One type of learning log is an observation log in which students make daily entries to track the growth of a plant or animal. Figure 6–3 presents a first grader's seed journal. In this journal, Tyler makes each entry on a new page. Drawing is as important as writing, and he uses invented spelling. Because several pages are difficult for adults to decipher, the text on each page has been translated into standard orthography.

ELL Teacher's Note: Assisting English Language Learners

How can older students who speak limited English keep learning logs? Have students draw a picture of a social studies or science topic and label it with key vocabulary words, or duplicate a photo or illustration from a content-area textbook or informational book and have students paste it in their learning log and label it. Later, students can dictate or write sentences using the vocabulary words.

A second type of learning log is one in which students make daily entries during a unit of study. Students may take notes during a presentation by the teacher or a classmate, after viewing a film, or at the end of each class period. Sometimes students make entries in list form, sometimes in clusters or charts, and at other times in paragraphs. A lab report is a third type of learning log. In these logs, students list the materials and procedures used in the experiment, present data on an observation chart, and then discuss the results.

Students also use learning logs to write about what they are learning in math (Salem, 1982). They record explanations and examples of concepts presented in class and react to any problems they may be having. Some upper-grade teachers allow students the last 5 minutes of math class to summarize the day's lesson and react to it in their learning logs (Schubert, 1987). Students write about what they have learned during class, the steps involved in solving a problem, definitions of mathematical terms, or things that confuse them. Writing in learning logs has several advantages over class discussion (Greesen, 1977): All students participate simultaneously in writing, and teachers can review written responses more carefully than oral ones. Also, students use mathematical vocabulary and become more precise and complete in their answers. They also learn how to reflect on and evaluate their own learning (Stanford, 1988).

Translation: We planted a plant.

Translation: We dug up the plant. It is fat.

Translation: We dug up the plant. It did not crack open.

Translation: We dug up the plant. It did not grow.

Figure 6–3 Independent writing: A first grader's seed log

continues

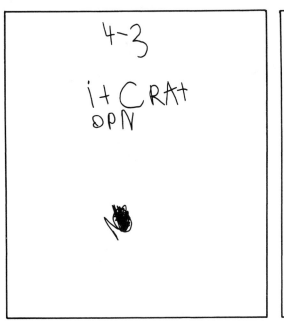

Translation: It cracked open

Translation: We dug up the seed. It grew a root.

Translation: It got fatter. It grew roots.

Translation: The plant grew roots. It grew leaves.

Figure 6–3 *continued*

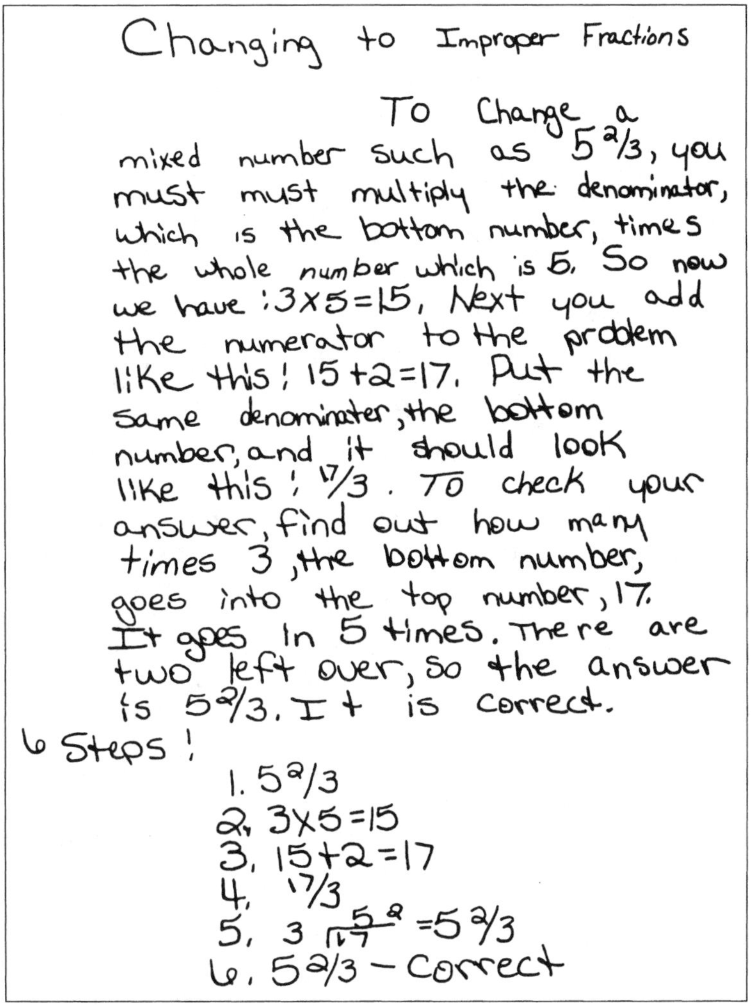

Changing to Improper Fractions

To Change a mixed number such as $5\,^2/_3$, you must must multiply the denominator, which is the bottom number, times the whole number which is 5. So now we have : $3 \times 5 = 15$, Next you add the numerator to the problem like this ! $15 + 2 = 17$. Put the same denominater, the bottom number, and it should look like this ! $^{17}/_3$. To check your answer, find out how many times 3, the bottom number, goes into the top number, 17. It goes in 5 times. There are two left over, so the answer is $5\,^2/_3$. It is correct.

6 Steps !

1. $5\,^2/_3$
2. $3 \times 5 = 15$
3. $15 + 2 = 17$
4. $^{17}/_3$
5. $3\sqrt{17} = 5\,^2/_3$
6. $5\,^2/_3$ — Correct

Figure 6–4 Independent writing: An excerpt from a sixth grader's math learning log

Figure 6–4 presents an entry from a sixth grader's learning log in which she describes how to change to improper fractions. Notice that after she describes the steps in sequence, she includes a review of the six steps.

In addition to the benefits to students, teachers use learning logs to informally assess students' learning. Through students' math entries, teachers

- assess what students already know about a concept before teaching
- help students integrate what they are learning and make the knowledge a part of their lives

- discover what students are really learning
- check on confusions and misconceptions
- monitor students' self-images and attitude toward math
- assess students' learning of a concept after teaching (McGonegal, 1987)

Sometimes teachers simply read these entries, and at other times, the learning logs become dialogue journals as teachers respond to students by clarifying misconceptions and offering encouragement.

Double-Entry Journals

For double-entry journals, students divide their journal pages into two parts and write different types of information in each part (Barone, 1990; Berthoff, 1981). Students can use double-entry journals for reading logs or for learning logs. When they make double-entry reading logs, students often write quotes from the story or other book they are reading in the left column and relate each quote to their own life and to literature they have read in the right column. Through this type of journal, students become more engaged in what they are reading, note sentences that have personal connections, and become more sensitive to the author's language.

Fifth graders drew and wrote in double-entry journals as they read *Bunnicula: A Rabbit-Tale of Mystery,* a hilarious Halloween story by Deborah and James Howe (1979). Before reading each chapter, students wrote predictions about what would happen in the chapter in one column, and after reading, they drew and wrote about what actually did happen. An excerpt from a fifth grader's journal is presented in Figure 6–5. This student's responses indicate that she is engaged in the story and is connecting the story to her own life as well as to another story she has read.

Double-entry journals can be used in several other ways. Instead of recording quotes from the book, students can write "Reading Notes" in the left column and then add "Reactions" in the right column. In the left column, students write about the events they read about in the chapter. Then they make personal connections to the events in the right column. As an alternative, students can use the heading "Reading Notes" for one column and "Discussion Notes" for the second column. Students write reading notes as they read or immediately after reading. Later, after they discuss the story or chapter of a longer book, students add discussion notes.

Younger students can use the double-entry format for a prediction journal. They label the left column "Predictions" and the right column "What Really Happened" (Macon, Bewell, & Vogt, 1991). In the left column, they write or draw a picture of what they predict will happen in the chapter before reading it. Then, after reading, they draw or write what actually happened in the right column.

Students also use the double-entry format in learning logs: They can write important facts in the left column and their reactions to the facts in the right

Chapter	Prediction	What Really Happened
3	I think that Chester will have night mares becose of the story.	They found a WHITE tomato.
4	I think that Chester will want to learn about vampires and he might even turn into one. ALL ABOUT VAMPIRES	He fond a Zuckini. It was white and it had 2 little holes in it.
5	I think they will find a white squash or some other vegatables.	Toby doont no that the rabbit is a VAMPIRE.

Figure 6–5 Independent writing: An excerpt from a fifth grader's double-entry journal on *Bunnicula: A Rabbit-Tale of Mystery*

column, or questions about the topic in the left column and answers in the right column. As with the other types of double-entry journals, it is in the second column that students make more interpretive comments. Figure 6–6 shows a sixth grader's double-entry journal written during a unit on drug prevention. In the left

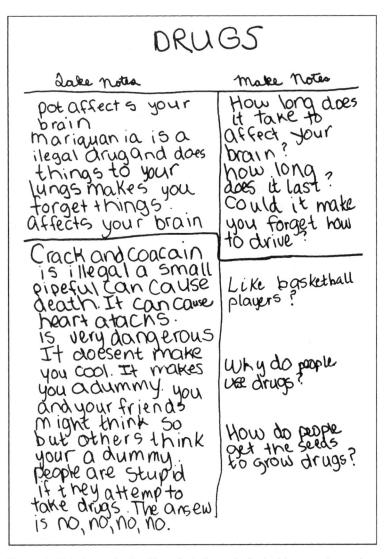

Figure 6–6 Independent writing: A sixth grader's double-entry journal page

column, the student wrote information she was learning, and in the right column, she made personal connections to the information.

Simulated Journals

In some children's books, such as *Catherine, Called Birdy* (Cushman, 1994) and *Stranded at Plimoth Plantation, 1626* (Bowen, 1994), the author assumes the role of a character and writes from the character's point of view. These books can be called simulated journals. They are rich with historical details and feature examples of both words and phrasing of the period. At the end of the book, authors often include information about how they researched the period and explanations about the liberties they took with the characters or events that are recorded. Scholastic Books has created four series of historical journals that are appropriate for fourth through eighth graders. The "Dear America" series features diaries written from girls' viewpoints, including *A Journey to the New World: The Diary of Remember Patience Whipple* (Lasky, 1996), *A Picture of Freedom: The Diary of Clotee, a Slave Girl* (McKissack, 1997), and *A Time for Courage: The Suffragette Diary of Kathleen Bowen* (Lasky, 2002a). The second series, "My Name Is America," features historical diaries written from boys' viewpoints, including *The Journal of Augustus Pelletier: The Lewis and Clark Expedition, 1804* (Lasky, 2000), *The Journal of Biddy Owens: The Negro Leagues, 1948* (Myers, 2001), and *The Journal of Patrick Seamus Flaherty: United States Marine Corps, Khe Sanh, Vietnam, 1968* (White, 2002). The third series, "My America," has shorter books with larger print that are written at the third-grade reading level. Most of the diaries in this series continue through two or three related books such as *Freedom's Wings: Corey's Underground Railroad Diary* (Book1) (Wyeth, 2001) and the continuation in *Flying Free: Corey's Underground Railroad Diary* (Book 2) (Wyeth, 2002). The fourth series, "The Royal Diaries," features the simulated diaries of Elizabeth I (Lasky, 2002b), Cleopatra (Gregory, 1999), and other famous queens from Europe, Africa, and Asia. Each of these books provides a glimpse into history from a child's perspective, and they are handsomely bound to look like an old journal. The paper is heavy and rough cut around the edges, and a ribbon page marker is bound into the book.

Elementary students, too, can write simulated journals. They can assume the role of another person and write from that person's viewpoint. As students read biographies or study social studies units, they can assume the role of a historical figure. As they read stories, they can assume the role of a character in the story. In this way, students gain insight into the lives of other people and into historical events. A look at a series of diary entries written by a fifth grader who has assumed the role of Betsy Ross shows how she carefully chose the dates for each entry and wove in factual information:

May 15, 1773

Dear Diary,

This morning at 5 o'clock I had to wake up my husband John to get up for work but he wouldn't wake up. I immediately called the doc. He came over as fast as he could. He asked me to leave the room so I did. An hour later he came out and told me he had passed away. I am so sad. I don't know what to do.

June 16, 1776

Dear Diary,

Today General Washington visited me about making a flag. I was so surprised. Me making a flag! I have made flags for the navy, but this is too much. But I said yes. He showed me a pattern of the flag he wanted. He also wanted six-pointed stars but I talked him into having five-pointed stars.

July 8, 1776

Dear Diary,

Today in front of Carpenter Hall the Declaration of Independence was read by Tom Jefferson. Well, I will tell you the whole story. I heard some yelling and shouting about liberty and everyone was gathering around Carpenter Hall. So I went to my next door neighbors to ask what was happening but Mistress Peters didn't know either so we both went down to Carpenter Hall. We saw firecrackers and heard a bell and the Declaration of Independence being read aloud. When I heard this I knew a new country was born.

June 14, 1777

Dear Diary,

Today was a happy but scary day. Today the flag I made was adopted by Congress. I thought for sure that if England found out that a new flag was taking the old one's place something bad would happen. But I'm happy because I am the maker of the first American flag and I'm only 25 years old!

Students can use simulated journals in two ways: as a tool for learning or as a project. When students use simulated journals as a tool for learning, they write the entries as they are reading a book in order to get to know the character better, or during a thematic unit as they are learning about the historical period. In these entries, students are exploring concepts and making connections between what they are learning and what they already know. These journal entries are less polished than when students write a simulated journal as a project. Students might choose to write a simulated journal as a culminating project for a literature focus unit or a thematic unit. For a project, students plan out their journals carefully, choose important dates, and use the writing process to draft, revise, edit, and publish their journals. They often add covers typical of the historical period. For example, a simulated journal written as part of a unit on ancient Greece might be written on a long sheet of butcher paper and rolled like a scroll, or a pioneer journal might be backed with paper cut from a brown grocery bag to resemble an animal hide.

Young Children's Journals

Young children can write in journals by drawing, or they can use a combination of drawing and writing (Hipple, 1985; McGee & Richgels, 1996; Nathan, 1987). Children may write scribbles, random letters and numbers, simple captions, or extended texts using invented spelling. These invented spellings often seem bizarre by adult standards, but they are reasonable in terms of children's knowledge of phoneme-grapheme correspondences and spelling patterns. Other children want parents and teachers to take their dictation and write the text. After the text is written, children can usually read it immediately, and they retain recognition of the words for several days.

Young children usually begin writing in personal or dialogue journals and then expand their repertoire of journal forms to include reading logs and learning logs. Four journal entries made by kindergartners are presented in Figure 6–7. The top two entries are from personal journals, and the bottom two are from reading logs. In the top left entry, this 5-year-old focuses on the illustration, drawing a detailed picture of a football game (note that the player in the middle right position has the ball); he adds five letters for the text so that his entry will have some writing. In the top right entry the kindergartner writes, "I spent the night at my dad's house." The child wrote the entry on the bottom left after listening to his teacher read *The Three Billy Goats Gruff* (Stevens, 1987). As he shared his entry with classmates, he read the text this way: "You are a mean bad troll." The kindergartner wrote the entry on the bottom right after listening to the teacher read *The Jolly Postman, or Other People's Letters* (Ahlberg & Ahlberg, 1986). This child drew a picture of the three bears receiving a letter from Goldilocks. She labeled the mom, dad, and baby bear in the picture and wrote, "I [am] sorry I ate your porridge."

Through a variety of forms and purposes, journal writing helps elementary students discover the power of writing to record information and explore ideas. Students usually cherish their journals and are amazed by the amount of writing they contain.

Teaching Students to Write in Journals

Students usually write in journal notebooks. Spiral-bound notebooks are used for long-term personal and dialogue journals and writing notebooks, and small booklets of paper stapled together are more often used for learning logs and simulated journals. Students often decorate the covers of these short-term journals, as Mrs. Wheatley's students did with their reading logs for *Tuck Everlasting*. Most teachers prefer to keep the journals in the classroom so they will be available for students to write in each day.

Figure 6–7 Independent writing: Entries from young children's journals

Students usually write in journals at a particular time each day. Many teachers have students make personal or dialogue journal entries while they take attendance or immediately after recess. Learning logs and simulated journals can be written in as part of a daily assignment or as part of social studies or science class. For example, students may go over to an incubator of quail eggs, observe them, and then make an entry in their learning log during their daily language arts time. Students who are writing simulated journals as part of a social studies unit on medieval life might make their entries during language arts time or during social studies class.

Introducing Children to Journal Writing

Teachers introduce students to journal writing using minilessons in which they explain the purpose of the journal-writing activity and procedures for gathering ideas, writing in a journal, and sharing with classmates. Teachers often model the procedure by writing a sample entry on the chalkboard or on chart paper as students observe. This sample demonstrates that the writing is to be informal, with content being more important than mechanics. Then students make their own first entries, and several read their entries aloud. Through this sharing, students who are still unclear about the writing activity have additional models on which to base their own writing.

Similar procedural minilessons are used to introduce each type of journal. Although all journals are informal, the purpose of the journal, the information included in the entries, and the point of view of the writer vary according to the type of journal. The minilesson feature on page 216 shows how a third-grade teacher introduces a new type of journal.

Journal writing can also be introduced with examples from literature. Characters in children's literature—such as Harriet in *Harriet the Spy* (Fitzhugh, 1964), Leigh in *Dear Mr. Henshaw* (Cleary, 1983), and Catherine Hall in *A Gathering of Days* (Blos, 1979)—keep journals in which they record the events in their lives, their ideas, and their dreams. A list of books in which characters and historical personalities keep journals is presented in Figure 6–8. In these books, the characters demonstrate the process of journal writing and illustrate both the pleasures and difficulties of keeping a journal. A good way to introduce journal writing is by reading one of these books.

Instructional Procedures for Journal Writing

Students use a variety of instructional procedures as they write in journals. Four of the most common ones are brainstorming, quickwriting, clusters, and data charts. Students also draw maps and diagrams, write key words, and draw pictures. None of the instructional procedures are better than the others. Students should choose the procedure that is most appropriate for the writing activity and the most useful for supporting their thinking and learning.

Altman, S. (1995). *My worst days diary*. New York: Bantam. (P)

Anderson, J. (1987). *Joshua's westward journey*. New York: Morrow. (M)

Banks, L. R. (2000). *Alice-by-accident*. New York: HarperCollins. (M)

Bowen, G. (1994). *Stranded at Plimoth Plantation, 1626*. New York: HarperCollins. (M–U)

Cartlidge, M. (1994). *A mouse's diary*. New York: Dutton. (P)

Cleary, B. (1983). *Dear Mr. Henshaw*. New York: Morrow. (M)

Cleary, B. (1991). *Strider*. New York: Morrow. (M)

Creech, S. (1995). *Absolutely normal chaos*. New York: HarperCollins. (U)

Cruise, R. (1998). *The top-secret journal of Fiona Claire Jardin*. San Diego, CA: Harcourt Brace. (M)

Cruise, R. (2000). *Fiona's private pages*. San Diego: Harcourt Brace. (U)

Cummings, P. (1992). *Petey Moroni's Camp Runamok diary*. New York: Bradbury.(P)

Cushman, K. (1994). *Catherine, called Birdy*. New York: Clarion. (U)

Denenberg, B. (1996). *When will this cruel war be over? The Civil War diary of Emma Simpson*. New York: Scholastic. (M–U)

Denenberg, B. (1999). *The journal of Ben Uchida: Citizen 13559, Mirror Lake Internment Camp*. New York: Scholastic. (M–U)

Fitzhugh, L. (1964). *Harriet the spy*. New York: Harper & Row. (M)

Frank, A. (1987). *Anne Frank: The diary of a young girl*. Philadelphia: Washington Square. (U)

Garland, S. (1998). *A line in the sand: The Alamo diary of Lucinda Lawrence*. New York: Scholastic. (M–U)

Gregory, K. (1996). *The winter of red snow: The Revolutionary War diary of Abigail Jane Stewart*. New York: Scholastic. (M–U)

Hest, A. (1995). *The private notebook of Katie Roberts, age 11*. Cambridge, MA: Candlewick Press. (M–U)

Hest, A. (1998). *The great green notebook of Katie Roberts: Who just turned 12 on Monday*. New York: Candlewick. (M–U)

Kalman, E. (1995). *Tchaikovsky discovers America*. New York: Orchard. (M–U)

Krupinski, L. (1995). *Bluewater journal: The voyage of the Sea Tiger*. New York: HarperCollins. (M–U)

Lasky, K. (1998). *Dreams in the golden country: The diary of Zipporah Feldman, a Jewish immigrant girl*. New York: Scholastic. (M–U)

Lewis, C. C. (1998). *Dilly's big sister diary*. New York: Millbrook. (P)

McKissack, P. C. (1997). *A picture of freedom: The diary of Clotee, a slave girl*. New York: Scholastic. (M–U)

Meyer, C. (2000). *Isabel: Jewel of Castilla*. New York: Scholastic. (M–U)

Moss, M. (1995). *Amelia's notebook*. New York: Tricycle. (P–M)

Moss, M. (2000). *Amelia's family ties*. New York: Pleasant. (M)

Murphy, J. (1998). *The journal of James Edmond Pease: A Civil War Union soldier*. New York: Scholastic. (M–U)

Murphy, J. (1998). *West to a land of plenty: The diary of Teresa Angelino Viscardi*. New York: Scholastic. (M–U)

Murphy, J. (2001). *My face to the wind: The diary of Sarah Jane Price, a prairie teacher*. New York: Scholastic. (M–U)

Figure 6–8 Books in which characters and historical personalities keep journals *continues*
P = primary grades (K–2), M = middle grades (3–5), U = upper grades (6–8).

Myers, W. D. (1999). *The journal of Scott Pendleton Collins: A World War II soldier.* New York: Scholastic. (M–U)

Parker, S. (1999). *It's a frog's life.* Pleasantville, NY: Reader's Digest. (P)

Philbrick, R. (2001). *The journal of Douglas Allen Deeds: The Donner party expedition.* New York: Scholastic. (M–U)

Platt, R. (1999). *Castle diary: The journal of Tobias Burgess, page.* Cambridge, MA: Candlewick Press. (U)

Rinaldi, A. (2000). *The journal of Jasper Jonathan Pierce: A Pilgrim boy.* New York: Scholastic. (U)

Roop, C., & Roop, P. (Eds.). (2000). *The diary of Mary Jemison, captured by the Indians.* New York: Benchmark. (M–U)

Roth, S. L. (1990). *Marco Polo: His notebook.* New York: Doubleday. (U)

Ruby, L. (1994). *Steal away home.* New York: Macmillan. (U)

Van Allsburg, C. (1991). *The wretched stone.* Boston: Houghton Mifflin. (M–U)

Weston, C. (2000). *The diary of Melanie Martin: Or how I survived Matt the brat, Michelangelo, and the leaning tower of pizza.* New York: Knopf. (M–U)

White, E. E. (1998). *Voyage on the great Titanic: The diary of Margaret Ann Brady.* New York: Scholastic. (M–U)

Wilson, J. (2001). *The story of Tracy Beaker.* New York: Delacorte. (M–U)

Yep, L. (2000). *The journal of Wong Ming-Chung: A Chinese miner.* New York: Scholastic. (M–U)

Figure 6–8 *continued*

Brainstorming.   Students generate a list of words or ideas on a topic when they brainstorm. They think about the topic and then list as many examples, descriptors, or characteristics as possible. Afterwards, students circle the most promising ideas to use in a writing activity. First graders generated these ideas about police officers before listening to their teacher read *Officer Buckle and Gloria* (Rathmann, 1995):

> **Teacher's Note: Assisting English Language Learners**
>
> Taking time to brainstorm a list of words with struggling writers before they begin to write a journal entry or another writing assignment often pays big dividends. The brainstorming activity activates background knowledge, provides direction for the writing assignment, and generates words and ideas that can be used in the writing activity. In addition, having the correct spelling of key words available ensures that students' writing will be more readable.

They have guns.
They put bad people in jail.
You have to do what they say.
Police officers will help you if you get lost.
They drive police cars with blue lights and sirens.
They fly in police helicopters.
They give tickets when your dad is speeding in the car.
They have handcuffs.
Don't be scared of them.

After reading the book, students added more information about police officers and then chose one idea to explore in a quickwrite.

Reading Logs

Mrs. Ford has taught a series of minilessons to her third graders about comprehension strategies, most recently about making connections. The students understand that good readers think while they are reading or listening to a book being read aloud and that they make personal, world, and book connections. Today she teaches a minilesson on writing about connections in their reading log entries.

1. Introduce the topic

Mrs. Ford reminds students that they have been learning to make connections, and the students identify the three types of connections.

2. Share examples

The third graders reread a chart they created that lists the connections they made after Mrs. Ford read *The Runaway Tortilla* (Kimmel, 2000), a southwestern version of "The Gingerbread Man" story. They recall that Arlene made a personal connection to the Mexican food that her grandmother cooks, Lupe made a world connection by locating Texas on the map of the United States, and Martee compared this version to the original "The Gingerbread Man" story.

3. Provide information

Mrs. Ford explains that students can write about the three types of connections in their reading logs by dividing a page into three columns and labeling them "Personal Connections," "World Connections," and "Book Connections." Mrs. Ford models the procedure: She divides a sheet of chart paper into three columns and labels each column. Then she asks Arlene, Lupe, and Martee to restate their connections as she writes them in the appropriate columns. Students read the chart and Mrs. Ford points out the qualities she expects to see in the students' reading log entries.

4. Guide practice

The next day, Mrs. Ford reads aloud *Chato's Kitchen* (Soto, 1995), a story about a cool cat named Chato who entices the barrio mice to come to his house by cooking lots of tasty Mexican food, and the third graders talk about the story and make all three types of connections. Then Mrs. Ford asks students to open their reading logs, divide a page into three columns, and write at least one connection in each column.

5. Assess learning

For the next week, Mrs. Ford reads aloud a picture book story each day and asks students to write connections. She monitors students' work and provides assistance as needed.

Quickwriting.   Students quickwrite when they write informally, rambling on paper, generating ideas, and making connections among the ideas. They often write on a topic for 5 to 10 minutes, letting their thoughts flow from their minds to their pens without focusing on mechanics or revisions. This strategy, originally called "freewriting" and popularized by Peter Elbow (1973), is a good way to help students focus on content rather than on mechanics. Young children can do "quickdraws" in which they use a combination of drawing and writing to explore concepts.

During a thematic unit on the solar system, third graders each chose a word from the word wall (a thematic list of words hanging in the classroom) to quickwrite about as an end-of-the-unit review. Here is one student's quickwrite on the sun:

> The sun is an important star. It gives the planets light. The sun is a hot ball of gas. Even though it appears large, it really isn't. It's pretty small. The sun's light takes time to travel to the planets so when you see light it's really from a different time. The closer the planet is to the sun the quicker the light reaches it. The sun has spots where gas has cooled. These are called sun spots. Sun spots look like black dots. The sun is the center of the universe.

Clusters.   Students make spider web–like diagrams called clusters to organize ideas and other information (Bromley, 1996; Rico, 1983). Clusters can be organized or unorganized. To make an organized cluster, students write the topic in the center circle on a sheet of paper and then draw out branches for main ideas. Then they add details to expand each main idea. A sixth grader's organized cluster on Poseidon is shown in Figure 6–9. In contrast, in unorganized clusters, ideas are not organized into main ideas and detail; instead, branches are drawn out from the center circle and the ideas are added in any order. A third-grade class's unorganized cluster on Saturn is shown in Figure 6–10. The steps in making a cluster are listed in the step-by-step feature on page 221.

Elementary students can use clusters in two ways: as tools for organizing thinking during prewriting, and as a report to present information. Figures 6–9 and 6–10 are examples of clusters used as finished pieces of writing, and they report information. Students used neat handwriting, conventional spelling, and artistic touches as they created these clusters.

Data Charts.   Students use data charts to categorize and record information about a topic. They make a data chart by drawing a grid and labeling the column headings with characteristics and the rows with examples. Then they fill in the boxes with information to complete the chart. Students can make data charts together as a class, in small groups, or individually. An excerpt from a fourth grader's data chart on the regions of California is shown

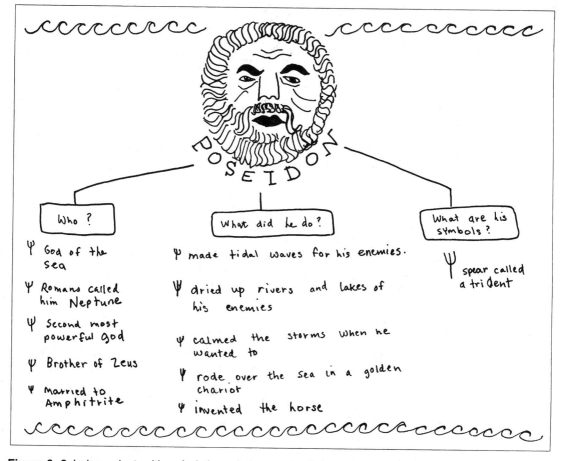

Figure 6–9 Independent writing: A sixth grader's organized cluster on Poseidon

in Figure 6–11. Students created the data charts at the beginning of a thematic unit on California, and then they added the information for each section after studying that region. Because the students followed the teacher's directions and demonstration as they created the chart and the teacher guided students as they completed each section, the figure is an example of guided writing.

Sustaining Journal Writing

Students write in journals on a regular schedule, usually daily. Once they know how to write the type of entry, students write independently. Although some

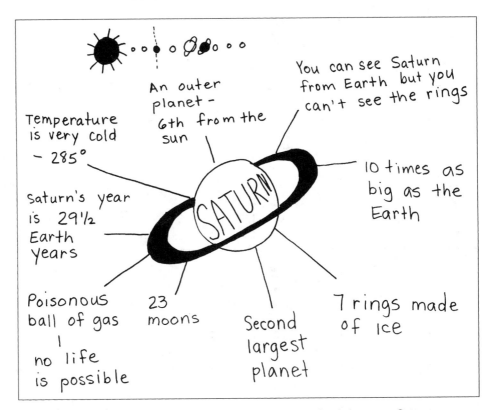

Figure 6–10 Shared writing: A third-grade class's unorganized cluster on Saturn

children prefer to write private journals, others will volunteer to read their journal entries aloud each day no matter what type of journal they are writing. Young children share their picture journal entries and talk about them. If the sharing becomes too time-consuming, several children can be selected each day on a rotating basis to share. Teachers and classmates may offer compliments about the topic, word choice, humor, and so on.

Students can select entries from their journals and develop them into polished compositions if they wish. However, the journal entries themselves are rarely revised and edited because the emphasis is on writing fluency and self-expression rather than on correct spelling and neat handwriting.

Students may continue to write in personal journals throughout the school year, but their writing in other types of journals starts and stops with particular literature focus units and theme cycles. Sometimes students seem to lose interest in personal journals. If this happens, many teachers find it useful to put

REGION	VEGETATION	ANIMALS	PLACES	HISTORY	ECONOMY
North	Redwood tres	Grizzly Bears Salmon	Eureka Napa Valley	Sutters Fort GOLD!	Logging Wine
North Coast	Redwood trees Giant Sequoia tres	seals Sea Otters Monarch Butterflies	San Francisco	Chinatown Cable Cars Earthquake	Computers Ghirardelli chocolate Levis
South Coast	Palm tres orange tres	Gray whales Condors	Los Angeles Hollywood	El Camino Real missions O.J. Simpson Earthquake	Disneyland TV + movies airplanes
Central Valley	Poppies	Quail	Fresno Sacramento	capital Pony Express Railroad	grapes Peaches Cotton Almond
Sierra Nevada	Giant Sequoia Lupine	Mule Deer Golden eagles Black Baers	Yosemite	John Muir	skiing

Figure 6–11 Guided writing: A fourth grader's data chart on California

Step by Step: Clusters

1. *Choose a topic.* Students choose a topic and write it in the center of a circle drawn on a chart or a sheet of paper. The center circle can be drawn in the middle or at the top of the sheet.

2. *Brainstorm words.* Students brainstorm as many words and phrases as they can that are related to the topic and write them on another sheet of paper. To complete an unorganized cluster, students write the words on rays drawn out from the center circle to make a diagram that looks like a sun.

3. *Organize the words.* For an organized cluster, students or the teacher identifies three to six categories and draws rays from the center circle for each category. Next students write the name of the category in a box or smaller circle at the end of the ray. Then they choose words from the brainstormed word list related to each category and write them on rays drawn out from the category box or circle.

4. *Complete the cluster.* Students reread the words and phrases recorded and brainstorm more ideas to complete the cluster. The teacher may prompt students for additional words and phrases. In addition, students sometimes complete the cluster with small drawings.

the journals away for several weeks and substitute another type of journal or free reading.

Assessing Children's Journals

Sometimes students write in journals independently with little or no sharing with the teacher, or at other times, they make daily entries that the teacher monitors or reads regularly. Typically, students are accustomed to having teachers read all or most of their writing, but the quantity of writing that students produce in their journals is often too great for teachers to keep up with. Some teachers try to read all entries, and others read selected entries and monitor remaining entries. Still others rarely check their students' journals. These three management approaches can be termed private journals, monitored journals, and shared journals. When students write private journals, they write primarily for themselves, and sharing with classmates or the teacher is voluntary. The teacher does not read the journals unless invited to do so by students. When students write monitored journals, they write primarily for themselves, but the teacher monitors the writing to ensure that entries are being made on a regular basis. The teacher may simply check that entries have been made and not read them unless they are specifically marked "Read me." When students write shared journals, they write primarily for the teacher; the teacher regularly reads all entries except for those personal journal entries marked "Private" and offers encouragement and suggestions.

The matter of how to grade journal entries is a concern. Because the writing is informal and usually not revised and edited, teachers usually do not grade the quality of the entries. One option is to give points for each entry made, especially with personal journals. For learning logs and simulated journals, though, some teachers grade the content because they can check to see if particular pieces of information are included in the entries. For example, when students write simulated journals about medieval life, they can be asked to include a specific number of pieces of historically accurate information in their entries. (It is often helpful to ask students to identify the pieces of information by underlining or highlighting them.) Rough draft journal entries should not be graded for mechanical correctness; students need to complete the writing process and revise and edit their entries if they are to be graded for mechanical correctness. A rubric for grading simulated journals that have been revised and edited is shown in Figure 6–12. When students develop simulated journals as a literature or theme project, it is appropriate to grade the entries.

ANSWERING TEACHERS' QUESTIONS ABOUT . . .

Journal Writing

1. My fourth graders get tired of writing in their personal journals. What can I do?

Many teachers report this problem. During the first month or two of the school year, students are eager to write in their journals, but then they get tired of it. There are several things you might try. First, you can alternate journal writing with independent reading activities so that students write in their journals only every other day, or give students a choice of reading a book or writing in their journals during this time. Second, change from personal journals to a different type of journal. Third, read aloud a book in which the main character keeps a journal, such as Beverly Cleary's *Dear Mr. Henshaw* (1983) (check the list of suggested books in Figure 6–8), and ask students to reflect on their journal-writing activities by comparing them to the character's.

2. How does quickwriting differ from personal journals? They seem like the same thing to me.

You're right. These two types of writing are very similar, and the differences between them can be confusing. Quickwriting is a specific strategy that students use to write more fluently. They can use quickwriting to write a journal entry, but they can use it for other informal writing activities as well. In contrast, a personal journal is a place where students write informally for themselves about almost any topic. They may use quickwriting or any other approach to writing these entries.

3. Which type of journal should I use with my fifth-grade class?

Choosing a type of journal depends on your purpose for having your students keep journals. If

Historical Journal Rubric
A   Excellent
• Assumes the "voice" of the historical figure. • Incorporates many words and phrases from the period in each entry. • Contains few, if any, capitalization, punctuation, spelling, or grammar errors. • Adds explanatory and decorative illustrations in the margins.
B   Good
• Writes detailed entries with at least three paragraphs. • Uses at least two vocabulary words related to the historical period in each entry. • Uses an easily understood sequence of events from entry to entry. • Contains only minor capitalization, punctuation, spelling, or grammar errors that do not interfere with understanding.
C   Adequate
• Organizes entries into at least two paragraphs. • Develops a sustaining idea in each entry. • Includes at least one vocabulary word related to the historical period in each entry. • Contains some capitalization, punctuation, spelling, or grammar errors that do not interfere with understanding.
D   Poor
• Recounts an event or a day's activity in each entry. • Writes at least one paragraph for each entry. • Writes from the first-person point of view. • Contains many capitalization, punctuation, spelling, or grammar errors that may interfere with understanding.
F Failing
• Does not accomplish what is expected for a D.

Figure 6–12 An eighth-grade rubric for writing simulated journals

you want your students to develop writing fluency, or if this is your students' first experience with journals, the personal journal is a good choice. If you want your students to gain writing practice and you also want to get to know them better, you might try dialogue journals. In connection with your literature focus units, try reading logs. If you want to use journals in content-area classes, learning logs or simulated journals are two options. Many teachers have students keep personal (or dialogue) journals and reading logs in separate notebooks throughout the school year and have them staple together booklets of paper for learning logs and simulated journals for thematic units.

4. My students don't like to write in reading logs when they're reading. They say they want to spend more time reading. What should I do?

Listen to what your students are telling you. The purpose of reading logs is to support students as they comprehend what they are reading; the logs shouldn't interfere with their reading. You might offer students more options in how often they write in their reading logs, or change the time when they write. Students might prefer to write after they discuss the book, or write journal entries at home after reading in school (or the other way around).

5. I have to disagree with not correcting errors in students' journals. I'm a teacher, and it's my job to correct students' spelling, capitalization, punctuation, and other errors.

Many teachers agree with you; it's difficult to ignore many of the errors in students' journal entries. But what good would the corrections do? Would the effect of your corrections be to teach students how to spell or use punctuation marks correctly, or would your emphasis on correctness convince students that they're "no good at this writing thing," a conclusion that causes many students to stop writing? Many teachers have found that focusing on students' mechanical errors rather than on the content of their writing teaches students that correctness is more important than meaning, and that is just not true. Journal entries are a form of personal and private writing, in contrast to public writing, in which mechanical correctness counts. In more formal types of writing, mechanics do count, and through the writing process, students learn to identify and correct their mechanical errors. If you focus on errors in students' journals, you are defeating the purpose of informal writing.

CHAPTER 7

Letter Writing

Preview

Purpose Students write friendly letters to develop relationships and share information. They write business letters to conduct business and to offer opinions. In simulated letters, students use their imagination to assume the role of another person and to reflect on their learning.

Audience Students usually write friendly letters to known audiences and business letters to more distant known or unknown audiences, and these letters should be mailed. Simulated letters are often written for a more limited audience—students themselves, teachers, and classmates.

Forms The two basic forms of letters are friendly letters and business letters. Students write friendly letters to pen pals, family members, teachers, classmates, favorite authors and illustrators, and other known audiences. They write business letters to companies, nonprofit organizations, and political leaders.

Instructional Preview: Letter Writing	
Grades	**Goals and Activities**
Kindergarten–Grade 2	**Goal 1:** Write friendly letters • Teachers set up mailboxes for each student in the class or a message board so that classmates can exchange messages. • Teachers write short messages to children and send them using the classroom mail system. • Teachers use interactive writing to model writing friendly letters. • Students write friendly letters to pen pals and authors.
	Goal 2: Write courtesy letters • Students write invitations to classroom and school events. • Students write thank-you notes. • Students make and send birthday, get well, and good-bye cards.
Grades 3–5	**Goal 1:** Learn the forms and uses of business letters • Students examine sample business letters to learn about their form and function. • Students write business letters to request information as part of theme studies.
	Goal 2: Correspond with pen pals • Students write friendly letters to students in another school. • Students send e-mail letters to pen pals. • Students become pen pals with college students learning to be elementary teachers. • Students write back and forth about a book they are reading or a thematic unit. • Students make postcards to send to relatives and friends.
	Goal 3: Correspond with authors and illustrators • Students write letters to favorite authors and illustrators as part of an author study. • Students write letters to favorite authors read during reading workshop.
Grades 6–8	**Goal 1:** Assume another point of view and write simulated letters • Students write simulated letters from one book character to another. • Students write simulated letters from one historical or scientific personality to another.
	Goal 2: Review friendly and business letters • Students compare the forms and purposes of the two types of letters. • Students write friendly and business letters as part of language arts and content-area classes.

Writing About Favorite Books

The students in Mrs. Donnelly's third-grade classroom spend 45 minutes after lunch in reading workshop with self-selected books from the classroom library. After reading two, three, or four books, students select and work on a project to extend their reading of one of the books. One of the most popular projects in Mrs. Donnelly's classroom is to make and mail a picture postcard to share information about a favorite book with a friend or relative. Students make the postcard using a piece of posterboard. On the front, they draw and color a picture of a scene from the book, and on the reverse, they write a message.

When Mrs. Donnelly introduced this project at the beginning of the school year, she taught three brief minilessons. One was about drawing pictures on postcards. The class examined Mrs. Donnelly's collection of picture postcards. Some were vacation postcards she had received from friends, and others were postcards advertising books of children's literature she had picked up at a convention. Together the class developed guidelines for the pictures they would draw on postcards: The picture should be about something special in the book, the picture should touch all four sides of the card, and the title and author should be listed. These three guidelines were recorded on a chart about postcards that was hung in the classroom.

The second minilesson was about how to address a postcard. The information about writing an address was added to the poster so that students could refer to it when they addressed their postcards. The third minilesson was on writing the message on the postcard. The students decided to include both personal information and information about the book in the message. Mrs. Donnelly also reviewed how to begin and end the message. This information was added to the chart.

Students used the writing process to create postcards. They began by reviewing the book to choose a high point or favorite episode for the illustration. They also planned what they would write on the postcard. Next, students drafted the message for the postcard on scratch paper and drew the picture on the postcard. Mrs. Donnelly encouraged students to begin the message with personal information but also to include information about the book. Many times, students' messages were persuasive, saying that they are sure this is a book the recipient of the postcard would enjoy reading.

Students met briefly with Mrs. Donnelly to revise and edit their messages before they made the final copy of the postcard. They also shared the picture they drew on the postcard with Mrs. Donnelly. Then students copied their message on the postcard and addressed the card.

Students shared their completed cards with the class during sharing time (the last 5 minutes of reading workshop), and then they were mailed.

One student's postcard about *Iktomi and the Berries* (Goble, 1989) is presented in Figure 7–1; both sides of the postcard, showing the picture and the message, are included in the figure. This postcard exemplifies many of the characteristics that Mrs. Donnelly taught through the series of minilessons on postcard projects: The picture is about the book, it covers the entire postcard, and the title and author are included. The student focuses on information about the book in the message and begins and ends the message appropriately for a letter to his parents. The address is also written correctly.

Writing and mailing postcards constitute an authentic writing activity because the cards are written for real people to read, not just for the teacher to grade. Mrs. Donnelly reports that her students really enjoy making the postcards and that community response to this project has been enthusiastic. Parents and grandparents are pleased to see this evidence of their children's reading and writing ability, and the children's friends also show more interest in reading after receiving these postcards.

PEOPLE WRITE POSTCARDS and other types of letters for genuine communicative purposes. Mrs. Donnelly's students wrote to get someone's attention, to sustain friendships, to share information, to persuade, and to recount events. Other purposes for letter writing include to ask questions, to ask permission, to apologize, to remind, and to request information (Karelitz, 1988).

Children's interest in letter writing often begins with writing notes. Young children often write "I love you" notes to their parents and messages to Santa Claus. Sometimes parents continue the practice by writing "Have a good day" notes to primary-grade children and then tucking them into lunch boxes for children to find and read at school. Reta Boyd (1985) is a firm believer in the value of note writing, and she encourages her elementary students to write notes and post them on a special message board in the classroom. The children write notes for a variety of purposes, but Boyd emphasizes their educational value: Children practice reading and writing skills, and they recognize the functional and social nature of writing. An added benefit is that through note writing, Boyd stays in touch with all students even though she may be working with a small group.

Letter writing is the logical extension of these informal notes. As with note writing, audience and function are important considerations, but in letter writing,

IKTOMI aND THE BErriES By Paul Goble

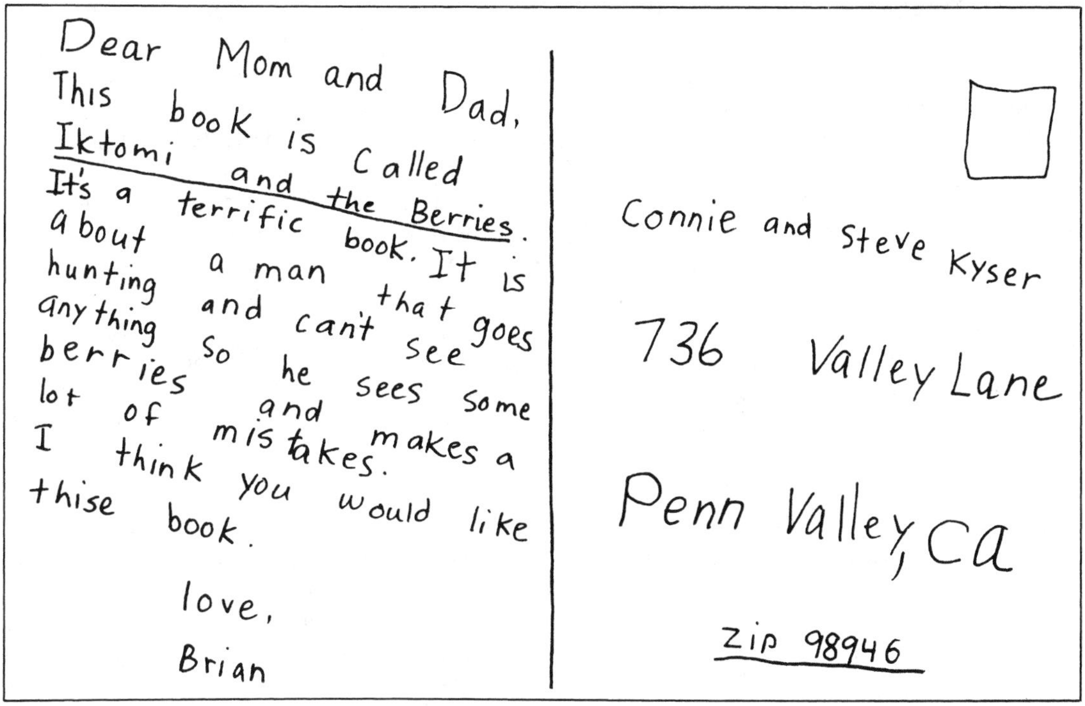

Dear Mom and Dad,
This book is Called
Iktomi and the Berries.
It's a terrific book. It is
about a man that goes
hunting and can't see
anything so he sees some
berries and makes a
lot of mistakes.
I think you would like
thise book.

love,
Brian

Connie and Steve Kyser

736 Valley Lane

Penn Valley, CA

Zip 98946

Figure 7–1 Guided writing: A third grader's postcard about *Iktomi and the Berries*

form also is important. Although letters may be personal, they involve a genuine audience of one or more persons. Not only do students have the opportunity to sharpen their writing skills through letter writing, but they also increase their awareness of audience. Because letters are written to communicate with a specific and important audience, students think more carefully about what they want to say, write more legibly, and are more inclined to use spelling, capitalization, and punctuation conventions correctly.

In this chapter, you will read about friendly, business, and simulated letters, the three types of letters that elementary students write, and you will learn how to teach students to write letters. The key points presented about letter writing are:

- Students write different types of letters for different purposes.
- Even young children can write letters.
- Teachers need to teach students how to write each type of letter.
- Teachers assess students' letters differently than other types of writing.

Types of Letters

Letters that elementary students write and mail are typically classified as friendly or business letters. The forms for friendly letters and business letters are presented in Figure 7–2. The choice of format depends on the function of the letter. When students write informal, chatty letters to pen pals or thank-you notes to a television newscaster who has come to the classroom to be interviewed, they use the friendly letter form. When they write letters to a cereal company requesting information about the nutritional content of breakfast cereals or letters to the mayor expressing an opinion about current events, they use the more formal, business letter form. Before students write either type of letter, they need to learn how to format the letter.

Friendly and business letter formats are accepted writing conventions, and most teachers simply explain the formats to students and prepare a set of charts to illustrate them. This attention to format should not suggest that form is more important than content; rather, it highlights the fact that elementary students are typically unfamiliar with the formatting aspects of letter writing.

Friendly Letters

Children write friendly letters to classmates, friends who live out of town, relatives, and pen pals. They may want to list addresses of people to whom they can write friendly letters on a special page in their journals or in address booklets. In these casual letters, students share news about events in their lives and ask questions to learn more about the person to whom they are writing and to encourage that person to write back. Receiving mail is the real reward of letter writing!

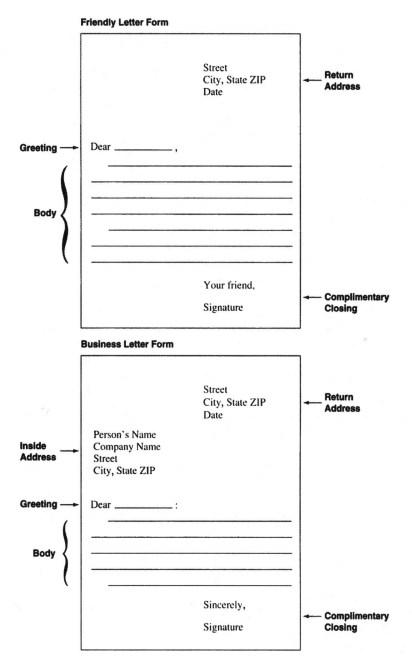

Figure 7–2 Forms for friendly and business letters

After being introduced to the friendly letter format, students need to choose a real person to write to. Writing authentic letters that are delivered is a much more valuable experience than writing practice letters to be graded by the teacher. Students may draw names and write letters to classmates, to pen pals (by exchanging letters with students in another class in the same school or in a school in another town), or to friends and relatives.

Students use the writing process in letter writing. In the prewriting stage, they decide what to say in their letters. Brainstorming and clustering are effective strategies to help students choose types of information to include and questions to ask in their letters. A cluster that a third-grade class developed for pen pal letters they were writing is presented in Figure 7–3. As a class, the students brainstormed a list of possible topics and finally decided on the four main idea rays ("Me and My Family," "My School," "My Hobbies," and "Questions"). Then each student completed a cluster by adding details to each main idea. As they wrote their rough drafts, students incorporated the information from one ray in the first paragraph, information from another ray in the second paragraph, and so on, for the body of their letters. After writing their rough drafts, students met in writing groups to revise the content of their letters, and then they edited their letters to correct mechanical errors with a classmate and later with the teacher. Last, they recopied the final draft of their letters, addressed envelopes, and mailed them. A sample letter is also presented in Figure 7–3. When you compare each paragraph of the letter with the cluster, you can see that by using the cluster, the student wrote a well-organized and interesting letter that was packed with information.

Pen Pal Letters.   Teachers can arrange for their students to exchange pen pal letters with students in another class by contacting a teacher in a nearby school, through local educational associations, or by answering advertisements in educational magazines. Sometimes teachers arrange for students to write to pen pals who are the same age, and sometimes they set up cross-age groups; both arrangements have benefits. When students write to same-age children, they have many things in common on which to build relationships. When they write to older or younger children, the relationship changes; younger children work to impress the older children, and older children assume a parental regard for their pen pals.

Students usually write about school activities and their families and friends in pen pal letters, but they can also write to pen pals about the literature they are reading. In an innovative reading-writing program in Houston, third graders write to pen pals about their thoughts and reactions to books they are reading (Dorotik & Betzold, 1992).

 Teacher's Note: Assisting English Language Learners

You may want to write collaborative letters with second-language learners who are unfamiliar with letter writing techniques and have limited English fluency. Use the interactive writing approach to teach students about English syntactic patterns and the courtesy phrases used in letters. Then they can work with you or another classmate to word process the letters.

Individual students can also arrange for pen pals by contacting one of the following organizations:

International Friendship League
22 Batterymarch
Boston, MA 02109

Student Letter Exchange
308 Second St. NW
Austin, MN 55912

League of Friendship
PO Box 509
Mt. Vernon, OH 43050

World Pen Pals
1690 Como Avenue
St. Paul, MN 55108

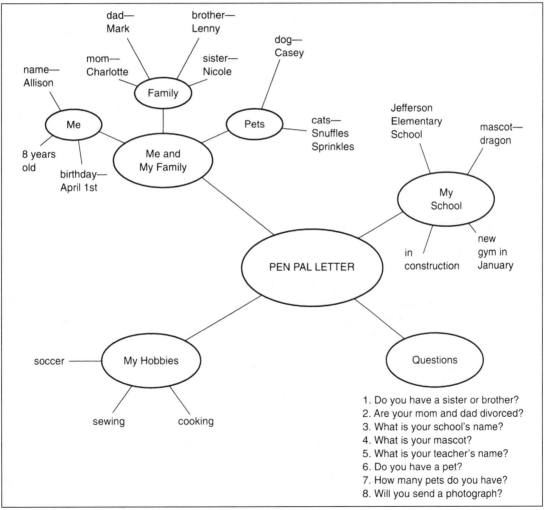

Figure 7–3 Guided writing: A third grader's cluster and pen pal letter *continues*

December 10

Dear Annie,

I'm your pen pal now. My name is Allison and I'm 8 years old. My birthday is on April 1st.

I go to Jefferson Elementary School. Our mascot is a dragon. We are in construction because we're going to have a new gym in January.

My hobbies are soccer, sewing, and cooking. I play soccer, sewing I do in free time, and I cook dinner sometimes.

My pets are two cats and a dog. The dog's name is Casey and he's a boy. He is two years old. The cat is a girl and her name is Snuffles. She is four years old. The kitten is a girl and her name is Sprinkles. She is two months old.

My dad's name is Mark and my mom's name is Charlotte. Her birthday is the day after Mother's Day. My brother's name is Lenny. He is 13 years old. My sister's name is Nicole. She is 3 years old.

I have some questions for you. Do you have a sister or a brother? Are your mom and dad divorced? Mine aren't. What is your school's name? What is your mascot? What is your teacher's name? Do you have a pet? How many pets do you have? Will you send me a photograph of yourself?

Your friend,
Allison

Figure 7–3 *continued*

Students write to one of the organizations, describing their interests and including their name, address, age, and sex. Also, they should ask if a fee is required and enclose a stamped, self-addressed envelope for a reply.

Another pen pal arrangement is for a class of elementary students to become pen pals with college students enrolled in teacher education programs. Over a semester, the elementary students and preservice teachers write to each other four, five, or six times and might arrange to meet each other at the end of the semester. The child has the opportunity to be a pen pal, and the college student has the opportunity to get to know an elementary student and examine the student's writing. In two studies (Berrill & Gall, 2000; Greenlee, Hiebert, Bridge, & Winograd, 1986), second graders became pen pals with groups of preservice teachers. The researchers investigated whether having a genuine audience would influence the quality of the letters the young students wrote. Second graders' letters were compared with letters written by a control group of students who wrote letters to imaginary audiences and received traditional teacher comments on their letters. The researchers found that the students who wrote pen pal letters wrote longer and more complex letters once they received responses to their letters. The results of these studies emphasize the importance of providing real audiences for student writing.

In another study (Crowhurst, 1992), sixth graders corresponded with preservice teachers, and students' letters showed similar growth. The sixth graders wrote increasingly longer letters, and their later letters were syntactically more complex with more adverbials and more embedded clauses. Only a few students wrote more than one paragraph in their first letters, but many used a series of paragraphs in later letters. Over the semester, students also experimented with more mature ways of beginning and ending letters and became more skillful in introducing new topics. In addition, the students themselves changed as writers: As they developed a sense of purpose and audience, they became more eager to write and more concerned about expressing themselves clearly.

E-mail Messages.   The Internet has created a completely new way for elementary students to send messages electronically to correspondents anywhere in the world when correspondents also have access to the Internet. It's a fast and simple way to send and reply to mail, and messages can be saved and stored on the computer, too. Students write in e-mail message boxes: They type the correspondent's e-mail address in the top window, specify a subject in the subject window, and then write their message in the large window. They begin by greeting their correspondent, and then they write their message. Students keep their messages short—no longer than one or two screens in length—so that they can easily be read on the computer screen. They end their messages with a closing, much as in other types of friendly letters.

Students can write e-mail messages to family members and friends, and they can become e-mail pen pals. A fifth-grade class became e-mail pen pals with another fifth-grade class in a distant state. The students were encouraged to focus on the books they were reading in their correspondence. Here is a series of brief e-mail messages between Mikey and his pen pal, William:

> Hey dude!
> What book are you reading now?
> Mikey
>
> Mikey,
> I'm reading Hatchet. What are you reading?
> Your friend,
> William
>
> Dude!
> I read Hatchet, too. I liked it:) Read The River next. It's good. I want to read the new Harry Potter book. I keep begging my Mom to buy it.
> Mikey
>
> Dude,
> Our teacher Miss Horsman read us Harry Potter and the Sorcerer's Stone but I haven't read it.
> Your friend,
> William

Hey William!
My mom got me Harry Potter and the Chamber of Secrets. I'm on page 24. I'll
tell you more after I read more.
Mikey

Courtesy Letters.   Invitations and thank-you notes are two other types of
friendly letters that elementary students write. They may write to parents to invite them to an after-school program, to the class across the hall to ask to visit
a classroom exhibit, or to a community person to be interviewed as part of a
content-area unit. Similarly, children write letters to thank people who have
been helpful.

A sixth-grade social studies class developed a multimedia presentation
about the United States Constitution and shared their presentation with a
fourth-grade class. The fourth graders wrote a thank-you note to each sixth
grader, and they included a question in their letters so that the sixth graders
would write back. One of the thank-you notes is presented in Figure 7–4 together with the sixth grader's response.

Letters to Authors and Illustrators.   Students write letters to favorite authors
and illustrators to share their ideas and feelings about the books they read.
They ask questions about how a particular character was developed or why
the illustrator used a certain art medium. Students also describe the books
they have written. A first grader's letter to Dr. Seuss is presented in Figure 7–5.
Most authors and illustrators will reply to children's letters; however, they receive thousands of letters from children every year and cannot be pen pals
with students.

Beverly Cleary's award-winning book *Dear Mr. Henshaw* (1983) provides a
worthwhile lesson about what students (and their teachers) can realistically expect from authors and illustrators. The following guidelines, adapted from
Cleary (1983, 1985), are suggested when writing to authors and illustrators:

- Follow the correct letter format with return address, greeting, body, clos-
  ing, and signature.
- Use the process approach to write, revise, and edit the letter. Be sure to
  proofread the letter and correct errors.
- Recopy the letter as a courtesy to the reader so that it will be neat and easy
  to read.
- Write the return address on the envelope and on the letter.
- Include a stamped, self-addressed envelope for a reply.
- Be polite in the letter, and use the words *please* and *thank you.*
- Write meaningful letters to share thoughts and feelings about the author's
  writing or the illustrator's artwork. Students should write only to authors
  and illustrators with whose work they are familiar.

Dear Marci,

You did a good job in
the play that we wa-
tched. Can you tell me what
union means please?
Also what does tranqu-
ility mean? Well I just
wanted to write you to
ask you questions and
tell you that you did
good. Well got to go
now. Bye.

Your friend,
Amy

Dear Amy,
Thank you for telling
me I was good. Union means
when all states get togther
and tranquility means
peace!

Your friend,
Marci

Figure 7–4 Independent writing: A fourth grader's thank-you note and the response by a sixth grader

Dear Dr. Seuss,
I like the SLEEP Book
Becos it is contagus
Amd the illustrations
Are the best of all.
I hav fourde Books
of yours and I have
rede them all.
              Love, Sara

Figure 7–5 Independent writing: A first grader's letter to an author

Avoid these pitfalls:

- Do not include a long list of questions to be answered.
- Do not ask personal questions, such as how much money the author earns.
- Do not ask for advice on how to become a better writer or artist.
- Do not send stories or artwork for the author or illustrator to critique.
- Do not ask for free books (authors and illustrators do not have copies of their books to give away).

Send letters to the author or illustrator in care of the publisher. Publishers' names are listed on the book's title page, and addresses are usually located on the copyright page (the page following the title page). If the complete mailing address is not listed, check *Books in Print* or *Literary Market Place*, reference books that are available in most public libraries.

Young Children's Letters.   Young children can write individual letters, as the first grader's letter to Dr. Seuss in Figure 7–5 illustrates. They prewrite as older students do, by brainstorming or clustering possible ideas before writing. A quick review of how to begin and end letters is also helpful. In contrast to older children's letters, kindergartners' and first graders' letters may involve only a single draft in which invented spellings and the artwork carry much of the message.

Primary-grade students also compose class letters. The children brainstorm ideas that the teacher records on a large chart. After the letter is finished, children add their signatures. They might write these collaborative letters to thank people from the community who have visited the class, to invite another class to attend a puppet show, or to compliment a favorite author. Class collaboration letters can also be used as pen pal letters to another class.

Business Letters

Students write business letters to seek information, to complain and compliment, and to transact business. These more formal letters are used to communicate with businesses, local newspapers, and governmental agencies. Students write to businesses to order products, ask questions, and complain about or praise specific products. They write letters to the editors of local newspapers and magazines to comment on recent articles and to express their opinions on a particular issue. It is important that students support their comments and opinions with facts if they hope to have their letters published. Students can also write to local, state, and national government leaders to express their concerns, make suggestions, or seek information.

Addresses of local elected officials are listed in the telephone directory, and the addresses of state officials are available in the reference section of the public library. The addresses of the President and United States senators and representatives are:

President's name
The White House
Washington, DC 20500

Representative's name
House of Representatives Office Building
Washington, DC 20515

Senator's name
Senate Office Building
Washington, DC 20510

Students can also write other types of business letters to request information and free materials. For example, they can write to NASA, the National Wildlife Federation, publishers, state tourism bureaus, and businesses to request materials as part of social studies and science units.

As part of an author unit on Laura Ingalls Wilder and her series of Little House books, a fourth-grade class decided to write a letter to the Laura Ingalls

Horace Mann Elementary School
1201 Whisenant Street
Duncan, Oklahoma 73533
February 23, 2003

Ms. Irene V. Lichty, Director
Laura Ingalls Wilder–Rose Wilder Lane
    Memorial Museum and Home
Mansfield, Missouri 65704

Dear Ms. Lichty:

My fourth grade class has been studying about Laura Ingalls Wilder because
February is the month of her birthday. We even have a learning center about her.
Our teacher has put a few chapters on tape of *The Little House in the Big Woods*.
It is a very good book.

We'd like to learn more about Laura. If you wouldn't mind, could you please send
our class some brochures about the museum and any other information about her?

Thank you.

Sincerely,

Kyle Johnson and
Mrs. Wilkins's Class

Figure 7–6 Shared writing: A fourth-grade class letter to a nonprofit organization

Wilder–Rose Wilder Lane Memorial Museum and Home in Missouri to request some information about the author and the museum. The class discussed what information needed to be included in the letter, and one child was selected to write the letter. A copy of this business letter is presented in Figure 7–6.

Teacher's Note: Supporting Struggling Writers

Who writes back to simulated letters? You can bring together a group of four or five struggling writers to work with you and write back as the recipients of simulated letters. This activity provides an opportunity to review a story the class is reading or a social studies topic as you work with the group to craft a reply and write the responses using shared writing.

Simulated Letters

Children write simulated letters, in which they assume the identity of a historical or literary figure and write letters from that point of view. As part of a social studies unit, they might write letters as though they were Davy Crockett defending the Alamo, or during a science unit as though they were Thomas Edison inventing the electric light. Students also assume the role of a character in a book they are reading and write from one book character to another. For example, after reading Patricia MacLachlan's *Sarah, Plain and Tall* (1985), third grader Adam assumed the persona of Sarah and wrote this letter to her brother William:

Dear William,

I'm having fun here. There was a very big storm here. It was so big it looked like the sea. Sometimes I am very lonesome for home but sometimes it is very fun here in Ohio. We swam in the cow pond and I taught Caleb how to swim. They were afraid I would leave. Maggie and Matthew brought some chickens.

Love, Sarah

Even though these letters are never mailed, they give students an opportunity to focus on a specific audience as they write. After students write simulated letters, they can exchange letters with a classmate who assumes the role of the respondent and replies to the letter.

Teaching Students to Write Letters

Teachers teach students to write friendly and business letters and involve students in a variety of letter-writing activities during language arts and content-area themes. For example, students write letters to children's authors, pen pal letters about books they are reading to children in another school, letters to governmental agencies and businesses requesting information and free materials, and simulated letters from one book character to another or from one historical personality to another.

Teaching students to write letters, however, involves more than just assigning letter-writing activities; teachers need to model how to write letters, teach minilessons on letter-writing formats and other skills and strategies, write collaborative letters with children, and have students use the writing process to write and send letters to real audiences.

Introducing Letter Writing

Many kindergarten and first-grade classrooms have classroom mailboxes or message boards so that children can write notes and other messages to classmates. The teacher begins by modeling how to write, deliver, and respond to short notes, and soon the children are exchanging messages. Teachers in middle-grade classrooms often introduce letter-writing activities by writing collaborative letters, as Mrs. Jacks did in the vignette at the beginning of Chapter 4.

Two books are very useful in introducing young children to letter writing. The Ahlbergs' *The Jolly Postman; or, Other People's Letters* (1986) is a fantastic storylike introduction to reasons why people write letters. It has small letters that children can remove from envelopes in the book and read. Lillian Hoban's story *Arthur's Pen Pal* (1982) is a delightful way to explain what it means to be a pen pal. Through books like these, kindergartners and other young children can learn about different letter formats and the types of information included in a letter. There are also books with letters that appeal to older children. Ann Turner's *Nettie's Trip South* (1987), for example, is a moving book-length letter about the horrors of slavery in the 1850s.

A list of books about letter writing is presented in Figure 7–7. Some of the books demonstrate how to write letters or be a pen pal; others present letters written to real people or to literary characters.

Writing Letters

For students to be successful in writing letters, teachers combine instruction about letter writing with authentic opportunities to write and send letters. Students use the process approach to write letters so that they can make their letters interesting, complete, and readable. The steps in teaching students to write a letter are listed in the step-by-step feature on page 244.

Teachers regularly teach minilessons so that students will know how to write letters and how the format and style of letters differ from those of stories, informational books, and journals. Topics for minilessons include using the letter-writing forms, focusing on audience, organizing information in the letter, and asking questions to encourage a response. Teachers also teach minilessons on capitalizing proper nouns, addressing an envelope, using paragraphs, and using courteous phrases. Two minilessons are presented: The minilesson on page 245 shows how Mr. Diaz teaches his second graders about writing interesting e-mail messages and the minilesson on page 246 shows how Mrs. Ramirez teaches her fifth-grade class about punctuation marks.

Assessing Students' Letters

Traditionally, students wrote letters that were turned in to the teacher to be graded. After they were graded, the letters were returned to the students, but they were never mailed. Educators now recognize the importance of having a real audience for student writing, and research suggests that students write better when they know their writing will be read by people other than the teacher. Although it is often necessary to assess student writing, it seems unimaginable for the teacher to place a grade at the top of the letter before mailing it. Instead of placing a grade on students' letters, teachers can develop a checklist to use in evaluating students' letters without marking on them.

Ada, A. F. (1998). *Yours truly, Goldilocks.* New York: Atheneum. (P)

Ada, A. F. (2001). *With love, Little Red Hen.* New York: Atheneum. (P)

Ahlberg, J., & Ahlberg, A. (1986). *The jolly postman, or other people's letters.* Boston: Little, Brown. (P)

Avi. (1991). *Nothing but the truth.* New York: Orchard. (U)

Ayres, K. (1998). *North by night: A story of the Underground Railroad.* New York: Delacorte. (M–U)

Beller, S. P. (2001). *The Revolutionary War.* New York: Benchmark. (M–U)

Bonners, S. (2000). *Edwina victorious.* New York: Farrar, Straus & Giroux. (M)

Boudalika, L. (1998). *If you could be my friend: Letters of Mervet Akaram Sha'ban and Galit Fink.* New York: Orchard. (M–U)

Cartlidge, M. (1993). *Mouse's letters.* New York: Dutton. (P)

Cartlidge, M. (1995). *Mouse's scrapbook.* New York: Dutton. (P)

Cherry, L. (1994). *The armadillo from Amarillo.* New York: Gulliver Green. (M)

Dahan, A. (2000). *Squiggle's tale.* San Francisco: Chronicle Books. (P)

Danziger, P., & Martin, A. M. (1998). *P.S. Longer letter later.* New York: Scholastic. (M)

Danziger, P., & Martin, A. M. (2000). *Snail mail no more.* New York: Scholastic. (M–U)

George, J. C. (1993). *Dear Rebecca, winter is here.* New York: HarperCollins. (M)

Hample, S. (Comp.) (1993). *Dear Mr. President.* New York: Workman. (M)

Harrison, J. (1994). *Dear bear.* Minneapolis: Carolrhoda. (P)

Heisel, S. E. (1993). *Wrapped in a riddle.* Boston: Houghton Mifflin. (M–U)

Hesse, K. (1992). *Letters from Rifka.* New York: Holt. (U)

Hobbie, H. (1997). *Toot and Puddle.* Boston: Little, Brown. (P)

Holub, J. (1997). *Pen pals.* New York: Grosset & Dunlap. (P)

Jakobsen, K. (1993). *My New York.* Boston: Little, Brown. (P–M)

James, E., & Barkin, C. (1993). *Sincerely yours: How to write great letters.* New York: Clarion. (M–U)

Johnston, T. (1994). *Amber on the mountain.* New York: Dial. (P–M)

Klise, K. (1998). *Regarding the fountain: A tale in letters, of liars and leaks.* New York: Avon. (U)

Klise, K. (1999). *Letters from camp.* New York: Avon. (U)

Langen, A., & Droop, C. (1994). *Letters from Felix: A little rabbit on a world tour.* New York: Abbeville Press. (M)

Lorbiecki, M. (1997). *My palace of leaves in Sarajevo.* New York: Dial. (M–U)

Lyons, M. E. (1992). *Letters from a slave girl: The story of Harriet Jacobs.* New York: Scribner. (U)

Lyons, M. E., & Branch, M. M. (2000). *Dear Ellen Bee: A Civil War scrapbook of two Union spies.* New York: Atheneum. (U)

Nichol, B. (1994). *Beethoven lives upstairs.* New York: Orchard. (M–U)

Pak, S. (1999). *Dear Juno.* New York: Viking. (P)

Pinkney, A. D. (1994). *Dear Benjamin Banneker.* San Diego, CA: Gulliver/Harcourt Brace. (M)

Pinkney, A. D. (2001). *Abraham Lincoln: Letters from a slave girl.* New York: Winslow. (M–U)

Potter, B. (1995). *Dear Peter Rabbit.* New York: Warne. (P–M)

Rabbi, N. S. (1994). *Casey over there.* San Diego, CA: Harcourt Brace. (P–M)

Schomp, V. (2001). *World War II.* New York: Benchmark. (M–U)

Figure 7–7 Books that include letters

continues

P = primary grades (K-2), M = middle grades (3-5), U = upper grades (6-8).

Stewart, S. (1997). *The gardener.* New York: Farrar, Straus & Giroux. (P)

Tryon, L. (1994). *Albert's Thanksgiving.* New York: Atheneum. (P)

Turner, A. (1987). *Nettie's trip south.* New York: Macmillan. (M–U)

Wheeler, S. (1999). *Greetings from Antarctica.* Chicago: Peter Bedrick Books. (M–U)

Whybrow, I. (1999). *Little Wolf's book of badness.* Minneapolis: Carolrhoda. (M)

Winthrop, E. (2001). *Franklin D. Roosevelt: Letters from a mill town girl.* New York: Winslow. (U)

Woodruff, E. (1994). *Dear Levi: Letters from the Overland Trail.* New York: Knopf. (M–U)

Figure 7–7 *continued*

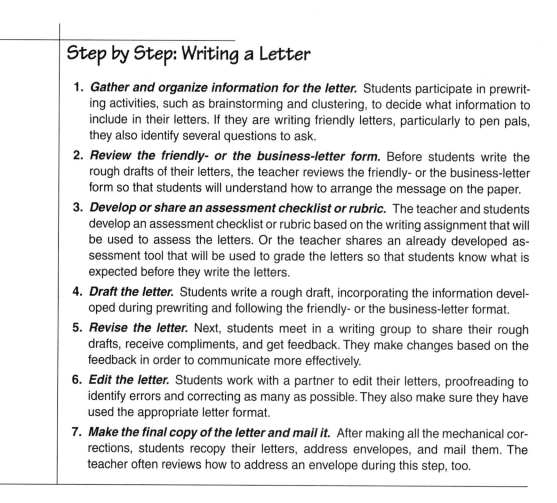

Step by Step: Writing a Letter

1. ***Gather and organize information for the letter.*** Students participate in prewriting activities, such as brainstorming and clustering, to decide what information to include in their letters. If they are writing friendly letters, particularly to pen pals, they also identify several questions to ask.

2. ***Review the friendly- or the business-letter form.*** Before students write the rough drafts of their letters, the teacher reviews the friendly- or the business-letter form so that students will understand how to arrange the message on the paper.

3. ***Develop or share an assessment checklist or rubric.*** The teacher and students develop an assessment checklist or rubric based on the writing assignment that will be used to assess the letters. Or the teacher shares an already developed assessment tool that will be used to grade the letters so that students know what is expected before they write the letters.

4. ***Draft the letter.*** Students write a rough draft, incorporating the information developed during prewriting and following the friendly- or the business-letter format.

5. ***Revise the letter.*** Next, students meet in a writing group to share their rough drafts, receive compliments, and get feedback. They make changes based on the feedback in order to communicate more effectively.

6. ***Edit the letter.*** Students work with a partner to edit their letters, proofreading to identify errors and correcting as many as possible. They also make sure they have used the appropriate letter format.

7. ***Make the final copy of the letter and mail it.*** After making all the mechanical corrections, students recopy their letters, address envelopes, and mail them. The teacher often reviews how to address an envelope during this step, too.

E-mail Messages

At the beginning of the year, Mr. Diaz taught his second graders to write e-mail messages, and his students became pen pals with students at another school in the district. Because he has noticed that the students' messages are getting shorter and less interesting, Mr. Diaz teaches this minilesson on how to write a good e-mail message.

1. Introduce the topic

Mr. Diaz explains that he's noticed that some of the students' e-mail messages to their pen pals are getting shorter and less interesting. Also, he points out that some of the students have complained to him that their pen pals don't write back regularly and speculates that the pen pals are not responding because they've lost interest in being pen pals.

2. Share examples

Mr. Diaz shares several very short and uninteresting e-mail messages, such as:

> Hi! How are you? I was sick but now I'm not.
>
> Bye.

He asks the students to tell him why the messages are not interesting.

3. Provide information

Mr. Diaz uses modeled writing to compose an interesting e-mail message:

> Hi Joey,
>
> My Grandma and Grandpa are visiting at my house. They live in Houston and they come to visit in the winter because they like to see some snow. My Grandma says that she likes to see it but not to drive in it. Ha! Ha! I have to sleep with my brother when they are here, but it's OK because Grandpa always gives me some money. Do you have grandparents that come to visit? Bye for now.

After reading the message aloud, the teacher asks the students to pick out the characteristics of an interesting message. The students recognize that Mr. Diaz's e-mail message includes five sentences, detailed information, and a question.

4. Guide practice

Together the students and Mr. Diaz develop a rubric with the characteristics of interesting e-mail messages, and the students use the rubric as they write e-mail messages to their pen pals.

5. Assess learning

Mr. Diaz asks the students to print out a copy of their e-mail messages and attach the rubric so that he can check that they wrote messages with at least four sentences and included detailed information and one or more questions.

Punctuation Marks

Mrs. Ramirez's fifth graders are writing letters to their favorite authors, and as many of the students move into the editing stage of the writing process, Mrs. Ramirez teaches this minilesson to review the punctuation marks used in letters and on envelopes.

1. Introduce the topic

Mrs. Ramirez asks her fifth-grade students to examine the chart with punctuation marks posted in the classroom and to name the punctuation marks that are commonly used in writing letters and addressing envelopes; they name period, comma, and colon. She writes one punctuation mark on each of three pieces of chart paper taped to the chalkboard.

2. Provide examples

Mrs. Ramirez passes out a collection of letters and envelopes; some are copies of letters written by students, and others are letters and envelopes she has received at home. She asks the students to examine the letters and envelopes and locate punctuation marks. She passes out highlighters for the fifth graders to use in highlighting the punctuation marks.

3. Provide information

The students work in small groups to make lists of the ways periods, commas, and colons are used in letters and on envelopes. After the groups have completed their lists, Mrs. Ramirez brings the class back together and they list the uses of the punctuation marks on the pieces of chart paper. Periods, for example, are used after abbreviations (e.g., Mr. and Jan.), and initials and at the ends of sentences.

4. Guide practice

Mrs. Ramirez asks her students to get out their language arts notebooks and turn to the page with letter-writing and envelope forms. She asks them to use their highlighters to mark all punctuation marks shown on the letter and envelope forms. Then she asks them to get out their rough drafts and check that they have used the punctuation marks correctly. Some of the students also trade papers and have classmates check their use of punctuation marks.

5. Assess learning

Mrs. Ramirez reminds the students that one item on the rubric she will use to assess their letters is "uses punctuation correctly in letters and on envelopes," so she will check that they have used punctuation marks correctly when she grades their work.

PEN PAL LETTER CHECKLIST

Name _____

		Yes	No
1.	Did you complete the cluster?	☐	☐
2.	Did you include questions in your letter?	☐	☐
3.	Did you put your letter in the friendly-letter form?	☐	☐

　　　　_____ return address
　　　　_____ greeting
　　　　_____ 3 or more paragraphs in the body
　　　　_____ closing
　　　　_____ salutation and name

		Yes	No
4.	Did you write a rough draft of your letter?	☐	☐
5.	Did you revise your letter with suggestions from people in your writing group?	☐	☐
6.	Did you proofread your letter and correct as many errors as possible?	☐	☐

Figure 7–8 A checklist for assessing students' pen pal letters

The third-grade teacher whose students wrote the pen pal letters described earlier developed the checklist presented in Figure 7–8. This checklist identifies specific behaviors and products that are measurable. The checklists are shared with students before they begin to write so they understand what is expected of them and how they will be graded. At an evaluating conference before the letters are mailed, the teacher reviews the checklist with each student. Then the letters are mailed without any evaluative comments or grades written on them, but the completed checklist is placed in students' writing folders. A grading scale can be developed from the checklist. For example, points can be awarded for each check mark in the yes column, or five check marks can be required for a grade of A, four check marks for a B, and so on.

ANSWERING TEACHERS' QUESTIONS ABOUT . . .

Letter Writing

1. Don't my students need to write practice letters before they write real pen pal letters that we mail?

　　Writing practice letters is a waste of time because the activity is artificial. When writing just for practice or for a grade, students feel little impetus to do their best work, but when they are writing to an authentic audience—their pen pals—they are careful about their writing because they want to communicate effectively. The instructional strategy for letter writing presented in this chapter provides the opportunity for teachers to introduce or review the friendly-letter format during the prewriting stage and to help students revise the content of letters after meeting in writing groups, and for students to identify and correct mechanical or formatting errors during the editing stage. With these activities built into the instructional strategy, students can eliminate most errors before they mail their letters, making the writing of practice letters unnecessary.

2. How can I tie letter writing to my literature-based reading program?

Here are three ways you can tie letter writing to literature study. First, students can write letters to you or to classmates about the books they are reading, or they can write postcards to friends and relatives, as Mrs. Donnelly's students did. In these letters, they share their reactions to the book, compare the book to others they have read or to others by the same author, or offer a recommendation about whether the reader would like the book. A second suggestion is for students to write letters to favorite authors and illustrators. Let students choose who they write to, and be sure to review the guidelines for writing letters to authors and illustrators before students begin writing. Third, students can assume the role of a character from a favorite book and write a simulated letter from one character to another. Then students can trade letters with classmates and write back and forth.

3. What do you think about having elementary students correspond using e-mail?

It's a terrific idea! Here is a wonderful example: Students in an elementary school on a naval base wrote and sent e-mail messages to their parents who were away at sea. Computers were a center at that school, and each day, students checked for messages from their parents and responded to the messages. Of course, students in other schools could use e-mail to write to pen pals.

4. I'd like to have my students write letters to an author, but I don't know how to do it. I mean, should all of my students write letters to the same author, or should they pick different authors?

Children should write to authors when they have something to say, not because it is an assignment. The letters shouldn't have a "My teacher is making me do this" tone. Instead, children should write when they have something that they really want to say to the author. Children who want to write letters to an author as a project after reading a book should do so. Other students should choose favorite authors to write to, perhaps as part of reading workshop activities. Children have a much better chance of getting a reply when they write an honest letter, with insightful comments and interesting questions.

5. I have a lot of things to teach in fifth grade. Are you saying that I need to do one unit on friendly letters, a second unit on business letters, and a third unit on simulated letters? That's a lot to do!

You don't need to do units on letter writing. Instead, incorporate letter writing as a tool for learning and communicating as part of other classroom activities. Students might write friendly letters because you have a pen pal program in your classroom, or they might write friendly letters to authors as part of your reading program. They could also write simulated letters as part of literature focus units or during social studies units. Your students might have opportunities to write business letters as part of social studies, science, or other community activities. Think of letters as tools for learning.

CHAPTER 8

Descriptive Writing

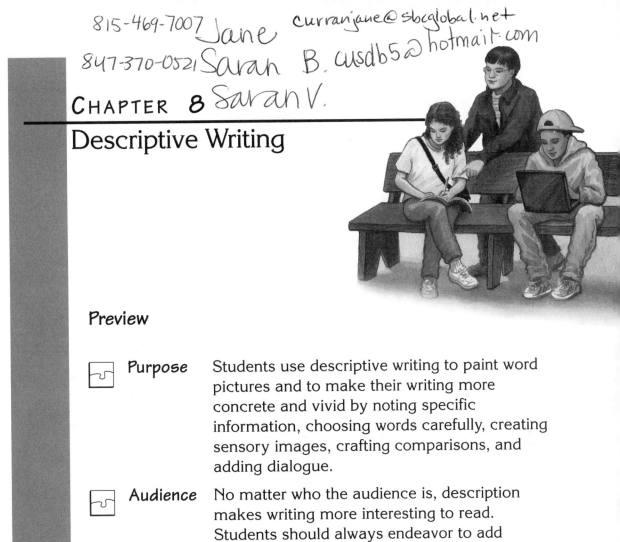

Preview

Purpose Students use descriptive writing to paint word pictures and to make their writing more concrete and vivid by noting specific information, choosing words carefully, creating sensory images, crafting comparisons, and adding dialogue.

Audience No matter who the audience is, description makes writing more interesting to read. Students should always endeavor to add descriptive words and phrases to their writing.

Forms Descriptive writing techniques are used in all genres, especially poetry and stories.

Instructional Preview: Descriptive Writing

Grades	Goals and Activities
Kindergarten–Grade 2	**Goal 1:** Create sensory images • Students brainstorm and cluster sensory words. • Students write five-senses poems. • Students write descriptive sentences.
	Goal 2: Add specific information • Students brainstorm lists of descriptive words for photos, paintings, and other illustrations and then choose the most appropriate words to use in sentences and poems. • Students build sentences and add specific information. • Students write sentences and paragraphs for wordless picture books.
Grades 3–5	**Goal 1:** Write dialogue • Students write dialogue to accompany photos and pictures. • Students add dialogue to stories they are writing. • Students write dialogue between characters in a story they are reading. • Students write dialogue for wordless picture books.
	Goal 2: Choose words carefully • Teachers introduce thesauri and demonstrate how to use this reference book. • Students brainstorm lists of synonyms. • Students make character clusters with carefully chosen descriptive words.
	Goal 3: Make comparisons • Students make charts about metaphors and similes. • Students identify examples of metaphors and similes in stories and poems they are reading. • Students write comparisons in sentences and paragraphs.
Grades 6–8	**Goal 1:** Use descriptive techniques • Students identify examples of descriptive techniques in books they are reading. • Students use descriptive techniques (e.g., word choice, comparisons) as they draft and revise their compositions.

Writing Vivid Descriptions

The sixth graders in Mrs. Ochs's class are studying life in ancient Egypt. Their study occupies much of the school day because language arts and social studies are integrated into a theme cycle. The students in Mrs. Ochs's class read books about life in ancient Egypt, and they write in response to their reading. The type of response varies—it may be a simulated journal or a learning log, an essay or report, a biography, or a simulated letter. Students work cooperatively in small groups on projects that may involve reading, writing, talking, art, music, and drama in addition to social studies. Students learn language arts and writing strategies and skills as they need them to respond to their reading or work on their projects. These are some of the specific activities:

- Students read informational books and keep a reading log.
- Each student researches an Egyptian god or goddess and makes a poster to share the information.
- Mrs. Ochs reads *The Egypt Game* (Snyder, 1967) aloud to the students, a chapter or two a day.
- Students work in small groups on various projects. One group creates a salt map of ancient Egypt; one dresses dolls in clothes like those worn by ancient Egyptians; one makes a time-line, chronicling the major events in the period; another designs a chart of hieroglyphic symbols.

One day, several students share with the class what they have learned about Howard Carter's discovery of King Tut's tomb in 1922 from *In Search of Tutankhamun* by Piero Ventura and Gian Paolo Ceserani (1985). Mrs. Ochs capitalizes on the class's interest and shows a videotaped film of Carter's discovery that she rented from a local video store. Several students express the wish that they could have been with Carter when the tomb was discovered. They discuss what this would have been like. The students' interest gives Mrs. Ochs an idea: She asks if the students would like to write a first-person "I was with Howard Carter" narrative of the discovery. Are the students interested? You bet they are!

Mrs. Ochs suggests that their writing, like the film, evoke a strong mood and focus on the description of the tomb. To gather words and ideas for writing, she and the students create a five-senses cluster on the chalkboard in which they brainstorm words for the sights, sounds, smells, tastes, and feelings they might have experienced as they entered the tomb. A copy of this collaborative cluster is presented in Figure 8–1. Taste was the most difficult sense for the students because the explorers did not eat in the tomb, but students recognized that the explorers might have tasted dryness, sandy grit, and even fear. The sense of touch evoked perhaps the most powerful images as students suggested that the explorers might have felt guilt about their trespassing.

With the background of knowledge gained from the unit on ancient Egypt and the clustering experience, students write the rough draft of their first-person narratives.

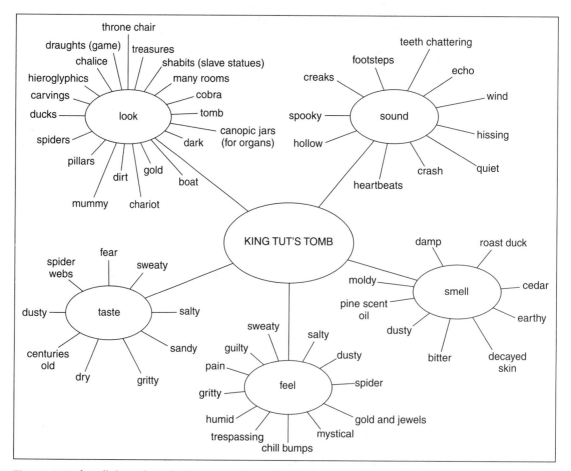

Figure 8–1 A collaborative cluster describing King Tut's tomb

After students finish their rough drafts, they meet in groups to share their writing. Mrs. Ochs asks students to focus on the mood created in the writing and the use of description as writing-group members comment about each other's writings.

In his writing group, Josh reads first:

> It was November 1922 and I was in Egypt with Howard Carter. We had uncovered one step in the Sahara Desert and then 15 more leading downward. As Howard and I walked down we heard the echo of our footsteps. When we got to the bottom we could not see our hands nor each other. I called, "Are you there, Howard?" And he called, "Yes." Both our voices echoed.
>
> As we waited for our eyes to adjust to the darkness we listened. It was quiet, so quiet. I could hear my heartbeat, and I think Howard could hear his too.
>
> My eyes had adjusted and I was amazed at what I saw. There was gold and jewels everywhere. There was a boat and a chariot. There were canopic jars, statues, tools, some kind of gameboards that looked like chess, and a child-size throne chair.
>
> Suddenly it hit me. I turned around and there it was—Tut's tomb!

There is a silence and then his writing group members beg, "Read it again." Josh willingly reads his piece a second time, this time more dramatically. When he finishes, Matt says, "I've got chill bumps like I was with Howard Carter. That's my compliment." Then Amber tells Josh she liked the part about hearing his heartbeat, and Becky Lee says she liked the dialogue.

Next it is Josh's turn, as the writer, to ask a question. He asks if his classmates think he included enough details as Mrs. Ochs suggested. They count the details from the cluster that he included and after they reach 10, they quit counting and conclude that he did.

Finally, Josh asks the writing group members for suggestions to improve his writing. "I think you should keep writing and get to the part about the cobra," suggests Matt. "That's the best part and you could give it a lot of mood!" Becky Lee suggests that Josh call the game by its real name *draughts* instead of describing it and saying it was like chess. Josh agrees to continue writing but explains to Becky Lee that he didn't name the game on purpose because if he was just exploring with Howard Carter, not studying Egypt in sixth grade, he might not know the name!

The other students take turns sharing their rough drafts, listening to compliments and suggestions from the writing-group members, and asking questions themselves. After everyone in the group has shared, they move back to their desks to make revisions. Later, they will edit and recopy their "I was with Howard Carter" writings and add them to a bulletin board display about King Tut.

Descriptive writing is painting pictures with words. Students need to be keen observers, attentive to word choices and sensory images, as Mrs. Ochs's students were when they wrote about King Tut's tomb. Her students added specific details, such as the number of steps at the entrance to King Tut's tomb, and used the sensations of sound, touch, smell, and taste to paint a vivid picture for readers. Sometimes descriptive writing is a phrase, sentence, or paragraph embedded within a composition, and sometimes it is an entire composition.

Ken Macrorie (1985) advises writers to show, not tell, as they write. When writers show, they paint word pictures with details, dialogue, and sensory images. Telling, in contrast, keeps readers at a distance, not as involved as they might be because they are observers on the sideline rather than actively experiencing what the writing is describing. Readers have to supply the missing details and create their own sensory images. However, it does little good to simply admonish students to "show, don't tell." Macrorie's advice must be translated into practice by teaching students how to write descriptively and by encouraging them to revise their compositions to paint more vivid word pictures.

In this chapter, you will learn how to help students add more description to their writing. The key concepts are:

- Students use five descriptive writing strategies to make their writing more vivid and interesting.

- Students learn to use a thesaurus to choose specific and appropriate words.

- Teachers teach minilessons about the descriptive writing strategies and provide opportunities for students to practice what they are learning in guided and independent writing activities.

Descriptive Techniques

Writers use specific techniques in descriptive writing to create vivid, multisensory word pictures. Five of these techniques are

- adding specific information
- choosing words carefully
- creating sensory images
- making comparisons (metaphors and similes)
- writing dialogue

These techniques help writers make their writing come alive for readers because they help writers shift from telling to showing.

Specific Information

Writers make their writing more descriptive when they add specific information and details. Rather than saying something is noisy, for example, the writer identifies the specific noise: a thunderstorm, a baby crying, a car engine roaring, or six dogs barking. Each of these noisy examples conjures up a distinct mental picture. Young writers can provide specific information in several ways:

ELL Teacher's Note: Assisting English Language Learners

Descriptive writing is especially difficult for second-language learners because they often lack a rich vocabulary, and without these words, they can't provide specific information to make their writing interesting. You can help your English learners by brainstorming a word bank of words and phrases with them at least twice during the writing process—during prewriting and again during revising.

---

1. *Identify specific activities and behaviors.* Instead of writing that "The bear was busy in the woods," the writer identifies the bear's activities: It climbed a tree, hunted for food, slept in its cave. Writers provide a wealth of information for readers when they identify specific activities rather than generalize with a word such as *busy.*

2. *Name the characters.* Instead of writing about "a little girl," the writer gives the character a name and provides details about the character's appearance and personality.

3. *Identify the setting.* Instead of writing "In a little town . . . ," the writer names the town or describes where it is located. The writer also identifies other aspects of setting, including weather, season, time of day, date, and day of the week.

4. *List attributes.* Rather than writing only that "The boy walked on the beach," the writer continues with details about the beach: noisy seagulls flying overhead, seashells spread across the sand like stars in the night sky, cold waves splashing against the boy's ankles. These attributes, or details, help the reader visualize the boy's walk on the beach.

As children write they need to incorporate specific information into their writing. Many books of children's literature can be used as examples of descriptive writing, and a list of useful books is presented in Figure 8–2. For example, in *The Best Town in the World* (1982), Byrd Baylor describes the town where her father grew up. Even though she does not name the town other than to say that it is in the Texas hills and that people called it "The Canyon," she shows, not tells, how the people lived and what the land was like. She writes about celebrations on the Fourth of July, going swimming in the creek, the toys the children played with, and the foods the people ate.

Word Choice

Students learn to choose words carefully in order to describe experiences and ideas effectively in their writing. Words that are specific and vivid give writing its energy, whereas more general nouns and weaker verbs force writers to use more

Babbitt, N. (1978). *Tuck everlasting.* New York: Farrar, Straus & Giroux. (U)
Barrett, J. (1987). *Cloudy with a chance of meatballs.* New York: Atheneum. (P–M)
Baylor, B. (1982). *The best town in the world.* New York: Aladdin Books. (M–U)
Bouchard, D. (1995). *If you're not from the prairie . . . .* New York: Simon & Schuster. (M)
Brown, R. (1996). *Toad.* New York: Puffin. (M–U)
Cooney, B. (1982). *Miss Rumphius.* New York: Viking. (M)
Fox, M. (1988). *Wilfred Gordon McDonald Partridge.* Brooklyn, NY: Kane/Miller. (M–U)
Houston, G. (1992). *My great-aunt Arizona.* New York: HarperCollins. (M)
Kalan, R. (1987). *Rain.* New York: Mulberry. (P)
King, E. (1990). *The pumpkin patch.* New York: Dutton. (P–M)
Martin, B., Jr., & Archambault, J. (1985). *The ghost-eye tree.* New York: Holt, Rinehart & Winston. (M)
Moss, T. (1993). *I want to be.* New York: Puffin. (P–M)
Polacco, P. (1988). *The keeping quilt.* New York: Simon & Schuster. (M–U)
Ringgold, F. (1991). *Tar beach.* New York: Crown. (M–U)
Rylant, C. (1985). *The relatives came.* New York: Bradbury Press. (P–M)
Say, A. (1989). *The lost lake.* Boston: Houghton Mifflin. (M–U)
Scillian, D. (2001). *A is for America: An American alphabet.* Chelsea, MI: Sleeping Bear Press. (M–U)
Shannon, D. (1998). *A bad case of stripes!* New York: Blue Sky Press/Scholastic. (P–M)
Showers, P. (1991). *The listening walk.* New York: HarperCollins. (P)
Siebert, D. (1989). *Heartland.* New York: Crowell. (M–U)
Soto, G. (1992). *Neighborhood odes.* San Diego: Harcourt Brace Jovanovich. (U)
Van Allsburg, C. (1984). *The mysteries of Harris Burdick.* Boston: Houghton Mifflin. (M–U)
Van Allsburg, C. (1985). *The polar express.* Boston: Houghton Mifflin. (M)
Wood, A. (1984). *The napping house.* San Diego: Harcourt Brace Jovanovich. (P)
Yolen, J. (1987). *Owl moon.* New York: Philomel. (M–U)
Zolotow, C. (1967). *Summer is . . . .* New York: Crowell. (P–M)

Figure 8–2 Children's books that use good descriptions
P = primary grades (K–2), M = middle grades (3–5), U = upper grades (6–8).

modifiers; using too many modifiers robs writing of its power and makes it sound unnatural. The most important guidelines for choosing the best words are:

1. *Choose specific nouns.* Nouns can be general or specific. General nouns paint a fuzzy picture, but specific nouns give readers a much more colorful and detailed picture. *Car,* for example, is a general noun; nouns that are more specific include *minivan, sports car, station wagon, convertible,* and *SUV.*

2. *Use vivid verbs.* Vivid verbs are more descriptive than ordinary verbs. *Walked,* for example, is an ordinary verb, but *trudged, hiked, marched, shuffled,* and *strutted* are more descriptive and give writing more energy. Students should also avoid the "to be" verbs—*is, are, was, were.* For example, instead of using *is* in the sentence *The snake is on the rock,* the verbs *sunbathes, sleeps,* and *lurks* are more vivid alternatives.

3. *Choose colorful adjectives and adverbs.* Adjectives modify and describe nouns, and adverbs describe the action of the verb. Students should incorporate adjectives and adverbs, but use them judiciously because they often use too many. For example, a sixth grader used too many modifiers in this sentence: *The tired and calm two-year-old child sat quietly in his lovely mother's lap to listen to a story at his 8 o'clock bedtime.* The sentence can be improved by shortening it and by substituting more specific nouns and verbs: *The tired toddler rested in his mother's lap listening to a bedtime story.*

4. *Use synonyms to avoid repetition.* A thesaurus lists synonyms, words with nearly identical or similar meanings, that writers can use to avoid repetition; however, writers must take care to choose a synonym to fit the meaning of the sentence. For example, synonyms for *famous* include *noted, prominent, eminent,* and *notorious,* but not all of these words would be appropriate substitutes for *famous* in this sentence: *Charles Lindbergh was a famous aviator.*

5. *Avoid "tired" words.* Students often overuse common words, such as *said, nice, bad, good, dumb, great,* and *pretty,* and they can choose fresher alternatives to make their writing more effective. For example, alternatives for *good* include *fine, excellent, outstanding, admirable, respectable,* and *splendid.* Students can use a thesaurus to locate alternatives for tired words when they are revising their writing.

6. *Differentiate among similar words.* Many similar word pairs and trios often confuse elementary students, and they must learn to choose the correct alternative. Some confusing words are homophones, words that sound alike but are spelled differently, such as *there–their–they're, capital–capitol, ant–aunt, through–threw,* and *it's–its.* Students confuse other word pairs, including *good–well, learn–teach, bring–take, lay–lie, who–whom,* and *leave–let* because of grammar and usage rules. In addition, students confuse word pairs that have similar spellings but do not sound alike, such as *desert–dessert* and *quiet–quite.*

Teachers help students learn to choose words carefully in a variety of ways. Whenever they read a book with students and focus on vocabulary through word wall activities or through minilessons in which they examine the author's word choice in excerpts from the book, they are emphasizing the importance of word choice. Books such as Julie Mammano's series of "Rhinos" books, including *Rhinos Who Surf* (1996) and *Rhinos Who Skateboard* (1999), and Ruth Brown's *Toad* (1996) show students how energized writing can be when authors use specific words. Teachers also teach students about word choice when they have them make charts of specific nouns, vivid verbs, and alternatives for overused words; study homophones and other confusing words; and learn how to use a thesaurus.

Sensory Images

Writers incorporate the senses into their writing to create stronger images and to make their word pictures more vivid. When Jane Yolen wrote about a father and child going owling on a cold winter night in *Owl Moon* (1987), she described how cold it was (touch), how the snow looked in the moonlight (sight), how the snow sounded as it crunched under their boots (hearing), how the wool scarf tied around the child's neck smelled (smell), and even how the fuzz from the scarf tasted (taste). Writers do not always use all five senses as Jane Yolen did; sometimes they include information about only one or two senses. Even so, the added sensory information makes the writing more memorable.

Too often, children's writing is limited to one sense—sight. Elementary students often write a narrative of what they have seen, as though their writing were a home movie without any sound. To combat this tendency, teachers should teach minilessons about writing sensory images and encourage children to incorporate more than one sense to enrich their writing. If a student is writing about a camping experience, for example, information about how things looked and sounded at night, how the food tasted, or how it felt sleeping in a sleeping bag on the ground might be included. The minilesson feature on page 259 shows how Mr. Uchida teaches his second-grade English language learners to add sound words to their writing.

Comparisons

One of the most powerful techniques that writers use to describe something is to compare it to something else. Good comparisons go beyond the conventional uses of words. In Alfred Noyes's poem "The Highwayman," the moon is called a *ghostly galleon* and the road *a ribbon of moonlight* (Noyes, 1983), and in Lois Lowry's *Anastasia Krupnik* (1979), Anastasia's nervousness when she begins to read a poem she has written to the class is compared to having ginger ale in her knees. These are fresh and unexpected comparisons.

Two types of comparisons are metaphors and similes. Metaphors are the more powerful because the comparison is made directly, as in "The toddler was a clown." Similes are less direct and are often signaled by the use of the words *like* and *as,* as in "The toddler acted like a clown." Another form of simile introduces an attribute to connect the subject and the thing it is compared to, as in "The toddler seemed as silly as a clown." Here the attribute that connects *toddler* and *clown* is *silly.*

Students often have difficulty interpreting comparisons in their reading. Readence, Baldwin, and Head (1987) explain that metaphors and similes can be difficult to understand because they are nonliteral comparisons. Students must be knowledgeable about the meanings of the two things being compared and their shared attribute to interpret the statement. Sometimes students recognize that the phrase they are

ELL Teacher's Note: Assisting English Language Learners

You have probably noticed that your English language learners rarely use comparisons in their writing, so encourage them to add comparisons during the revision stage of the writing process. Because they're often not familiar with our trite "butterflies in your stomach"-type comparisons, the ones they come up with are often unique and powerful. You may want to prompt them, by asking, "What is ____ like?" or "What does ____ make you think of?"

Sound Words (Onomatopoeia)

The English language learners in Mr. Uchida's second-grade classroom are interested in words. For the past week, they have been collecting sound words from cartoons and books they are reading and adding them to a word wall in the classroom. They like collecting words, but so far they have not begun to use the words in their speech or writing. Mr. Uchida's goal for today's minilesson is for his students to begin using sound words in sentences that they say and write.

1. Introduce the topic

Mr. Uchida reads aloud *Slop Goes the Soup: A Noisy Warthog Word Book* (Edwards, 2001), and the second graders repeat the sound words, giggling and savoring them.

2. Share examples

As Mr. Uchida rereads the book, the students add the sound words to their sound words word wall, and they take turns dramatizing each word and using it in a sentence.

3. Provide information

The teacher has copied sentences from the book and created others following the pattern used in the book (e.g., *Splash goes the water*) on sentence strips, omitting the sound words. He reads each sentence aloud and passes the sentence strip to a student. Then he asks the students to add a sound word to complete the sentence. Mr. Uchida encourages students to choose several sound words that are appropriate for each sentence (e.g., *swoosh, splish-splash, drip,* or *squirt goes the water*), but he corrects them when they choose an inappropriate word (e.g., *clatter goes the water*).

4. Guide practice

Mr. Uchida suggests that students make up a new noisy warthog story, beginning with this sentence: "Clip-clop, a warthog walks down the street . . . ." Graciela begins the oral story, "Chatter, chatter go the people on the sidewalk. They see a bad warthog." The students invent a silly story about the warthog's visit to Los Angeles that is full of sound words.

5. Assess learning

After the minilesson, the second graders begin writing workshop, and Mr. Uchida encourages them to write sound stories about the warthog or to add sound words to stories they are writing. He explains that he will ask them about their use of sound words at their next writing conference.

reading is a comparison and that two words are being compared, but they cannot figure out the relationship between them.

During the elementary grades, children grow in their understanding of figurative language and their ability to say, read, and write metaphors (Geller, 1985). Books, such as *Quick as a Cricket* (Wood, 1982), are a good way to introduce primary-grade children to traditional comparisons. In this book, a child is described using 22 comparisons, including "loud as a lion" and "wild as a chimp." From this introduction to traditional comparisons, middle- and upper-grade students begin to notice traditional comparisons and then fresh comparisons in the books and poems they are reading. Figure 8–3 presents a list of poems with fresh comparisons that are appropriate for middle- and upper-grade students. At the same time, students begin writing their own comparisons, as these third graders did about their classmates:

> Eleanor's bangs are as curly as the ocean waves.
> Joey is as smart as a computer.
> Sanjay is as quiet as a burning candle.
> Tim is as big as King Kong.
> Sandra's hair shines like a black Corvette.

Dialogue

Another way writers show, not tell, is by adding dialogue to their writing instead of summarizing what the characters talked about. For example, instead of writing "The boy hesitantly asked Veronica for a date," the student writes, "The boy asked, 'Veronica, I, um, will you go to the dance with me?' " In this way, the student shows the boy's hesitation through the dialogue. Macrorie (1985) notes that dialogue gives force to writing and introduces a tension between characters.

Many examples of dialogue can be found in children's literature. In *The Ghost-Eye Tree* (Martin & Archambault, 1985), for example, a recounting of two children's spooky trip to get a pail of milk, the dialogue of the children is realistic: They use childlike language, with the big sister calling her little brother "a fraidy cat" and the boy's hat "dumb." The lines of talk are short, highlighting the children's fear. The anxious feeling created by the book would not be as strong without the dialogue.

Teaching Students to Write Descriptively

Students learn about descriptive techniques through minilessons. Teachers explain the techniques, share examples of descriptive writing in stories and poems, and then encourage students to practice the techniques in their own writing. After lessons on the descriptive techniques, students focus on making their writing more descriptive, especially during the revising stage of the writ-

From *Eric Carle's Animals Animals.*
　　"Bat," by Lawrence, D. H. (The bat is compared to a glove.)
　　"Tiger," by Worth, V. (The tiger's black stripes are compared to flames from a
　　　　black sun.)

From Beatrice Shenk de Regniers's *Sing a Song of Popcorn: Every Child's Book
of Poems*
　　"The steam shovel," by Bennett, R. (A steam shovel is compared to a dinosaur.)
　　"Dragon smoke," by Moore, L. (A person's cold breath is described as "dragon's
　　　　smoke.")
　　"Clouds," by Rossetti, C. G. (Clouds are called white sheep and the sky a blue hill.)

From X.J. and Dorothy Kennedy's *Knock at a Star: A Child's Introduction to Poetry*
(rev. ed.)
　　"Dreams," by Hughes, L. (Broken dreams are compared to an injured bird and
　　　　to a barren field.)
　　"The sidewalk racer or, on the sidewalk," by Morrison, L. (A sidewalk is
　　　　compared to an asphalt sea and a skateboarder to an automobile.)
　　"My fingers," by O'Neill, M. (Fingers are compared to antennae.)
　　"The eagle," by Tennyson, A. (An eagle is compared to a thunderbolt.)
　　"Dad," by Wong, J. S. (A father is compared to a turtle.)

The Highwayman, by Alfred Noyes, (The moon is called a "ghostly galleon," the road
"a ribbon of moonlight.")

From Jack Prelutsky's *The Random House Book of Poetry for Children: A Treasury of
752 Poems for Today's Child*
　　"Dandelion," by Conkling, H. (A dandelion is compared to a soldier.)
　　"The base stealer," by Francis, R. (A base stealer is compared to a tightrope
　　　　walker.)
　　"Air traveler," by Morrison, L. (An airplane is called "a silver cigar.")
　　"What is orange?" by O'Neill, M. (The color orange is described as many things,
　　　　including a parrot's feather, zip, and a marigold.)
　　"What is red?" by O'Neill, M. (The color red is described as many things,
　　　　including blood, embarrassment, and a valentine heart.)
　　"Fog," by Sandburg, C. (Fog is compared to a cat.)
　　"The toaster," by Smith, W. J. (A toaster is called a dragon.)
　　"Zebra," by Thurman, J. (A fire escape on a city building is compared to a zebra.)

Figure 8–3 Poems that use interesting comparisons

ing process, whether they are writing in connection with theme studies or in
writers' workshop.

Teaching Minilessons

In the lessons on the five descriptive techniques, teachers provide basic information about the technique, share examples from literature, and involve students

in writing activities. Teachers may want to refer to the list of books in Figure 8–2 and poems in Figure 8–3 for these minilessons. Six descriptive writing activities are shown here:

1. Creating five-senses clusters
2. Listing attributes
3. Building sentences
4. Crafting comparisons
5. Creating dialogue
6. Adding words to wordless picture books

These activities can be incorporated into minilessons on the descriptive writing techniques.

Creating Five-Senses Clusters.   To help students focus on the senses, they can create five-senses clusters. In this activity, students focus on each of the five senses as they explore an object or a concept and brainstorm words related to each sense. A step-by-step feature explaining how to create a five-senses cluster is presented on page 264. A class of first graders examined apples as part of a study of Johnny Appleseed and created a five-senses cluster for apples as shown in Figure 8–4. The teacher drew the cluster on a large piece of chart paper and then added the attributes that the children suggested. Later, children can use words and phrases from the cluster in writing about apples.

Food is a very effective stimulus for a five-senses cluster because it evokes a response for each sense. Students can write about apples, pumpkins, popcorn, and other foods. For example, a fourth grader wrote this paragraph after doing a five-senses cluster about popcorn:

> I love to see popcorn pop. It looks like little white firecrackers. Sometimes it looks like a little white bunny. And it feels like bumpy little clouds shooting toward the sky. And they all get together and make one big smooth soft cloud. I like to hear it popping. It sounds like little stars falling from the sky and when they land it makes a whole bunch of popcorn for you to share with your friends. I love to eat it, too.

In this paragraph, the student incorporated three senses—sight, touch, and hearing—and made several comparisons. A seventh grader wrote the following poem about popcorn after making a five-senses cluster:

> **Life Span of Popcorn**
> In the beginning, I was a golden teardrop.
> An ancient, petrified, golden teardrop.
> I was tossed into a fountain of youth
> where I became a sizzling teenager.
> Suddenly, the ground beneath me

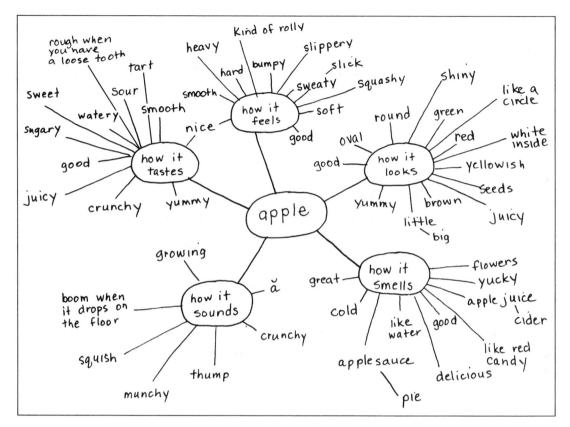

Figure 8–4 A first-grade class's five-senses cluster for apples

became hot—unbearably hot.
I jumped into the air and P O P
my dull, indifferent shape
became unique—individual.
I was fluffy and almost weightless.
Filled with life,
I jumped into the air again and again
until I suddenly felt tired.
I could jump no more,
exhausted and old.
Now I lay in a bowl awaiting my inevitable fate—
the human being.

This sophisticated poem contains a metaphor: The popping of popcorn is compared to a person's life. The sensory images come from the words this student wrote on her five-senses cluster as she examined a few kernels of

Step by Step: Five-Senses Cluster

1. *Draw a cluster diagram with five main idea circles.* On the chalkboard, on a poster, or on an overhead transparency, the teacher draws a cluster consisting of a larger topic circle in the middle of the page and five smaller, main idea circles around the central circle.

2. *Label the diagram.* The teacher labels the circle in the center of the cluster with the topic to be examined and lists the five senses, one in each of the main idea circles. The teacher can use the five-senses labels (i.e., *see, touch, smell, hear,* and *taste*) or write questions or phrases in each main idea circle (e.g., *what we hear* or *What do you hear?*). Teachers may also ask students to write the labels.

3. *Brainstorm ideas about the topic.* Students discuss the topic using as many descriptive words as possible as they recall background knowledge, and the teacher draws their attention to other characteristics or features.

4. *Complete the cluster.* The teacher directs students to think about each of the five senses and to brainstorm words related to each sense. The teacher or a student writes the words on lines drawn out from the main idea circles. It is usually easier to begin with the most concrete sense, sight, and move to smell, hear, and touch before taste. Even if the topic is not something that students can eat or hear, for example, they can still think of sensory words.

unpopped corn, observed the popcorn being popped, and ate some of the popped popcorn.

The class can gradually move on to more sophisticated sensory writings. For example, after reading a story about courage, students can cluster sensory details related to this abstract concept. Or, for a social studies theme cycle on freedom, students can ask, What does freedom look like? sound like? feel like? smell like? taste like? A class of fifth graders wrote this class collaboration about freedom and what it means to them, incorporating sensory details:

The men and women who fought in the American Revolution made America a free country, but many people today take freedom for granted. They shouldn't, but they do. Freedom is hard to explain, but when you see people pledging allegiance to the flag, going to the church they want to go to, and writing letters to the editor of the newspaper, you are seeing freedom. On the Fourth of July, freedom tastes like hot dogs and apple pie and it sounds like bands and fireworks. But every day, it smells like fresh air and sounds like people speaking their minds. George Washington and Abraham Lincoln and Martin Luther King, Jr. symbolize freedom for many people, but we think we do, too. The pride and love we feel for the United States of America is our expression of freedom.

Listing Attributes.   Writers are careful observers of life. They incorporate the attributes of people, places, and events in their writing so that readers feel as though they are eyewitnesses. Students need opportunities to develop observational skills and learn how to give eyewitness quality to their writing. They can observe classroom pets and list attributes from their observations, cut pictures from magazines and list attributes from the picture, or watch a film or video about a historical event and write a description of it.

Another way to help students develop observational skills and the words they need to express these observations is through examining art prints. A sixth-grade class brainstormed these attribute words and phrases as they looked at a large print of Vincent van Gogh's famous painting *Starry Night:*

whirlwinds of light	lonely town
bursting out	darkness
cypress trees dancing	stars sparkle
frustration	glittering moon
anger	swirling
dark	round and round
few lights	scary
empty	frightening

> **Teacher's Note: Supporting Struggling Writers**
>
> Too often, struggling writers don't like writing because they view it as a long, tedious process. They even complain that their hands get tired when they write. These students can write powerful descriptive sentences and poems because they typically have the necessary vocabulary and these writing projects are short. Try using strips or small pieces of paper to emphasize that the writing doesn't have to be long.

Then students wrote quickwrites describing the print, trying to incorporate many of the attributes from the brainstormed list. They shared their quickwrites with a classmate and highlighted favorite descriptive sentences using highlighter pens. Then in a class read-around, students took turns reading their highlighted descriptive sentences, including the following:

In the sky above, stars are bursting with light.
The stars are whirlwinds of light.
Clouds are swirling round and round.
Sparkles of brightness shoot out of the moon as it gleams in the sky.
The wind swiftly swings through the darkness.
Cypress trees on a hillside are dancing in the wind.
The coldness of the air puts ice into my bones.
All I can see is the frustration of the sky on a gusty night.
The sky above a small lonely town shatters the darkness.
The sky waves good night.

These sentences are powerful because the students were studying descriptive writing. They focused on how authors use description in books and practiced the descriptive techniques themselves.

Building Sentences.   Students can practice building sentences to see the power of specific information, sensory images, and comparisons. Teachers present an outline for a sentence, such as A _____ horse _____ _____. Students brainstorm a list of words and phrases for each blank and then choose words and phrases from the three lists to create descriptive sentences. Here are some sentences that a fifth-grade class created using sentence building:

A startled horse reared up into the air when he heard the crash of thunder.
The white stallion ran like the wind.
The ancient chestnut horse snoozed contentedly in his stall in the barn.
The hungry colt gobbled the oats in his feed bucket.
The black and white horse pranced jauntily as he pulled the carriage down the drive.
The mare gently licked her foal dry.

These sentences demonstrate some of the possible images that students can create about a horse in a single sentence. Students are often amazed by the variety of sentences their classmates create. Other topics for sentences might include an actor, a tree, a car, a space capsule, a cat, and other nouns that can inspire a range of images.

Crafting Comparisons.   Teachers should be alert to figurative language and provide opportunities for children to craft comparisons. After reading the folktale *Jack and the Beanstalk,* for instance, the teacher can encourage students to identify other things that grow as quickly as a beanstalk or things that are as big as a giant. Building on a shared experience and providing the attribute for the comparison (e.g., *fast* or *big*) are good ways to help elementary students practice inventing comparisons. Even young children can create comparisons (Geller, 1981, 1985). For example, after petting a bunny and remarking on how soft the tail was, a kindergartner said, "My blue sweater is as soft as a bunny's tail." Then classmates began to name other things that were as soft as a bunny's tail.

To help students say and write comparisons once they have a subject, ask: What does _____ make you think of? What is it like? Students brainstorm several comparisons and then select the one that seems most powerful to them. Children exploring a Hershey's Kiss have compared it to a teepee, a mountain, a pyramid, an upside-down raindrop or tornado, a bell, the nose cone of a rocket, a volcano, and a castle. As they write, students add a phrase to complete the comparison or build a piece of writing around the comparison as this second grader did:

Hershey's Kiss
I like to eat Hershey's kisses.
It is a chocolate mountain.

My teeth climb up the mountain
and my tongue sits on the pointy tip.
Then I eat it.
I like to eat Hershey's kisses.

Another second grader wrote:

Yummy Little Chocolate Kiss
A little brown raindrop
Good, chocolate, and sweet.
A yummy chocolate kiss
Dressed in silver.
The little brown raindrop
Melting in my mouth.
Yummy, yummy in my tummy!

In the first poem, the Hershey's Kiss is called a mountain, and in the second, it is called a raindrop. These second graders are using comparison (metaphor) effectively in crafting their poems.

Poet Kenneth Koch (2000) has taught elementary students to write poems using metaphors and similes. To begin, Koch asked the students to pretend something was like something else and to compare the two things using *like* or *as*. One child wrote "An octopus looks like a table and chair" (p. 104). Some students wrote a different and unrelated comparison in each line of their poems, and others took one comparison and expanded on it in each line of the poem. After experience with similes, students tried metaphors. Koch asked them to think of a comparison and instead of saying one thing was like the other, to say that one thing *was* the other. Examples of students' poems are collected in *Wishes, Lies and Dreams: Teaching Children to Write Poetry* (Koch, 2000). For more information about wordplay and writing poetry, see Chapter 12, "Poetry Writing."

Creating Dialogue. Elementary students gain experience in creating dialogue by drawing a picture of a scene from a favorite story and adding talk balloons for the characters they show. A fifth grader's drawing inspired by Chris Van Allsburg's fantasy *Jumanji* (1981), featuring a dialogue between two children (and a warning from a friendly sun), is shown is Figure 8–5.

Students can also practice writing dialogue on story boards. Story boards can be made by cutting pages from two copies of a picture book, backing the pictures with posterboard, and then laminating them. Students examine the story boards and write dialogue for the characters on stick-on notes, which they then attach to the story boards. The next step is for students to write about the story by referring to the pictures and adding the dialogue they have written on the notes, as well as other descriptions, to the composition. Students can collect all the writings, arrange them in sequence, and compile them to make a class retelling of the book.

Figure 8–5 A fifth grader's dialogue picture based on Van Allsburg's *Jumanji*

Adding Words to Wordless Picture Books. In wordless books, authors tell the entire story using only pictures. A variety of wordless books are available today, and students at all levels enjoy "reading" these books and making up a text to accompany the pictures. A favorite book is *Frog Goes to Dinner* (Mayer, 1974), a hilarious story of a frog who goes to a fancy restaurant hidden in a small boy's jacket pocket. At the restaurant, the frog jumps out of the boy's pocket and causes all sorts of mayhem. A list of wordless picture books is presented in Figure 8–6.

Students can practice the descriptive writing techniques they are learning with wordless books. They brainstorm descriptive words and phrases on small

Alexander, M. (1968). *Out! Out! Out!* New York: Dial. (P)
Alexander, M. (1970). *Bobo's dream.* New York: Dial. (P)
Anno, M. (1978). *Anno's Italy.* New York: Collins. (M–U)
Anno, M. (1978). *Anno's journey.* New York: Philomel. (M–U)
Anno, M. (1982). *Anno's Britain.* New York: Philomel. (M–U)
Anno, M. (1983). *Anno's USA.* New York: Philomel. (M–U)
Aruego, J. (1971). *Look what I can do.* New York: Scribner. (P)
Bang, M. (1980). *The grey lady and the strawberry snatcher.* New York: Four Winds. (M–U)
Banyai, I. (1995). *Zoom.* New York: Viking. (M–U)
Blake, Q. (1996). *Clown.* New York: Holt. (M)
Briggs, R. (1980). *The snowman.* New York: Random House. (P)
Day, A. (1985). *Good dog, Carl.* New York: Green Tiger Press. (M)
Day, A. (1998). *Carl goes shopping.* New York: Farrar, Straus & Giroux. (P–M)
de Groat, D. (1977). *Alligator's toothache.* New York: Crown. (P–M)
de Paola, T. (1978). *Pancakes for breakfast.* New York: Harcourt Brace Jovanovich. (P)
de Paola, T. (1981). *The hunter and the animals: A wordless picture book.* New York: Holiday House. (P–M)
Dupasquier, P. (1988). *The great escape.* Boston: Houghton Mifflin. (M–U)
Goodall, J. S. (1975). *Creepy castle.* New York: Macmillan. (M)
Goodall, J. S. (1983). *Above and below stairs.* New York: Atheneum. (U)
Goodall, J. S. (1987). *The story of a high street.* London: Andre Deutsch. (M–U)
Goodall, J. S. (1988). *Little Red Riding Hood.* New York: McElderry Books. (P–M)
Henstra, F. (1983). *Mighty mizzling mouse.* New York: Lippincott. (P–M)
Hoban, T. (1988). *Look! Look! Look!* New York: Greenwillow. (P)
Hutchins, P. (1971). *Changes, changes.* New York: Macmillan. (P)
Krahn, F. (1977). *The mystery of the giant footprints.* New York: Dutton. (P–M)
Krahn, F. (1978). *The great ape.* New York: Penguin. (P–M–U)
Mayer, M. (1967). *A boy, a dog, and a frog.* New York: Dial. (P–M)
Mayer, M. (1974). *Frog goes to dinner.* New York: Dial. (P–M)
McCully, E. A. (1987). *School.* New York: Harper & Row. (P)
McCully, E. A. (1988). *New baby.* New York: Harper & Row. (P)
Monro, R. (1987). *The inside-outside book of Washington, D.C.* New York: Dutton. (M–U)
Peddle, D. (2000). *Snow day.* New York: Doubleday. (P)
Rohmann, E. (1994). *Time flies.* New York: Crown. (M)
Prater, J. (1987). *The gift.* New York: Viking. (P–M)
Spier, P. (1977). *Noah's ark.* New York: Doubleday. (P–M–U)
Spier, P. (1982). *Rain.* New York: Doubleday. (P–M–U)
Tafuri, N. (1985). *Rabbit's morning.* New York: Greenwillow. (P)
Tafuri, N. (1986). *Have you seen my duckling?* New York: Viking. (P)
Turkle, B. (1976). *Deep in the forest.* New York: Dutton. (P–M)
Weitzman, J. P. (2002). *You can't take a balloon into the Museum of Fine Arts.* New York: Dial. (M–U)
Wiesner, D. (1988). *Free fall.* New York: Lothrop, Lee & Shepard. (M–U)
Wiesner, D. (1991). *Tuesday.* New York: Clarion. (M)
Wiesner, D. (1999). *Sector 7.* New York: Clarion. (M–U)
Winters, P. (1976). *The bear and the fly.* New York: Crown. (P–M–U)
Young, E. (1984). *The other bone.* New York: Harper & Row. (P–M)

Figure 8–6 Wordless picture books

stick-on notes and attach a note to each page in the book, or they can write dialogue on the notes. Then they incorporate the notes they have written into their retelling of the book. Here is an excerpt from a third grader's retelling of *Frog Goes to Dinner*:

 Page 3: The boy is dressed in his Sunday best clothes. He bends over to pat his dog's head. "Good-bye and I will be home from the restaurant very soon," he says. He does not see the silly frog jump into his pocket.

Page 15: The lady wearing a flower hat puts a fork full of lettuce into her mouth. Then she looks down to the plate, and she sees the silly frog sitting in her salad. He has a smile on his face, but the woman screams anyway.

This is a very effective retelling because the student clearly conveys the plot and has incorporated descriptive words and dialogue.

Using the Writing Process

As students work in writers' workshop or on writing projects connected with theme studies, they apply the descriptive writing techniques they are learning. Students gather descriptive words and phrases during prewriting and incorporate them during drafting, but the revising stage is probably the most important for descriptive writing. During the revising stage, students compliment classmates on their use of description—vivid sensory images, specific details, dialogue, and comparisons—and they suggest where writers can add more description to their writing. Students then have the opportunity to return to their rough drafts to make changes.

In Theme Studies

In literature, social studies, or science theme studies, students often use descriptive writing. A fourth-grade class, for example, was reading *Bunnicula: A Rabbit-Tale of Mystery* (Howe & Howe, 1979). In a minilesson, students learned about the roles of characters in a story and then chose their favorite character from *Bunnicula* to examine. They began by making a character map, or cluster. The character's name was written in a circle in the middle of a piece of paper, and then rays or lines were drawn out from the center circle. At the end of each ray, students wrote specific bits of information about the character. One student's character map for Harold, the literary dog in *Bunnicula,* is shown in Figure 8–7. The activity can end with the character map, or the student can use the information to write a paragraph-length description of Harold.

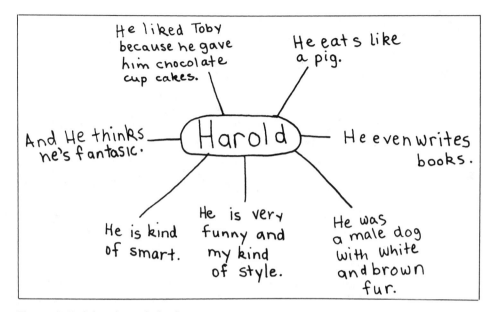

Figure 8–7 A fourth grader's character map

Another example is from a sixth-grade class that was involved in an author study of Chris Van Allsburg. Students each chose one of the illustrations from *The Mysteries of Harris Burdick* (1984), a collection of fantastic, surrealistic illustrations, and wrote a description of it. The teacher had taught several mini-lessons on descriptive writing before students wrote their descriptions, and students were encouraged to experiment with descriptive techniques. One student wrote about the illustration titled "Under the Rug":

It was Tuesday evening and Harold Grimsley had had his dinner. He'd put on an old, comfortable sweater and his favorite leather slippers. He was in the family room reading the *People* magazine when he thought he heard a squeaky noise in the living room. So he went in to investigate. There was a round lump under the gray wall-to-wall carpet. It was the same thing that happened two weeks ago. Now it was back? Harold grabbed a chair from the dining room and hit the lump over and over. The lump squeaked louder and louder and grew larger and larger. Finally it broke through the carpet and a kind of fog spread throughout the room. Harold threw the chair down and ran out of the room and kept on running. He slammed the front door closed as he ran out of the house.

In Writing Workshop

As students write on self-selected topics and work on projects during writing workshop, they often use description, whether they are describing a trip to New York City, the pizza they had for dinner last night, or the hermit crab living in a terrarium in the classroom. During a fourth-grade theme cycle on Antarctica, for instance, two students chose to write a poem about penguins during writers' workshop. This is the procedure they followed. Their work at each stage is shown in Figure 8–8.

1. *Prewriting.* The students collected books about penguins from the class library and looked at the pictures. They brainstormed a list of words as they looked at the illustrations.

2. *Drafting.* Drawing on the words in their list, the students wrote four sentences about penguins.

3. *Revising.* Students shared the sentences with their writing group and decided to "unwrite" (delete unnecessary words) to make a poem from the sentences. After unwriting, they met with their writing group again to share their poem. Classmates complimented the students on the word picture they had created and commented that the first line was the weakest one, offering commonly known information. Afterwards, the students revised their poem by strengthening the first line and making several other changes.

4. *Editing.* The students proofread their poem and noted that they had misspelled *lichen.* They made the correction and met with the teacher for a final editing. Then they wrote their final copy, which is shown at the bottom of Figure 8–8.

5. *Publishing.* The students pasted the final copy of their poem on a picture of a penguin they had drawn, colored, and cut out. At the class sharing time, the two students showed their final product and read their poem aloud to the class.

Assessing Students' Writing

Teachers assess students' descriptive writing in several ways. As they observe and conference with students, teachers use informal assessment procedures and note whether or not students use descriptive techniques. They examine students' use of specific information, careful choice of vocabulary words, sensory images, comparisons, and dialogue to show, not tell, in their writings.

Teachers also develop checklists and rubrics to assess students' use of descriptive techniques in their writing. Figure 8–9 shows a fifth-grade teacher's descriptive writing checklist. As part of a series of lessons about descriptive

Prewriting	Feathers rock orange chubby belly
	feet yellow gray black black
	wing black penguin funny
	beak white red likens
Drafting	① The penguins belly is white its back is black.
	② The penguin has yellow and orange head feathers sticking out of its head.
	③ The rock is covered with likens.
	④ The penguin is up on a rock ledge in the sunshine.
Revising	The Penguin
	White belly and black back
	yellow and orange head feather
	sticking out of the side of its head.
	Up on a liken rock
	in the sunshine.
Final Copy	The Penguin
	White chubby belly.
	yellow and orange head feathers
	sticking out of the side of its head
	Up on a lichen-covered rock
	Standing in the sunshine.

Figure 8–8 The writing process used by two fourth graders in writing a poem about penguins

writing, the fifth graders used the checklist to assess descriptive paragraphs they wrote about photos of lions, tigers, and other big cats cut from calendars. Students assessed whether or not they had overused the descriptive techniques in their writing. In addition, teachers often incorporate one or more items about word choice and description in the rubrics they create for different writing genres because descriptive techniques play an important role in all types of writing.

Too few	Just right	Too many	
			1. Choose vivid describing words.
			2. Include five senses words.
			3. Make comparisons.
			4. Describe emotions.
			5. Choose strong verbs.
			6. Use dialogue.

Figure 8–9 Descriptive writing checklist

ANSWERING TEACHERS' QUESTIONS ABOUT . . .

Descriptive Writing

1. When should I teach descriptive writing?

Descriptive writing should be taught at all grade levels beginning in kindergarten. Five- and six-year-olds can dictate lists of attributes, learn about the five senses, and use informal drama and puppets to create dialogue. Older students continue to write lists of attributes, develop five-senses clusters, and write dialogue, and they learn about other techniques as well. Through the elementary grades, children become increasingly capable of incorporating description into their writing.

2. When students are writing dialogue, how important is it that they use quotation marks correctly?

When students begin to include dialogue in their writing, teachers should focus on the achievement, rather than criticizing them for not marking the dialogue with punctuation marks. However, teachers should build on students' interest in dialogue and give a series of minilessons on how to use quotation marks. Also, you can introduce quotation marks during the editing stage of the writing process and demonstrate their use by marking them on the student's rough draft.

3. What about students trite expressions—*pretty* and *nice?* They use those words over and over!

Teaching students about descriptive writing will help them find alternatives for *pretty* and *nice*. As students brainstorm lists of words and draw five-senses clusters, they will realize that there are many better alternatives for these overworked words. Another way to combat the problem is to suggest to students in their writing groups (during the revising stage) that they substitute more descriptive words.

4. Is descriptive writing a separate genre, or is it part of every type of writing?

That's a good question. Some people consider it a genre, but others don't. Teaching students how to write more descriptively is more important than deciding whether or not it is a genre, and teachers usually find that it is more effective to focus students' attention on descriptive writing separately from other genres. Students can learn how to improve their word choice, write comparisons and dialogue, and create sensory images, and then they practice writing descriptive sentences and paragraphs. After this practice, students are more likely to add description to other genres.

5. I've seen students who start using a thesaurus and then their writing gets worse because they substitute inappropriate words—words they don't even know the meaning of—for the words they've written. I don't think students should use a thesaurus during the elementary grades.

This is a common occurrence, but a thesaurus is an important writing tool, so students should be introduced to it. Students need to learn how and when to use a thesaurus and why they should never change a word in their compositions to an unfamiliar word. When they consult a thesaurus, students learn new vocabulary words and shades of meaning for familiar words. This new knowledge will make students better readers and writers.

CHAPTER 9
Biographical Writing

Preview

Purpose Children use biographical writing to chronicle events in their own and other people's lives, to reflect on experiences, and to draw generalizations about life.

Audience The audience for personal narratives is often the writers themselves and their classmates and families. Autobiographies and biographies are more sophisticated forms of biographical writing, and these compositions are often shared with wider audiences.

Forms Forms are personal narratives, autobiographies, and biographies.

Instructional Preview: Biographical Writing	
Grades	**Goals and Activities**
Kindergarten–Grade 2	**Goal 1:** Write personal narratives • Students write personal narratives during writing workshop. • Students apply the writing process as they write and refine their personal narratives. • Students bind writings into books and place them in the classroom library for classmates to read.
	Goal 2: Write autobiographies • Students write "All About Me" books. • Students collect materials for life boxes.
Grades 3–5	**Goal 1:** Write biographies • Students read biographies and examine the genre. • Students choose personalities to write about and make life lines. • Students write simulated journal entries from the person's viewpoint. • Students make biography clusters. • Students write multichapter biographies. • Students give oral presentations as their personalities.
	Goal 2: Write autobiographies • Students read autobiographies and examine the genre. • Students make "me" quilts. • Students write chapter book autobiographies.
Grades 6–8	**Goal 1:** Write biographies • Students compare and contrast biographies and autobiographies. • Students choose personalities to study and read biographies and collect other information. • Students write simulated journal entries from the person's viewpoint. • Students create multigenre biographies with at least three genres (e.g., simulated journal, biographical sketch, life line, collection of objects, poems, and photos).

Writing a Class Biography

Mrs. Jordan's first-grade class is studying plants, and as part of the theme study, the students want to learn about people who work with plants. They take a field trip to a local plant nursery, interview an agricultural extension agent, and learn about George Washington Carver. Mrs. Jordan reads Aliki's *A Weed Is a Flower: The Life of George Washington Carver* (1988), and after listening to the book read aloud, the students get into a circle for a grand conversation to talk about the book.

Mrs. Jordan starts by asking, "Who would like to begin our conversation about George Washington Carver?" and then the first graders take turns sharing ideas and asking questions. They talk about how Carver was born a slave and was taken away from his mother, how he struggled to learn about plants, and the many uses he found for common plants such as peanuts and sweet potatoes. One child asks why Carver has George Washington's name, another asks if the class can make a meal entirely from peanuts like the botanist did, and another child says that Carver reminds her of Martin Luther King, Jr., whom they had studied earlier in the school year.

Mrs. Jordan seizes this opportunity to review the concept of biography. She asks students if they know what kind of book *A Weed Is a Flower* is, and when no one recalls the term *biography,* she writes the word on the chalkboard and pronounces it. Then one child remembers that a biography "is a story of someone's life," and another child says, "It's a book that tells about the important things that happened in somebody's life." A third child recalls that a biography "tells why a person is remembered today."

Mrs. Jordan suggests that the students brainstorm a list of reasons why George Washington Carver is special and remembered today. One child suggests, "He invented stuff like peanut butter," another says, "He was a scientist," and a third child comments, "People admired him a lot." Then Mrs. Jordan points out that people like Carver are also a lot like us. The students make a second list of the ways that Carver is "just like us." The list includes "he liked peanut butter," "he was black," "he was good," "he went to college and I'm going to college too," and "he wanted people to like him." Each child chooses something from the "special" list or the "just like us" list as the topic for a quickwrite or a quickdraw.

Mrs. Jordan has a set of eight paperback copies of Aliki's book, and children reread the book in small groups with her. Several children remember Carver's saying, "A weed is a flower growing in the wrong place," and after rereading the book, they decide to make a mural about it. Other students work together in a group to make a life line (a line marked into 10-year intervals on a long sheet of chart paper) of Carver's life, noting the most important events, from his birth in 1864 to his death at age 79 in 1943. Students take turns identifying important events in Carver's life and writing them on the chart. Mrs. Jordan shares other information about the famous botanist and adds some of the information to complete the life line. For the year 1890, for instance, one child wrote, "GWC finally earned enough money to go to college in Ames, Iowa." Another group of students marked the locations that Carver traveled to on the large laminated map of the United States that hangs in the classroom, and several others made mobiles about the uses of peanuts. After they finish work, students share their projects with the class.

The class then plans two special whole-class activities: They plan and cook a meal made entirely of vegetables, including peanut butter, and they make a class book about the great botanist. Individually or with a classmate, students choose events from Carver's life to write about. On each page, students write a sentence or two about an event in the botanist's life and add an illustration. Students use the writing process to make their class book the best it can be. They begin by drawing their illustration on "good" paper and writing a rough draft of their text on "draft" paper.

Then the class gets into a circle, arranging themselves so the pages of the book are in sequential order, and students take turns reading their pages. They read through the entire book; then each page is reread and students offer compliments and suggestions about how to communicate more effectively. As students find gaps in their biography, several children volunteer to do additional pages to complete the book. Then students make revisions and meet with the teacher to edit their compositions. Finally, students add the text to the illustrations they have already done and the book is compiled. They line up to sequence the pages, one child makes a cover and a title page, and then the book is bound with a plastic spiral. One page from the collaborative biography is presented in Figure 9–1.

Mrs. Jordan inserts a blank page at the back of most books for students, parents, and other readers to make comments after reading. Students read the book during independent reading, and they take turns taking the book home for parents to read. Here is a sampling of comments on the "Readers' Comments" page:

This book is so good I read it twice!!
The writers and illustrators of this book did a great job!
The children really learned a lot about George Washington Carver.
Cool, dude.
We have enjoyed each of the books this year.
This book was very interesting; we never get too old to learn.
Very, very good book!

Mrs. Jordan teaches thematically, and she ties reading and writing into science and social studies activities. She uses the themes to introduce genres of literature, such

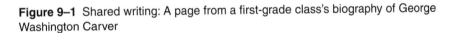

George had a traveling School. He went across Alabama telling farmers how to plant cowpeas, sweet potatoes, cotton, and peanuts.

Figure 9–1 Shared writing: A page from a first-grade class's biography of George Washington Carver

as biography, and as jumping-off places for writing activities. Mrs. Jordan's students use informal writing as they brainstorm lists and quickwrite in learning logs, and they use the writing process as they write biographies. Her students used the writing process to write their class biography of George Washington Carver, and because each student or pair of students wrote one page, Mrs. Jordan could model the writing process and complete the book in four days.

BIOGRAPHICAL WRITING IS WRITING ABOUT PEOPLE. Elementary students enjoy sharing information about their lives and learning about the lives of well-known personalities. In this chapter, we focus on three types of biographical writing: personal narratives, autobiographies, and biographies. Personal narratives are accounts of events from writers' own lives, told much like a story. Primary-grade students' first writings are typically personal narratives, and older writers continue to write personal narratives when they write about and reflect on happenings in their own lives. Autobiographies are more sophisticated, multiple-episode life stories about the writer, and biographies are other people's life stories.

In biographical writing, writers combine elements of expository (or informational) writing with narrative (or story) writing. Writers take information from a person's life—dates, places, events, and people—and weave the factual details and sometimes dialogue into an entertaining account that readers can relate to. Through the events they write about, writers portray the person's character or demonstrate why the person is remembered today.

In this chapter, you will learn about biographical writing and how to teach students to write three types of biographies. The key concepts are:

- Personal narratives are the first biographies that children write; in these compositions, children write about themselves and their experiences.
- Children write about their own lives in autobiographies.
- Children write about other people's lives in biographies.
- Teachers share trade book versions of personal narratives, autobiographies, and biographies with children.
- Teachers teach children to use a process approach to writing biographies.

Types of Biographical Writing

Personal Narratives

Personal narratives are often one of the first types of sustained writing that children do. In this form of biographical writing, students write about themselves and their experiences in the community in which they live. Students in the primary grades as well as older students (and even adults!) become more active, engaged writers as they write about themselves in personal narratives (Steinberg, 1991). One reason that students are so successful in writing personal narratives is that they can draw on what they know best—themselves.

Teachers do not assign topics for personal narratives; instead, students draw from their own lives and experiences and write about things that interest them. A writing might begin as a journal entry about a field trip to the zoo or a birthday party and then be developed and polished through writing process activities. In the writing workshop approach, students keep a list of possible topics in their writing notebooks. They choose a topic from this list or an event in their life and work through the writing process stages to organize, draft, revise, edit, and publish their writing.

In contrast, very young writers often use an abbreviated writing process. They draw and write their personal narratives directly into a booklet of paper stapled together. Drawing the pictures is their prewriting activity, and writing the words is drafting. They usually omit the revising and editing stages, but they increasingly make changes while they are drafting. In fact, children's desire to go back and make some changes is the best indication that they are becoming aware of their audience and can handle all five stages of the writing process. Whether or not students revise and edit, they publish and share their books, usually with classmates and their families.

Young children's personal narratives are often written with an illustration and a line of text on each page. First grader Jessica, for example, writes a line of text on each page of her "We Went to the Zoo" book:

Page 1: We went to the zoo.
Page 2: We saw a turtle.
Page 3: We saw a bunny and we saw a snake.
Page 4: We saw a monkey.

Jessica wrote this book after a class trip to the zoo, and her experiences are evident in the text and accompanying illustrations.

Young children also write books of lists. Sometimes they write lists of favorite toys, family members, or things they like to do. One example of a book of lists is first grader Jason's "I Like" book:

Page 1: I like pizza.
Page 2: I like ice cream.
Page 3: I like cookies.
Page 4: I like salad.
Page 5: I like fish.
Page 6: But I don't like spinach.

In both of these personal narratives, the first-grade writers repeated a pattern ("We saw," "I like"), which structures the text and simplifies the writing task.

Older students and more experienced writers are able to sustain their account without a sentence pattern, as third grader Sean's account demonstrates:

When I was three and a half years old, my mother and I had a discussion about cleaning my room. She was a little on the upset side. She told me I couldn't play until I cleaned my room up. She went into the kitchen to cook and left me to clean my room up. About ten minutes later I walked in the kitchen and stood there. My mother asked, "That was fast. Did you already get your room cleaned?" I said, "God told me that I didn't have to clean my room." With a shocked look on my mom's face, she asked again, "What? God will forgive me this day, so get back in your room and get it cleaned up!"

Sean is a more experienced and more fluent writer than the first graders. He wrote several drafts to develop his account and shared the drafts with classmates, each

Teacher's Note: Assisting English Language Learners

Have you noticed that English learners tend to write the same personal narratives using the same familiar vocabulary words over and over? Teachers can break this cycle by helping children brainstorm other topics and the vocabulary words to describe them. Children need opportunities to talk about a new topic to develop it before they begin to write. With support and guidance, English learners can move on to new topics, vocabulary, and sentence structures.

time revising his writing to extend and elaborate his account in order to communicate more effectively. He also met with the teacher to edit his writing and add conventional spelling, capitalization, and punctuation.

Teachers typically call personal narratives "stories" even though they rarely have the plot and character development of a story. However, it is a disservice to children to call all writing "stories" when the writing might be a report, a poem, or a personal narrative because the terminology is confusing and children are less likely to learn to distinguish the various genres or writing forms.

Some picture books written in the first person that tell about realistic life events might be classified as personal narratives; Jane Yolen's *Owl Moon* (1987), an account of a child's walk into the woods on a snowy night to see a great horned owl, is one example, and Cynthia Rylant's *The Relatives Came* (1985), about a time when relatives came from Virginia for a visit and everyone had a good time, is another. A list of children's books that are written like personal narratives is presented in Figure 9–2. These books might be shared

Barbour, K. (1987). *Little Nino's pizzeria.* San Diego: Harcourt Brace Jovanovich. (P)

Baylor, B. (1982). *The best town in the world.* New York: Aladdin Books. (M–U)

Brown, R. (1986). *Our cat Flossie.* New York: Dutton. (P)

Bunting, E. (1990). *The wall.* New York: Clarion Books. (M–U)

Giff, P. R. (1980). *Today was a terrible day.* New York: Puffin Books. (See also other books in the same series.) (P–M)

Kellogg, S. (1986). *Best friends.* New York: Dial. (P–M)

Martin, B., Jr., & Archambault, J. (1985). *The ghost-eye tree.* New York: Holt, Rinehart & Winston. (M–U)

Mayer, M. (1968). *There's a nightmare in my closet.* New York: Dial. (P)

Ringgold, F. (1991). *Tar beach.* New York: Crown. (P–M)

Rylant, C. (1985). *The relatives came.* New York: Bradbury Press. (M)

Viorst, J. (1971). *The tenth good thing about Barney.* New York: Atheneum. (See other books by the same author.) (M–U)

Waber, B. (1988). *Ira says goodbye.* Boston: Houghton Mifflin. (P–M)

Williams, V. B. (1982). *A chair for my mother.* New York: Mulberry. (See other books in the same series.) (P–M)

Wood, A. (1982). *Quick as a cricket.* London: Child's Play. (P)

Yolen, J. (1987). *Owl moon.* New York: Philomel. (M–U)

Figure 9–2 Books that are written like personal narratives
P = primary grades (K–2), M = middle grades (3–5), U = upper grades (6–8).

with students as examples of published personal narratives that have the same characteristics as the personal narratives the children write.

Autobiographies

An autobiography is the story of a person's life narrated by that person. In writing an autobiography, students relive and document events in their lives, usually in chronological order. They describe memorable events, the ones that are necessary to understand their personalities. A limited number of autobiographies have been written for children, and these life stories of scientists, entertainers, sports figures, and others provide useful models of the autobiography form. A list of recommended autobiographies for elementary students is presented in Figure 9–3.

Autobiographical writing grows out of children's personal narratives and "All About Me" books that they write in kindergarten and first grade. Children's greatest source of information for writing is their own experiences, and when they write autobiographies, they draw from this wealth of experiences. Students can also share their life stories by collecting items that represent their lives in life boxes and me quilts.

"All About Me" Books.   Children in kindergarten and first grade often compile "All About Me" books. These first autobiographies usually contain information such as the child's birthday, family members, friends, and favorite activities, with drawings as well as text used to present the information. Two pages from a first grader's "All About Me" book are presented in Figure 9–4. In these books, children and the teacher decide on the topic for each page, and after brainstorming possible ideas for the topic, children draw a picture and write about the topic. Children may also need to ask their parents for information about their birth and events during their preschool years. In Figure 9–4, for example, first grader Jana reports that it was her father who told her she was choosy about the clothes she wore when she was 5.

Life Boxes.   Autobiographies don't have to be written in books. Students can collect four or five small items that represent themselves and events in their lives and place these things in a shoebox, cereal box, or other box (Fleming, 1985). Items such as a baby blanket, a stuffed animal, family photos, postcards from a vacation, pictures of favorite toys or other items cut from magazines, maps showing places the child has visited, a letter from grandma, a mask worn on Halloween, a favorite book, or an award the child has received might be included. Students write a label to explain each item and attach the labels to the things. They also decorate the box and add an appropriate title. They can use a favorite color of paper, drawings of life events, words and pictures cut from magazines, or wallpaper scraps to decorate the box. Students can share the items with classmates orally or use the items in writing an autobiography.

Bunting, E. (1995). *Once upon a time.* Katonah, NY: Richard C. Owen. (M)

Caras, R. (1994) *A world full of animals: The Roger Caras story.* New York: Chronicle Books. (U)

Cole, J., & Saul, W. (1996). *On the bus with Joanna Cole: A creative biography.* Portsmouth, NH: Heinemann. (M–U)

Collins, M. (1976). *Flying to the moon and other strange places.* New York: Farrar, Straus & Giroux. (M–U)

Dahl, R. (1984). *Boy.* New York: Farrar, Straus & Giroux. (M–U)

de Paola, T. (1989). *The art lesson.* New York: Putnam. (P–M)

de Paola, T. (1999). *26 Fairmount Avenue.* New York: Putnam. (P)

de Paola, T. (2000). *Here we all are.* New York: Putnam. (P)

de Paola, T. (2001). *On my way.* New York: Putnam. (P)

Dewy, J. O. (1995). *Cowgirl dreams: A western childhood.* Honesdale, PA: Boyds Mill. (M–U)

Ehlert, L. (1996). *Under my nose.* Katonah, NY: Richard C. Owen. (P–M)

Filipovic, Z. (1994). *Zlata's diary: A child's life in Sarajevo.* New York: Viking. (U)

Fleischman, S. (1996). *The abracadabra kid: A writer's life.* New York: Greenwillow. (M–U)

Fritz, J. (1982). *Homesick: My own story.* New York: Putnam. (M–U)

Fritz, J. (1992). *Surprising myself.* Katonah, NY: Richard C. Owen. (M)

Gish, L. (1988). *An actor's life for me.* New York: Viking. (U)

Goble, P. (1994). *Hau kola/Hello friend.* Katonah, NY: Richard C. Owen. (M)

Goodall, J. (1988). *My life with the chimpanzees.* New York: Simon and Schuster. (M)

Herrera, J. F. (2000). *The upside down boy/El nino de cabeza.* San Francisco: Children's Press. (P)

Hopkins, L. B. (1992) *The writing bug.* Katonah, NY: Richard C. Owen. (M)

Howe, J. (1994). *Playing with words.* Katonah, NY: Richard C. Owen. (M)

Huynh, Q. N. (1982). *The land I lost: Adventures of a boy in Vietnam.* New York: Harper & Row. (M–U)

Ippisch, H. (1996). *Sky: A true story of resistance during World War II.* New York: Simon & Schuster. (U)

James, N. (1979). *Alone around the world.* New York: Coward. (U)

Jimenez, F. (2001). *Breaking through.* Boston: Houghton Mifflin. (M–U)

Kehret, P. (1996). *Small steps: The year I got polio.* New York: Whitman. (M–U)

Lowry, L. (1998). *Looking back: A book of memories.* New York: Delacorte. (M–U)

Lu, C. F., & White, B. (2001). *Double luck: Memoirs of a Chinese orphan.* New York: Holiday House. (M–U)

Maiorano, R. (1980). *Worlds apart: The autobiography of a dancer from Brooklyn.* New York: Coward. (U)

Myers, W. D. (2001). *Bad boy: A memoir.* New York: HarperCollins. (U)

O'Grady, S., & French, M. (1997). *Basher five-two: The true story of F-16 fighter pilot Captain Scott O'Grady.* New York: Doubleday. (M–U)

O'Kelley, M. L. (1983). *From the hills of Georgia: An autobiography in paintings.* Boston: Little, Brown. (P–M–U)

Paulsen, G. (2001). *Guts: The true stories behind Hatchet and the Brian Books.* New York: Delacorte. (M–U)

Polacco, P. (1994). *Firetalking.* Katonah, NY: Richard C. Owen. (M)

Rudolph, W. (1977). *Wilma: The story of Wilma Rudolph.* New York: New American Library. (U)

Schulz, C. M. (with R. S. Kiliper). (1980). *Charlie Brown, Snoopy and me: And all the other Peanuts characters.* New York: Doubleday. (M–U)

Stine, R. L., & Arthur, J. (1997). *It came from Ohio! My life as a writer.* New York: Scholastic. (M–U)

Tallchief, M. (1999). *Tallchief: America's prima ballerina.* New York: Viking. (M–U)

ZIndel, P. (1992). *The pigman and me.* New York: HarperCollins. (M–U)

Figure 9–3 Recommended autobiographies for elementary students

This is me wen I'm, five. I'm, reading a book. My mom comes in and puts out my cloths for me to wear but I didn't, wat to wear them. I became very picky about my cloths my dad said.

This is my Grammy's house. I have my own room in it. Sometimes I sleep on the love seat. I like to see papa, Sometimes my papa takes me fishing. I love to go fishing. My Grammy makes me feel special.

Figure 9–4 Independent writing: Two pages from a first grader's "All About Me" book

Students can also make a life box after reading a biography. As with autobiographical life boxes, students collect or make three, four, or five items that represent a person's life, add labels to explain the objects, and place them in a decorated box. Life boxes are effective as a first biographical project because students think more critically about the important events in a person's life as they read and plan the items they will use to symbolize the person's life.

Me Quilts. Me quilts are another autobiography project. Students draw a self-portrait and a series of eight pictures to symbolize special events in their lives. Then they attach the pictures to a large sheet of butcher paper to look like a quilt with the self-portrait in the middle, as shown in Figure 9–5. Students write paragraphs to describe each picture, add these to the quilt, and then share their quilts with classmates. They can display their quilts on the classroom wall or present them orally to the class, explaining the pictures and what they represent.

Students can also make biographical quilts with a picture of a well-known person in the center and eight pictures representing special events or objects related to that person's life. Students add paragraphs describing each picture, following the same procedure as with me quilts.

Chapter Books. Students can write chapter books about important events in their lives. They choose three, four, or five important events to write about and

My name is Corrina Anne. I was born on August 6, 1991. I was born at Clovis Community Hospital.

I was born to my parents, Cecilia and Steve Uyeda. The one who showed me all the girly stuff was my sister, Adrienne.

I went to a private school called St. Helen's School. Then in first grade I went to Eaton Elementry. I was really shy.

When I was 6 I got my first pet. It was a black Labrador. Her name was Shadow.

In second grade I made the greatest friend ever. Her name is Jaclyn. We are really good friends.

I second grade I had a really nice teacher. She soon moved to Morro Bay. Her name was Mrs. Worthley.

In fourth grade I had my first male teacher. His name was Mr. Jones.

Now in fifth grade I am in a combo class with Mrs. Ohashi.

Figure 9–5 Independent writing: A fifth grader's "me" quilt

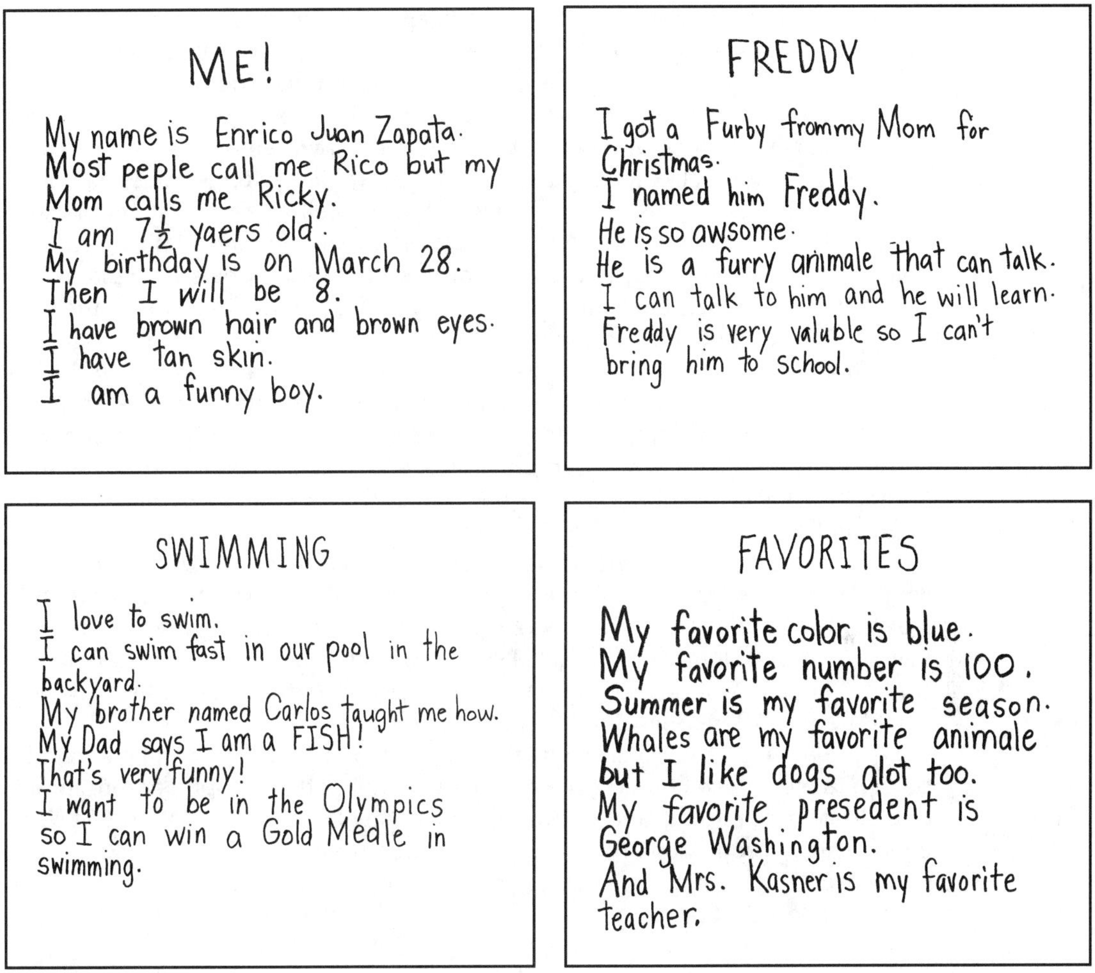

ME!

My name is Enrico Juan Zapata.
Most peple call me Rico but my
Mom calls me Ricky.
I am 7½ yaers old.
My birthday is on March 28.
Then I will be 8.
I have brown hair and brown eyes.
I have tan skin.
I am a funny boy.

FREDDY

I got a Furby frommy Mom for
Christmas.
I named him Freddy.
He is so awsome.
He is a furry animale that can talk.
I can talk to him and he will learn.
Freddy is very valuble so I can't
bring him to school.

SWIMMING

I love to swim.
I can swim fast in our pool in the
backyard.
My brother named Carlos taught me how.
My Dad says I am a FISH!
That's very funny!
I want to be in the Olympics
so I can win a Gold Medle in
swimming.

FAVORITES

My favorite color is blue.
My favorite number is 100.
Summer is my favorite season.
Whales are my favorite animale
but I like dogs alot too.
My favorite president is
George Washington.
And Mrs. Kasner is my favorite
teacher.

Figure 9–6 Independent writing: An excerpt from a second grader's autobiography, "A Story About Me"

use the writing process to develop and refine their compositions. A second grader's autobiography is presented in Figure 9–6. In this autobiography, you learn about Rico through four chapters in which he describes himself and his toys, his hobbies, and his "favorites."

Biographies

A biography is an account of a person's life written by someone else. Writers strive to make this account as accurate and authentic as possible. In researching biographies, they consult a variety of sources of information. The best source of information, of course, is the person himself or herself, and through interviews, writers can learn many things about the person. Other primary sources include diaries and letters written by the person, photographs, mementos, historical records, and recollections of people who know that person. Secondary sources are books, newspapers, and films about the person written by someone else.

Biographies of well-known people such as explorers, kings, queens, scientists, sports figures, artists, and movie stars, as well as ordinary people who have endured hardship and shown exceptional courage, are available for elementary students to read. A list of recommended biographies is presented in Figure 9–7. Jean Fritz has written many biographies for middle-grade students, two of which are included in the list.

Authors use several approaches in writing biographies (Fleming & McGinnis, 1985). The most common one is historical. In this approach, the writer focuses on the dates and events of the person's life and presents them in chronological order. Many biographies that span the person's entire life, such as *Michelangelo* (Stanley, 2000) and *A Picture Book of Helen Keller* (Adler, 1990), follow this pattern.

A second approach is the sociological approach. Here the writer describes what life was like during a historical period, providing information about family life, food, clothing, education, economics, transportation, and so on. For instance, in *Molly Bannaky* (McGill, 1999), the author describes how difficult life was in Colonial America for an indentured servant named Molly Bannaky, who would become Benjamin Banneker's mother.

A third approach is psychological; the writer focuses on the conflicts that the person faces. These conflicts may be with oneself, other people, nature, or society. (For more information about conflict, see Chapter 11, "Narrative Writing.") This approach has many elements in common with stories and is most often used in the shorter event or phase biographies. One example is Jean Fritz's single-event biography *And Then What Happened, Paul Revere?* (1973), in which Paul Revere faces conflict with the British army.

Biographies may be categorized as contemporary or historical. Contemporary biographies are written about a living person, especially a person whom the writer can interview. In contrast, historical biographies are written about persons who are no longer alive.

When students study someone else's life to prepare for writing a biography, they need to become personally involved in the project (Zarnowski, 1988). There are several ways to engage students in biographical study—that is, to help them walk in the footsteps of the other person. For contemporary biographies, meeting and interviewing the person is the best way. For other biography projects, students read books about the person, view films and videos, dramatize events from the person's life, and write about the personalities they are studying. An especially valuable activity is simulated journals, in which students assume the persona of the person they are studying and write journal

Adler, D. A. (1990). *A picture book of Helen Keller.* New York: Holiday House. (P–M)

Adler, D. A. (1996). *A picture book of Davy Crockett.* New York: Holiday House. (P–M)

Adler, D. A. (2000). *A picture book of Sacagawea.* New York: Holiday House. (P)

Adler, D. A. (2001). *Dr. Martin Luther King, Jr.* New York: Holiday House. (P)

Aliki. (1965). *A weed is a flower: The life of George Washington Carver.* Englewood Cliffs, NJ: Prentice-Hall. (M)

Anderson, J. (1991). *Christopher Columbus: From vision to voyage.* New York: Dial. (M)

Adronik, C. M. (2001). *Hatshepsut, his majesty, herself.* New York: Atheneum. (M–U)

Brown, D. (2000). *Uncommon traveler: Mary Kingsley in Africa.* Boston: Houghton Mifflin. (P–M)

Burleigh, R. (1985). *A man named Thoreau.* New York: Atheneum. (U)

Christensen, B. (2001). *Woody Guthrie: Poet of the people.* New York: Knopf. (P–M)

Cooper, F. (1996). *Mandela: From the life of the South African statesman.* New York: Philomel. (M–U)

Dash, J. (2001). *The world at her fingertips: The story of Helen Keller.* New York: Scholastic. (U)

Demi. (2001). *Gandhi.* New York: McElderry. (M–U)

Ellsworth, M. E. (1997). *Gertrude Chandler Warner and the boxcar children.* New York: Whitman. (M–U)

Fisher, L. E. (1999). *Alexander Graham Bell.* New York: Antheneum. (M–U)

Freedman, R. (1987). *Lincoln: A photobiography.* New York: Clarion. (M–U)

Freedman, R. (1996). *The life and death of Crazy Horse.* New York: Holiday House. (M–U)

Fritz, J. (1973). *And then what happened, Paul Revere?* New York: Coward. (P–M)

Fritz, J. (1999). *Why not, Lafayette?* New York: Putnam. (M–U)

Giblin, J. C. (2000). *The amazing life of Benjamin Franklin.* New York: Scholastic. (M–U)

Gilliland, J. H. (2000). *Steamboat! The story of Captain Blanche Leathers.* New York: DK Ink. (P)

Golenbock, P. (1990). *Teammates.* San Diego: Harcourt Brace Jovanovich. (M)

Hodges, M. (1997). *The true story of Johnny Appleseed.* New York: Holiday House. (P)

Jakes, J. (1986). *Susanna of the Alamo: A true story.* New York: Harcourt Brace Jovanovich. (M)

Levinson, N. S. (2001). *Magellan and the first voyage around the world.* New York: Clarion. (M–U)

Marrin, A. (2000). *Sitting Bull and his world.* New York: Dutton. (U)

Mayo, M. (2000). *Brother sun, sister moon: The life and stories of St. Francis.* Boston: Little, Brown. (P–M)

Mitchell, B. (1986). *Click: A story about George Eastman.* Minneapolis: Carolrhoda Books. (M)

Myers, W. D. (2000). *Malcolm X: A fire burning brightly.* New York: HarperCollins. (M–U)

Pinkney, A. D. (1996). *Bill Pickett: Rodeoridin' cowboy.* New York: Gulliver. (M)

Provensen, A., & Provensen, M. (1984). *Leonardo da Vinci.* New York: Viking. (A movable book) (M–U)

Rappaport, D. (2001). *Martin's big worlds: The life of Dr. Martin Luther King, Jr.* New York: Hyperion/Jump. (P–M)

Reef, C. (2001). *Sigmund Freud: Pioneer of the mind.* New York: Clarion. (U)

Rockwell, A. (2000). *Only passing through: The story of Sojourner Truth.* New York: Knopf. (M–U)

Sís, P. (1995). *Starry messenger.* New York: Farrar, Straus & Giroux. (P–M)

Stanley, D. (1999). *Peter the Great.* New York: Morrow. (M–U)

Stanley, D., & Vennema, P. (2001). *Good Queen Bess: The story of Elizabeth I of England.* New York: HarperCollins. (M–U)

Szabo, C. (1997). *Sky pioneer: A photo biography of Amelia Earhart.* Washington, DC: National Geographic Society. (U)

Wallner, A. (1997). *Laura Ingalls Wilder.* New York: Holiday House. (P)

Wallner, A. (2001). *Abigail Adams.* New York: Holiday House. (P)

Winter, J. (1991). *Diego.* New York: Knopf. (M)

Winter, J. (1999). *Sebastian: A book about Bach.* New York: Browndeer. (P)

Figure 9–7 Recommended biographies for elementary students

entries from that person's viewpoint. (See Chapter 6 for more information about simulated journals.)

Life Lines.   Students sequence the information they gather for a biography on a life line or a time line about a person's life. A fourth grader's life line for Benjamin Franklin is shown in Figure 9–8. This activity helps students identify the milestones and other events in the person's life. Students can use the information on the life line to identify topics for the biography, or the life line can be the entire biography project if students write a sentence or paragraph about each event and add illustrations.

Teacher's Note: Supporting Struggling Writers

Biographies are especially difficult for struggling writers because they need a great deal of background knowledge in order to write successfully. Teachers can assist by reading aloud information about the personality or by showing a film or video. Struggling writers may also need assistance in taking notes. Rather than requiring these students to write a chapter-book biography, have them try making life lines, biography boxes, and posters. These biography projects require less writing but still demonstrate learning.

Bio Boxes.   Students make "bio" or biography boxes similar to me boxes. They begin by identifying items that represent the person, then collect them and put them in a box they have decorated. They also write cards to put with each object, explaining the object's significance to the person. A fifth grader created a bio box for Paul Revere and decorated the box with aluminum foil, explaining that it looked like silver and Paul Revere was a silversmith. Inside the box, he placed the following items:

a spoon to represent Paul Revere's career as a silversmith
a toy horse to represent his famous midnight ride
a tea bag to represent his involvement in the Boston Tea Party
a copy of Longfellow's poem "The Midnight Ride of Paul Revere"
an advertisement for Revere pots and pans along with an explanation that Paul Revere is credited with inventing the process of layering metals
a portrait of the patriot
photos of Boston, Lexington, and Concord that were downloaded from the Internet
a life line the student had drawn marking important events in Paul Revere's life

The student wrote a card describing the relationship of each object to Paul Revere and attached it to the item.

Biography Posters.   Students present the information they have learned about the subject of their biography project on a poster. Posters can include a portrait of the person and information about the person's life and accomplishments. Students in an eighth-grade class made a biography quilt with paper squares, and each square was modeled after the illustrations in *My Fellow Americans: A Family Album,* by Alice Provensen (1995). One student's square about Martin Luther King, Jr., is presented in Figure 9–9. This student drew a portrait of the civil rights leader set in Washington, DC, on August 28, 1963, the day he delivered

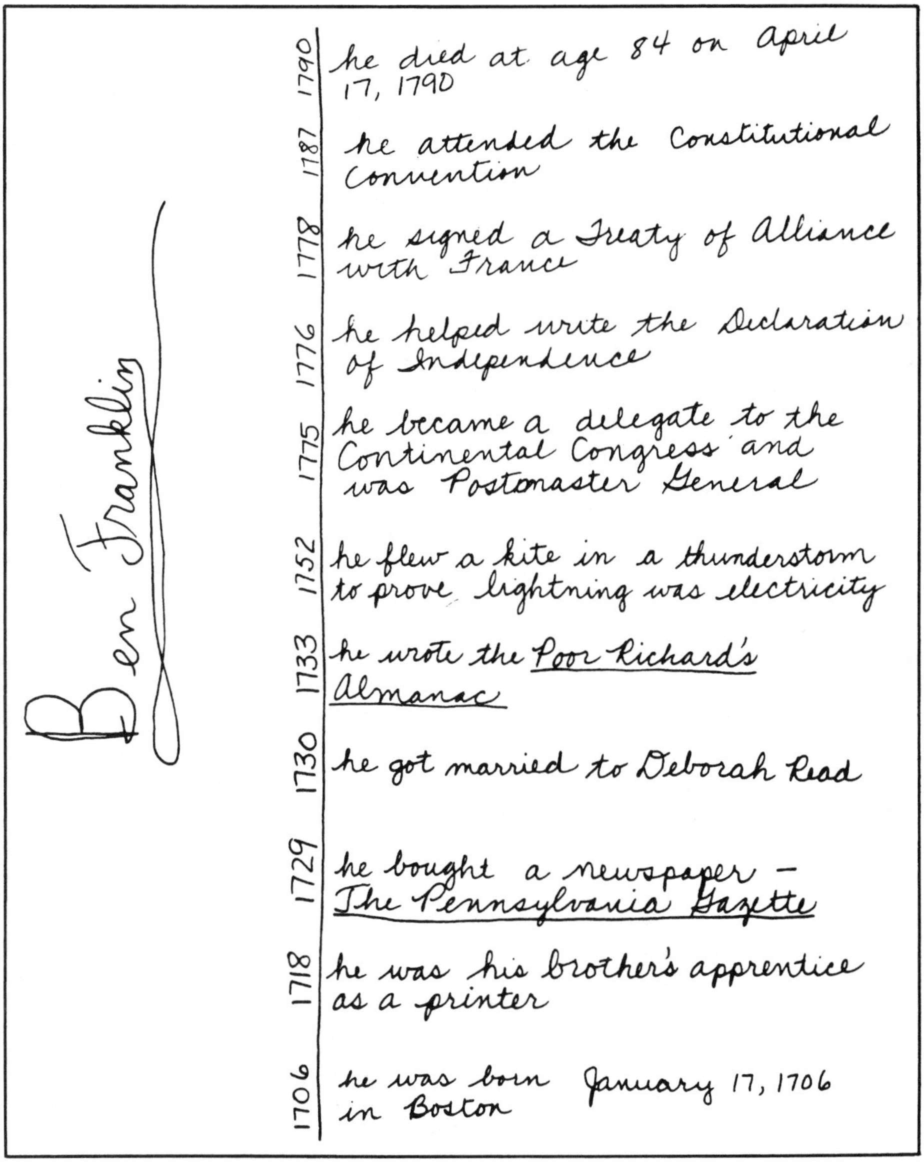

1790	he died at age 84 on April 17, 1790
1187	he attended the Constitutional Convention
1778	he signed a Treaty of Alliance with France
1776	he helped write the Declaration of Independence
1775	he became a delegate to the Continental Congress and was Postmaster General
1752	he flew a kite in a thunderstorm to prove lightning was electricity
1733	he wrote the Poor Richard's Almanac
1730	he got married to Deborah Read
1729	he bought a newspaper — The Pennsylvania Gazette
1718	he was his brother's apprentice as a printer
1706	he was born January 17, 1706 in Boston

Ben Franklin

Figure 9–8 Independent writing: A fourth grader's life line of Benjamin Franklin

Figure 9–9 Independent writing: A biography poster about Martin Luther King, Jr.

his famous "I Have a Dream" speech. The student also added well-known sayings and other phrases related to Martin Luther King, Jr., around the outside.

Collaborative Biographies.   Students share the writing, as Mrs. Jordan's first graders did in the vignette at the beginning of the chapter, when they write collaborative biographies. They divide the biography into pages or chapters, and students each write one section, using the writing process to draft and refine their writing. A second-grade class interviewed their principal, Mrs. Reno, and compiled a picture-book biography that became the most popular book in the school. Before the interview, the second graders brainstormed questions and each child selected a question to ask. Then Mrs. Reno came to the classroom and answered the children's questions. After the interview, the students wrote pages

Figure 9–10 Shared writing: A page from a second-grade class's collaborative biography of the school principal

Estelle asked, "Are you married?"

Mrs. Reno answered, "Yes. I am."

with their questions and Mrs. Reno's answers and compiled the pages into a book. A page from their collaborative biography is presented in Figure 9–10. You will also notice that the students practiced using quotation marks in their report.

Multigenre Biographies. Students write and draw a variety of pieces about a person to create a multigenre biography, which is like a multigenre report (Romano, 1995, 2000). Students collect and create some of the following items for a multigenre biography:

life line	found poem or other poem	story
quotations	open-mind portrait	poster
photographs	report	newspaper articles
collection of objects	maps	advertisements
simulated journal	letters	

Each item is a complete piece by itself and contributes to the overall impact of the biography. Students compile their biographies on posters or in notebooks. Figure 9–11 presents excerpts from a seventh grader's multigenre biography of Maya Angelou.

Maya Angelou

In Maya's Heart

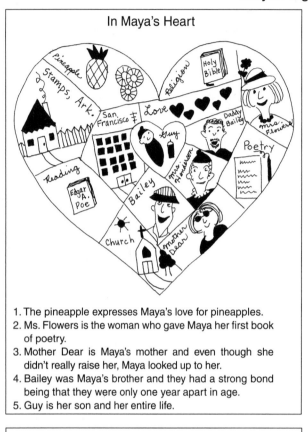

1. The pineapple expresses Maya's love for pineapples.
2. Ms. Flowers is the woman who gave Maya her first book of poetry.
3. Mother Dear is Maya's mother and even though she didn't really raise her, Maya looked up to her.
4. Bailey was Maya's brother and they had a strong bond being that they were only one year apart in age.
5. Guy is her son and her entire life.

Quotes

"Cleanliness is next to Godliness."

"God blessed everyone with an intelligent mind. Only we can decide how we use it."

Dear Diary,
One night I was scared and momma let me sleep in the bed with her and Mr. Freeman. Then when momma left early to run an errand, I felt a strange pressure on my left leg. I knew it wasn't a hand because it was much too soft. I was afraid to move and I didn't budge. Mr. Freeman's eyes were wide open with both hands above the covers. He then said, "Stay right here, Rite, I'm not gonna hurt you." I really wasn't afraid, a little curious, but not afraid. Then he left and came back with a glass of water and poured it on the bed. He said, "see how you done peed in the bed." Afterwards, I was confused and didn't understand why Mr. Freeman had held me so gently, then accused me of peeing in the bed.
Marguerite

Dear Diary,
While I was sitting talking to Miss Glory, Mrs. Cullinan called for someone. She said, "Mary P." We didn't know who she was calling, but my name is Marguerite. Now I settled for Margaret, but Mary was a whole nother name. Bailey told be bout Whites and how they felt like they had the power to shorten our names for their convenience. Miss Glory told me her name used to be Hallelujah and Mrs. Cullinan shortened it to Glory. Mrs. Cullinan sent me on an errand, which was a good idea because I was upset and anything was bound to come out of my mouth at the time.
Marguerite

Dear Diary,
Graduation day was a big event in Stamps. The high school seniors received most of the glory. I'm just a twelve year old 8th grader. I'm pretty high-ranked in my class along with Henry Reed. Henry is also our class valedictorian. The tenth grade teacher helped him with his speech. Momma was even going to close the store. Our graduation dresses are a lemon yellow, but momma added ruffles and cuffs with a crocheted collar. She added daisy embroideries around the trim before she considered herself finished. I just knew all eyes were going to be on me when graduation day came.
Marguerite

Figure 9–11 Excerpts from a seventh grader's multigenre biography of Maya Angelou

Teaching Children to Write Biographies

Teachers prepare their students for writing biographies by teaching them about the organization of information in biographies and by sharing trade book versions of biographies. With this experience, elementary students can write personal narratives, autobiographies, and biographies using the writing process.

Introducing Biography With Personal Narratives

Children usually write personal narratives during writing workshop when they are free to choose their own topics for writing and write about topics that are important to them. It is important that children choose topics they care about and want to write about. Otherwise, writing workshop can seem like an assembly line with children producing book after book without thoughtful work or careful bookmaking. Children get ideas for their writing as they listen to classmates sharing their books and from books of children's literature they are reading. The writing process itself also helps to nurture students' interest in writing because children learn how to develop and refine their compositions.

The teaching strategy for writing personal narratives is described in the step-by-step feature on page 298.

Writing Biographies and Autobiographies

Children write life stories as part of literature focus units and social studies and science thematic units. During an author unit, children might write a biography of a favorite author, or during a unit on the American Revolution, children read and write biographies of Paul Revere, George Washington, and other historical personalities. They also write biographies of scientists in connection with science themes. Children write autobiographies as part of literature focus units, writing workshop, and thematic units on self-awareness, families, and change.

The steps in the teaching strategy are described in the step-by-step feature on page 299. Although the teaching strategy involves steps similar to those used for writing autobiographies and biographies, these two writing forms are different and should be taught separately.

Assessing Students' Biographies

Personal narratives are often the first type of sustained writing that young children do, and teachers watch for this accomplishment as a significant development in children's growth as writers. Teachers should look for the following traits in children's first personal narratives:

- There is a common thread through the book.
- There is one line of text and an illustration on each page.
- The illustrations and the text are coordinated.
- The writer uses the first person.
- The child willingly shares the book with classmates.

As elementary students gain more writing experience and begin working through all five stages of the writing process, their personal narratives become more developed and polished. Their writings should display many of these qualities:

Step by Step: Personal Narratives

1. ***Introduce personal narratives.*** Teachers use minilessons to teach children how to write personal narratives. In one minilesson, teachers explain that children write about events in their own lives and about topics of special interest. They may share examples that students in a previous class have written or books written like personal narratives. In another minilesson, teachers help children brainstorm a list of possible writing topics such as a family trip, birth of a baby brother or sister, a pet, a hobby, an accident, a special holiday, a scary experience, or a grandparent's visit. Children keep this list in a writing notebook or a writing workshop folder and update the list periodically during the year.

2. ***Use the writing process.*** Children use the writing process to write personal narratives. They begin by making a cluster or drawing a series of pictures to gather and organize their ideas. Then they write a rough draft, meet with classmates in a writing group, and revise their drafts based on feedback they receive from classmates. Next they proofread to identify and correct spelling, capitalization, and punctuation errors. Finally, children write the final draft of their composition, add a title page, and compile the pages to make a book. Children move through these activities at their own pace in writing workshop.

3. ***Publish and share the writing.*** Children publish their personal narratives in books. Minilessons might focus on how to make and bind books. Teachers share examples of books other students have made and show various sizes and shapes of books. They also demonstrate how to make book covers by covering pieces of cardboard with wallpaper, cloth, contact paper, or wrapping paper, and how to compile pages in a book.

   Children also share their books with the class. Often they sit in an author's chair to read their books aloud to a group of classmates. Sharing is an important part of the writing process because it emphasizes that writers write for listeners and readers and that writers are successful when their audience enjoys the book. They might also place their books in the classroom library for classmates to read and reread.

- The account focuses on one event or experience.
- Specific people, locations, and objects are named.
- Sensory details about the people, locations, and events are included.
- Actions are described.
- Dialogue or monologue is included.
- The events are arranged in an appropriate sequence.
- There is suspense or a surprise at the end.

These qualities do not develop simultaneously, nor does any one personal narrative necessarily incorporate all of them. Think back to the three personal nar-

Step by Step: Autobiographies and Biographies

1. *Examine the format and the unique conventions of autobiographies and biographies.* Students read autobiographies and biographies to examine how authors organize and format life stories. In particular, students note which events the author focuses on, how the author presents information and feelings, and what the author's viewpoint is.

2. *Gather information about the life story.* Students gather information in several ways. For autobiographical writing, the students themselves are the best source of information about their lives, but they may need to ask parents and other family members for additional information. For biographical writing, students read books and view videotapes and movies to learn about the person and the time period in which he or she lived. If students are researching a living person, it might be possible to interview him or her in person or by e-mail. As they conduct research, students take notes about information they learn.

3. *Organize the information for the life story.* Students usually choose three, four, or five important events in their subject's life and develop clusters with these important events as the main ideas. Then they complete the cluster by adding details from the information they have gathered. Or, students can use life lines or life boxes to organize their writing. They make life lines about their own lives or the life of a historical personality and sequence their writing in time order. Or, they choose three, four, or five objects or photos from their life boxes and brainstorm ideas about each one.

4. *Write the life story using the writing process.* Students use the clusters they developed to write their rough drafts: The main ideas become topic sentences and details are expanded into supporting sentences. After they write their rough drafts, students meet in writing groups to get feedback on their writing and then make revisions. Next, they edit their writing and recopy it or word process it. They add drawings, photographs, or other memorabilia. For biographies, students also add a bibliography, listing the sources of information they consulted.

ratives presented earlier in the chapter; each of the accounts includes some of these qualities. Jessica's "We Went to the Zoo" piece, for instance, focuses on a single event, and Jason's "I Like" account has a surprise at the end. Sean's personal narrative is sequential, uses dialogue, and describes actions.

A second-grade checklist for assessing students' personal narratives is presented in Figure 9–12. Students use this checklist as they revise and edit their writing.

Before they begin work, students need to understand the requirements for their autobiography or biography project and how they will be graded. Teachers often create a rubric or assessment checklist with students so that they will understand what is expected of them. A seventh-grade teacher developed the rubric shown

	Yes	No
Story Structure I used the "I" point of view. I wrote a beginning, middle, and end. I described the characters. I described the setting. I told why it was important to me.		
Ideas I wrote about one event. I wrote about the event in sequence. I added vivid details. I chose descriptive words to paint a picture.		
Mechanics I spelled most words correctly. I capitalized the beginning of sentences and names. I used punctuation marks correctly. I used complete sentences. I indented paragraphs.		

Figure 9–12 Second-grade personal narrative checklist

in Figure 9–13 for a multigenre biography project. She began by listing these seven components on the chalkboard: genres, information, vocabulary, mechanics, writing process, design/graphics, and bibliography. She and her students discussed each component, and the teacher explained her expectations for their assignment. For example, for the genres component, the students knew that they had to include at least three genres—a report of information, a simulated journal with five entries, and a poem. Then they developed the genres component of the rubric. Three genres was the *C* expectation; if they wrote fewer genre pieces, their grade would be a *D* or *F*. For a *B*, students needed to write four genre pieces, and for an *A*, they needed to write five. Together as a class, the students brainstormed the genres they might use. Then they repeated the process with each of the other six components. Through this activity, the students developed the rubric and the teacher reviewed the requirements for each grade.

Teachers usually give students copies of checklists and rubrics to keep in their writing folders so that they can check their work against the guidelines. At the end

A	**Genres:** The biography includes five genres. **Information:** The information presented in the "voice" of the personality. **Vocabulary:** The compositions are rich with specific vocabulary terms. **Mechanics:** There are few, if any, mechanical errors. **Writing Process:** Rough drafts are attached and provide evidence of the writing process. **Design/Graphics:** The design is eye-catching, and four or more graphics extend into the text. **Bibliography:** There are five or more references, and one is an Internet reference.
B	**Genres:** The biography includes four genres. **Information:** The information is accurate, detailed, and interesting. **Vocabulary:** The compositions include many specific vocabulary words used correctly. **Mechanics:** There are a few mechanical errors, but they do not interfere with understanding. **Writing Process:** Rough drafts are attached and provide evidence of the writing process **Design/Graphics:** The design is attractive, and three or more graphics support the text. **Bibliography:** There are four or more references and one is an Internet reference.
C	**Genres:** The biography contains three genres. **Information:** The information is accurate and interesting. **Vocabulary:** The compositions include a few specific vocabulary words. **Mechanics:** There are some mechanical errors, but they do not interfere with understanding. **Writing Process:** Rough drafts are attached and provide evidence of the writing process. **Design/Graphics:** The design is attractive, and two or more graphics support the text. **Bibliography:** There are three or more references.
D	**Genres:** The biography includes two genres. **Information:** A lot of information is confusing. **Vocabulary:** Very few specific vocabulary words are used. **Mechanics:** There are many mechanical errors. **Writing Process:** The rough drafts are not attached. **Design/Graphics:** The design is confusing, and there is one graphic. **Bibliography:** There are two references.
F	**Genres:** The biography includes one genre. **Information:** Very little information is provided or it is not accurate. **Vocabulary:** No specific vocabulary words are used. **Mechanics:** There are many mechanical errors. **Writing Process:** The rough drafts are not attached. **Design/Graphics:** The biography has no design and there are no graphics. **Bibliography:** There is one reference or none at all.

Figure 9–13 Assessment rubric for a multigenre biography

of the project, students self-assess their work and attach the checklists and rubrics to their work. Through this approach, students assume a greater responsibility for their own learning and better understand why they receive a particular grade.

ANSWERING TEACHERS' QUESTIONS ABOUT . . .

Biographical Writing

1. My second graders are writing personal narratives. In fact, that's all most of them write. How can I get them into writing stories, poems, letters, and other writing forms?

Choose one of the forms you mentioned and introduce it to your students, perhaps using a class collaboration. Then invite your students to use the form for a genuine writing purpose. For example, they might become pen pals with students in another school. The first letter might be a class letter, and you can demonstrate how to write a friendly letter as you compose the letter together with your students. Then they can write individual letters to their pen pals several times during the school year. Then continue to introduce other writing forms in connection with literature the students are reading or social studies and science units.

2. At which grade levels do you think elementary students should write biographies and autobiographies?

Primary-grade students can do almost all types of writing, including biographical writing. First graders typically write personal narratives, and they can also begin writing collaborative biographies, as Mrs. Jordan's first graders did in the vignette at the beginning of the chapter (see Figure 9–1). Second graders (see Figure 9–6) can write chapter autobiographies, and some experienced first-grade writers might also. Most students write personal narratives throughout the elementary grades, but they shouldn't have to write an autobiography or a biography in every grade. During the elementary grades, students can write a chapter autobiography once or twice and several biographies in connection with science and social studies themes.

3. Can I use stories such as *Johnny Tremain* (Forbes, 1970) and *Sarah, Plain and Tall* (MacLachlan, 1985) for biographical writing?

The two books that you mentioned are stories, not biographies, so they should not be used as examples of biographical writing. Like biographies, however, both stories focus on the main character, and the main character might even be based on a real person. The line between historical fiction and biography can sometimes be fuzzy, but biographies are written about people who actually lived, and the events described in them really happened and have been researched, not invented, by the author.

4. I don't have my students write autobiographies because they aren't middle class. Many of them are homeless. Others have parents who are in jail or deal in drugs. They don't have anything good to write about. What do you think?

It is important to be sensitive to your students and their family life; however, all children have some experiences they could share in an autobiography. If you don't think it's appropriate for your students, you might have them read and write biographies instead.

5. I like the idea of having my fourth graders write biographies or autobiographies, but do you have any ideas other than written books?

Sure! Writing an autobiography or biography is just one of many ways of presenting biographical information. After your students collect information, they can make life boxes, draw life lines, or make biography posters.

CHAPTER 10
Expository Writing

Preview

Purpose   Students use expository writing to learn and to share information.

Audience   Expository writing is often done for a wide, unknown audience. Reports in book format can be placed in the school library. Information presented on posters, in diagrams, and on other charts can be displayed in the hallways of the school or in the community.

Forms   The forms include reports, "All About . . . " books, ABC books, riddles, posters, diagrams, charts, and cubes. Students can also incorporate information into stories and poems that they write.

Instructional Preview: Expository Writing

Grades	Goals and Activities
Kindergarten– Grade 2	**Goal 1:** Recognize and use the description, sequence, and comparison structures • Students notice examples of the structures when reading. • Students use graphic organizers to record information. • Students use the structures to organize their writing. • Students use the cue words to signal use of the structure.
	Goal 2: Share information they have learned in reports • Students write "All About . . ." books. • Students write class collaborative reports. • Students write riddles. • Students make posters, diagrams, and charts.
Grades 3–5	**Goal 1:** Recognize and use all five expository text structures • Students notice examples of the structures when reading. • Students use graphic organizers to record information. • Students use the structures to organize their writing of paragraphs and longer compositions. • Students use the cue words to signal use of the structure.
	Goal 2: Research and write reports • Students write small-group collaborative reports. • Students write class ABC books as part of thematic units. • Students write riddles using social studies or science information they have learned. • Students make posters, diagrams, and charts. • Students write individual reports. • Students participate in developing class multigenre projects.
Grades 6–8	**Goal 1:** Research and write reports • Students write small-group collaborative reports that are structured using the expository text structures. • Students write individual reports that are structured using the expository text structures. • Students write cubes to explore a topic from different perspectives. • Students use diagrams and charts to report information.
	Goal 2: Create multigenre projects • Students explore a topic by writing, using several genres. • Students use three or more genres and graphics to create a multigenre project on a poster or in a book.

Traveling the Oregon Trail

As part of their unit on pioneers, Mr. Garcia's fifth-grade class is playing *The Oregon Trail* (1997), a CD-ROM simulation game, on the computers in the classroom. Students play in small-group teams, assuming the role of pioneers and traveling 2,000 miles from Independence, Missouri, to the Willamette Valley in Oregon in 1848. As they play the game, Mr. Garcia's students learn about the geography of the Oregon Trail, dangers that the pioneers faced along the way, and how the pioneers solved problems. They make decisions about their travel, and a trail log with their decisions and important events is generated by the computer.

Tyler, Luz, Marianne, Stacy, and George form one team; they call themselves the "Oregon or Bust" team. They choose to begin their simulated journey on April 1, 1848, and buy supplies, including 5 oxen, 500 bullets, and 250 pounds of food. Four days later, they reach the Kansas River and hire a ferry to take their wagon across. As they travel to Fort Laramie and then to Independence Rock, one member of their team dies from a snakebite and another breaks an arm. Periodically they run short of food and have to hunt deer, rabbits, and buffalo. They get lost twice and deal with not having grass for the oxen to eat. They travel past the Grande Ronde in the Blue Mountains, Fort Boise, The Dalles, and then reach the Columbia River. After resting for several days, the remaining members of the team decide to raft down the Columbia River. The river is treacherous, but at first the team navigates it well. Then disaster strikes, their wagon falls off the raft and into the river, and all but one person is drowned. At the end of the game, that person reaches the Willamette Valley safely on August 5, 1848.

The teams take turns using the three computers in the classroom to play the simulation game, and students who have completed the game are involved in a variety of related activities: They make maps of their journey, read books from a text set about pioneer life, write letters home from some point on the trail, work on a classroom display of trail life, and create a simulated journal using information from the game's trail log. Here are four entries from the "Oregon or Bust" team's collaborative journal:

April 1, 1848
Dear Diary,
Today we left Independence, Missouri, for the Oregon Trail. It was sad when we had to say good-bye to our families. We may never see them again, but we really want to go west because we are adventurers. We have lots of supplies. We have 5 oxen, 5 sets of clothing, 500 bullets (in case we get in a fight with the Indians), 2 wagon wheels, 2 wagon axles, 1 wagon tongue, 250 pounds of food, and more than $900. We are strong and healthy and young. We want to make it to Oregon by October before the snows begin.

May 17, 1848
Dear Diary,
Life on the trail is very hard now. Everyone is too tired to sing or dance. We have been out of water until we thought we would go crazy and die. There was no water for us or for the animals. Now we have reached Fort Bridger and we drank and drank lots of water. We rested for two days and drank lots more water. We used some of our money to buy more food at the store in the fort. Now we have decided to continue.

August 3, 1848
Dear Diary,
Today we are resting beside the Columbia River. It is a great and dangerous river. We want to be strong before we raft down it to the Willamette Valley. We think it will take us three days to reach Oregon. We have talked to lots of people here to get advice about how to travel on the river. It will be very dangerous because there are rocks and broken wagons and other stuff in the river. There are still four of us who are alive on this wagon. We are sure that we will make it to Oregon now.

August 5, 1848
Dear Diary,
It's just me, Stacy, now. I am alive and I made it to the Willamette Valley. It was terrible on the Columbia River. We were doing fine and then what happened is that the side of our raft hit a rock and it turned over. All the oxen drowned real fast. We tried to swim to shore but I was the only good swimmer. When I got to shore, I tried to look for them but I couldn't find them. I saw some pioneers on another raft and they came to the shore and picked me up. They let me go with them. I'm happy for me but I am sad for my friends.

After all teams complete their journey on the Oregon Trail, they have a class meeting to share their experiences. Each team recounts its trip and whether or not everyone on the team survived to reach Oregon. Students talk about the decisions they made, what they learned, and how they would play the game differently next time.

Mr. Garcia smiles as he listens to them talk knowledgeably about the Oregon Trail. They have learned so much about the Oregon Trail, and now they are ready to write reports. It's one of the language arts standards for fifth-grade level in his district, and he has planned an innovative expository writing project: guidebooks for pioneers who travel the Oregon Trail. "I know what we should do next," Mr. Garcia explains. "You've learned so much about the Oregon Trail, I think you'd really enjoy writing a guidebook for pioneers who travel on the Oregon Trail. You could write the most important information that you've learned about life on the trail."

His enthusiasm is contagious, and Mr. Garcia's students agree eagerly. "We could share these guides with the other fifth-grade classes before they play *The Oregon Trail.* And you could give the guides to your students to read before they play the game next year," the children suggest.

The students are eager to share what they have learned, and Mr. Garcia reviews the form, purpose, and audience for this project. They will fold two sheets of paper in half and staple them together to make a guidebook. He shows the children several travel guidebooks from his trip to Europe several years ago. After examining the guides, the class brainstorms these topics that they might include in their guides:

- Map of the Oregon Trail
- Lists of supplies to bring
- Information about the dangers
- Advice about how to pack a covered wagon, how to caulk a wagon to cross a river, how to find the trail when you get lost, and how to hunt for food
- Directions for medical emergencies
- A calendar showing the best months to travel the Oregon Trail
- Questions and answers
- Quotes from pioneers who made the trip

Mr. Garcia explains that each team will create one guidebook, and students can choose topics from this list or think of other important information to include in their guides. The students use the writing process to create their guidebooks. They create rough draft guides and share them with Mr. Garcia. Some teams write the guides by hand, and others use the computers in the classroom for some or all of their guidebooks. They revise and edit their guides, draw the illustrations, and make the final copies of the guidebooks. Then each team shares its guide with the class. Two pages from the "Oregon or Bust" team's guide are shown in Figure 10–1. One page shows the cover, and the other presents information about food.

Mr. Garcia also developed a rubric with the students soon after they began creating their guides. As a class, they decide which qualities the guides should exemplify: useful and interesting information, attention-getting design, historically accurate and technical vocabulary, mechanical correctness, and illustrations that support and extend the text. Mr. Garcia divides a sheet of butcher paper into six rows and five columns. In the top row, he writes the scores 1 (Poor) to 4 (Great), and down the left column, he writes labels for the five qualities the class identified, as shown in Figure 10–2. Then Mr. Garcia and the class talk about the characteristics of each of the five qualities and choose descriptors to complete the rubric. With this information, the children are better able to create quality guides.

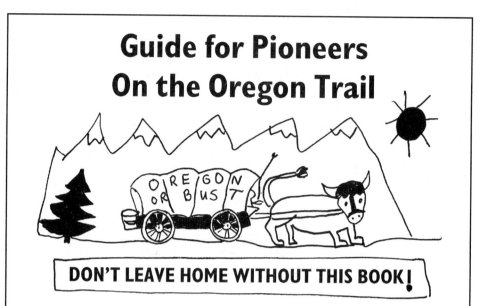

Guide for Pioneers
On the Oregon Trail

DON'T LEAVE HOME WITHOUT THIS BOOK!

Written by Pioneers Who Know First Hand
The Hardships of the Trail

Food

You must take lots of food with you. Take food that does not spoil quickly because if the food is spoiled you have to throw it away. Never eat spoiled food or you will get sick or die! You can only do three things to get more food on the Oregon Trail:

1. You can hunt for food. You will need bullets so that you can hunt for deer, birds, rabbits, and buffalo. Don't be greedy because you can only carry some food like one deer back to your wagon. Remember that the food you hunt is perishable. It will spoil fast.

2. You can buy food at the forts. You need money to buy food. The food at the fort is not perishable but you might get sick of eating it.

3. You can trade for food, but you must have something that Indians or pioneers want or no one will trade with you.

Figure 10–1 Shared writing: Two pages from a collaborative guide on the Oregon Trail

	1 Poor	2 Satisfactory	3 Good	4 Great
Information	Little information or incorrect information	Some useful information and no incorrect information	More useful information	Lots of very detailed and useful information
Design of the guide	Confusing arrangement and no headings	Organized into sections with some headings	Attractive organization with headings for every section	Attention-getting organization and headings make it easy to read
Vocabulary and style	No special words and hard to read	A few special words	More special words and easy to read	Lots of special words and interesting to read
Mechanics • **spelling** • **capitals** • **punctuation**	Many errors	Some errors	A few errors	No errors
Illustrations	No pictures or pictures aren't related to the Oregon Trail	A few pictures or charts	Useful pictures and charts	Very detailed pictures and charts

Figure 10–2 Rubric for assessing students' Oregon Trail guides

LIKE OTHER WRITERS, MR. GARCIA'S STUDENTS use expository writing to share information with readers. The information might be about traveling on the Oregon Trail, the steps in building a road, the problems involved in cleaning up an oil spill in Alaska's Prince William Sound, or a comparison of Paul Revere's and Jack Joulett's Revolutionary War rides. Elementary students are interested in learning about the world around them, and informational books help them satisfy their curiosity. Researchers report that even kindergartners enjoy and learn from informational books (Pappas, 1991).

Expository writing forms are also used to write about literature. When students research the setting of a book (for example, the Holocaust after reading *Number the Stars* [Lowry, 1989]), compare book and film versions of a novel (such as *Tuck Everlasting* [Babbitt, 1975]), or investigate a topic related to a story (perhaps owls after reading *Owl Moon* [Yolen, 1987]), they are using expository writing. Britton (1970a) says this type of writing is intended "to interact with people and things and to make the wheels of the world, for good or ill, go round" (p. 8).

In this chapter, you will learn about expository or informational writing and how to teach children to write reports and other types of informational books. The key concepts are:

- Informational books are organized using five expository text structures.
- Children can identify the expository structures in informational books and write informational books following the structural patterns used in them.
- Reports are the most common type of expository writing, and elementary students can write both collaborative and individual reports.
- Other types of expository writing are ABC books, riddles, posters, diagrams, charts, and cubes.

Expository Text Structures

Writers organize different kinds of writing in different ways. When they write to share information, writers use expository patterns or text structures. In each pattern, information is organized in a particular way, and words often signal the structure. Five of the most commonly used patterns are description, sequence, comparison, cause and effect, and problem and solution (Meyer & Freedle, 1984; Niles, 1974).

Description

Writers describe a topic by listing characteristics, features, and examples. Phrases such as *for example* and *characteristics are* cue this structure. When students delineate any topic, such as cobras, the planet Jupiter, and Russia, they use description.

Sequence

Writers list items or events in numerical or chronological order. Words that signal the sequence structure include *first, second, third, next, then,* and *finally.* Students use this structure when they write directions for completing a math problem, steps in the life cycle of a plant or animal, or events in a biography.

Comparison

Writers explain how two or more things are alike or how they are different. *Different, in contrast, alike, same as,* and *on the other hand* are words and phrases that signal this structure. When students compare and contrast book and movie versions of a story, insects with spiders, or life in colonial America with life today, they use this organizational pattern.

Cause and Effect

Writers explain one or more causes and the resulting effects. *Reasons why, if . . . then, as a result, therefore,* and *because* are words and phrases that signal this structure. Students write explanations of why the dinosaurs became extinct, the effects of pollution on the environment, or the causes of the American Revolution using the cause-and-effect pattern.

Problem and Solution

Writers state a problem and provide one or more solutions to the problem. A variation is the question-and-answer format, in which the writer poses a question and then answers it. Cue words and phrases include *the problem is, the puzzle is, solve,* and *question . . . answer.* When students write about why money was invented, saving endangered animals, and building dams to stop flooding, they use this structure. Also, students often use the problem-and-solution pattern in writing advertisements and other persuasive writing. These patterns are summarized in Figure 10–3.

Diagrams called graphic organizers can be created to help students organize ideas for these organizational patterns (P. L. Smith & Tompkins, 1988). Sample diagrams of the graphic organizers are also presented in Figure 10–3.

Reading researchers identified these five patterns by examining content-area reading materials to devise ways to help students comprehend those materials more easily. Most of the research on expository text structures has focused on

Pattern	Description	Graphic Organizer	Sample Passage
Description	The author describes a topic by listing characteristics, features, and examples. Cue words are: *for example* *characteristics are*		The Olympic symbol consists of five interlocking rings. The rings represent the five continents—Africa, Asia, Europe, North America, and South America—from which athletes come to compete in the games. The rings are colored black, blue, green, red, and yellow. At least one of these colors is found in the flag of every country sending athletes to compete in the Olympic games.
Sequence	The author lists items or events in numerical or chronological order. Cue words are: *first, second, third* *next* *then* *finally*	1. ___ 2. ___ 3. ___ 4. ___ 5. ___	The Olympic games began as athletic festivals to honor the Greek gods. The most important festival was held in the valley of Olympia to honor Zeus, the king of the gods. It was this festival that became the Olympic games in 776 B.C. These games were ended in A.D. 394 by the Roman Emperor who ruled Greece. No Olympic games were held for more than 1,500 years. Then the modern Olympics began in 1896. Almost 300 male athletes competed in the first modern Olympics. In the games held in 1900, female athletes were allowed to compete. The games have continued every four years since 1896 except during World War II, and they will most likely continue for many years to come.
Comparison	The author explains how two or more things are alike and/or how they are different. Cue words are: *different* *in contrast* *alike* *same as* *on the other hand*		The modern Olympics is very unlike the ancient Olympic games. Individual events are different. While there were no swimming races in the ancient games, for example, there were chariot races. There were no female contestants and all athletes competed in the nude. Of course, the ancient and modern Olympics are also alike in many ways. Some events, such as the javelin and discus throws, are the same. Some people say that cheating, professionalism, and nationalism in the modern games are a disgrace to the Olympic tradition. But according to the ancient Greek writers, there were many cases of cheating, nationalism, and professionalism in their Olympics, too.

Figure 10–3 The five expository text structures

Pattern	Description	Graphic Organizer	Sample Passage
Cause and Effect	The author lists one or more causes and the resulting effect or effects. Cue words are: *reasons why* *if . . . then* *as a result* *therefore* *because*	Cause → Effect #1, Effect #2, Effect #3	There are several reasons why so many people attend the Olympic games or watch them on television. One reason is tradition. The name *Olympics* and the torch and flame remind people of the ancient games. People can escape the ordinariness of daily life by attending or watching the Olympics. They like to identify with someone else's individual sacrifice and accomplishment. National pride is another reason, and an athlete's or a team's hard-earned victory becomes a nation's victory. There are national medal counts and people keep track of how many medals their country's athletes have won.
Problem and Solution	The author states a problem and lists one or more solutions for the problem. A variation of this pattern is the question-and-answer format in which the author poses a question and then answers it. Cue words are: *problem is* *dilemma is* *puzzle is* *solved* *question . . .* *answer*	Problem → Solution	One problem with the modern Olympics is that it has become very big and expensive to operate. The city or country that hosts the games often loses a lot of money. A stadium, pools, and playing fields must be built for the athletic events and housing is needed for the athletes who come from around the world. And all of these facilities are used for only 2 weeks! In 1984, Los Angeles solved these problems by charging a fee for companies who wanted to be official sponsors of the games. Companies like McDonald's paid a lot of money to be part of the Olympics. Many buildings that were already built in the Los Angeles area were also used. The Coliseum where the 1932 games were held was used again and many colleges and universities in the area became playing and living sites.

Figure 10–3 *continued*

older students' use of these patterns in reading; however, elementary students also use the patterns and cue words in their writing.

How Children Apply the Patterns

Just as children develop a concept of story and learn specific information about story structures, they learn about the organization of informational books and apply what they have learned as they write about information. A class of second graders examined the five expository text structures and learned that authors use cue words as a "secret code" to signal the structures. They read informational books exemplifying each of the expository text structures, and after reading, they wrote paragraphs to share what they had learned. Working in small groups, they developed graphic organizers and added main ideas and details from their reading. Then they wrote paragraphs modeling each of the five organizational patterns. These graphic organizers and paragraphs are presented in Figure 10–4. The cue words in each paragraph appear in boldface type. The minilesson feature on page 318 shows how an eighth-grade teacher used the sequence structure in a minilesson about writing instructions.

Types of Expository Writing

Contrary to the popular assumption that young children's first writing is narrative, educators have found that kindergartners and first graders write many nonnarrative compositions in which they provide information about familiar topics, such as "Signs of Fall," or write directions for familiar activities, such as "How to Feed Your Pet" (Bonin, 1988; Sowers, 1985). Children in the middle grades continue to use expository writing to search for answers to questions that interest them and write both class and individual reports (Krogness, 1987; Queenan, 1986). Through early, successful experiences with expository writing, students not only learn how to write research reports but also gain knowledge in different subject areas.

"All About . . ." Books

Young children write entire booklets on a single topic, and these small booklets are known as "All About . . ." books. Usually one piece of information and an illustration are presented on each page. An example of an "All About . . ." book is presented in Figure 10–5. First grader David wrote an "All About . . ." book about sea animals as a part of a unit on the sea. Notice that David numbered each page of his book, 1 through 4, in the upper right corner of the page. Then he added a cover, and after a minute of confusion, he added a zero to the cover so that each page would be numbered. David used invented spelling for many words in his report, but the information can be deciphered easily. Also, on page

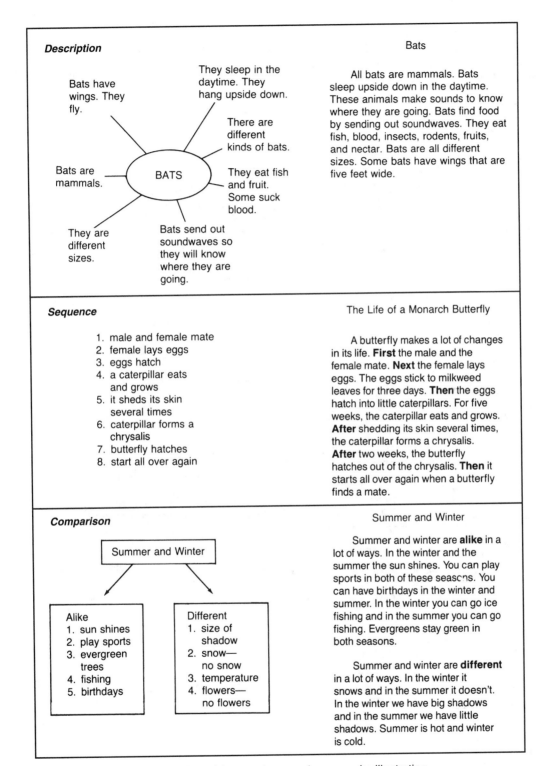

Description

Bats have wings. They fly.

They sleep in the daytime. They hang upside down.

There are different kinds of bats.

Bats are mammals.

BATS

They eat fish and fruit. Some suck blood.

They are different sizes.

Bats send out soundwaves so they will know where they are going.

Bats

All bats are mammals. Bats sleep upside down in the daytime. These animals make sounds to know where they are going. Bats find food by sending out soundwaves. They eat fish, blood, insects, rodents, fruits, and nectar. Bats are all different sizes. Some bats have wings that are five feet wide.

Sequence

1. male and female mate
2. female lays eggs
3. eggs hatch
4. a caterpillar eats and grows
5. it sheds its skin several times
6. caterpillar forms a chrysalis
7. butterfly hatches
8. start all over again

The Life of a Monarch Butterfly

A butterfly makes a lot of changes in its life. **First** the male and the female mate. **Next** the female lays eggs. The eggs stick to milkweed leaves for three days. **Then** the eggs hatch into little caterpillars. For five weeks, the caterpillar eats and grows. **After** shedding its skin several times, the caterpillar forms a chrysalis. **After** two weeks, the butterfly hatches out of the chrysalis. **Then** it starts all over again when a butterfly finds a mate.

Comparison

Summer and Winter

Alike
1. sun shines
2. play sports
3. evergreen trees
4. fishing
5. birthdays

Different
1. size of shadow
2. snow— no snow
3. temperature
4. flowers— no flowers

Summer and Winter

Summer and winter are **alike** in a lot of ways. In the winter and the summer the sun shines. You can play sports in both of these seasons. You can have birthdays in the winter and summer. In the winter you can go ice fishing and in the summer you can go fishing. Evergreens stay green in both seasons.

Summer and winter are **different** in a lot of ways. In the winter it snows and in the summer it doesn't. In the winter we have big shadows and in the summer we have little shadows. Summer is hot and winter is cold.

Figure 10–4 Second graders' graphic organizers and paragraphs illustrating the five expository text structures

continues

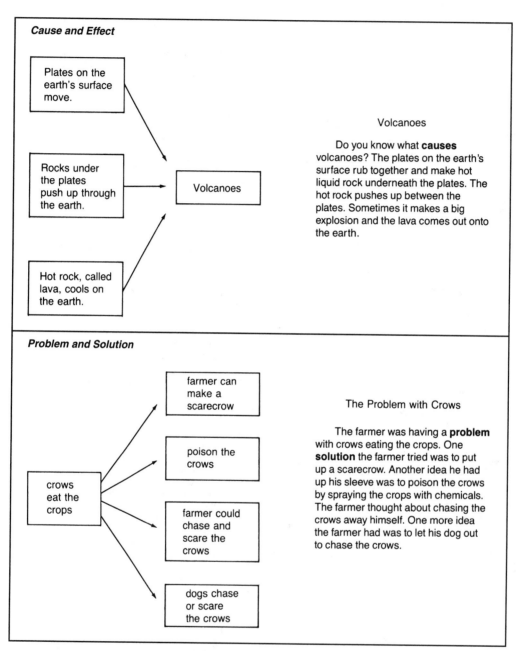

Cause and Effect

Plates on the earth's surface move.

Rocks under the plates push up through the earth. → Volcanoes

Hot rock, called lava, cools on the earth.

Volcanoes

Do you know what **causes** volcanoes? The plates on the earth's surface rub together and make hot liquid rock underneath the plates. The hot rock pushes up between the plates. Sometimes it makes a big explosion and the lava comes out onto the earth.

Problem and Solution

farmer can make a scarecrow

poison the crows

crows eat the crops

farmer could chase and scare the crows

dogs chase or scare the crows

The Problem with Crows

The farmer was having a **problem** with crows eating the crops. One **solution** the farmer tried was to put up a scarecrow. Another idea he had up his sleeve was to poison the crows by spraying the crops with chemicals. The farmer thought about chasing the crows away himself. One more idea the farmer had was to let his dog out to chase the crows.

Figure 10–4 *continued*

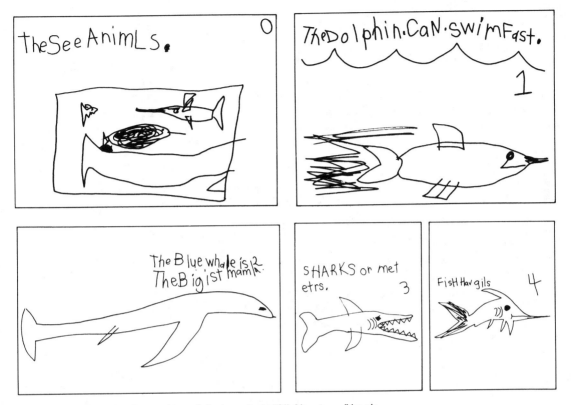

Figure 10–5 Independent writing: A first grader's "All About . . ." book

1, David was experimenting with word boundaries and chose to use a dot to mark the division between words that he recognized as separate. He considered "The dolphin" and "swim fast" as single units. When he wrote other pages, David's attention changed and he focused on other dimensions of writing.

An "All About . . ." book can be a collaborative production in which each child contributes one page for the book. For example, as part of the unit on insects, primary-grade children collected some ladybugs to observe in the classroom and read several books about these distinctive insects. Then, working in small groups, children brainstormed a list of facts they had learned about ladybugs. Next, the children each chose one fact from the list, or another piece of information if they preferred, for their page. They wrote the information interactively and added an illustration. Their teacher collected the pages, included a sheet at the end of the book called "How We Learned about Ladybugs," and then added a cover made of construction paper. Here is the group's report:

Page 1: There are about 600 kinds of ladybugs.
Page 2: Ladybugs are supposed to bring you good luck.

Writing Instructions

Mr. LeBeau's eighth graders are learning to write instructions in preparation for his district's quarterly writing assessment. The students began by examining instructions on food packages, games, and household appliances and identifying the characteristics of clear, well-sequenced instructions. Next, they wrote instructions for making a peanut butter and jelly sandwich, and their classmates tried to follow the instructions to actually make a sandwich. Afterwards, they revised their instructions to make them clearer. The purpose of today's minilesson is for the students to assess the sandwich-making instructions written by students in another of Mr. LeBeau's classes using the district's rubric for technical writing.

1. Introduce the topic

Mr. LeBeau explains that he has made copies of five students' sandwich-making instructions that he wants them to read and assess. (The students' names were covered before the copies were made.)

2. Share examples

Mr. LeBeau passes out copies of two students' papers and asks the students to read the papers and compare them. The students discuss the papers and agree that the second one is stronger because the instructions are more concise and easier to follow. Then he passes out a third paper for the students to read and compare to the other two. This paper, the students conclude, is even better than the other two because the student has used spatial detail words, such as *underneath* and *top.*

3. Provide information

The teacher passes out copies of the district's 4-point technical writing rubric and the students use it to score the three papers. One paper is ranked a 2, the second a 3, and the third a 4. The students provide reasons for ranking each paper as they did.

4. Guide practice

Students divide into groups of two to read and assess two more student papers. They score one paper as a 2 and the other as a 3 and give reasons to support their scores. Next, Mr. LeBeau asks students how they might revise these papers to improve the scores.

5. Assess learning

Students use the rubric to self-assess their compositions and then make revisions if they do not score at least a 3, because a score of 3 is considered "on grade level." Later, Mr. LeBeau conferences with students to discuss their rankings.

Page 3: Ladybugs pretend to be dead when frightened.

Page 4: Ladybugs like the rain.

Page 5: Ladybugs spend the winter in pinecones, cracks, under leaves, and even in houses sleeping and waiting for spring.

Page 6: Ladybugs don't bite!

Page 7: How We Learned about Ladybugs:

    1. We watched three ladybugs that we kept in a jar in our classroom.

    2. We read these books: *Insects* by Illa Podendorf, 1981. *Ladybug, Ladybug, Fly Away Home* by Judy Hawes, 1967.

Collaborative Reports

Small groups of children work together to write collaborative reports. Each child writes a section, and then they compile their sections to form the report. Students benefit from writing a group report, first, because the group provides a scaffold or support system, and second, because the laborious parts of the work are shared by group members.

A group of four fourth graders wrote a collaborative report on hermit crabs. These children sat together at a table and watched the hermit crabs that lived in a terrarium on their table. They cared for these crustaceans for 2 weeks and recorded their observations in learning logs. After this period, the children were bursting with questions about the hermit crabs and were eager for answers. They wanted to know what the crabs' real habitat was, what the best habitat was for them in the classroom, how they breathed air, why they lived in borrowed shells, why one pincer was bigger than the other, and so on. Their teacher gave some answers and directed them to books that would provide additional information. As they collected information, the students created a cluster that they taped to their table next to the terrarium. Soon the cluster wasn't an adequate way to report information, so they decided to share their knowledge by writing a book they called "The Encyclopedia About Hermit Crabs." This book and the cluster used in gathering information for it are presented in Figure 10–6.

The children decided to share the work of writing the book, and they chose four main ideas, one for each student to write. The four main ideas were what hermit crabs look like, how they act, where they live, and what they eat. One student wrote each section and then returned to the group to share the rough draft. The children gave each other suggestions for revisions. Next they edited their report with the teacher and added an introduction, a conclusion, and a bibliography.

> **ELL** **Teacher's Note: Assisting English Language Learners**
>
> Second-language learners are often more successful when they write collaborative reports because they benefit from working with a partner or in a small group. Students share content-area knowledge and vocabulary, English fluency, and writing skills when they collaborate. In addition, the teacher is not overwhelmed trying to help students to revise and edit their writing because students are not writing as many compositions at the same time.

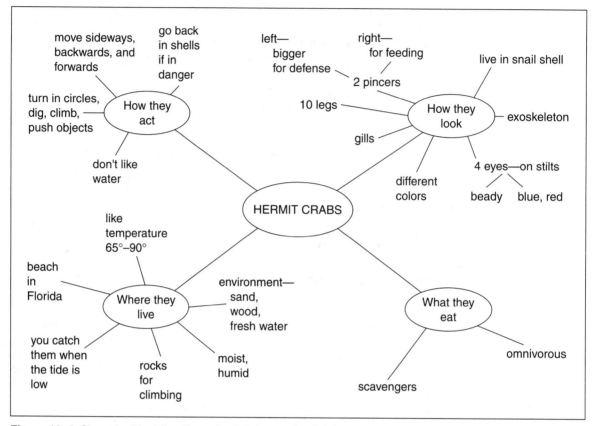

Figure 10–6 Shared writing: Fourth graders' cluster and collaborative report on hermit crabs

Finally, they recopied their report and added illustrations in a clothbound book that they read to each class in the school before adding it to the school library.

Individual Reports

Toby Fulwiler (1985) recommends that children do authentic research in which they explore topics that interest them or hunt for answers to questions that puzzle them. As children become immersed in thematic units, questions arise that they want to explore. For example, students in a fourth-grade class were studying dinosaurs, and they quickly asked more questions than the teacher could answer. She encouraged them to search for answers in the books they had

---

The Encyclopedia About Hermit Crabs

How They Look
Hermit crabs are very much like regular crabs but hermit crabs transfer shells. They have gills. Why? Because they are born in water and when they mature they come to land and kill snails so they can have a shell. They have two beady eyes that look like they are on stilts. Their body is a sight! Their shell looks like a rock. Really it is an exoskeleton which means the skeleton is on the outside. They have two pincers. The left one is bigger so it is used for defense. The right one is for feeding. They also have ten legs.

Where They Live
Hermit crabs live mostly on beaches in Florida where the weather is 65°–90°. They live in fresh water. They like humid weather and places that have sand, wood, and rocks (for climbing on). The best time to catch hermit crabs is a low tide.

What They Eat
Hermit crabs are omnivorous scavengers which means they eat just about any-thing. They even eat left-overs.

How They Act
Hermit crabs are very unusual. They go back into their shell if they think there is danger. They are funny because they walk sideways, forwards, and backwards. They can go in circles. They can also get up when they get upside down. And that's how they act.

Figure 10–6 *continued*

checked out of the school and community public libraries. As they located answers to their questions, the children were eager to share their new knowledge and decided to write reports and publish them as books.

A fourth grader's "The World of the Dinosaurs" is presented in Figure 10–7. His report is divided into three chapters, and he also included a table of contents, a bibliography, and an "All About the Author" page at the end. Each chapter focuses on a question he examined. The first chapter, "The Death Star," was written to answer his question about how the dinosaurs became extinct. He wrote the chapter on the three periods to answer his question about whether or not the dinosaurs all lived at the same time. In the third chapter, the child wrote a description of the pterodactyl, an unusual flying lizard that lived when the dinosaurs did. He chose this topic after locating an interesting book about these flying lizards.

The World of the Dinosaurs

Chapter 1
The Death Star

Over the years scientists have noticed that almost all stars have a sister star. But what about the sun? Scientists have found out that the sun does have a sister star. It's darker than the sun, and it takes 28 million years to orbit around our solar system. They named it Nemesis after the Greek god of revenge. When Nemesis reaches its closest point to the sun, it makes the asteroid belt go beserk! Asteroids and comets were flying everywhere! The earth was a disaster! Scientists have studied and found out that if a comet or an asteroid hit the earth it would be like dropping an atomic bomb (or a thousand billion tons of dynamite) on the earth. Whenever that happens, almost everything on the face of the earth is destroyed. The next time Nemesis reaches its closest point to the sun will be in about fifteen million years.

Chapter 2
The Three Periods: Triassic, Jurassic, and Cretaceous

There were three periods when the dinosaurs came, and then they were just wiped off the face of the earth. It may have been the Death Star. Whatever the reason, nobody knows. The three periods were the Triassic, Jurassic, and the Cretaceous.

Most of the smaller animals like Orniholestes and Hysilophodon came in the Triassic Period. They were mostly plant eaters.

Most of the flying dinosaurs like Pteradactyl and Pteranadon came in the Jurassic Period. A number of the big plant eaters like Brontosaurus and Brachiosaurus also came in that period. A lot of sea reptiles came in that time, too.

The bigger dinosaurs like Tyrannosaurus Rex and Trachodon came in the Cretaceous Period. Most of these were meat eaters.

Chapter 3
Pterodactyl: The Flying Lizard

The Pterodactyl is a flying lizard that lived millions of years ago when the dinosaurs lived. Pterodactyl means "flying lizard." It was a huge animal. It had skin stretched between the hind limb and a long digit of the forelimb. It didn't have any feathers. Some had a wingspan of 20 feet. Some paleontologists think Pterodactyl slept like a bat, upside down, because of the shape of its wings. It had a long beak and very sharp teeth. When it would hunt for food, it would fly close to the water and look for fish. When it saw one, it would dive in and get it. It also had sharp claws that helped it grab things. The Pterodactyl had a strange looking tail. It was long with a ball shape at the end. Some people say it really looked like a flying lizard.

Figure 10–7 Independent writing: A fourth grader's dinosaur report

ABC Books

Children can use the letters of the alphabet to organize the information they want to share in an ABC (or alphabet) book. These report books incorporate the sequence structure because the pages are arranged in alphabetical order. ABC books such as *Ashanti to Zulu: African Traditions* (Musgrove, 1976), about African cultures, *Eight Hands Round: A Patchwork Alphabet* (Paul, 1991), about quilting, and *Illuminations* (Hunt, 1989), about medieval life, can be used as models. Children begin by brainstorming information related to the topic being studied and identify a word or fact for each letter of the alphabet. Then children work individually, in pairs, or in small groups to compose pages for the book. The format for the pages is similar to the one used in ABC books by professional authors: Students write the letter in one corner of the page, draw an illustration, and write a sentence or paragraph to describe the word or fact. The text usually begins "_____ is for _____," and then a sentence or paragraph description follows. The *H* page from a sixth-grade class's ABC book is presented in Figure 10–8.

Riddles

Children can compose riddles to share information they have discovered. Riddles use a question-and-answer format and incorporate two or three facts, or clues, in the question part. Sometimes the answer is written upside down on the page, on the back of the page with the question, or on the next page of a book. The writing process is important for creating riddles, and during the revising stage, students make sure they have provided essential descriptive information and that the information is correct.

Small groups of children or the whole class can compose books of riddles related to social studies or science themes. During a study of life in the desert, first graders wrote these riddles as part of a class book:

I live in underground cities of tunnels.
I get my name from my barking cry.
I eat grass and other plants.
What am I? (a prairie dog)

I fly in wide circles above the earth.
I sometimes am called a buzzard.
What am I? (a vulture)

Posters, Diagrams, and Charts

Children can make posters, diagrams, and charts to learn and share information. They might make murals, design clusters, draw Venn diagrams, make graphs, draw maps, and do many other types of projects. In these projects,

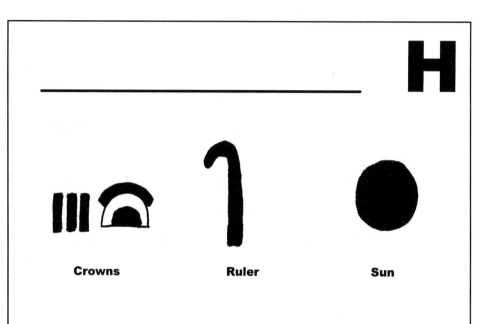

Figure 10–8 Guided writing: A page from a sixth-grade ABC book on ancient Egypt

 Teacher's Note: Assisting
English Language Learners

Is report writing too much for your English language learners? These students may be able to make a visual report that combines words and drawing to share their knowledge. Students use a process approach to design and make a poster, diagram, or chart. Many English language learners show artistic flair, and teachers can help students take advantage of their strengths when they create visual reports individually or in small groups.

students combine drawing and writing to apply the expository text structures. Here are some examples:

- *Description.* As part of a study of medieval life, seventh graders draw diagrams and label the parts of a castle or fortress. Second graders make a poster with information and a drawing of an insect.

- *Sequence.* After reading *The Very Hungry Caterpillar* (Carle, 1969), first graders draw circle diagrams to illustrate the life cycle of a butterfly.
- *Comparison and contrast.* Fourth graders make Venn diagrams (two interlocking circles, one labeled "Then" and the other "Now") to compare and contrast pioneer life with life today. Kindergartners make posters to illustrate each of the four seasons.
- *Cause and effect.* As a part of a drug abuse program, sixth graders make posters to point out the effects of smoking, drugs, and drinking.
- *Problem and solution.* During a thematic unit on ecology, eighth graders work in small groups to brainstorm a chart of ecological problems and ways to solve them. Third graders make posters showing ways to save energy as part of a science theme on natural resources.

Cubes

A cube has six sides, and in this expository writing activity, students explore a topic from six dimensions or sides by doing the following:

1. *Describe it.* Describe its colors, shapes, and sizes.
2. *Compare it.* What is it similar to or different from?
3. *Associate it.* What does it make you think of?
4. *Analyze it.* Tell how it is made or what it is composed of.
5. *Apply it.* What can you do with it? How is it used?
6. *Argue for or against it.* Take a stand and list reasons supporting it.

Almost any topic can be examined from these six dimensions, from earthquakes to the California gold rush, from eagles to microcomputers, from the Great Wall of China to ancient Egypt. Figure 10–9 presents a sixth-grade class's cube on junk food that was written as part of a theme on nutrition.

Children often work together in small groups to do a cube. Students divide into six groups, and each group examines the topic from one dimension. Together, they develop a paragraph or two to explore their dimension. Children brainstorm ideas, use the ideas to develop a paragraph or two, revise, and edit. Then one student in the group writes the final copy. All six groups share their writing with the class. The final copies can be taped to a large square box and displayed in the classroom.

Multigenre Projects

Students explore a science or social studies topic through several genres in a multigenre project (Allen, 2001; Romano, 1995, 2000). They combine content-area study with writing in significant and meaningful ways. Tom Romano

Junk Food

1. Describe It

Junk food is delicious! Some junk food is made of chocolate, like chocolate ice cream and brownies. Some junk food is salty, like potato chips and pretzels. Other junk food is usually sweet or sugary, like sugar cookies, sweet rolls, or soft drinks. Junk food packages are colorful and often show you what's inside to get your attention. Most of the packages are made of paper or plastic, and they make crinkly sounds.

2. Compare It

Junk food tastes better than nutritious food, but nutritious food is better for you. Nutritious food is less sweet and salty. Parents would rather you eat nutritious food than junk food because nutritious food keeps you healthy, but kids would rather eat junk food because it tastes better and is more fun to eat.

3. Associate It

Most often you eat junk food at get-togethers with friends. At parties, junk food such as chips and dip and soft drinks are served. At movies, you can buy popcorn, candy, nachos, and many other kinds of junk food. Other places where people get together and eat junk food are skating rinks, sporting events, and concerts.

4. Analyze It

Junk food is not good to eat because of all the oils, sugar, salt, and calories. Most of them have artificial colorings and flavorings. Many junk foods are low in vitamins and protein, but they have a high percentage of fats.

5. Apply It

The most important thing you can do with junk food is to eat it. Some other uses are popcorn decorations at Christmas time, Halloween treats, and Easter candy. You can sell it to raise money for charities, clubs, and schools. Last year we sold junk food to raise money for the Statue of Liberty.

6. Argue for or Against It

We're for junk food because it tastes good. Even though it's not good for you, people like it and buy it. If there were no more junk food, a lot of people would be unemployed, such as dentists. Bakeries, convenience stores, fast food restaurants, grocery stores, and ice cream parlors would lose a lot of business if people didn't buy junk food. The Declaration of Independence guarantees our rights and freedoms, and Thomas Jefferson might have said, "Life, Liberty, and the Pursuit of Junk Food." We believe that he who wants something pleasing shall have it!

Figure 10–9 Guided writing: A sixth-grade collaborative cubing on junk food
From "Rx for Writer's Block," by G. E. Tompkins and D. J. Camp, 1988, *Childhood Education, 64,* p. 213. Copyright © 1988 by the Association for Childhood Education International. Reprinted with permission.

(2000) explains that the benefit of this approach is that each genre offers ways of learning and understanding that the others do not. Students gain different understandings, for example, by writing a simulated journal entry and by writing a riddle. Teachers or students identify a repetend, a common thread or unifying feature for the project, which helps students move beyond the level of remembering facts to a deeper, more analytical or critical comprehension level.

Students use a variety of genres for their projects, depending on the information they want to present and their repetend. Figure 10–10 presents a list of 25 genres, including clusters, reports, poems, maps, letters, and data charts, that elementary students can use in their multigenre projects. Students usually incorporate three or more genres in a multigenre project and include both textual and visual genres. What matters most is that the genres amplify and extend the repetend.

The design of a third-grade class's multigenre project on honeybees is presented in Figure 10–11. The class studied bees as part of an agriculture unit, and they learned how the insects help farmers pollinate crops. The multigenre project included these seven textual and visual genres:

1. *Collage.* Students created a collage of honeybee words and pictures cut from magazines, and the title was printed over the collage.

2. *True or False Flip Books.* Students used facts on the KWL chart to write flip books with true or false statements about honeybees. The statement is written on the first page and the answer on the second page. For example:

First page: Bees do not communicate.
Second page: False. Bees communicate by dancing.

3. *Advertisements.* Students wrote advertisements from the viewpoint of a farmer who needs bees to pollinate the crops or from the viewpoint of a bee who offers the colony's services to farmers.

4. *I Can Poems.* Students assumed the role of a queen, drone, or worker bee and wrote a poem from that bee's viewpoint. For example:

I am a busy worker bee.
I gather food for the colony.
I build combs with wax from my body.
I defend the hive from our enemies.
I am a brave worker bee.

5. *Honeybees Help Us! Chart.* Students drew pictures of four ways honeybees help people and wrote paragraph-long explanations to accompany the pictures.

6. *Word Cards.* Students wrote key vocabulary words on word cards and drew and wrote definitions. Words included *pollinate, drone, migrate, hive, communicate, comb, metamorphosis,* and *swarm.*

acrostics	Students spell a key word vertically and then write a phrase or sentence beginning with each letter to create a poem or other composition.
biographical sketch	Students write a biographical sketch of a person related to the topic being studied.
cartoons	Students draw a cartoon or copy a published cartoon from a book or Internet article.
charts	Students organize and display textual and visual information on a chart.
clusters	Students draw clusters or other diagrams to display information concisely.
cubes	Students examine a topic from six perspectives.
data charts	Students create a data chart to list and compare information.
found poems	Students collect words and phrases from a book or article and arrange the words and phrases to make a poem.
"I am" poems	Students create an "I am" poem about a person or a topic.
letters	Students write simulated letters or make copies of real letters related to the topic.
life lines	Students draw life lines and mark important dates related to a person's life.
maps	Students make copies of actual maps or draw maps related to the topic.
newspaper articles	Students make copies of actual newspaper articles or write simulated articles related to the topic.
open-mind portraits	Students draw open-mind portraits of people related to the topic.
photos	Students download photos from the Internet or make copies of photos in books.
postcards	Students create postcards with a picture on one side and a message on the other.
questions-answers	Students write a series of questions and answers related to the topic.
quotes	Students collect quotes about the topic from materials they are reading.
riddles	Students write riddles with information related to the topic.
simulated journals	Students write simulated-journal entries from the viewpoint of a person related to the topic.
songs	Students write lyrics about the topic that are sung to familiar tunes.
stories	Students write stories related to the topic.
time lines	Students draw time lines to sequence events related to the topic.
Venn diagrams	Students draw Venn diagrams to compare the topic with something else.
word wall	Students make an alphabetized word wall or word cards of key words related to the topic.

Figure 10–10 Genres for multigenre projects

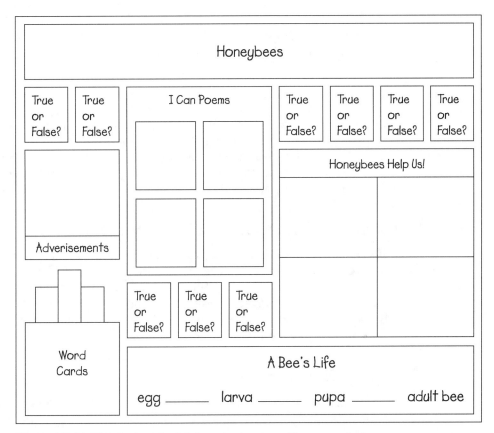

Figure 10–11 The design of a third-grade class's multigenre project

7. *Life Line.* Students drew a bee's life cycle, showing the stages that bees move through during the first 21 days of their lives from egg to adult.

The teacher displayed the multigenre project in the classroom, and the students often stopped to reread the true-false booklets, review the word cards, look at the advertisements placed in a pocket on the chart, or study some other part of the project.

Not only can elementary students create multigenre projects, but some authors/illustrators use the technique in children's trade books; *The Magic School Bus on the Ocean Floor* (Cole, 1992) and other books in the Magic School Bus series are examples of multigenre books. Each book features a story about Ms. Frizzle and her students on a fantastic science adventure, and on the side panels of pages, a variety of explanations, charts, diagrams, and essays are presented. Together, the story and the informational side panels present a more complete, multigenre presentation or project. Other multigenre books for older students are *To Be a Slave* (Lester, 1998), *Nothing But the Truth* (Avi, 1991), *Tears of a Tiger* (Draper, 1994), and *Ernest Lawrence Thayer's Casey at the Bat: A Ballad of the Republic Sung in the Year 1888* (Bing, 2000).

Teaching Children About Expository Writing

Expository writing is an important component of writing programs for elementary students because children enjoy learning information during thematic units and sharing the information in books they write. Teachers introduce children to the five expository text structures and provide many opportunities for them to write a variety of informational books.

Introducing the Expository Text Structures

Children learn to recognize expository patterns and use them to improve their reading comprehension as well as to organize their writing (Flood, Lapp, & Farnan, 1986; McGee & Richgels, 1985; Piccolo, 1987). Teachers teach students about the five expository text structures through a series of minilessons that involve both reading and writing. The steps in the instructional strategy are listed in the step-by-step feature on page 331.

Writing Collaborative Reports

Students learn how to write reports through a series of minilessons and several experiences writing class collaboration reports. Through the minilessons, teachers explain how to choose a topic, design research questions, use the writing process to develop and refine the report, and write a bibliography. Then students practice what they have learned as they work with partners or in small groups to write collaborative reports. Through these experiences, students gain both the expertise and the confidence to write individual reports.

Children use the writing process as they search for answers to questions about a topic and then compose a report to share what they have learned. Reports are usually written in connection with theme studies, but some students enjoy expository writing or have special interests that they research and write about during writing workshop. Sometimes thematic units extend throughout much of the school day, and students read books related to the theme during reading workshop and write a research report related to the theme during writing workshop.

Teacher's Note: Supporting Struggling Writers

Is plagiarism a problem in your classroom? Struggling writers sometimes resort to copying information from encyclopedias and other reference books when they don't know how to write a report. Learning to use the process approach to writing is the answer. Students need to learn how to take notes from books using a graphic organizer and then develop the notes into sentences and paragraphs when they write the rough draft.

Step by Step: Expository Text Structures

1. *Introduce an organizational pattern.* Teachers explain the pattern and when writers use it, note cue words that signal the pattern, share an example of the pattern, and then describe the graphic organizer for that pattern.

2. *Analyze examples of the pattern in trade books.* Students locate examples of the expository text structure in informational books, not in stories. A list of informational books illustrating the five expository structures is presented in Figure 10–12. Sometimes the pattern is signaled clearly using titles, topic sentences, and cue words, and sometimes it is not. Students identify cue words when they are used, and they talk about why writers may or may not explicitly signal the structure. They also diagram the structure using a graphic organizer. Moss, Leone, and DiPillo (1997) report that students learn about expository text by reading and examining informational books.

3. *Write paragraphs using the pattern.* After students analyze examples of the pattern in informational books, they write paragraphs using the pattern. The first writing activity may be a whole-class activity. Later, students write paragraphs in small groups and individually. For prewriting activities, students choose a topic, gather information, and organize it using a graphic organizer. Next, they write a rough draft of the paragraph, inserting cue words to signal the structure. Then they revise, edit, and write a final copy of the paragraph.

4. *Repeat for each pattern.* Students repeat the first three steps for each of the five expository text structures. Once students have learned the organizational patterns, they are ready to use them in their writing.

5. *Choose the most appropriate pattern to communicate effectively.* After students learn to use each of the five expository text structures, they need to learn to choose the most appropriate pattern to communicate effectively. Students can experiment to see the appropriateness of various patterns by writing paragraphs using different organizational patterns for one set of information. For example, information about igloos might be written as a description, as a comparison with Indian teepees, or as a solution to a housing problem in the Arctic region.

Children work with partners or in small groups to write collaborative reports in connection with theme studies. Class collaboration reports are a good way for students to learn the steps involved in writing a report and to gain experience working through the writing process without the complexities of writing individual reports. The steps are explained in the step-by-step feature on page 333.

Description

Arnosky, J. (1995). *All about owls.* New York: Scholastic. (P–M)

de Bourgoing, P. (1995). *Under the ground.* New York: Scholastic. (P)

Fowler, A. (1990). *It could still be a bird.* Chicago: Childrens Press. (P–M)

Gibbons, G. (1995). *Sea turtles.* New York: Holiday House. (P)

Patent, D. H. (1992). *Feathers.* New York: Cobblehill. (M–U)

Pringle, L. (1995). *Coral reefs: Earth's undersea treasures.* New York: Simon & Schuster. (U)

Sequence

Aliki. (1992). *Milk from cow to carton.* New York: HarperCollins. (P–M)

Gibbons, G. (1995). *Planet earth/inside out.* New York: Morrow. (M)

Matthews, D. (1995). *Arctic foxes.* New York: Simon & Schuster. (P)

Provensen, A. (1990). *The buck stops here.* New York: HarperCollins. (M–U)

Steltzer, U. (1995). *Building an igloo.* New York: Holt. (P–M)

Wadsworth, G. (1995). *Giant sequoia trees.* Chicago: Lerner. (P–M)

Comparison

Gibbons, G. (1984). *Fire! Fire!* New York: Harper & Row. (P–M)

Lasker, J. (1976). *Merry ever after: The story of two medieval weddings.* New York: Viking. (M–U)

Markle, S. (1993). *Outside and inside trees.* New York: Bradbury Press. (M)

Rauzon, M. J. (1993). *Horns, antlers, fangs, and tusks.* New York: Lothrop, Lee & Shepard. (P–M)

Singer, M. (1995). *A wasp is not a bee.* New York: Holt. (P)

Spier, P. (1987). *We the people.* New York: Doubleday. (M–U)

Cause and Effect

Branley, F. M. (1985). *Volcanoes.* New York: Harper & Row. (P–M)

Branley, F. M. (1986). *What makes day and night?* New York: Harper & Row. (P–M)

Casey, D. (1995). *Weather everywhere.* New York: Macmillan. (P)

Heller, R. (1983). *The reason for a flower.* New York: Grosset & Dunlap. (M)

Lauber, P. (1995) *Who eats what? Food chains and food webs.* New York: HarperCollins. (M)

Showers, P. (1985). *What happens to a hamburger?* New York: Harper & Row. (P–M)

Zoehfeld, K. W. (1995). *How mountains are made.* New York: HarperCollins. (M)

Problem and Solution

Arnosky, J. (1995). *I see animals hiding.* New York: Scholastic. (P)

Colman, P. (1995). *Rosie the riveter: Women working on the home front in World War II.* New York: Crown. (U)

Geisert, B. (1995). *Haystack.* Boston: Houghton Mifflin. (P)

Heller, R. (1986). *How to hide a whippoorwill and other birds.* New York: Grosset & Dunlap. (P–M)

Johnson, S. A. (1995). *Raptor rescue! An eagle flies free.* New York: Dutton. (M)

Lauber, P. (1990). *How we learned the earth is round.* New York: Crowell. (P–M)

Rounds, G. (1995). *Sod houses on the Great Plains.* New York: Holiday House. (M)

Combination

Aliki. (1981). *Digging up dinosaurs.* New York: Harper & Row. (M)

Coombs, K. M. (1995). *Flush! Treating wastewater.* Minneapolis: Carolrhoda. (M–U)

George, J. C. (1995). *Everglades.* New York: HarperCollins. (M)

Guiberson, B. Z. (1991). *Cactus hotel.* New York: Henry Holt. (P–M)

Patent, D. H. (1995). *Why mammals have fur.* New York: Cobblehill. (P)

Figure 10–12 Informational books representing the expository text structures
P = primary grades (K–2), M = middle grades (3–5), U = upper grades (6–8).

Step by Step: Collaborative Reports

1. **_Choose a topic._** The teacher chooses a broad topic related to what students are studying or want to study for the collaborative research project. Almost any topic in social studies or science that can be subdivided into 4 to 10 parts works well for class reports.

2. **_Design research questions._** As students study the topic, research questions emerge. Partway through the unit, students brainstorm a list of possible questions that are posted on a chart in the classroom, and new questions are added as they are suggested.

3. **_Write one section together as a class._** The teacher chooses a question that no one has chosen and models how to write a section of the report, demonstrating the procedures that students are to use.

4. **_Gather and organize information._** Students choose a research question from the brainstormed list and work in pairs or small groups to read and find answers to their question. These questions provide the structure for data collection. Students take notes and use clusters or other graphics to organize the data they collect before beginning to write.

5. **_Write sections of the report._** Students use the writing process to draft, revise, and edit their sections of the report using information they have gathered and organized. One child in the group serves as the scribe and the other children dictate the sentences and paragraphs. Then each group shares its rough draft in a whole-class revising group and uses the feedback it receives to revise its writing. Then the children proofread their draft and correct as many mechanical errors as possible. Last, they meet with the teacher for an editing conference to correct any remaining errors.

6. **_Complete the report._** The students meet as a class and write the introduction and conclusion to the report. Next they decide on the order for the sections of the report and make a table of contents and a cover. After all the parts are compiled, the entire report is read aloud so children can catch any inconsistencies or redundant passages. Older students also compile the bibliography at this time.

7. **_Publish the report._** Students prepare the final copy of their sections and compile them. The introduction and conclusion are also added. Next, they add page numbers. If the report has been word processed, it is easy to print out the final copy, and the report looks very professional. Copies of the report are made for each child.

Writing Individual Reports

Writing an individual report is similar to writing a collaborative report. Children design research questions, gather information to answer the questions, and then report what they have learned. However, writing individually makes two significant changes necessary: Children must narrow their topics and then assume the entire responsibility for writing the report. The steps in writing individual research reports are presented in the step-by-step feature on page 336.

Assessing Children's Expository Writing

Children need to know what the requirements are for the writing project and how they will be assessed or graded. Many teachers develop a checklist or grading sheet with the requirements for the project and distribute this to students before they begin working. In this way, students know what is expected of them and assume responsibility for completing each step of the assignment. For an individual report, the checklist might include these observable behaviors and products:

- Choose a narrow topic.
- Identify four or five research questions.
- Use a cluster to gather information to answer the questions.
- Write a rough draft with a section (or chapter) to answer each question.
- Meet in writing groups to share your report.
- Make at least three changes in your rough draft.
- Complete an editing checklist with a partner.
- Add a bibliography.
- Write the final copy of the report.
- Share the report with someone.

This checklist can be made simpler or more complex depending on the age and experiences of the students. Figure 10–13 shows two assessment checklists for expository writing projects. The first is a checklist for a second grader's report poster on an insect, and the second is for the sixth-grade ABC book project. For both of these checklists, children were involved in developing the checklists, and they received copies of the checklists at the beginning of the writing projects. Then they checked off the items as they worked and turned in the checklists with their completed projects.

Students staple the checklist to the inside cover of the folder in which they keep all the work for the project; as each requirement is completed, they check it off. In this way, students monitor their own work and learn that writing is a process, not just a final product.

Insect Poster Checklist

Name _____ Insect _____

☐ 1. Draw and color an insect.

☐ 2. Label the drawing.

☐ 3. Write 3 facts in sentences.

☐ 4. Add a title and your name.

☐ 5. Make the poster attractive.

The ABC Book Project

Name _____ Your Letter _____

   As you create your page for our class ABC book on ancient Egypt, check off each item on this assessment checklist. Keep the checklist in your project folder and turn it in with your project.

_____ 1. Brainstorm a list of at least three things beginning with your letter, and then choose the word for your page.

_____ 2. Research your word and gather information in a cluster.

_____ 3. Write a rough draft paragraph explaining the word for your page at the computer station. Begin with _____ is for _____.

_____ 4. Design your page and sketch an illustration.

_____ 5. Share your paragraph in writing group and revise based on feedback that you receive.

_____ 6. Edit your paragraph and proofread for spelling errors.

_____ 7. Print out your paragraph at the computer station.

_____ 8. Add illustrations.

Figure 10–13 Two assessment checklists

Step by Step: Individual Reports

1. **Choose and narrow a topic.** Students choose topics for reports from content-area units, hobbies, or other interests. After choosing a general topic, such as cats or the human body, they need to narrow their topic so that it is manageable. The broad topic of cats might be reduced to pet cats or tigers, and the human body might be narrowed to one organ or organ system.

2. **Design research questions.** Students brainstorm a list of questions for which they want to find answers. Then they review their list, combine some questions, delete others, and finally arrive at four to six questions that are worthy of answering. As they conduct their research, new questions may be added and others deleted if they reach a dead end.

3. **Gather and organize information.** Children read, take notes, and use clusters, data charts, or other graphics to gather and organize information. For upper-grade students, data charts with their rectangular spaces for writing information serve as a transition between clusters and note cards.

4. **Draft the report.** Children write a rough draft using the information they gathered in the previous step. Each research question can become a paragraph, a section, or a chapter in the report. As they draft each section of the report, children organize their writing using an appropriate text structure.

5. **Revise and edit the report.** Children meet in writing groups to share their rough drafts, and they make revisions based on the feedback they receive from their classmates. After they make the needed revisions, children use an editing checklist to proofread their reports and identify and correct mechanical errors.

6. **Publish the report.** Children recopy their reports in books and add bibliographic information. Reports can also be published in several other ways. For example, children can give an oral presentation using PowerPoint, produce a video presentation, or create a series of illustrated charts or dioramas.

When the project is completed, children submit their entire folder to the teacher to be assessed. All of the requirements listed on the checklist are considered in determining the grade. If the checklist has 10 requirements, each requirement might be worth 10 points, and the grading can be done objectively on a 100-point scale. Thus, if the child's project is complete with all required materials, the child scores 100 or a grade of A. Points can be subtracted for work that is sloppy or incomplete. If additional grades are necessary, each item on the checklist can be graded separately. If a quality assessment of the final copy of the research report is needed, then a second grade can be awarded.

Teachers also develop rubrics to assess the quality of children's reports, as Mr. Garcia did in the vignette at the beginning of the chapter. Sometimes teachers use general criteria about good writing to create the rubric, and at other times, they create a rubric for the specific writing project, such as the rubric for guidebooks shown in Figure 10–2.

It is more important that students understand how to conduct research to find answers to questions that puzzle them than it is for them to be successful on one particular report-writing project. McGinley and Madigan (1990) recommend that students reflect on the research process they used and write about that process in order to appreciate that the research process is a powerful learning tool. Students can write about each step in the research and writing process in their learning logs or write a reflective analysis of their work after they complete a research project.

ANSWERING TEACHERS' QUESTIONS ABOUT . . .

Expository Writing

1. You must be kidding! My second graders can't write reports. They still need to learn basic reading and writing skills.

The writing samples in this chapter show that second graders can write research reports. The question you seem to be asking is *why* second graders should write reports. Writing collaborative and individual reports is not frivolous! Children learn basic reading and writing skills as they develop research questions, read to find answers, and then write a report to share what they have learned. What is more basic than having children read to find answers to research questions? They apply decoding and comprehension skills as they read, searching for answers to their questions. What is more basic than having children share their findings through writing? They use the writing process to write their reports. Report writing is authentic and meaningful, the kind of activity that promotes basic reading and writing skills.

2. When do I teach outlining?

Outlining is a sticking point for many writers. Because the format of an outline seems so formidable, children often write it *after* completing the report. Generally speaking, outlining should not be taught to elementary students because it is unnec-

essary. Instead, have children use clusters and data charts to organize their writing. These forms are more effective and flexible than outlining. If you do teach outlining, have children make a cluster first and then transfer the information from the cluster to the outline. Each main idea from the cluster becomes a main idea in the outline and is marked with a roman numeral. The details are listed under the main ideas and are marked with uppercase letters. If additional details have been added, they are marked with numerals and written under the particular detail. For example, the "How they act" section of the cluster on hermit crabs presented in Figure 10–6 can be rewritten this way as an outline:

  A. How they act
    1. Move sideways, backwards, and forwards
    2. Turn in circles, dig, climb, push objects
    3. Go back in shells if in danger
    4. Don't like water

3. Why do you insist that children, even first graders, should add a bibliography to their reports?

Children should give credit to the sources they used in their reports. Adding a bibliography lends credibility to the report and helps assure the reader that the information is accurate. Adding a bibliography to a report is not a complicated matter, even though some junior and senior high school students who have never written a report before seem overwhelmed when asked to write a bibliography—a word they often confuse with biography. In contrast, elementary students accept the responsibility easily when it has been a natural part of report writing since kindergarten. Young children simply add a page at the end of their reports to tell everyone who reads it how they became experts about the subject and found answers to their research questions. It is sufficient if primary-grade students list only the name and author of the book. Students at each grade level gradually add more information; upper-grade students include author, title, city of publication, publisher, and copyright date for the books they reference.

Another benefit is that middle graders begin to note that the authors of the informational books they read have references, too, and they become more critical readers when they look for evidence of the accuracy of information they are reading.

4. I teach fifth grade and I want my students to write reports as part of our unit on colonial life. Which type of report should I use?

You could use any of the types described in this chapter. Teachers choose the type of report depending on their students' prior experiences with expository writing, the amount of time available for the project, and their goals for the writing activity. When students haven't had many report-writing experiences, a collaborative report or ABC book might be a good choice. When time is limited, you might choose riddles or ABC books. If you want to help students think more critically about a topic or make connections to other curricular areas, cubes or charts might be a good choice. When you want students to learn to write a conventional report, individual reports are a good choice.

5. I think multigenre projects are a good idea for older students, but I have a kindergarten–first grade combination class. My students couldn't do them.

Many kindergarten and first-grade teachers develop multigenre projects with their classes. The students participate in a variety of writing activities, and then the teacher puts the display board or display book together using samples of the students' work. Working together as a class, young children can write reports and poems interactively, make clusters and other diagrams, and create new song lyrics. They can also work independently to draw pictures and write words and sentences.

CHAPTER 11
Narrative Writing

Preview

 Purpose   Students use narrative writing to create both fictitious and true stories that entertain readers. A fully developed story involves a problem, which is introduced in the beginning, becomes more complicated in the middle, and is resolved at the end. Students retell familiar stories, write sequels and new episodes for favorite characters, and compose original stories.

 Audience   Students write stories for classmates, their families, and other well-known and trusted audiences. They also publish their stories as books that are placed in the class library or school library.

 Forms   Stories are often bound into books and may be written as class collaborations or individual stories, or as scripts for puppet shows and readers theatre.

Instructional Preview: Narrative Writing

Grades	Goals and Activities
Kindergarten–Grade 2	**Goal 1:** Recognize the beginning-middle-end of stories and use this structure to organize stories • Students examine the characteristics of beginnings, middles, and ends of stories. • Students dramatize familiar stories in beginning, middle, and end parts. • Students make storybooks by drawing pictures of the beginning, middle, and end of stories. • Students write retellings of familiar stories in beginning, middle, and end parts. • Students write personal narratives with beginning, middle, and end parts. • Students write original stories with beginning, middle, and end parts.
	Goal 2: Identify characters and settings in stories and include characters and settings in the stories students write • Students draw portraits of characters. • Students make character clusters with information about what the character looks like, what he/she does, what he/she says, and what he/she thinks. • Students draw setting maps and make tabletop displays of settings. • Students identify the characters and settings in stories they write.
Grades 3–5	**Goal 1:** Analyze the four ways authors develop characters in stories and how students use these methods in their stories • Students examine the four ways authors develop characters. • Students make open-mind portraits. • Students write character sketches. • Students create well-developed characters in the stories they write.

Instructional Preview: Narrative Writing	
Grades	**Goals and Activities**
Grades 3–5	**Goal 2:** Analyze the ways authors develop setting in stories and how students use setting in their stories • Students examine location, weather, and other components of setting. • Students consider how the story would be different if the setting were different. • Students make setting maps.
	Goal 3: Analyze how authors develop plot in stories and how students use plot in their stories • Students examine the four conflict situations. • Students make a plot profile as they read a novel. • Students draw story mountains.
Grades 6–8	**Goal 1:** Identify explicit and implicit themes in stories • Students read Aesop's fables (without the morals) and guess the moral. • Students write brief fablelike stories and provide a moral. • Students make a theme cluster to explore a one-word theme (e.g., friendship). • Students write an essay to explain how the author developed a theme in a story.
	Goal 2: Identify the four points of view in stories and analyze the effect of viewpoint on the story • Students analyze the four viewpoints in stories they are reading. • Students consider how the story would differ if told from a different viewpoint. • Students rewrite familiar folktales and short stories from different viewpoints.
	Goal 3: Analyze story structure • Students review the elements of story structure. • Students analyze the author's use of story structure in a familiar story. • Students analyze their use of story structure in stories they have written.

Retelling and Writing Stories

"*C*lever trick number 4!" cries LaWanda. "That mean ol' crocodile is pretending to be a picnic bench."

"Don't worry, Trunky is going to warn the kids," replies Ashton.

The children in Ms. Dillen's first-grade classroom are listening to their teacher reread a favorite story, Roald Dahl's *The Enormous Crocodile* (1978), as part of a focus unit on the book. They eagerly listen to the crocodile's four clever (but unsuccessful) attempts to catch a fat and juicy child to eat for supper, and they join in as Ms. Dillen reads, predicting the failure of the crocodile's tricks again and again. Although many adults find Dahl's story repulsive, these first graders love it.

Recognizing the students' interest in this story, Ms. Dillen decides to use the story to introduce her first graders to the most basic components of plot. She explains that stories have three parts: a beginning, a middle, and an end. She and the children retell the beginning, middle, and end of *The Enormous Crocodile.* Next, she draws a cluster on the chalkboard with the title of the story in a circle and three rays marked "Beginning," "Middle," and "End." The children identify the events that belong in each story part and complete the story cluster as shown in Figure 11–1.

The following day, Ms. Dillen asks the children if they want to write their own version of the story in a big book (a large book made out of sheets of posterboard that the class can read together). They shout and clap their enthusiasm. Ms. Dillen begins by reviewing the story with the children, using the story cluster to organize the retelling. The children decide to write a six-page book, with one page for the beginning, one page for each of the four tricks, and one page for the end. (Later, a title page will be added.) Next, she divides the chalkboard into six columns and asks the students to dictate the story. She records their dictation on the chalkboard, page by page. Then the children reread their story and suggest several changes. Using proofreaders' marks, Ms. Dillen incorporates the changes agreed upon by the class. After a final reading, the children draw and write the big book. Some children draw illustrations on large sheets of posterboard, and others write the text above or below the illustrations on each page. Another illustrator and writer create the title page. Then

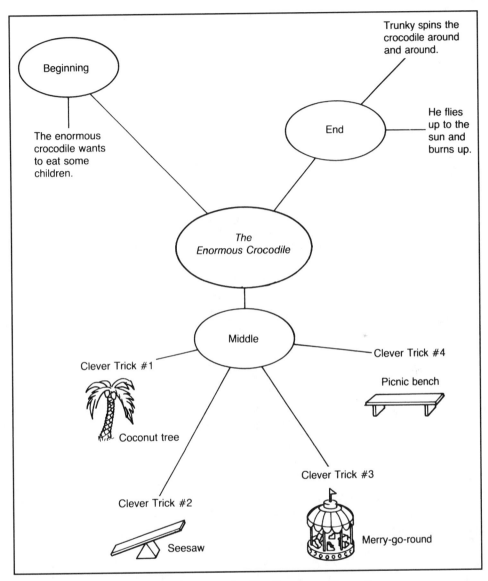

Figure 11–1 Shared writing: Story cluster for *The Enormous Crocodile*

the pages are compiled and bound. Here is the text of their completed story, "The Enormous Crocodile in Ms. Dillen's Classroom":

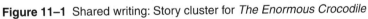

Page 1:   The enormous crocodile wanted to eat the children in Ms. Dillen's class.

Page 2:   The enormous crocodile made himself look like a coconut tree. The trick didn't work.

Page 3: The crocodile tried another trick. He made himself into a seesaw. But Muggle-Wump warned the children.

Page 4: The crocodile turned himself into a merry-go-round. The Roly-Poly Bird warned the kids. Clever trick three didn't work!

Page 5: The crocodile was a picnic bench. Trunky warned the children. Clever trick four did not work either.

Page 6: Trunky spun the enormous crocodile around and around. He threw him up into the sun.

The children personalized the story by having the enormous crocodile want to eat the children in their class rather than the children in the nearby town, as Roald Dahl wrote in his version of the story, and they used the repetition of clever tricks to recall the story events.

Several days later, the children participate in other projects. Some make finger puppets to use in retelling the story. They draw pictures of the characters, cut them out, and tape the pictures to strips of paper that they fit around their fingers. As soon as the puppets are made, students break into small groups to tell the story to each other. Others write retellings of the story, with one page for the beginning, four pages for the middle, and one page for the end. Then they add a cover and staple their completed booklets together. Barry's retelling is presented in Figure 11–2.

Next, Ms. Dillen suggests that they write another class story using clever tricks. They brainstorm a list of clever tricks and discuss possible plots. The class decides to write a story about six hungry rabbits who use clever tricks to fool a fox so they can eat the vegetables in the garden. The students decide on three clever tricks and develop a story cluster with a beginning, middle, and end. With this preparation, they dictate the story to Ms. Dillen, who records it on the chalkboard. They refine their story, and then Ms. Dillen makes copies for each child. Here is their story, "The Hungry Rabbits":

Page 1: Once there were six rabbits. They wanted carrots and lettuce. But the fox chased the rabbits out of the garden.

Page 2: The rabbits think of clever tricks. They tell the fox there's a deer in the forest so the fox will chase the deer instead of them. But the trick didn't work.

Page 3: The rabbits dig a hole trying to get to the garden but they didn't dig far enough. They were only by the fence.

Page 4: Then the rabbits ran to the briar patch and jumped over it. The fox tried to jump over it but landed in it. "Ouch, ouch," cried the fox. He couldn't get out.

Page 5: So the rabbits jumped real high over the briars and got the carrots and lettuce. And they lived happily ever after.

As the children are finishing their class story, many are already talking about clever trick stories they want to write. Ms. Dillen provides the guidelines. Like their class story, children's individual stories should have a beginning, three (or more) clever

Figure 11–2 Independent writing: A first grader's retelling of *The Enormous Crocodile*

tricks in the middle, and an ending. Children stack five, six, or more pages of paper on their desks and begin to work. Some begin illustrating their stories, some begin writing, and others mark their papers with the words "beginning," "middle–1," "middle–2," "middle–3," and "end" before writing or drawing.

Eddie has his story already in mind. He quickly sets to work drawing a picture in the top half of each page. Then he writes his story, using the pictures he has drawn, much as an adult uses an outline. As he writes, using a combination of invented and standard spelling, Eddie becomes more and more animated. As soon as he finishes writing, he gets construction paper for a cover and staples his storybook together. He goes over to Barry's desk to share his story with his best friend. "Hey, Bar', listen to this. You're gonna love it," he says. And Barry does. Other children crowd around to read Eddie's story, and soon Ms. Dillen moves this group of children over to the author's chair to share their stories. They clap as each story is read and offer compliments about their classmates' use of clever clues and surprise endings.

This is Eddie's story, "The Dog," written in standard spelling:

Page 1: The little dog is very, very hungry and he sees a little rabbit. He chases the rabbit but he ran too fast.

Page 2: Clever trick no. 1. The dog jumped on the rabbit's tail but the trick didn't work.

Page 3: Clever trick no. 2. He hid under the bushes and jumped out of the bush but he missed the rabbits and they ran away.

Page 4: Clever trick no. 3. The dog dressed up into a carrot and the rabbit walked by the dog and the dog ate him.

Page 5: That's the end.

Eddie's story is well developed: He established a conflict between the hungry dog and the rabbit in the beginning; in the middle, he presented three attempts to catch the rabbit; and with the third attempt, the dog is successful. Although the ending is not as elaborate as it might be, it follows the style often used in folktales (e.g., "Snip, snap, snout, this tale's told out!") and in television cartoon shows (e.g., "That's all, folks!").

THE FIRST GRADERS IN MS. DILLEN'S CLASS are learning about stories by listening to stories read aloud, examining how authors organize their stories, and writing stories themselves. Distinguished British educator Harold Rosen (1986) pleads for elementary teachers to provide more opportunities, or "generous space," for storytelling—both oral and written—to teach children about narrative discourse, its meaning, voice, and seduction. In this chapter we examine children's concept of story, discuss five elements of story structure, and suggest strategies for teaching students to write stories.

Even before they enter school, young children have a rudimentary awareness of what makes a story; that is, they have a concept of story or story schema. Children's concept of story includes some understanding of the elements of story structure, such as character, plot, and setting, as well as the conventions that authors use in stories. This knowledge is usually intuitive; that is, children are not conscious of what they know. Golden (1984) describes children's concept of story as part of their cognitive structure: "a mental representation of story structure, essentially an outline of the basic story elements and their organization" (p. 578).

Researchers have documented that children's concept of story begins in the preschool years, and that children as young as 2½ years of age have a rudimentary sense of story (Applebee, 1978, 1980; Pitcher & Prelinger, 1963). Children acquire this concept of story gradually, first through listening to stories read to them, later by reading stories themselves, and then by telling and writing stories. Not surprisingly, older children have a better understanding of story structure and conventions than younger children do. Similarly, the stories that older children tell and write are increasingly more complex; the plot structures are more tightly organized, and the characters are more fully developed. Yet Applebee (1980) found that by the time children begin kindergarten, they have already developed a concept of what a story is, and these expectations guide them as they respond to stories and tell their own stories. For example, he found that kindergartners could use three story markers: the convention "Once upon a time . . . " to begin a story, the past tense for telling a story, and formal endings such as "The End" and "they lived happily ever after."

Most of the research examining children's understanding of story structure and conventions has been applied to reading. Children's concept of story plays an important role in their ability to comprehend and recall information from the stories they read (Mandler & Johnson, 1977; Rumelhart, 1975; Stein & Glenn, 1979). However, children's concept of story is equally important in writing (Golden, 1984). Just as they draw on their concept of story in reading stories, children use this knowledge in writing stories. Dressel (1990) found that children who read and discussed higher-quality stories wrote stories of greater literary quality than did children who read low-quality stories.

In this chapter, you will read about the elements of story structure and how to teach students to recognize and analyze them in stories they read and to incorporate them in the stories they write. The key concepts are:

- The five elements of story structure are plot, setting, characters, theme, and point of view.
- Teachers introduce each element and have students analyze how authors use them in stories.
- Teachers support students as they write stories incorporating the elements they have studied.
- Teachers and students use checklists and rubrics to assess students' stories.

Elements of Story Structure

Stories have unique elements of structure that distinguish them from other forms of writing. In fact, the structure of stories is quite complex because authors manipulate character, plot, setting, and other elements to produce an interesting story. Five elements of story structure—plot, setting, characters, theme, and point of view—are discussed in this section, with familiar and award-winning trade books used to illustrate each element.

Plot

Plot is the sequence of events involving characters in conflict situations in the beginning, middle, and end of a story. The plot is based on the goals of one or more characters (Lukens, 1999). The main character (or characters) wants to achieve a certain goal or to solve a problem, and other characters try to prevent the main character from being successful. The story is put into motion as the main character attempts to overcome obstacles to reach the goal or solve the problem.

Beginning-Middle-End.   The most basic aspect of plot is the division of the main events of a story into three parts: the beginning, the middle, and the end. (With upper-grade students, the terms often used are introduction, development or complication, and resolution.) In *Where the Wild Things Are* (Sendak, 1963), for instance, the three story parts can be picked out easily. As the story begins, Max plays a mischievous wolf and is sent to his room for misbehaving. In the middle, Max magically travels to the land of the wild things to become their king. Then Max feels lonely and returns home to find his supper waiting and still hot—the end of the story. A cluster for *Where the Wild Things Are* is presented in Figure 11–3.

Authors include specific types of information in each part of the story. In the beginning, they introduce the characters, describe the setting, and present a problem. The author uses the characters, setting, and events to develop the plot and sustain the theme through the story. In the middle, authors introduce conflict; they create roadblocks that keep the characters from solving their problems. How the characters deal with these obstacles adds suspense, which keeps readers interested. In the end, readers learn whether or not the characters' struggles are successful.

Conflict.   Conflict is the tension or opposition between forces in the plot, and it is usually the element that entices readers to continue reading the story. Conflict usually takes one of four forms (Lukens, 1999):

1. Conflict between a character and nature
2. Conflict between a character and society
3. Conflict between characters
4. Conflict within a character

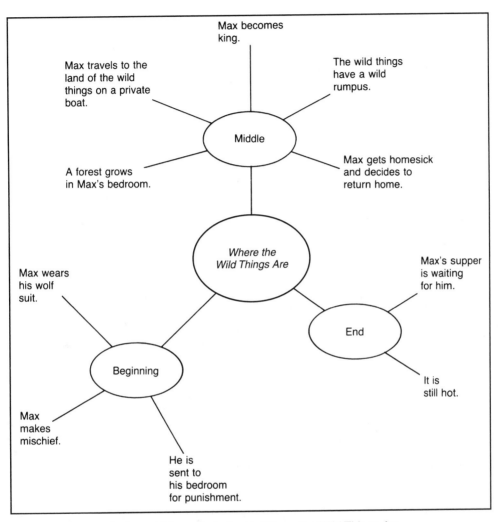

Figure 11–3 A beginning-middle-end cluster for *Where the Wild Things Are*

Conflict between a character and nature is represented in stories in which severe weather plays an important role, as in Jean Craighead George's *Julie of the Wolves* (1972), and in stories set in isolated geographic locations, such as Scott O'Dell's *Island of the Blue Dolphins* (1960), in which the Indian girl Karana struggles to survive alone on a Pacific island. In some stories, a character's activities and beliefs are different from those held by other members of the society, and these differences cause conflict. One example of this type of conflict is Elizabeth Speare's *The Witch of Blackbird Pond* (1958), in which Kit Tyler is accused of being a witch because she continues, in a New England

Puritan community, activities that were acceptable in the Caribbean community where she grew up. Conflict between characters is commonly used in children's literature. In Judy Blume's *Tales of a Fourth Grade Nothing* (1972), for instance, the never-ending conflict between Peter and his little brother Fudge is what makes the story interesting. The fourth type of conflict is conflict within a character, and stories such as Bernard Waber's *Ira Sleeps Over* (1972) and Betsy Byars's *The Summer of the Swans* (1970) are examples. In *Ira Sleeps Over,* 6-year-old Ira must decide whether to take his teddy bear with him when he goes next door to spend the night with a friend. In *The Summer of the Swans,* Sara feels guilty when her mentally retarded brother wanders off and is lost. A list of stories representing the four types of conflict is presented in Figure 11–4.

Plot Development.   Authors develop plot through the introduction, development, and resolution of the conflict. Plot development can be broken down into four steps:

1. A problem that introduces conflict is presented in the beginning of a story.
2. Characters face roadblocks as they attempt to solve the problem in the middle of the story.
3. The high point in the action occurs when the problem is about to be solved. This high point separates the middle and the end of the story.
4. The problem is solved and the roadblocks are overcome at the end of the story.

The problem is introduced at the beginning of the story, and the main character (or characters) is faced with trying to solve it. This problem determines the conflict. In *The Pied Piper of Hamelin* (Mayer, 1987), the problem is that the town of Hamelin is infested with rats, and conflict develops between the townspeople and the Pied Piper, who has been hired to rid the town of the rats. This conflict can be characterized as a conflict between characters.

Once the problem has been introduced, the author throws roadblocks in the way of an easy solution. As one roadblock is removed, another emerges to thwart the main character. Postponing the solution by introducing roadblocks is the core of plot development. Stories may contain any number of roadblocks, but children's stories typically contain three, four, or five.

In *The Pied Piper of Hamelin,* the first conflict comes when the townspeople demand that the mayor get rid of the rats. The mayor promises to do something, but he doesn't know what to do. Next, the piper visits the mayor and offers to rid the town of the rats. The mayor promises to pay the piper 1,000 pieces of silver. Third, the piper gets rid of the rats: He plays a mesmerizing tune on his pipe, and the rats follow him out of town and are drowned in a nearby river. Fourth, it appears that the problem is solved, but the mayor belittles the piper's accomplishment and refuses to pay the agreed-upon reward. When the mayor refuses, the piper threatens terrible consequences if he is not paid.

Conflict Between a Character and Nature

George, J. C. (1972). *Julie of the wolves.* New York: Harper & Row. (M–U)

O'Dell, S. (1960). *Island of the blue dolphins.* Boston: Houghton Mifflin. (M–U)

Paulsen, G. (1987). *Hatchet.* New York: Bradbury Press. (M–U)

Polacco, P. (1990). *Thundercake.* New York: Philomel. (P–M)

Sperry, A. (1968). *Call it courage.* New York: Macmillan. (U)

Steig, W. (1987). *Brave Irene.* New York: Farrar, Straus & Giroux. (M)

Conflict Between a Character and Society

Brett, J. (1994). *Town mouse, country mouse.* New York: Putnam. (P–M)

Bunting, E. (1994). *Smoky night.* San Diego: Harcourt Brace. (P–M)

Lowry, L. (1989). *Number the stars.* New York: Atheneum. (M–U)

Lowry, L. (1993). *The giver.* Boston: Houghton Mifflin. (U)

Nixon, J. L. (1987). *A family apart.* New York: Bantam. (M–U)

O'Brien, R.C. (1971). *Mrs. Frisby and the rats of NIMH.* New York: Atheneum. (M)

Speare, E. G. (1958). *The witch of Blackbird Pond.* Boston: Houghton Mifflin (M–U)

Uchida, Y. (1971). *Journey to Topaz.* Berkeley, CA: Creative Arts. (U)

Conflict Between Characters

Blume, J. (1972). *Tales of a fourth grade nothing.* New York: Dutton. (M)

Bunting, E. (1994). *A day's work.* New York: Clarion. (P–M)

Cohen, B. (1983). *Molly's pilgrim.* New York: Lothrop, Lee & Shepard. (M)

Cushman, K. (1994). *Catherine, called Birdy.* New York: HarperCollins (U)

Hoban, R. (1970). *A bargain for Frances.* New York: Scholastic. (P)

Lester, H. (1988). *Tacky the penguin.* Boston: Houghton Mifflin. (P)

Say, A. (1995). *Stranger in the mirror.* Boston: Houghton Mifflin. (M–U)

Steig, W. (1982). *Doctor De Soto.* New York: Farrar, Straus & Giroux. (M)

Zelinsky, P. O. (1986). *Rumpelstiltskin.* New York: Dutton. (P–M)

Conflict Within a Character

Bauer, M. D. (1986). *On my honor.* Boston: Houghton Mifflin. (M–U)

Byars, B. (1970). *The summer of the swans.* New York: Viking. (M)

Carle, E. (1995). *The very lonely firefly.* New York: Philomel. (P)

Fritz, J. (1958). *The cabin faced west.* New York: Coward-McCann. (M)

Henkes, K. (1991). *Chrysanthemum.* New York: Greenwillow. (P)

Naylor, P. R. (1991). *Shiloh.* New York: Atheneum. (M–U)

Pinkney, A. D. (1995). *Hold fast to dreams.* New York: Morrow. (U)

Taylor, T. (1969). *The cay.* New York: Doubleday. (U)

Waber, B. (1972). *Ira sleeps over.* Boston: Houghton Mifflin. (P)

Figure 11–4 Stories that illustrate the four types of conflict

P = primary grades (K–2), M = middle grades (3–5), U = upper grades (6–8)

The high point of the action comes when the solution of the problem hangs in the balance. Tension is high, and readers continue reading to learn whether or not the main characters will solve the problem. In *The Pied Piper of Hamelin,* readers experience some relief because the town of Hamelin has been saved, but tension exists because of the disagreement between the mayor and the piper. The piper plays his pipe again, this time enticing all the children to follow him out of Hamelin. They follow him to a nearby mountain, which they enter through a magic door. The mayor and other townspeople are left with their money but without their children.

At the end of the story, the problem is solved. Only one little lame boy, whom the piper cures, returns to tell the story and remind everyone that "a promise is a promise" and "the piper must be paid."

Second-grade Riley wrote this animal story (called "Charge!") for a district writing competition. Notice how clearly he identifies a problem in the beginning of the story and uses the problem to drive the plot through the middle and end:

It was a beautifully sunny day with the sun up bright 'n early. And so was the president! He was getting married! So as you probably already know, everybody else was up, too.

But the president was a worrywart, so as I'm sure you know, he was worried about what was on the front page of the newspaper. It said:

Rhino Escaped from Zoo!

1,000,000 Dollar Reward

"What if it blows down our wedding?" the president asked his future wife.

"Oh, but it won't, honey," she replied.

But she found out how wrong those very words could be. Right when he slipped the ring on her finger, the door blew down and the missing rhino (now not missing) came charging through the church. Pews were flyin', the church got shattered, and the rhino had its horn engraved in the organ, which it was shattering as well.

"Run for your lives!" someone shouted.

"Break for it!" shouted someone else.

"It's the rhino that escaped from the zoo!" shouted another.

All of the people but twelve got out. Those twelve, all mighty and strong if you hope to know, were trying to pick up the rambunctious rhino. After an hour and a half, they hauled off the mighty being. So they returned the rhino, got the million, split it up, and went home to tell the tale.

The president did the marriage again (without the rhino), and Washington had other marriages (without the rhino), and it lived happily ever after (without the rhino).

The rhino presents the conflict in this story, and it is classified as conflict between characters and nature. This story shows how even primary-grade students can create effective stories using the elements of plot structure, including conflict. This story is even more charming because of Riley's sophisticated vocabulary, expressions, and asides to the reader.

Setting

In some stories, the setting is barely sketched: this is called a backdrop setting. In many folktales, for example, the setting is relatively unimportant, and the convention "Once upon a time . . . " may be used to set the stage. In other stories, however, the setting is elaborate and is integral to the story's effectiveness; these settings are called integral settings (Lukens, 1999). Whether or not the setting is important to plot and character development determines how much attention writers give to describing the setting. Some stories could take place anywhere, and the setting requires little description; others, however, require a specific setting, and authors must take care to ensure the authenticity of the historical period or geographic location in which the story is set.

Of the elements of story structure, setting is the one many people feel most comfortable with. Often they think that setting is simply where the story takes place. Certainly location is an important dimension of setting, but there are three other dimensions as well: weather, time, and time period.

Location.   Location is a very important dimension of setting in many stories. The Boston Commons in *Make Way for Ducklings* (McCloskey, 1969), the Alaskan North Slope in *Julie of the Wolves* (George, 1972), and New York City's Metropolitan Museum of Art in *From the Mixed-up Files of Mrs. Basil E. Frankweiler* (Konigsburg, 1983) are integral to these stories' plots. The settings are artfully described by the authors and add something unique to the story. In contrast, many stories take place in everyday settings that do not contribute to the story's effectiveness.

Weather.   Weather is a second dimension of setting and, like location, is crucial in some stories. For example, a rainstorm is essential to the plot development in both *Bridge to Terabithia* (Paterson, 1977) and *Sam, Bangs and Moonshine* (Ness, 1966). At other times, the author may not even mention the weather because it does not have an impact on the story. Many stories take place on warm, sunny days. Think about the impact weather could have on a story; for example, what might have happened if a snowstorm had prevented Little Red Riding Hood from reaching her grandmother's house?

Time.   The third dimension, time, involves both time of day and the passage of time within a story. The time of day is not significant in many children's stories, except for Halloween or ghost stories, which typically take place after dark. In stories that take place at night, such as the folktale *The Teeny-Tiny Woman* (Galdone, 1984), time is a more important dimension than in stories that take place during the day because events that happen at night seem scarier than those that happen during the day.

Many short stories span a brief period of time, often less than a day, and sometimes less than an hour. In Chris Van Allsburg's *Jumanji* (1981), for instance, Peter and Judy's bizarre adventure in which their house is overtaken by an exotic jungle lasts only the several hours their parents are at the opera. Other stories, such as *The Ugly Duckling* (Andersen, 1979), span a time period long enough for the main character to grow to maturity.

Time Period.   The fourth dimension of setting is the time period in which a story is set. The time period is important in stories that are set in the past or in the future. If *The Witch of Blackbird Pond* (Speare, 1958) and *Beyond the Divide* (Lasky, 1983) were set in different eras, for example, they would lose much of their impact. Today, few people would believe that Kit Tyler is a witch, and travel across the United States would not be nearly so difficult today with modern conveniences. Other stories, such as *A Wrinkle in Time* (L'Engle, 1962), take place in the future where events occur that are not possible today. A list of stories with integral settings is presented in Figure 11–5. These stories illustrate the four dimensions of setting—location, weather, time, and time period.

Even though settings are often taken for granted in stories, an integral setting exerts a great deal of influence on the story. Watson (1991) recommends that teachers help students to recognize the importance of setting as a literary element and to see the connections between setting and plot, character, and other elements. For example, in *Number the Stars* (Lowry, 1989), a story of two friends—a Christian child and a Jewish child—set in Denmark during World War II, the setting is integral to the development of the story. The time period influences the plot development because readers expect that the Nazis will try to relocate the Jewish girl and her family and that the Christian girl and her family will try to protect or rescue the Jewish family. Readers also have expectations about the characters. The Christian girl and the Jewish girl may have different physical features, but it is likely that both will be called upon to perform courageous actions. The minilesson feature on page 356 shows how a sixth-grade teacher helped her students create historically accurate settings.

Characters

Characters are the people or personified animals who are involved in the story. Often character is the most important element of story structure because the experience the author creates for readers is centered on a character or group of characters. Usually, one fully rounded character and two or three supporting characters are introduced and developed in a story. Fully developed main characters have all the characteristics of real people. A list of fully developed main characters in children's stories is presented in Figure 11–6.

The supporting characters may be individualized, but they will be portrayed much less vividly than the main character. The extent to which the supporting characters are developed depends on the author's purpose and the needs of the

Babbitt, N. (1975). *Tuck everlasting.* New York: Farrar, Straus & Giroux. (M–U)

Bunting, E. (1994). *Smoky night.* San Diego: Harcourt Brace. (P–M)

Cauley, L. B. (1984). *The city mouse and the country mouse.* New York: Putnam. (P–M)

Choi, S. N. (1991). *Year of impossible goodbyes.* Boston: Houghton Mifflin. (U)

Curtis, C. P. (1995). *The Watsons go to Birmingham—1963.* New York: Delacorte. (M–U)

Cushman, K. (1994). *Catherine, called Birdy.* New York: HarperCollins. (U)

Cushman, K. (1996). *The ballad of Lucy Whipple.* New York: Clarion. (M–U)

Fleischman, P. (1993). *Bull Run.* New York: HarperCollins. (U)

Fleischman, S. (1963). *By the great horn spoon!* Boston: Little, Brown. (M–U)

George, J. C. (1972). *Julie of the wolves.* New York: Harper & Row. (M–U)

Harvey, B. (1988). *Cassie's journey: Going west in the 1860s.* New York: Holiday House. (M)

Johnston, T. (1994). *Amber on the mountain.* New York: Dial. (P–M)

L'Engle, M. (1962). *A wrinkle in time.* New York: Farrar, Straus & Giroux. (U)

Lester, H. (1989). *Tacky the penguin.* Boston: Houghton Mifflin. (P–M)

Lowry, L. (1989). *Number the stars.* Boston: Houghton Mifflin. (M–U)

Lowry, L. (1993). *The giver.* Boston: Houghton Mifflin. (U)

McCloskey, R. (1969). *Make way for ducklings.* New York: Viking. (P)

Mead, A. (1995). *Junebug.* New York: Farrar, Straus & Giroux. (M–U)

Myers, W. D. (1988). *Scorpions.* New York: Harper & Row. (U)

Paterson, K. (1977). *Bridge to Terabithia.* New York: Crowell. (M–U)

Paulsen, G. (1987). *Hatchet.* New York: Simon & Schuster. (U)

Polacco, P. (1988). *The keeping quilt.* New York: Simon & Schuster. (M)

Polacco, P. (1988). *Rechenka's eggs.* New York: Philomel. (P–M)

Ringgold, R. (1991). *Tar beach.* New York: Crown. (P–M)

Roop, P., & Roop, C. (1985). *Keep the lights burning, Abbie.* Minneapolis: Carolrhoda. (P–M)

Ryan, P. M. (1998). *Riding Freedom.* New York: Scholastic. (M–U)

Sachar, L. (1998). *Holes.* New York: Farrar, Straus & Giroux. (U)

Say, A. (1990). *El Chino.* Boston: Houghton Mifflin. (M)

Speare, E. G. (1958). *The witch of Blackbird Pond.* Boston: Houghton Mifflin. (M–U)

Speare, E. G. (1983). *The sign of the beaver.* Boston: Houghton Mifflin. (M–U)

Stanley, D. (1996). *Saving Sweetness.* New York: Putnam. (P–M)

Uchida, Y. (1993). *The bracelet.* New York: Philomel. (P–M)

Wilder, L. I. (1971). *The long winter.* New York: Harper & Row. (M)

Yep, L. (1975). *Dragonwings.* New York: Harper & Row. (U)

Figure 11–5 Stories with integral settings

story. In *Queenie Peavy* (Burch 1966), for instance, Queenie is the main character, and we get to know her as a real person. She pretends that she is tough, as she does when the other children taunt her because her father is in the chain gang, but actually Queenie is a sensitive girl who wants a family to care for her. In contrast, the author tells us very little about the supporting characters in the story: Queenie's parents, her neighbors, her classmates, and her teachers. This

Creating a Historically Accurate Setting

As part of a semester-long unit on ancient civilizations, Mrs. Clay's sixth-grade students are working in small groups to make multigenre projects that focus on each of the civilizations, and each project will include a story set in that civilization. Mrs. Clay has emphasized that their stories must be historically accurate. She is meeting with the small groups during revising to help them examine the settings they have created. Today she is meeting with the "Greek Civilization" group.

1. Introduce the topic

Mrs. Clay explains that an important characteristic of historical fiction is that the setting is detailed and historically accurate. Today, she'd like the students to examine the historical information included in their story.

2. Share examples

Mrs. Clay distributes copies of the rough draft of the story to each student. She also passes out highlighter pens. While one student reads aloud, the other students highlight words and phrases about life in Athens in the story. Then students take turns sharing what they have highlighted.

3. Provide information

The teacher commends the students for their use of many historical words, particularly at the beginning of the story, but she calls their attention to the fact that most of their highlighted words and phrases are on the first page of the story. She suggests the students draw a series of pictures to illustrate the story and add as many historical details to their drawings as possible. Then they can go back and add historically accurate words and phrases to the story.

4. Guide practice

The students each take a section of the story to illustrate and decide to add phrases using words from the word wall to mark the historical details in their drawings, for example, citizens wearing linen tunics at the Temple of Nike on the Acropolis, vendors at the crowded agora selling goats and sheep, women in the looming room making clothes for their family, altars to Zeus in the courtyard of the home, and slaves who are craftsmen making pottery and shields. Then the students add many of these historical details to their story.

5. Assess learning

Mrs. Clay will assess students' use of historically accurate information and vocabulary when she reads the final draft of their story.

Character	Story
Ramona	Cleary, B. (1981). *Ramona Quimby, age 8.* New York: Morrow. (M)
Birdy	Cushman, K. (1994). *Catherine, called Birdy.* New York: HarperCollins. (U)
Lucy	Cushman, K. (1996). *The ballad of Lucy Whipple.* New York: Clarion. (M–U)
Amber	Danziger, P. (1994). *Amber Brown is not a crayon.* New York: Putnam. (M)
Livingston	Edwards, P. D. & Cole, H. (1996). *Livingston Mouse.* New York: HarperCollins. (P)
Little Willy	Gardiner, J. R. (1980). *Stone Fox.* New York: Harper & Row. (M–U)
Chrysanthemum	Henkes, K. (1991). *Chrysanthemum.* New York: Greenwillow. (P)
Swamp Angel	Isaacs, A. (1994). *Swamp Angel.* New York: Dutton. (P–M)
Sarah	MacLachlan, P. (1985). *Sarah, plain and tall.* New York: Harper & Row. (M)
Marty	Naylor, P. R. (1991). *Shiloh.* New York: Atheneum. (M–U)
Karana	O'Dell, S. (1960). *Island of the blue dolphins.* Boston: Houghton Mifflin. (M–U)
Brian	Paulsen, G. (1987). *Hatchet.* New York: Viking. (U)
Babushka	Polacco, P. (1988). *Rechenka's eggs.* New York: Philomel. (P–M)
Officer Buckle	Rathmann, P. (1995). *Officer Buckle and Gloria.* New York: Putnam. (P)
Stanley	Sachar, L. (1998). *Holes.* New York: Farrar, Straus & Giroux. (U)
Maria	Soto, G. (1993). *Too many tamales.* New York: Putnam. (P)
Matt	Speare, E. (1983). *The sign of the beaver.* Boston: Houghton Mifflin. (M–U)
Maniac	Spinelli, J. (1990). *Maniac Magee.* New York: Scholastic. (U)
Irene	Steig, W. (1986). *Brave Irene.* New York: Farrar, Straus & Giroux. (P–M)
Cassie	Taylor, M. (1976). *Roll of thunder, hear my cry.* New York: Dial. (U)
Moon Shadow	Yep, L. (1975). *Dragonwings.* New York: Harper & Row. (U)

Figure 11–6 Stories with fully developed main characters

story focuses on Queenie and how this lonely 13-year-old copes with times that have "turned off hard" in the 1930s.

Authors must determine how to develop and present characters to involve readers in the experiences they are writing about. They develop characters in four ways: through appearance, action, dialogue, and monologue.

Appearance.   Authors describe how their characters look as the story develops; however, they generally provide some physical description when characters are introduced. Readers learn about characters by the description of their facial features, body shapes, habits of dress, mannerisms, and gestures. For example, Roald Dahl vividly describes James's two wicked aunts in *James and the Giant Peach* (1961): Aunt Sponge is fat and short. She has "small piggy eyes, a sunken mouth," and a "white flabby face that looked exactly as though it had been boiled" (p. 7). Aunt Spiker is just the opposite. She is tall and lean, and has "steel-rimmed spectacles that fixed onto the end of her nose with a clip" (p. 7). Dahl's descriptions bring these two despicable characters vividly to life. He has carefully chosen the specific details to influence readers to appreciate James's dismay at having to live with these two aunts.

Action.   What a character does is the best way of knowing about that character. In Betsy Byars's story about three unwanted children, *The Pinballs* (1977), 15-year-old Carlie is described as being "as hard to crack as a coconut" (p. 4), and her dialogue is harsh and sarcastic; however, Carlie's actions belie these other ways of knowing about her. She demonstrates through her actions that she cares about her two fellow pinballs and the foster family who cares for them. For example, she gets Harvey a puppy as a birthday present and sneaks it into the hospital.

Dialogue.   Another important technique that authors use to develop their characters is dialogue. What characters say is important, but so is the way they speak. The level of formality of the language that characters use is generally determined by the social situation; a character might speak less formally with a friend than with respected elders or characters in positions of authority. The geographic location of the story and the socioeconomic status of the characters also determine the way the characters speak. For example, in *Roll of Thunder, Hear My Cry* (Taylor, 1976), Cassie and her family speak Black English, and in *Ida Early Comes Over the Mountain* (Burch, 1980), Ida's speech is characteristic of rural Georgia, and she says, "Howdy-do?" and "Yes, sir-ee."

Monologue.   Authors also provide insight into their characters by revealing the characters' thoughts. In *Anastasia Krupnik* (Lowry, 1979), for example, Lois Lowry shares 10-year-old Anastasia's thinking with the reader. Anastasia has enjoyed being an only child, and she is very upset that her mother is pregnant. To deal with Anastasia's feelings of sibling rivalry, her parents suggest that she choose a name for the new baby, and Anastasia agrees. Through monologue, readers learn why Anastasia has agreed to choose the name: She will pick the most awful name she can think of for the baby. Lowry also has

Anastasia keep a journal in which she lists things she likes and hates, another reflection of her thinking.

Theme

Theme is the underlying meaning of a story and embodies general truths about society or human nature. According to Lehr (1991), the theme "steps back from the literal interpretation" to state more general truths (p. 2). The theme usually deals with the characters' emotions and values.

Themes can be stated explicitly or implicitly (Lukens, 1999). Explicit themes are stated openly and clearly in the story, whereas implicit themes are suggested through the characters' actions, dialogue, and monologue as they strive to resolve their problems. Friendship, responsibility, courage, and kindness to others are common topics around which authors build themes in children's literature.

In *Charlotte's Web* (1980), E. B. White builds a theme around the topic of friendship. Wilbur, who is grateful for Charlotte's encouragement and protection, remarks that "friendship is one of the most satisfying things in the world" (p. 115). Wilbur's statement is an example of an explicitly stated theme. Friendship is also central to *Bridge to Terabithia* (Paterson, 1977), but it is implied through Jess and Leslie's enduring friendship rather than explicitly stated in the text.

During the elementary grades, children develop and refine their understanding of theme. Kindergartners have a very rudimentary sense of theme, and through a wide exposure to literature and many opportunities to discuss books, students grow in their ability to construct and talk about themes (Au, 1992). Even so, students in the middle and upper grades often think about theme differently than adults do (Lehr, 1991). Older children and adults become more sensitive to the structure of stories, develop a greater ability to generalize the events of the story, increasingly understand the characters' motivations and the subtleties of the plot, and expand their own worldviews and ability to interpret literature.

Many stories have more than one theme, and as students talk about stories, they may head toward a different theme than the one the teacher had in mind. Teachers thus can gain new insights about themes from their students (Au, 1992).

Point of View

People see other people and the world from different points of view. Listening to several people recount an event they have all witnessed proves the impact of viewpoint. The focus of the narrator determines to a great extent readers'

First-Person Viewpoint

Bunting, E. (1994). *Smoky night*. San Diego: Harcourt Brace. (P–M)

Cushman, K. (1994). *Catherine, called Birdy*. New York: HarperCollins. (U)

Howard, E. F. (1991). *Aunt Flossie's hats (and crab cakes later)*. New York: Clarion. (P)

Howe, D., & Howe, J. (1979). *Bunnicula: A rabbit-tale of mystery*. New York: Atheneum. (M)

MacLachlan, P. (1985). *Sarah, plain and tall*. New York: Harper & Row. (M)

Rylant, C. (1992). *Missing May*. New York: Orchard Books. (U)

Stanley, D. (1996). *Saving Sweetness*. New York: Putnam. (P–M)

Viorst, J. (1977). *Alexander and the terrible, horrible, no good, very bad day*. New York: Atheneum. (P)

Omniscient Viewpoint

Babbitt, N. (1975). *Tuck everlasting*. New York: Farrar, Straus & Giroux. (M–U)

Grahame, K. (1961). *The wind in the willows*. New York: Scribner. (M)

Lewis, C. S. (1981). *The lion, the witch and the wardrobe*. New York: Macmillan. (M–U)

Myers, W. D. (1988). *Scorpions*. New York: Harper & Row. (U)

Steig, W. (1982). *Doctor De Soto*. New York: Farrar, Straus & Giroux. (P)

Limited Omniscient Viewpoint

Cleary, B. (1981). *Ramona Quimby, age 8*. New York: Morrow. (M)

Gardiner, J. R. (1980). *Stone Fox*. New York: Harper & Row. (M)

Lionni, L. (1969). *Alexander and the wind-up mouse*. New York: Pantheon. (P)

Lowry, L. (1989). *Number the stars*. Boston: Houghton Mifflin. (M–U)

Lowry, L. (1993). *The giver*. Boston: Houghton Mifflin. (U)

Sachar, L. (1998). *Holes*. New York: Farrar, Straus & Giroux. (U)

Objective Viewpoint

Allard, H. (1997). *Miss Nelson is missing!* Boston: Houghton Mifflin. (P–M)

Cauley, L. B. (1988). *The pancake boy*. New York: Putnam. (P)

Lester, H. (1988). *Tacky the penguin*. Boston: Houghton Mifflin. (P–M)

Lobel, A. (1972). *Frog and Toad together*. New York: Harper & Row. (P)

Meddaugh, S. (1992). *Martha speaks*. Boston: Houghton Mifflin. (P)

Zemach, M. (1983). *The little red hen*. New York: Farrar, Straus & Giroux. (P)

Multiple Viewpoints

Avi. (1991). *Nothing but the truth: A documentary novel*. New York: Orchard. (U)

Dorris, M. (1992). *Morning girl*. New York: Hyperion. (U)

Fleischman, P. (1991). *Bull Run*. New York: HarperCollins. (U)

Rowland, D. (1991). *Little red riding hood/The wolf's tale*. New York: Birch Lane Press. (P–M)

Figure 11–7 Stories illustrating the four points of view

understanding of the story—the characters, the events—and whether or not readers will believe what they are being told. The student author must decide who will tell the story and then follow that viewpoint consistently. Four points of view are first-person viewpoint, omniscient viewpoint, limited omniscient viewpoint, and objective viewpoint (Lukens, 1999). A list of stories written from each point of view is presented in Figure 11–7. Sometimes authors tell stories from the viewpoints of two characters, as in Fleischman's *Bull Run* (1991), or by providing letters or other documents that display multiple viewpoints, as in Avi's *Nothing But the Truth: A Documentary Novel* (1991). These multiple viewpoint books are also listed in Figure 11–7.

First-Person Viewpoint.   Authors use the first-person viewpoint when they tell the story through the eyes of one character using the first-person pronoun *I*. This point of view is used so that the reader can live the story as the narrator tells it. The narrator, usually the main character, speaks as an eyewitness and a participant in the events. For example, in *The Slave Dancer* (Fox, 1973), Jessie tells the story of his kidnapping and frightful voyage on a slave ship, and in *Alexander and the Terrible, Horrible, No Good, Very Bad Day* (Viorst, 1977), Alexander tells about a day when everything seemed to go wrong for him. One limitation to this viewpoint is that the narrator must remain an eyewitness.

Omniscient Viewpoint.   Here the author is godlike, seeing and knowing all. The author tells the readers about the thought processes of each character without worrying about how the information is obtained. William Steig's *Doctor De Soto* (1982), a story about a mouse dentist who outwits a fox with a toothache, is an example of a story written from the omniscient viewpoint. Steig lets readers know that the fox is thinking about eating the dentist as soon as his toothache is cured and that the mouse dentist is aware of the fox's thoughts and plans a clever trick.

Limited Omniscient Viewpoint.   Authors use this point of view to overhear the thoughts of one of the characters without being all-knowing and all-seeing. The story is told in third person, and the author concentrates on the thoughts, feelings, and significant past experiences of the main character or another important character. Robert Burch uses the limited omniscient viewpoint in *Queenie Peavy* (1966), and Queenie is the character Burch concentrates on, showing why she has a chip on her shoulder and how she overcomes it.

Objective Viewpoint.   Authors using the objective viewpoint write as though they were making a film of the story and can learn only from what is visible and audible and from what others say about the characters and situations. Readers are eyewitnesses to the story and are confined to the immediate scene. A limitation is that the author cannot probe very deeply into characters. *Cinderella* (Brown, 1954) and *The Little Red Hen* (Zemach, 1983) are examples of stories told from the objective viewpoint. In these stories, authors focus on recounting the events of the story rather than on developing the personalities of the characters.

These five elements are the building blocks of stories. With this structure, authors—both children and adults—can let their creativity flow and combine ideas with structure to craft a good story.

Comparison	Authors compare one thing to another or view something in terms of something else. When the comparison uses the word *like* or *as*, it is a simile; when the comparison is stated directly, it is a metaphor. For example, "the ocean is like a playground for whales" is a simile; "the ocean is a playground for whales" is a metaphor. Metaphors are stronger comparisons because they make more direct comparisons.
Hyperbole	Authors use hyperbole when they overstate or stretch the truth to make obvious and intentional exaggerations for a special effect. "It's raining cats and dogs" and "my feet are killing me" are two examples of hyperbole. American tall tales also have rich examples of hyperbole.
Imagery	Authors use descriptive or sensory words and phrases to create imagery or a picture in the reader's mind. Sensory language stirs the reader's imagination. Instead of saying "the kitchen smelled good as grandmother cooked Thanksgiving dinner," authors create imagery when they write "the aroma of a turkey roasting in the oven filled grandmother's kitchen on Thanksgiving."
Personification	Authors use personification when they attribute human characteristics to animals or objects. For example, "the moss crept across the sidewalk" is personification.
Symbolism	Authors often use a person, place, or thing as a symbol to represent something else. For example, a dove symbolizes peace, the Statue of Liberty symbolizes freedom, and books symbolize knowledge.
Tone	Authors create an overall feeling or effect in the story through their choice of words and use of other literary devices. For example, *Bunnicula: A Rabbit-Tale of Mystery* (Howe & Howe, 1979) and *Catherine, Called Birdy* (Cushman, 1994) are humorous stories, and *Babe the Gallant Pig* (King-Smith, 1995) and *Sarah, Plain and Tall* (MacLachlan, 1985) are uplifting, feel-good stories.

Figure 11–8 Literary devices

Literary Devices

In addition to the five elements of story structure, authors use literary devices to make their writing more vivid and memorable. Without these literary devices, writing can be dull (Lukens, 1999). A list of six literary devices that elementary students learn about is presented in Figure 11–8. Imagery is probably the most commonly used literary device; many authors use imagery as they paint rich word pictures that bring their characters and settings to life. Authors use metaphors and similes to compare one thing to another, personification to endow animals and objects with human qualities, and hyperbole to exaggerate or stretch the truth. They also create symbols as they use one thing to represent something else. In Chris Van Allsburg's *The Wretched Stone* (1991), for example, the glowing stone that distracts the crew from reading, from spending time with their friends, and from doing their jobs symbolizes television or, perhaps, computers. For students to understand the theme of the story, they need to recognize symbols. The author's style conveys the tone or overall feeling in a story; some stories are humorous, some are uplifting celebrations of life, and others are sobering commentaries on society.

Young children focus on the events and characters as they read and write stories, but during the elementary grades, students become more sophisticated readers and writers. They learn to notice both what the author says and how he or she says it. Teachers facilitate students' growth by directing their attention to literary devices and to the author's style as they discuss stories they are reading and by encouraging students to use these devices in their own writing.

Teaching Children to Write Stories

Children develop their concept of story through listening to stories read aloud and telling stories during the preschool years. With this introduction to narratives, elementary students are ready to learn more about how stories are organized and how authors use the elements of story structure to create stories. Children use this knowledge to compose the stories they write as well as to comprehend stories they read.

> **Teacher's Note: Supporting Struggling Writers**
>
> Too often, struggling writers won't even attempt to write a story because they don't think they know how to write one. To build both their confidence and their knowledge base, write a collaborative story with a small group of struggling writers and offer guidance and support through each stage of the writing process. After several collaborative writing activities, struggling writers are more likely to be successful when they write a story independently.

The teaching strategy presented in this section builds on children's concept of story by examining the elements of story structure—plot, setting, character, theme, and point of view—in connection with a literature-based reading program and then having students apply these elements in writing stories. Rather than a collection of cookbook-like activities, this strategy is an integrated approach in which children read, listen to, talk, view, visually represent, and write stories. The reading-writing connection is particularly crucial. As readers, children consider how the author used a particular structure and consider its impact; then, as writers, they experiment with the structure in the stories they write and consider the impact on their classmates who read the stories.

Step by Step: Elements of Story Structure

1. **Introduce the element.** Teachers introduce the element of story structure and develop charts to define the element and/or list its characteristics. Figure 11–9 on pp. 366–367 presents sample charts that can be developed for each element of story structure. Next, teachers read several stories illustrating the element to children or have children read the stories themselves. After reading, teachers and children have a grand conversation to discuss the story, and teachers ask questions to probe children's awareness of how the author used the element in constructing the story.

2. **Analyze the element in stories.** Children read or listen to one or more stories that illustrate the element. After reading, children analyze how the author used the element in each story. They should tie their analyses to the definition and the characteristics of the element presented in the first step.

3. **Participate in exploration activities.** Children participate in exploration activities in which they investigate how authors use the element in particular stories. Possible activities include retelling stories orally, with drawings, and in writing; dramatizing stories with puppets and with informal drama; and drawing clusters to graphically display the structure of stories. (These exploration activities are described in the next section.)

4. **Review the element.** Teachers review the characteristics of the element being studied using the charts introduced earlier, and they ask children to restate the definition and characteristics of the element in their own words, using one book they have read to illustrate the characteristics.

5. **Write a class collaboration story.** Children apply what they have learned about the element of story structure by writing a class (or group) collaboration story. A collaborative story provides children with a rehearsal before they write stories independently. Teachers review the element of story structure and refer to the appropriate chart as the story is being written. They encourage children to offer ideas for the story and explain how to incorporate the element into the story. Next, children follow the writing process stages by writing a rough draft on the chalkboard, chart paper, or overhead transparency. Then they revise the story, working both to improve the content and to check that the element of story structure being studied has been incorporated. Next, children edit the story and make a final copy to be shared with all class members.

6. **Write individual stories.** Using the process approach, children write individual stories incorporating the element being studied and other elements of story structure that they have already learned.

Teaching an Element of Story Structure

Teachers introduce children to an element of story structure using the stories illustrating the element that they collect and the instructional materials they develop. Children read stories and analyze how authors use the element in them. Next, they participate in exploration activities, such as retelling stories and drawing clusters, in which they investigate how authors used the element in particular stories. With this background, children write collaborative and individual stories applying what they have learned about the element. The teaching steps are presented in the step-by-step feature on page 364.

Exploration Activities

Children investigate how authors use plot, character, setting, theme, and point of view through exploration activities. As they retell and dramatize stories, compare versions of stories, and write new versions, children are elaborating their concepts of story and gaining the experience necessary to write well-developed stories. Here are 10 useful exploration activities:

1. *Class collaboration retelling of stories.* Teachers choose a favorite story that children have read or listened to several times, and have each student draw or write a retelling of a page or short part of the story. Then they collect the contributions and compile them to make a class book. Younger children can draw pictures and dictate their retellings, which the teacher prints in large type. Then these pictures and text can be attached to sheets of posterboard to make a big book that children can read together.

2. *Retelling and telling stories.* Children retell familiar stories to small groups of classmates using simple hand or finger puppets or with pictures on a flannel board. Similarly, children can create their own stories to tell. A gingerbread boy might become a gingerbread bunny that runs away with a basket of Easter eggs, or Max might make a second trip to visit the wild things.

3. *Retelling stories with pictures.* Children retell a favorite story by drawing a series of pictures and compiling them to make a wordless picture book. Young children can make a booklet by folding one sheet of drawing paper in quarters like a greeting card. Then they write the title of the book on the front; on the three remaining pages, they draw illustrations to represent the beginning, middle, and end of the story. A sample four-sided booklet is presented in Figure 11–10 on p. 368. Older children can produce a film of a favorite story by drawing a series of pictures on a long sheet of butcher paper and scrolling the film on a screen made out of a cardboard box.

4. *Retelling stories in writing.* Children write retellings of favorite stories in their own words. Predictable books—stories that use repetition—are often the easiest to retell. Children do not copy the text out of a book; rather, they retell

Chart 1

Stories

Stories have three parts:

1. A beginning
2. A middle
3. An end

Chart 2

Beginnings of Stories

Writers put these things in the beginning of a story:

1. The characters are introduced.
2. The setting is described.
3. A problem is established.
4. Readers get interested in the story.

Chart 3

Middles of Stories

Writers put these things in the middle of a story:

1. The problem gets worse.
2. Roadblocks thwart the main character.
3. More information is provided about the characters.
4. The middle is the longest part.
5. Readers become engaged with the story and empathize with the characters.

Chart 4

Ends of Stories

Writers put these things in the end of a story:

1. The problem is resolved.
2. The loose ends are tied up.
3. Readers feel a release of emotions that were built up in the middle.

Chart 5

Conflict

Conflict is the problem that characters face in the story. There are four kinds of conflict:

1. Conflict between a character and nature
2. Conflict between a character and society
3. Conflict between characters
4. Conflict within a character

Chart 6

Plot

Plot is the sequence of events in a story. It has four parts:

1. A Problem: The problem introduces conflict at the beginning of the story.
2. Roadblocks: Characters face roadblocks as they try to solve the problem in the middle of the story.
3. The High Point: The high point in the action occurs when the problem is about to be solved. It separates the middle and the end.
4. The Solution: The problem is solved and the roadblocks are overcome at the end of the story.

Figure 11–9 Charts for the elements of story structure

Chart 7

Setting

The setting is where and when the story takes place.

1. Location: Stories can take place anywhere.
2. Weather: Stories take place in different kinds of weather.
3. Time of Day: Stories take place during the day or at night.
4. Time Period: Stories take place in the past, at the current time, or in the future.

Chart 8

Characters

Writers develop characters in four ways:

1. Appearance: How characters look
2. Action: What characters do
3. Dialogue: What characters say
4. Monologue: What characters think

Chart 9

Theme

Theme is the underlying meaning of a story.

1. Explicit Themes: The meaning stated clearly in the story.
2. Implicit Themes: The meaning is suggested by the characters, action, and monologue.

Chart 10

Point of View

Writers tell the story according to one of four viewpoints:

1. First-Person Viewpoint: The writer tells the story through the eyes of one character using "I."
2. Omniscient Viewpoint: The writer sees all and knows all about each character.
3. Limited Omniscient Viewpoint: The writer focuses on one character and tells that character's thoughts and feelings.
4. Objective Viewpoint: The writer focuses on the events of the story without telling what the characters are thinking and feeling.

Figure 11–9 *continued*

Figure 11–10 Independent writing: A four-sided booklet retelling *The Tale of Peter Rabbit*

a story that they know well. A sixth grader wrote the following retelling of "Little Red Riding Hood." Notice that her sentences are written in alphabetical order: The first sentence begins with *A*, the second with *B*, the third with *C*, and so on.

 "Another plain day," said Little Red Riding Hood. "Boy, oh boy, oh boy," she wondered. "Could I do something fun today?"

"Dear," called her mother to Little Red Riding Hood. "Eat your breakfast and then take these goodies to grandma's house."

"Fine, I'll do it. Great," said Little Red Riding Hood, "my first time I get to go through the forest."

"Hold it," said a wolf in the forest. "I want to look in that basket of yours."

"Just stay out of there, you wolf. Keep your hands off me! Let go of me, you wolf." Mighty and brave, she slapped the wolf. Not knowing what to do, she ran down the path to grandma's house.

Open minded, the wolf ran to grandma's house. Putting his hands through the window, he climbed in and swallowed grandma. Quietly he jumped in her bed.

> Running to grandma's house, still scared from the wolf, Little Red Riding Hood knocked on grandma's door. Silently the wolf came to meet her. Too late for Red Riding Hood to run, she panicked and yelled. Unaware she was. Very loudly her yell traveled through the forest.
>
> Wondering what it was, a woodsman heard it and came to grandma's house and killed the wolf. X-raying the body of the wolf, he saw grandma.
>
> "Your help sure has paid off," said Little Red Riding Hood after the woodsman saved her. Zooming from grandma's house came Little Red Riding Hood, to tell her mom what had just happened.

After writing, children can point out how they used the element of story structure being studied in their retelling. They can point out the conflict situation; the point of view; repeated words; or the beginning, middle, and end parts. This activity is a good confidence builder for children who can't seem to continue a story to its conclusion. By using a story they are familiar with, they are more successful.

5. *Dramatizing stories.* Children dramatize favorite stories or use puppets to retell a story. These dramatizations should be informal; fancy props are unnecessary, and students should not memorize or read dialogue.

6. *Drawing story clusters and other diagrams.* Children draw beginning-middle-end story clusters, repetition clusters, and plot diagrams for stories they have read.

7. *Comparing versions of stories.* Children compare different versions of folktales and fairy tales such as "The Hare and the Tortoise" and "Cinderella." They can compare the beginning, middle, and end of each version. For example, in one version of "The Hare and the Tortoise," the beginning is much longer as the author describes the elaborate plans for the race, whereas in other versions, the beginning is brief. Children can also compare the events in each story. In one version of "Cinderella," for instance, the heroine attends two balls.

8. *Creating open-mind portraits.* Children choose a character and create an open-mind portrait showing both what the character looks like and what the character is thinking. A fourth grader's open-mind portrait for Sarah, the mail-order bride in *Sarah, Plain and Tall* (MacLachlan, 1985), is shown in Figure 11–11. Children begin by drawing and cutting out a portrait of the character, as shown in the left part of the figure. Then they trace an outline of the character's head on another piece of paper and draw pictures and write words inside the outline to show what the character is thinking, as shown in the right part of the figure. In Figure 11–11, Sarah is thinking about things that she loves: the ocean, her cat named Seal, her new family—Papa, Anna, and Caleb—and two kinds of dunes. Then children staple the portrait at the top of the mind drawing so that it opens from the bottom like a flip book.

9. *Writing dialogue.* Children choose an excerpt from a favorite story and create a script with dialogue, then they read the script to classmates as a readers theatre presentation. Also, children can draw comic strips for an excerpt from a

Figure 11–11 Guided writing: A fourth grader's open-mind portrait of Sarah, the main character of *Sarah, Plain and Tall*

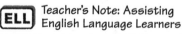
Teacher's Note: Assisting English Language Learners

Looking for ways to get your English learners involved in story writing activities? These 10 activities are as appropriate for second-language learners as they are for other young children because they offer opportunities for students to become actively involved with stories and use talk, drama, and drawing to learn about the structure of stories. In addition, students who need more support can work with classmates on their activities.

story and add dialogue. They might also try varying the register of the language, from informal to very formal, from standard to nonstandard English, to appreciate the power of language.

10. *Retelling stories from different points of view.* Children experiment with point of view to understand how the author's viewpoint can slant a story. To demonstrate how the story changes according to the perspective of the person telling the story, read Judy Blume's *The Pain and the Great One* (1974) to children. In this book, the same brief story is told twice, first from the viewpoint of "the great one," an 8-year-old sister, and then from the viewpoint of "the pain," the 6-year-old brother. Even children in the primary

grades are struck by how different the two versions are and how the narrator filters the information.

Another way to demonstrate the impact of different viewpoints is for children to retell or rewrite a familiar story, such as *Little Red Riding Hood* (Galdone, 1974), from different points of view—through the eyes of Little Red Riding Hood, her sick, old grandmother, the hungry wolf, or the woodsman. As they shift the point of view, children learn that they can change some aspects of a story but not others. To learn how these changes affect a story, children can retell short episodes of a story such as C. S. Lewis's *The Lion, the Witch and the Wardrobe* (1950), which is told from the omniscient viewpoint, from the viewpoint of each character or from the four basic viewpoints. The omniscient viewpoint is a good one to start with because in this viewpoint, the readers learn all. As children shift to other points of view, they must decide what to leave out according to the new perspective. They must decide whether to tell the story in first or third person and what kinds of information about the characters they are permitted to share.

Assessing Stories That Children Write

Assessing the stories that children write involves far more than simply judging the quality of the finished stories. Any assessment should also take into account children's activities and learning as they study the element of story structure as well as the activities children engage in as they write and refine their stories. Three components should be considered in assessing children's stories:

1. Students' knowledge about and application of the element in writing
2. Students' use of the writing process
3. The quality of students' finished stories

The first component is children's knowledge of the element of story structure and their application of the element in the stories they write. Determining whether children applied what they have learned in their stories is crucial in assessing their stories. Consider the following points:

- Can the child define or identify the characteristics of the element?
- Can the child explain how the element being studied was used in a particular story?
- Did the child apply the element in the story he or she has written?

Children's use of the process approach to write their stories is the second component of evaluation. Learning about the element is a prewriting activity, and afterward, children draft, revise, edit, and share their stories as they do with other types of writing. Teachers assess children's use of the writing process by observing them as they write and by asking these questions:

- Did the child participate in a writing group?

- Did the child revise the story according to feedback received from the writing group?
- Did the child proofread the story and correct as many mechanical errors as possible?
- Did the child share the story?

The third component is the quality of the story. Quality is difficult to measure, but it is often described as creativeness or inventiveness. In addition, a second aspect of quality is organization. Children who write high-quality, interesting stories use the elements of story structure to their advantage. Ask these questions to assess the quality of children's stories:

- Is the story interesting?
- Is the story well organized?

These three components and the questions listed under each can be used to develop rubrics and checklists to assess children's stories. Assessing or grading children's stories is more than simply evaluating the quality of the finished product, and any assessment should reflect all components of children's involvement with stories.

Figures 11–12 and 11–13 present two assessment instruments that teachers developed for their students to assess their use of story structure in stories they

| Name _____ | |
Story _____	
Who is the main character?	Who are the other characters?
How did you develop the main character? _____ How the character looks _____ What the character does _____ What the character says _____ What the character thinks	What is the most important thing about your main character?

Figure 11–12 Third graders' self-assessment character checklist

Name _____

Story _____

1. Which element of story structure did you focus on in your story?

2. What did you know about this element?

3. How did you focus on the element in your story?

4. Why is your story better because of your focus on this element?

Figure 11–13 An eighth-grade story structure assessment sheet

are writing. Figure 11–12 shows a character checklist that a third-grade teacher developed for students to self-assess how well they had developed the characters in the stories they are writing. Figure 11–13 shows an eighth-grade story structure assessment sheet that students use to examine their use of any element of story structure in stories they are writing. Students typically use the checklists during the revising stage of the writing process and make revisions based on their self-assessment.

Narrative Writing

1. It sounds as if this approach is very time-consuming, and I don't have any time to spend on teaching writing. What can I do?

Your concern is a common one. Many teachers feel frustrated as they try to squeeze writing instruction into an already full school day. One way to make time to teach children about the elements of story structure and have them write stories is to incorporate the activities discussed in this chapter into the reading program. Stories in basal reading texts illustrate many of the elements of story structure, and they can be supplemented with class sets of some of the stories suggested in this chapter, stories that you read aloud to the entire class, and library books that students read independently. As children read the stories in the basal readers or in trade books, focus the discussion on the elements of story structure rather than on questions provided in teacher manuals. If you teach creatively, you can use a combination of basal readers and trade books to teach students about stories.

2. I told my sixth graders about plot and then they wrote stories. I was very disappointed with their stories. They weren't very good.

It sounds as if you explained plot to the children rather than helping them analyze stories to see how authors use plot. It is important to follow the instructional strategy laid out in this chapter and allow time for children to examine and experiment with plot before they write stories. It isn't enough to explain an element of story structure to children.

Did children write a class collaboration story before they wrote individual stories? Writing a collaborative story is an important step because it gives you an opportunity to see if the children understand the element and how to apply it in their stories.

3. Is there a sequence I should follow in teaching the elements of story structure, or can I teach them all together?

Each element of story structure should be taught separately, and it is best to teach the elements in the order presented in this chapter. Plot (and the concept of beginning-middle-end in particular) is the most basic element of story structure. Even older children need to understand this basic organizational pattern before examining the other elements. If children haven't been taught about plot, setting, characters, theme, and point of view, they need to study each element and write stories incorporating each.

4. What should I do when Wilson can't write a story?

You should work with Wilson to find out why he can't write a story. First, check his understanding of the elements of story structure. Can he explain an element and give examples? If not, he is not prepared to write a story incorporating that element and should be involved in additional activities to examine it. Second, check Wilson's ability to retell a story he has read that incorporates the element. Can he retell a story orally? If not, read a short story to him or have him read one himself and retell it to you. If he can retell a story success-fully, you might want to have him retell a story in writing instead of writing an original story. Third, check to see if he has an idea for his story. If he doesn't, talk to him about possible story ideas, encourage him to write a sequel to a story he has read, or, if all else fails, suggest that he retell a favorite story. It is important for Wilson to write something so he can overcome his writer's block.

5. My third graders spend an hour each day in writing workshop and they write personal narratives. I don't have time to teach them about story elements.

Teaching your third graders about the elements of story structure would fit well within your writing workshop structure. You can teach minilessons about the elements of story structure as part of writing workshop and then have them apply what they are learning in their writing. You'll find that your students' personal narratives will become more sophisticated when they apply information about plot, characters, setting, and the other elements of story structure. There are benefits for reading, too, because knowing about story structure also improves their reading comprehension.

CHAPTER 12
Poetry Writing

Preview

Purpose Students write poetry to play with words, create images, explore feelings, and entertain.

Audience Poems are usually shared orally so that the audience can appreciate the wordplay, rhythm, and other poetic devices. Often students share their poems and other wordplays with classmates by reading them aloud or preparing an anthology.

Forms Forms include formula poems, free-form poems, syllable- and word-count poems, rhymed verse forms, and poems modeled on other poems. Most children like to write poetry, but when they equate poetry with rhymed verse, the poems they compose are stilted and artificial. As they experiment with poetic forms and devices, students write interesting poems because of their spontaneity and playfulness with language.

Instructional Preview: Poetry Writing

Grades	Goals and Activities
Kindergarten–Grade 2	**Goal 1:** Identify rhyming words and create rhyming wordplays • Students identify rhyming words in familiar songs and poems. • Students create silly rhyming couplets (e.g., I see a spoon flying over the moon). • Students use the pattern of a familiar rhyming poem to create a new, collaborative poem.
	Goal 2: Write collaborative and individual formula poems • Students write "I wish . . ." poems. • Students write color poems. • Students write five-senses poems. • Students write "If I were . . ." poems.
	Goal 3: Create collaborative and individual word pictures • Students use words to draw a picture. • Students write a word artistically to illustrate its meaning. • Students write sentences in shapes of objects to create word pictures. • Students write concrete poems.
Grades 3–5	**Goal 1:** Identify syllables in words and write syllable-count poems • Students break multisyllabic words into syllables. • Students write collaborative and individual haiku and cinquains.
	Goal 2: Recognize the multiple meanings of words • Students read books of riddles and analyze how words with multiple meanings are used to create the riddle and its answer. • Students use multiple meanings of words to create riddles. • Students compare the meanings of homophones (e.g., *sun* and *son*). • Students analyze the literal and figurative meanings of idioms. • Students create posters to illustrate multiple meanings of words.
	Goal 3: Develop a repertoire of poetic forms • Teachers review poetic forms taught in the primary grades. • Students write formula poems. • Students write free-form poems. • Students write found poems from books they are reading. • Students write poems for two voices related to stories and thematic units.

Instructional Preview: Poetry Writing

Grades	Goals and Activities
Grades 6–8	**Goal 1:** Analyze poems written by adult poets and write new poems modeled on them • Students examine a poem written by an adult poet and create poems following its form. • Students write model poems.
	Goal 2: Analyze how poets use poetic devices and incorporate poetic devices in poems students write • Students choose favorite poems and examine them to determine which poetic devices the poets used. • Students write alliterative sentences and tongue twisters. • Students examine poems they have written to look for poetic devices or revise these poems to add one or more poetic devices.
	Goal 3: Review poetic forms • Teachers teach a series of minilessons on various poetic forms. • Students add information about each form to a poetry notebook. • Students write poems as part of writing workshop or as projects in literature focus units and thematic units.

Reading and Writing Poetry

Miss Clark's sixth-grade class is reading and writing poetry during a 4-week genre unit. During the first week, students focus on Jack Prelutsky and his poems. They read poems during reading workshop and write responses to them. Through minilessons, they learn about the poet and his poems. Then they apply what they have learned as they write poems during writing workshop. The daily schedule is as follows:

8:45–9:30	***Reading Workshop*** Students read poems independently and write responses in poetry logs.
9:30–9:45	***Sharing*** Students share poems they have read, and the class uses choral reading to reread favorite Prelutsky poems copied onto chart paper.
9:45–10:10	***Minilesson*** Miss Clark teaches reading and writing minilessons about Prelutsky and his poems, poetic forms, and poetic devices.
10:10–10:45	***Writing Workshop*** Using the writing process, students write poems, some of which are modeled on Prelutsky's poems.
10:45–11:00	***Sharing*** Students read poems they have written to the class.

During reading workshop, students read self-selected books from a text set (or collection) of poetry books written by Jack Prelutsky that are displayed in a special poetry box in the classroom library. Figure 12–1 presents a list of the books in Miss Clark's text set. She has several copies of each book available for students to read. After independent reading time, students gather together to share some of the poems they have read. Three favorite poems are "The New Kid on the Block," "Mean Maxine," and "Louder Than a Clap of Thunder!"—all from Prelutsky's *The New Kid on the Block* (1984). Students have copied these poems on large chart paper, and the class rereads the poems as a choral reading or sings them to familiar tunes such as "Yankee Doodle" almost every day.

The baby uggs are hatching. (1982). New York: Mulberry.
The beauty of the beast: Poems from the animal kingdom. (1997). New York: Knopf.
Circus. (1974). New York: Macmillan.
The headless horseman rides tonight. (1980). New York: Greenwillow.
It's Christmas. (1981). New York: Greenwillow.
It's Halloween. (1977). New York: Greenwillow.
It's snowing! It's snowing! (1984). New York: Greenwillow.
It's Thanksgiving. (1982). New York: Greenwillow.
It's Valentine's Day. (1983). New York: Greenwillow.
My parents think I'm sleeping. (1985). New York: Greenwillow.
The new kid on the block. (1984). New York: Greenwillow.
Nightmares: Poems to trouble your sleep. (1976). New York: Greenwillow.
Rainy rainy Saturday. (1980). New York: Greenwillow.
Ride a purple pelican. (1986). New York: Greenwillow.
Rolling Harvey down the hill. (1980). New York: Greenwillow.
Something big has been here. (1990). New York: Greenwillow.
The snopp on the sidewalk and other poems. (1977). New York: Greenwillow.
Toucans two and other poems. (1979). New York: Macmillan.
Tyrannosaurus was a beast. (1988). New York: Greenwillow.
Zoo doings. (1983). New York: Greenwillow.

Figure 12–1 Text set of poetry books written by Jack Prelutsky

Each day, students write in a poetry log about the poems they are reading during reading workshop. In these entries, students write about poems they like, record observations about Prelutsky as a poet, list poetic devices that Prelutsky uses, and comment on relationships between the poems and their own lives. Here is one student's response to "Louder Than a Clap of Thunder!" from *The New Kid on the Block:*

> I love this poem. It's cool to read because you can sort of yell and it's the truth for my dad. He snores real loud, real, real loud. And I think Jack Prelutsky was smart to use comparisons. He keeps you guessing until the last line that it is all about snoring. I think that's why the title is just the first line of the poem because if he called it "My Father's Snoring" it would give away the surprise. It's not a very good title. Sort of boring. I would call it "Can You Beat This?" I'm going to write a poem like this but change it to softer than and write about how soft my cat is when she tiptoes across my bed. Or when she curls up in my lap.

Miss Clark teaches a minilesson each day, and she uses Prelutsky's poems as examples for the concepts she is teaching. On Monday, her minilesson focuses on the poet and his life. Because rhyme is an important device in Prelutsky's poems, she makes this her topic for the minilesson on Tuesday. Miss Clark shares several poems with different rhyme schemes, and students examine the arrangements. They also talk about repetition and imagery as alternatives to rhyme.

On Wednesday, Miss Clark reads "The Baby Uggs Are Hatching" (Prelutsky, 1982) and teaches a minilesson on inventing words. She suggests that students might want to create creatures like the uggs, invent names for them, and write their own verses following the format of the poem during writing workshop. On Thursday, she teaches a minilesson on alliteration after sharing several poems from Prelutsky's *The Headless Horseman Rides Tonight* (1980). Students especially enjoy these spooky poems, and Prelutsky uses alliteration effectively in the poems to evoke a frightening mood.

In the fifth minilesson, on Friday, Miss Clark explains how to write color poems after reading "What Happens to the Colors?" in *My Parents Think I'm Sleeping* (1985) and sharing other color poems from *Hailstones and Halibut Bones* (O'Neill, 1989). Later, during writing workshop, students write color poems in which they begin each line or stanza with the name of the color. Here is one student's poem about gray:

Gray is smoke,
  billowing from a burning house,
  Or clouds in a stormy sky,
  Gray is my Grandma's hair
  permed at the beauty salon,
  Or rocks on a mountainside.
  Gray is an elephant's hide
  wrinkled and covered with dust,
  Or me when I'm feeling down.

During writing workshop, students write their own poems. They experiment with the poetic forms that Miss Clark teaches and with other forms that they have learned previously. They draft their poems, meet in writing groups to revise their poems, edit them with Miss Clark, and then write the final copy in the second half of their poetry logs.

One day during writing workshop, students work together as a class to write a new version of Prelutsky's poem "I'm Thankful" (1984). They follow Prelutsky's format, even the "except" arrangement of the last line. Here is an excerpt from the class poem "I'm Thankful":

I'm thankful for my telephone.
  It hardly ever rings.
I'm thankful for my cat.
  He scratched me in the face.
I'm thankful for my basketball.
  It broke my mother's vase.
I'm thankful for my bicycle.
  I ran into a car.

I'm thankful for my skateboard.
I fell and scraped my knees.
I'm thankful for so many things
Except, of course, for peas!

Students also prepare a reading-writing project at the end of the week. Miss Clark and the class brainstorm a list of more than 20 possible projects, and students work individually or in small groups on self-selected projects. Some students write letters to Jack Prelutsky, and others make a collection of favorite Prelutsky poems. One group videotapes a choral reading of several Prelutsky poems to share with the class. Others write their own poems and compile them in an anthology or turn a Prelutsky poem into a picture book with one stanza illustrated on each page.

CHILDREN ARE NATURAL POETS. They have a natural affinity for songs, verses, and rhymes. Babies and preschoolers respond positively when their parents repeat Mother Goose rhymes, read A. A. Milne's Winnie-the-Pooh stories, and sing songs to them. Elementary students continue this interest in poetry as they create jump-rope rhymes and other ditties on the playground. Miss Clark's students affirm this interest in poetry: they are enthusiastically involved in reading and writing poetry and think of themselves as poets. Jack Prelutsky and other poets who write for children have created many collections of poems that spark students' interest in poetry. These poets write about topics that appeal to children, such as poltergeists, parents, and dinosaurs. When students know how to write poems and use poetic devices, they can create vivid word pictures, powerful images, and emotional expressions.

In this chapter, the focus is on teaching students how to write poetry. You will learn about the types of poems elementary students can write and how to help them learn to play with words and craft poems. The key points presented in this chapter are:

- Children explore the power of words and phrases and create word pictures through wordplay activities.
- During the elementary grades, children learn to write five types of poems—formula poems, free-form poems, syllable- and word-count poems, rhymed verse poems, and model poems.
- Teachers teach students how to write different types of poems.
- Teachers provide opportunities for students to read and write poetry during reading and writing workshop, literature focus units, and social studies and science theme cycles.

Wordplay

Students play with words as they put words together in unusual ways, invent new words, learn that words can have many meanings, and experiment with the sound of words. These experiences help children to appreciate what a powerful tool words are for creating images, communicating ideas, and reflecting on life. They learn to compare figurative and literal meanings of idioms, appreciate riddles, and play with rhyme. Many examples of wordplay can be found in children's books, and these books demonstrate how people experiment, laugh, and create pictures with language. In Bernard Most's *A Dinosaur Named After Me* (1991), for example, children use their own names to invent new dinosaur names. A list of wordplay books is presented in Figure 12–2.

Learning the Meaning of Words

The meaning of words is crucial in wordplay. Many riddles, for instance, depend on words with multiple meanings. A familiar riddle asks, "How are children and fish alike?" and the answer is "Both are in school." The word *school* is ambiguous, and understanding this riddle requires knowledge of the second meaning of *school*—a group of fish or aquatic animals traveling together. Although young children often assume a one-to-one relationship between words and their meanings, as elementary students gain more experience with language, they learn that words have multiple meanings, that the sound of certain words called homophones doesn't predict meaning, and that some words have both literal and figurative meanings. This ability to understand and appreciate multiple meanings makes wordplay possible for children.

Words With Multiple Meanings.   One of the concepts about words that children learn during the elementary grades is that words can have more than one meaning. The word *bank,* for example, has at least 12 meanings:

1. a piled-up mass of snow or clouds
2. the slope of land beside a lake or river
3. the slope of a road on a turn
4. the lateral tilting of an airplane in a turn
5. to cover a fire with ashes for slow burning
6. a business establishment that receives and lends money
7. a container in which money is saved
8. a supply for use in emergencies (e.g., blood bank)
9. a place of storage (e.g., computer's memory bank)
10. to count on

Agee, J. (1992). *Go hang a salami! I'm a lasagna hog! and other palindromes.* New York: Farrar, Straus & Giroux. (U)

Barrett, J. (1983). *A snake is totally tail.* New York: Atheneum. (P–M)

Bayer, J. (1984). *A my name is Alice.* New York: Dial. (P–M)

Brown, M. (1983). *What do you call a dumb bunny?* Boston: Little, Brown. (P–M)

Cole, J., & Calmenson, S. (1995). *Yours till banana splits: 201 autograph rhymes.* New York: Morrow. (M–U)

Cox, J. A. (1980). *Put your foot in your mouth and other silly sayings.* New York: Random House. (P–M)

Eiting, M., & Folsom, M. (1980). *Q is for duck: An alphabet guessing game.* New York: Clarion. (P–M)

Fakih, K. O. (1995). *Off the clock: A lexicon of time words and expressions.* New York: Clarion. (M)

Gwynne, F. (1970). *The king who rained.* New York: Dutton. (M–U)

Gwynne, F. (1976). *A chocolate moose for dinner.* New York: Dutton. (M–U)

Gwynne, F. (1980). *The sixteen hand horse.* New York: Prentice-Hall. (M–U)

Gwynne, F. (1988). *A little pigeon toad.* New York: Simon & Schuster. (M–U)

Hall, K., & Eisenberg, L. (1992). *Spacey riddles.* New York: Dial. (P)

Hartman, V. (1992). *Westward ho ho ho! Jokes from the wild west.* New York: Viking. (M–U)

Houget, S. R. (1983). *I unpacked my grandmother's trunk: A picture book game.* New York: Dutton. (P–M)

Juster, N. (1982). *Otter nonsense.* New York: Philomel. (P–M)

Kellogg, S. (1987). *Aster Aardvark's alphabet adventures.* New York: Morrow. (P–M)

Lewis, J. P. (1996). *Riddle-icious.* New York: Knopf. (M)

Maestro, G. (1984). *What's a frank Frank? Tasty homograph riddles.* New York: Clarion. (P–M)

McMillan, B. (1990). *One sun: A book of terse verse.* New York: Holiday House. (M)

Most, B. (1992). *Zoodles.* San Diego: Harcourt Brace Jovanovich. (M)

Perl, L. (1988). *Don't sing before breakfast, don't sing in the moonlight.* New York: Random House. (M–U)

Rees, E. (1995). *Fast Freddie frog and other tongue twister rhymes.* Honesdale, PA: Wordsong. (P)

Schwartz, A. (1992). *Busy buzzing bumblebees and other tongue twisters.* New York: Harper Collins. (P–M)

Smith, W. J., & Ra, C. (1992). *Behind the king's kitchen: A roster of rhyming riddles.* Honesdale, PA: Wordsong. (M–U)

Sterne, N. (1979). *Tyrannosaurus wrecks: A book of dinosaur riddles.* New York: Crowell. (M)

Terban, M. (1982). *Eight ate: A feast of homonym riddles.* New York: Clarion. (P–M)

Terban, M. (1983). *In a pickle and other funny idioms.* New York: Clarion. (M)

Terban, M. (1985). *Too hot to hoot: Funny palindrome riddles.* New York: Clarion. (M–U)

Terban, M. (1992). *Funny you should ask: How to make up jokes and riddles with wordplay.* New York: Clarion. (M–U)

Terban, M. (1995). *Time to rhyme: A rhyming dictionary.* Honesdale, PA: Wordsong. (M)

Van Allsburg, C. (1987). *The z was zapped.* Boston: Houghton Mifflin. (M)

Wilbur, R. (1995). *Runaway opposites.* San Diego: Harcourt Brace. (P)

Figure 12–2 Wordplay books

P = primary grades (K–2), M = middle grades (3–5), U = upper grades (6–8).

11. similar things arranged in a row (e.g., a bank of elevators)

12. to arrange things in a row

Why do some words have many different meanings? The meanings of *bank* in this example come from three sources. The first five meanings come from a Viking word and deal with something slanted or making a slanted motion. Meanings 6 through 10 come from the Italian word *banca,* which originally meant a money changer's table. These meanings deal with financial banking, except meaning 10, "to count on," which requires a bit more thought. We use the saying "to bank on" figuratively to mean "to depend on," but it began more literally, from the actual counting of money on a table. Meanings 11 and 12 come from the Old French word *banc,* meaning "bench." Words acquire multiple meanings as society becomes more complex and finer shades of meaning become necessary. For example, meanings 8 and 9, "an emergency supply" and "a storage place," are fairly new. As with many other words with multiple meanings, it is a linguistic accident that three original words from three languages with their related meanings came to be spelled the same way.

Words assume additional meanings when affixes are added or they are compounded (used together with another word). Consider the word *night* and the variety of words and phrases that incorporate *night,* such as *night blindness, nightcap, nightclub, night crawler, nightfall, nightgown, nightingale, nightlife, nightly, nightmare, night owl, night school, nightstick,* and *nighttime.* Students can compile a list of related words or make a booklet illustrating the words. Figure 12–3 presents a list of 84 *down* words that a sixth-grade class compiled.

Homophones. Homophones are words that sound alike but are spelled differently, such as *fairy* and *ferry.* In most cases, these homophones happen by chance; they develop from entirely different root words and even from words in two languages (Tompkins & Yaden, 1986). Other homophones, such as *flower* and *flour* or *flea* and *flee,* are related etymologically; the first word in each pair is derived from the second. Homophones are confusing because the two words sound alike and their spellings sometimes differ only by a letter or two.

Primary-grade students often notice homophones in books they are reading and ask questions about them. This interest often cues teachers to explain homophones in a minilesson or to plan a series of minilessons and other activities that focus on these sound-alike words. Teachers often share homophone riddle books, including Terban's *Eight Ate: A Feast of Homonym Riddles* (1982) and *Hey, Hay: A Wagonful of Funny Homonym Riddles* (1991), and then students often make their own homophone books in which they draw pictures to illustrate pairs of homophones and use confusing word pairs in sentences. A page comparing *night* and *knight* from a second grader's homophone book is

"Down" Words			
downtown	climb down	reach down	downward
touchdown	down payment	write down	hunt down
get down	sit down	settle down	knock down
chow down	throw down	down it	breakdown
shake down	cut down	goose down	sundown
squat down	downhill	hop down	fall down
showdown	low down	hands down	tear down
lie down	slow down	downfall	turn down
quiet down	down right	close down	push down
shut down	beam down	run down	downstairs
shot down	downy	pin down	look down
cool down	downer	come down	inside down
crackdown	downslope	slam down	zip down
countdown	kickdown	slap down	pour down
pass down	stare down	hoe down	down pour
pass me down	boogy down	lock down	tape down
burn down	put down	water down	downgrade
downbeat	wrestle down	downturn	downstream
down to earth	flop down	stuff down	mow down
shimmey down	hung down	downcast	downhearted
downtrodden	chase down	hurl down	beat down

Figure 12–3 A sixth-grade class collaboration list of *down* words

presented in Figure 12–4. On the page shown in the figure, the student has drawn pictures of the two homophones and used both words in a sentence.

Idioms. Idioms are figurative sayings such as "It's raining cats and dogs" and "I'm all ears." They are sometimes confusing for children, especially those who are learning English as a second language, because the phrases have both literal and figurative meanings. Children must move beyond the literal meaning of the individual words in order to understand the idiom.

Teachers can introduce idioms by sharing books such as Fred Gwynne's *The King Who Rained* (1970), *A Chocolate Moose for Dinner* (1976), *The Sixteen Hand Horse* (1980), and *A Little Pigeon Toad* (1988). These picture books present literal interpretations of well-known idiomatic sayings, and students enjoy guessing the figurative meaning. Together the class talks about what the words in an idiom say—the literal meaning—and what the words mean—the figurative meaning. After students become familiar with idioms, they can compile a list of them on a chart to hang in the classroom. Students often incorporate idioms into their journal entries and even choose idioms to explain in

Figure 12–4 Guided writing: A page from a second grader's homophone book

their journals. One fourth grader wrote this about the saying "I have a frog in my throat":

 I remember that my Gramps used to always say, "I have a frog in my throat." I know it sounds silly, but I used to think he really did and I would ask him to let me look in his throat to see it. That always made him laugh but one time he let me. He opened his mouth and I looked and looked but I couldn't see any frog. I thought it was hiding under his tongue. I was a little kid then so that was why I was thinking the literal meaning.

Students also design posters to illustrate the literal meaning of favorite idiomatic phrases. A fourth grader's poster illustrating the literal meaning of "Hold your horses" is presented in Figure 12–5. After students share their idiom posters with classmates, they add explanations to their posters. This information was added to the poster shown in Figure 12–5:

 "Hold your horses" is an all-American saying. At first it was just literal and it meant that people should hold their horses so that they didn't run away. That was when people rode on horseback or in buggies and wagons. It was part of the best of the American West! But now people don't hold horses much

Figure 12–5 Independent writing: A fourth grader's idiom poster

any more but they still say, "Hold your horses!" Now it is figurative and it means "Do not get too excited!" or "Hey, you calm down!"

Students often become curious about how and why idioms developed, and teachers can share *Put Your Foot in Your Mouth and Other Silly Sayings* (Cox, 1980) and Marvin Terban's *In a Pickle and Other Funny Idioms* (1983), *Mad as a Wet Hen! and Other Funny Idioms* (1987), and *Punching the Clock: Funny Action Idioms* (1990). These books provide easy-to-read and understandable information about the origins of many familiar idioms.

"Thumbs up" and "thumbs down," for example, originated in ancient Rome. Spectators at gladiator contests voted with their thumbs on whether the losers of the fights should live or die. "Cut off your nose to spite your face" is another old idiom; It has been traced to King Henry IV of France, who in 1593 considered making war on his own citizens until his advisers changed his mind. Other idioms are American: "Left holding the bag" comes from a trick country boys played on city boys in the 1800s; "too big for your britches" refers to the hand-me-down pants American boys wore a hundred years ago; and "like greased lightning" is an American expression for something that is very fast. Pioneers greased wagon wheels to make them go faster, so what could be faster than greased lightning? Teachers can also consult Funk's *A Hog on Ice and Other Curious Expressions* (1984), though most students will not be able to read it on their own.

Laughing With Language

As children learn that words have the power to amuse, they enjoy reading, telling, and writing riddles and jokes. Linda Gibson Geller (1985) researched children's humorous language and identified two stages of riddle play that elementary students move through: Primary-grade children experiment with the riddle form and its content, and middle- and upper-grade students explore the paradoxical constructions in riddles. Riddles are written in a question-and-answer format, but young children may only ask questions or ask questions and offer unrelated answers. With more experience, children provide both questions and related answers, and their answers may be either descriptive or nonsensical. An example of the descriptive answer to the question "Why did the turtle go out of his shell?" is "because he was getting too big for it." An example of a nonsensical answer involving an invented word for the riddle "Why did the cat want to catch a snake?" is "because he wanted to turn into a rattle-cat" (Geller, 1981, p. 672). Many primary-grade students' riddles seem foolish by adult standards, but this wordplay is an important precursor to creating true riddles.

Riddles depend on manipulating words with multiple meanings or similar sounds and on using metaphors. The Opies (1959) identified five riddle strategies used by elementary students:

1. Using multiple referents for a noun: "What has an eye but cannot see? (a needle)"

2. Combining literal and figurative interpretations for a single phrase: "Why did the clockmaker throw the clock out the window? (because he wanted to see time fly)"

3. Shifting word boundaries to suggest another meaning: "Why did the cookie cry? (because its mother was a wafer so long)"

4. Separating a word into syllables to suggest another meaning: "When is a door not a door? (when it's a jar)"

5. Creating a metaphor: "What are polka dots on your face? (pimples)"

ELL **Teacher's Note: Assisting English Language Learners**

You probably won't be surprised to learn that wordplay is particularly difficult for students learning English. Many second-language learners don't laugh at jokes and can't solve riddles because they don't understand idioms and multiple meanings of words. It's essential, therefore, to involve students learning English in wordplay activities and to take time to explain jokes and riddles so that they can laugh along with their classmates.

Children begin riddle play by telling familiar riddles and reading riddles written by others. Several excellent books of riddles to share with elementary students are *Tyrannosaurus Wrecks: A Book of Dinosaur Riddles* (Sterne, 1979), *What Do You Call a Dumb Bunny? And Other Rabbit Riddles, Games, Jokes, and Cartoons* (Brown, 1983), and *Eight Ate: A Feast of Homonym Riddles* (Terban, 1982). Soon children are composing their own riddles by adapting riddles they have read and creating new ones.

Figure 12–6 Independent writing: A sixth grader's wordplay cartoon

Others turn jokes into riddles. An excellent book for helping children write riddles is *Fiddle With a Riddle: Write Your Own Riddles,* by Joanne E. Bernstein (1979).

Larissa, a third grader, wrote this riddle using two meanings for Milky Way: "Why did the astronaut go to the Milky Way? Because he wanted a Milky Way Bar." Terry, a fifth grader, wrote this riddle using the homophones *hair* and *hare:* "What is gray and jumpy and on your head? (a gray hare)." The riddles children write may have a visual component; a sixth grader created the humorous cartoon presented in Figure 12–6 based on two meanings of *sidekick.*

Creating Word Pictures

In the primary grades, children learn to write words in horizontal lines from left to right and from top to bottom across a sheet of paper, just as the lines in a book are printed. However, they enjoy breaking this pattern and creating pictures out of the words themselves. These literal, or concrete, word pictures can be single-word pictures or a string of words or a sentence arranged in a picture. Four types of concrete word pictures are described here, and examples are presented in Figure 12–7.

- *Using words to draw a picture.* Children use words instead of lines to draw a picture. Children first draw the picture using lines and then place a second sheet of paper over the drawing and replace all or most of the lines with repeated words.

- *Writing a word to illustrate its meaning.* Children write descriptive words so that the arrangement, size, and intensity of the letters in the word illustrate the meaning. They also write the names of objects and animals so that features of the thing being named are illustrated in the name.

Figure 12–7 Independent writing: Students' word pictures

- *Writing sentences to create word pictures.* Children compose a descriptive phrase, sentence, or paragraph; write it in the shape of an object; and use an asterisk to indicate where to start reading the word picture.
- *Representing words and sayings in pictures.* Children represent a word or idiom with a picture.

Writing Sentences to Create Word Pictures

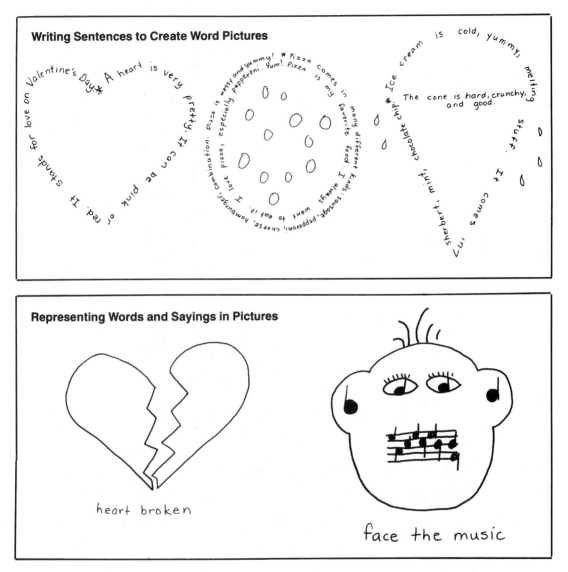

Representing Words and Sayings in Pictures

heart broken

face the music

Figure 12–7 *continued*

Playing With Rhyme

Through their experience with Dr. Seuss stories, finger plays, and nursery rhymes, young children enjoy creating rhymes. Unfortunately, many children equate rhyme with poetry, and often their dependence on rhyme thwarts their attempts to write poetry. Nonetheless, rhyme is a special kind of wordplay and one that children enjoy. A small group of first graders created their own version of *Oh, A-Hunting We Will Go* (Langstaff, 1974). After reading the book, they identified the refrain (lines 1, 2, and 5) and added their own rhyming couplets. Here is an excerpt from their collaborative version:

Oh, a-hunting we will go,
a-hunting we will go.
We'll catch a little bear
and curl his hair,
and never let him go.

Oh, a-hunting we will go,
a-hunting we will go.
We'll catch a little snake
and hit him with a rake,
and never let him go.

Oh, a-hunting we will go,
a-hunting we will go.
We'll catch a little mole
and put him in a hole,
and never let him go.

Oh, a-hunting we will go,
a-hunting we will go.
We'll catch a little bug
and give him a big hug,
and never let him go.

Oh, we'll put them in a ring
and listen to them sing
and then we'll let them go.

The first graders wrote this collaboration with the teacher taking dictation on a large sheet of paper. After the rough draft was written, students reread it, checking the rhymes and changing a word here or there. Then each child chose one stanza to copy and illustrate. The pages were collected and compiled to make a collaborative book.

Hink-Pinks.   Hink-pinks are short rhyming riddles or expressions that describe something; they are composed of two one-syllable rhyming words. Hinky-pinkies have two two-syllable words, and hinkity-pinkities have two three-syllable words (Geller, 1981). Two books of hink-pinks are *Play Day: A Book of Terse Verse* (McMillan, 1991), for primary students, and *The Hink Pink Book* (Burns, 1981), for older students. Here are two examples of hink-pinks written by upper-grade students:

Gas station   What do you call an astronaut?
Car Bar   A sky guy.

Poetic Forms

On St. Patrick's Day, Mrs. Garner hangs a large sheet of green paper on the wall and asks her second graders to help write a poem about the color green. The children eagerly suggest things that are green: grasshoppers, frogs, leprechauns, alligators, aliens, and so on. Then Mrs. Garner demonstrates how to use items from the list in a poem and writes: "Green is aliens from outer space." Quickly Naomi suggests another line: "Green is the paper you're writing on for St. Patrick's Day." Other children grasp the pattern and suggest additional lines. Mrs. Garner reads the poem in a dramatic voice, lengthening some words, softening others, but she ends the list abruptly. Spontaneously, Antoine adds: "And that's what is green!" The children clap their hands as Mrs. Garner adds the line to complete their green poem, "Too Much Green":

Green is aliens from outer space.
Green is the paper you're writing on for St. Patrick's Day.
Green is a caterpillar climbing up the trunk of a tree.
Green is a fierce alligator.
Green is a shiny apple.
Green is Kool-aid that you drink.
Green is a leaping grasshopper.
Green is a hopping frog.
Green is the grass that a leprechaun steps on.
And that's what is green!

Children write poetry successfully using poetic formulas. They write formula poems by beginning each line with particular words (as in color poems), and they count syllables for haiku and create word pictures in concrete poems. Because these poems are brief and written quickly, children use the writing process to revise, edit, and share their writing more easily than with other types of writing. Poetry also allows children more freedom in how they use punctuation, capitalization, and page arrangement.

Many types of poetry that children write do not use rhyme. Rhyme is the sticking point for many would-be poets. In searching for a rhyming word, children often create inane verse:

I see a funny little goat
Wearing a blue sailor's coat
Sitting in an old motorboat.

This is not to suggest that children should not be allowed to write rhyming poetry, but rhyme should never be imposed as a criterion for acceptable poetry. Children should be encouraged to incorporate rhyme when it fits naturally into their writing. As children write poetry, they are searching for their own voices, and they need freedom to do that. Using poetic forms, children create sensitive word pictures, vivid images, and unique comparisons in their poems.

Five types of poetic forms are presented in this section: formula poems, free-form poems, syllable- and word-count poems, rhymed poems, and model poems. Elementary students' poems illustrate each poetic form. The poems written by kindergartners and first graders may seem little more than lists of sentences compared to the more sophisticated poems written by older students. The range of poems, however, shows effectively how children grow in their ability to write poetry through these writing activities.

Formula Poems

Poetic formulas may seem like recipes to be followed rigidly, but that is not how they are intended. Rather, they provide a skeleton for students' poems. After collecting words, images, and comparisons through brainstorming, clustering, or another prewriting strategy, students craft their poems, choosing words and arranging them to create a message. Meaning is always most important; form follows the search for meaning.

Poet Kenneth Koch (2000) worked with students in the elementary grades and developed some simple formulas that make it easy for nearly every child to become a successful poet. Some of these forms seem more like sentences than poems, but the line between poetry and prose is blurry, and these poetry experiences help direct children toward poetic expression. Koch's forms involve repetition, a stylistic device that can be much more effective than rhyme for young poets.

"I Wish . . ." Poems.   Children begin each line of their poems with the words "I wish" and then complete the line with a wish (Koch, 2000). In this second-grade class collaboration, children simply listed their wishes:

   I wish I had all the money in the world.
I wish I was a star fallen down from Mars.
I wish I were a butterfly.
I wish I were a teddy bear.
I wish I wouldn't rain today.
I wish I didn't have to wash a dish.
I wish I had a flying carpet.
I wish I could go to Disney World.
I wish I could go outside and play.

Then children choose one of their wishes and expand on the idea in several more lines. Seven-year-old Brandi chose her wish, "I wish I were a teddy bear," and wrote:

I wish I were a teddy bear
Who sat on a beautiful bed
Who got a hug every night
By a little girl or boy.

Maybe tonight I'll get my wish
And wake up on a little girl's bed
And then I'll be as happy as can be.

Color Poems. Students begin each line of their poems with a color. The same color may be repeated in each line, or a different color may be used (Koch, 2000). For example, second grader Cheyenne describes yellow in this color poem:

Yellow is bright,
Yellow is light.
Yellow glows in the dark,
Yellow likes to lark.
Yellow is an autumn tree,
Yellow is giving to you and me.

In her poem, Cheyenne uses rhyming words effectively, and in searching for a rhyming word for dark, she creates a particularly powerful line, "Yellow likes to lark." Older students, like seventh grader Nancy in the following poem, expand each of their ideas into a stanza:

Black

Black is a deep hole
sitting in the ground
waiting for animals
that live inside.

Black is a beautiful horse
standing on a high hill
with the wind
swirling its mane.

Black is a winter night sky
without stars
to keep it company.

Black is a panther
creeping around a jungle
searching for its prey.

Mary O'Neill's book of color poems, *Hailstones and Halibut Bones: Adventures in Color* (1989), can also be shared with students; however, O'Neill uses rhyme, and it is important to emphasize that students' poems need not rhyme.

Teacher's Note: Supporting Struggling Writers
Formula poems may be the answer for your students who don't like writing. Struggling writers often first feel that they are successful writers when they write color poems or other formula poems. The structure of formula poems almost always ensures that students will be successful, and students report that they like formula poems because they're short and easy to write, and they don't have to rhyme.

Writing color poems can be coordinated with teaching young children to read and write the color words. Instead of having kindergartners and first graders read color words on worksheets and then color pictures with the designated colors, students can create color poems in booklets of paper stapled together. They write and illustrate one line of the poem on each page.

Five-Senses Poems.   Children write about a topic by describing it with each of the five senses. These poems are usually five lines long, with one line for each sense, as the following poem, "Winter," written by a seventh grader, demonstrates:

> Winter smells like chimney smoke.
> Winter tastes like ice.
> Winter looks like heaven.
> Winter feels like a deep freeze.
> Winter sounds like a howling wolf.

Sometimes students add a line at the beginning or end of a poem, as sixth grader Amy did in this poem entitled "Valentine's Day":

> Smells like chocolate candy
> Looks like a flower garden
> Tastes like sugar
> Feels like silk
> Sounds like a symphony orchestra
> Too bad it comes only once a year!

It is often helpful to have students develop a five-senses cluster to collect ideas for each sense. From the cluster, students select the strongest or most vivid idea for each sense to use in a line of the poem.

"If I Were . . . " Poems.   Children write about how they would feel and what they would do if they were something else—a tyrannosaurus rex, a hamburger, or sunshine (Koch, 2000). They begin each poem with "If I were" and tell what it would be like to be that thing. For example, 8-year-old Jeff writes about what he would do if he were a giant:

> If I were a giant
> I would drink up the seas
> And I would touch the sun.
> I would eat the world
> And stick my head in space.

In composing "If I were . . . " poems, students use personification, explore ideas and feelings, and consider the world from a different vantage point.

"I Used to . . . /But Now . . . " Poems.   In these contrast poems, students begin the first line (and every odd-numbered line) with "I used to" and the second

line (and every even-numbered line) with "But now" (Koch, 2000). Using this formula, students can explore ways in which they have changed as well as how things in the world change. Eighth grader Sondra writes from the point of view of a piece of gold ore:

> I used to be a hunk of gold sitting in
> A mine having no worries
> Or responsibilities.
> Now I'm a wedding band bonding
> Two people together, with all
> The worries in the world.

A third-grade teacher adapted this formula for her social studies class, and her students wrote a class collaboration poem using the pattern "I used to think . . . / But now I know . . ." and information they had learned during a unit on the Plains Indians. Here is their poem:

> I used to think that Indians always wore beads,
> but now I know they didn't until the white men came.
> I used to think that Indians used pouches to carry their babies,
> but now I know that they used cradle boards, too.
> I used to think that Indians didn't paint their teepees,
> but now I know that they did.
> I used to think that one chief ruled all the tribes,
> but now I know that there are different chiefs for each tribe.
> I used to think that Indians had guns,
> but now I know that Indians didn't before the white men came.
> I used to think that Indians burned wood,
> but now I know they burned buffalo chips.
> I used to think that Indians caught their horses,
> but now I know they got them from the Spaniards.

"_____ Is . . ." Poems. In description or definition poems, students describe what something is or what something or someone means to them. To begin, the teacher or students identify a topic, filling in the blank with a word such as *anger, a friend, liberty,* or *fear.* Then students start each line in the same way and describe or define the thing they have chosen. Ryan, a sixth grader, wrote the following poem in which he described fear:

> Fear is not knowing what's around the next corner.
> Fear is strange noises scratching on my window at night.
> Fear is a cold hand touching you in an old, dusty hallway.
> Fear is being in a jet that's losing altitude at 50,000 feet.
> Fear is the earth blowing up.

Ryan evoked strong, concrete images of fear in his poem. Children often write very powerful poems using this formula when they move beyond "Happiness is . . ." and "Love is . . . ."

Preposition Poems. Students begin each line of preposition poems with a preposition, and a delightful poetic rewording of lines often results. A fourth grader wrote this preposition poem, "We Ran Forever," about a race with a friend:

> About noon one day
> Along came my friend
> To say, "Want to go for a run?"
> Below the stairs my mom said, "Go!"
> Without waiting, I flew out the door,
> Down the steps,
> Across the lawn, and
> Past the world we ran, forever.

It is helpful for children to brainstorm a list of prepositions to refer to when they write preposition poems. As they write, students may find that they need to drop the formula for a line or two to give the content of their poems top priority, or they may mistakenly begin a line with an infinitive (e.g., "to say") rather than a preposition, as in the third line of "We Ran Forever." The forms presented in this section provide a structure or skeleton for students' writing that should be adapted as needed.

Free-Form Poems

Children put words and phrases together in free-form poems to express a thought or tell a story without concern for rhyme, repetition, or other patterns. The number of words in a line and use of punctuation vary. In the following poem, eighth grader Bobby poignantly describes loneliness using only 15 well-chosen words:

> A lifetime
> Of broken dreams
> And promises
> Lost love hurt
> My heart
> Cries
> In silence

In contrast, Don, a sixth grader, writes a humorous free-form poem about misplaced homework:

> **Excuse for Not Having Homework**
> Oh no, my English homework
> Cannot be found—
> Nor my science book.
> Did my dog eat it?
> Or maybe I dropped my mitt on it.
> Possibly, Martians took it away,
> Or it fell deep down in the hay.

Maybe it's lost or shut in the door.
Oh no, I broke my rule—
I forgot and left it at school!

Students can use several methods for writing free-form poems. First, they can select words and phrases from brainstormed lists and clusters they have written and compile them to create a free-form poem. As an alternative, they write a paragraph and then "unwrite" to create the poem by deleting unnecessary words. The remaining words are arranged to look like a poem. Eighth grader Craig wrote his poem, "A Step Back in Time," this way:

It is late evening
On a river bank.
The sky has clouds
That seem to be moving
Towards the moon.
The only light is my lantern,
Which gives enough glare to see
A few feet in front of me.
Several sounds are heard
In the distance: an owl
Hooting in the trees,
A deer crossing the river.
Life overflows around me
Like many different colored bugs.
The wind is chilly,
Making the large pines dance.
The sand is damp.
It's like the beginning of time,
Before man existed,
Just animals and plants.

Concrete Poems. Students create concrete poems by arranging words pictorially on a page or by combining art and writing. Words, phrases, and sentences can be written in the shape of an object, or word pictures can be inserted within poems that are written left to right and top to bottom on a sheet of paper. These concrete poems are extensions of the word pictures discussed earlier in this chapter. Three examples of concrete poems are presented in Figure 12–8. In the "Washington Monument" poem, fourth graders brainstormed a list of facts about the monument and then combined their ideas to form the sentence that was written in the shape of the Washington, DC, landmark. In the "Key" and "Lightbulb" poems, seventh graders used the same approach to create their concrete poems.

Found Poems. Students create poems by culling words from other sources, such as newspaper articles, songs, and stories. Seventh grader Eric found this poem in an article about racecar driver Richard Petty:

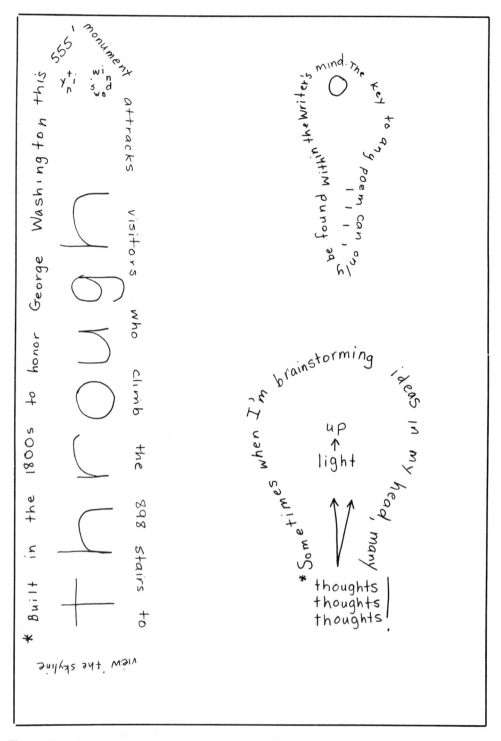

Figure 12–8 Independent writing: Students' concrete poems

Fast Moving

Moving down the track,
faster than fast, is Richard Petty
seven-time winner of the crowned jewel
Daytona 500.
At 210 mph—dangerous—
pushing his engine to the limit.
Other NASCARs running fast
but Richard Petty takes the lead
at last.
Running across the line
with good time.

Eric developed his poem by circling powerful words and phrases in the 33-line newspaper article and then writing the words in a poetic arrangement. After reading over the draft, he deleted two words and added three other words not included in the newspaper article that were needed for transitions in the poem. By writing found poems, students have the opportunity to manipulate words and sentence structures they don't write themselves.

Poems for Two Voices.   Poems for two voices are a unique type of free verse. These poems are written in two columns, side by side, and the columns are read together by two readers or two groups of readers. One reader reads the left column, and the other reader reads the right column. When both readers have words—either the same words or different words—written on the same line, they read them simultaneously so that the poem sounds like a musical duet.

The two best-known books of poems for two readers are Paul Fleischman's *I Am Phoenix: Poems for Two Voices* (1985), which is about birds, and his New-bery Award–winning *Joyful Noise: Poems for Two Voices* (1988), which is about insects. Children, too, can write poems for two voices; Loraine Wilson (1994) suggests that topics with contrasting viewpoints are the most effective.

A class of second graders wrote this poem for two voices about Halloween:

Halloween is coming!	Halloween is coming!
Let's have some fun.	
	Fun! Fun! Fun!
Where are the black cats?	
	Hiss-ss.
	Me-ow.
You're here.	We're here.
	We're ready for some fun.
Where are the spooky ghosts?	
	Boo-oo.
	Boo-oo.
You're here.	We're here.
	We're ready for some fun.

Where are the bony skeletons?

Rat-tle.
Rat-tle.
We're here.
We're ready for some fun.

You're here.

Where are the scary witches?

Hocus Pocus.
Hocus Pocus.
We're here.
We're ready for some fun.

You're here.

Where are the children?

Trick or treat.
Trick or treat.
We're here.
We're ready for some fun.

You're here.

Happy Halloween!
Fun! Fun! Fun!

Fun! Fun! Fun!
Happy Halloween!

Syllable- and Word-Count Poems

Haiku and other syllable- and word-count poems provide a structure that helps students succeed in writing; however, the need to adhere to the formula in these poems may restrict students' freedom of expression. In other words, the structure of these poems may both help and hinder students. The exact syllable counts force students to search for just the right words to express their ideas and feelings and provide a valuable opportunity for students to use a thesaurus and a dictionary.

Haiku. The best-known syllable-count poem is haiku (high-KOO), a Japanese poetic form consisting of 17 syllables arranged in three lines of 5-7-5. Haiku deals with nature and presents a single clear image. It is a concise form, much like a telegram. Ten-year-old Shawn wrote this haiku about the feeling of mud swishing between his toes:

 The mud feels slimy
As it splashes through my toes
Making them vanish.

Books of haiku poems to share with students include *Black Swan/White Crow* (J. P. Lewis, 1995), *Spring: A Haiku Story* (Shannon, 1996), and *Shadow Play: Night Haiku* (Harter, 1994). The photographs and artwork used in these trade books may provide students with ideas for illustrating their haiku poems. Richard Lewis (1968, 1970) has written about the lives of two of the greatest Japanese haiku poets, Issa and Basho. He provides biographical information as well as a collection of poems in these books.

Cinquains. A cinquain (SIN-cane) is a five-line poem containing 22 syllables in a 2-4-6-8-2 syllable pattern. Cinquains usually describe something, but they may also tell a story. Encourage students to search for words and phrases that are precise, vivid, and sensual. Have students ask themselves what their subject looks like, smells like, sounds like, and tastes like and record their ideas using a five-senses cluster. The formula is

Line 1: a one-word subject with two syllables
Line 2: four syllables describing the subject
Line 3: six syllables showing action
Line 4: eight syllables expressing a feeling or observation about the subject
Line 5: two syllables describing and renaming the subject

This cinquain poem was written by sixth grader Kevin:

Wrestling
skinny, fat
coaching, arguing, pinning
trying hard to win
tournament

If you compare Kevin's poem to the cinquain formula, you'll notice that some lines are short a syllable or two; Kevin bent some of the guidelines in choosing words to create a powerful image of wrestling. The message of the poem is always more important than adhering to the formula.

An alternative cinquain form contains five lines but does not follow the syllable count. Instead, each line contains a specified number of words rather than syllables. The first line contains a one-word title, the second line has two words that describe the title, the third line has three words that express action, the fourth line has four words that express feelings, and the fifth line contains a two-word synonym for the title.

Diamantes. Iris Tiedt (1970) invented the diamante (dee-ah-MAHN-tay), a seven-line contrast poem written in the shape of a diamond. In this poetic form, students apply their knowledge of opposites and parts of speech. The formula is

Line 1: one noun as the subject
Line 2: two adjectives describing the subject
Line 3: three participles (ending in *-ing*) telling about the subject
Line 4: four nouns (the first two related to the subject and the second two related to the opposite)
Line 5: three participles telling about the opposite
Line 6: two adjectives describing the opposite
Line 7: one noun that is the opposite of the subject

When the poem is written, it is arranged in a diamond shape. Sixth grader Shelley wrote the following diamante about heaven and hell:

HEAVEN
happy, love
laughing, hunting, everlasting
pearly gates, Zion, Satan, netherworld
burning, blazing, yelling
pain, fire
HELL

Shelley created a contrast between heaven, the subject represented by the noun in the first line, and hell, the opposite in the last line. Creating the contrast gives students the opportunity to play with words and extend their understanding of opposites. The third noun, *Satan,* in the fourth line marks the transition from heaven to hell.

Rhymed Verse Poems

Several rhymed verse forms, such as limericks and clerihews, can be used effectively with middle- and upper-grade students. In using these forms, it is important that teachers try to ensure that the rhyme schemes do not restrict students' creative and imaginative expressions.

Limericks.   The limerick is a form of light verse that uses both rhyme and rhythm. The poem consists of five lines. The first, second, and fifth lines rhyme, and the third and fourth lines rhyme with each other and are shorter than the other three lines. The rhyme scheme is a-a-b-b-a. Often the last line contains a funny or surprise ending, as shown in the following limerick written by eighth grader Angela:

There once was a frog named Pete
Who did nothing but sit and eat.
He examined each fly
With so careful an eye
And then said, "You're dead meat."

Writing limericks can be a challenging assignment for many upper-grade students, but middle-grade students can also be successful with this poetic form, especially when they work together and write a class collaboration. This class collaboration limerick, "Leprechaun," was written by fourth graders:

There once was a lucky leprechaun
That rode on a big, fat fawn.
He ate a cat,
And got so fat,
To lose some weight he had to mow the lawn.

Limericks were popularized in the 19th century by Edward Lear (1812–88). Teachers often introduce limericks by reading aloud some of Lear's verses so that students can appreciate the rhythm (stressed and unstressed syllables) of the verse. Two collections of Lear's limericks are *Daffy Down Dillies: Silly Limericks by Edward Lear* (Lear, 1995) and *Lots of Limericks* (Livingston, 1991). Arnold Lobel has also written a book of unique pig limericks, *Pigericks* (1983). After sharing Lobel's pigericks, children often write "birdericks" or "fishericks."

Clerihews. A clerihew (KLER-i-hyoo) is a four-line rhymed verse that describes a person. The form is named for Edmund Clerihew Bentley (1875–1956), a British detective writer who invented it. The formula is

Line 1: the person's name
Line 2: rhymes with the first line
Lines 3 and 4: rhyme with each other

Clerihews can be written about anyone—historical figures, characters in stories, and even the students themselves. The following clerihew was written by an eighth grader named Johnny about another John:

> John Wayne
> Is in the Cowboy Hall of Fame.
> In movies he shot his gun the best,
> And that's how he won the west.

Model Poems

Students can write poems that are modeled on poems composed by adult poets. Kenneth Koch suggests this approach in *Rose, Where Did You Get That Red?* (1990). According to this approach, students read a poem and then write their own poems using the same theme expressed in the model poem. For other examples of model poems, see Paul Janeczko's *Poetry From A to Z: A Guide for Young Writers* (1994) and Nancy Cecil's *For the Love of Poetry: Poetry for Every Learner* (1994).

Apologies. Using William Carlos Williams's poem "This Is Just to Say" as the model, children write a poem in which they apologize for something they are secretly glad they did (Koch, 1990). Middle- and upper-grade students are very familiar with offering apologies, and they enjoy writing humorous apologies to inanimate things. For example, fifth grader Clay wrote an apology to his eraser:

> Dear Eraser,
> This is just to say
> I'm so sorry
> for biting you off
> my pencil
> and eating you

and putting you
in my digestive system.
Forgive me!
Forgive me p-l-e-e-e-a-s-e-e-e.

Apology poems don't have to be humorous; they may be sensitive, genuine apologies as in this poem, "Open Up," written by seventh grader Angela:

> I didn't open
> my immature eyes
> to see the pain
> within you
> a death had caused.
> Forgive me,
> I misunderstood
> your anguished
> broken heart.

Invitations.   Students write poems in which they invite someone to a magical, beautiful place full of sounds and colors and where all kinds of marvelous things happen. The model poem is William Shakespeare's "Come Unto These Yellow Sands" (Koch, 1990). The guidelines for writing an invitation poem are that it must be an invitation to a magical place and include sound or color words. The following invitation poem, "The Golden Shore," written by seventh grader Nikki, follows these two guidelines:

> Come unto the golden shore
> Where days are filled with laughter,
> And nights filled with whispering winds.
> Where sunflowers and sun
> Are filled with love.
> Come take my hand
> As we walk into the sun.

Prayers From the Ark.   Students write a poem or prayer from the viewpoint of an animal following the model poems *Prayers From the Ark* (1992) by Carmen Bernos de Gasztold, who wrote poems in the persona of animals on Noah's ark. Children can write similar poems in which they assume the persona of an animal. Second grader Candice assumes the persona of the Easter Bunny for her poem:

> Dear Lord,
> I am the bunny.
> Why did you make me so fluffy?
> I thank you for keeping the carrots
> sweet and orange so I can be strong.
> Thank you for making me the Easter Bunny.
> Oh, I almost forgot, bless you
> for last month's big crop of carrots.

"If I Were in Charge of the World." Students write poems in which they describe what they would do if they were in charge of the world; Judith Viorst's poem "If I Were in Charge of the World" (1981) is the model for this form. Children are eager to share ideas about how they would change the world, as this fourth-grade collaborative poem illustrates:

> If I were in charge of the world
> School would be for one month,
> Movies and video games would be free, and
> Foods would be McCalorieless at McDonalds.
> Poor people would have a home,
> Bubble gum would cost a penny, and
> Kids would have cars to drive.
> Parents wouldn't argue,
> Christmas would be in July and December, and
> We would never have bedtimes.
> A kid would be president,
> I'd meet my long lost cousin, and
> Candybars would be vegetables.
> I would own the mall,
> People would have as much money as they wanted, and
> There would be no drugs.

Poetic Devices

Good poets choose words carefully. They create strong images when they use unexpected comparisons, repeat sounds within a line or stanza, imitate sounds, repeat words and phrases, and choose rhyming words. These techniques are called poetic devices. Many children notice these devices when they read poems, and they need to be aware of them before they can use them in their writing. Knowledge of the appropriate terminology—*comparison, alliteration, onomatopoeia, repetition,* and *rhyme*—is also helpful in writing groups, when students compliment classmates on their use of a device or suggest that they try a particular device. The minilesson on page 410 shows how Ms. Cook, a fifth-grade teacher, teaches her students about poetic devices.

Comparison. Children use comparisons—metaphors and similes—to describe images, feelings, and actions in the poems they write. As discussed in Chapter 8, "Descriptive Writing," a metaphor compares two things by implying that one thing is something else, and a simile is an explicit comparison of one thing to another, signaled by the use of *like* or *as.* Children learn traditional comparisons, such as "high as a kite" and "soft as a feather," during the primary grades, and then they experiment with creating new comparisons, such as this metaphor:

> Anger is a volcano
> Erupting with poisonous words.

Poetic Devices

The fifth graders in Ms. Cook's class are reading and writing poems during their workshop period. Ms. Cook has taught a series of minilessons on repetition, rhyme, alliteration, comparison, and onomatopoeia; as part of each minilesson, the students made a chart about the poetic device and posted it in the classroom. In today's minilesson, Ms. Cook asks her fifth graders to apply what they've learned about poetic devices to analyze some familiar poems and some new ones, too.

1. Introduce the topic

Ms. Cook asks, "I'm wondering what poets do to craft a good poem . . . ?" The students offer a variety of responses, including this one from Heather: "Poets choose the best words and sometimes make you laugh."

2. Share examples

The teacher shares three familiar poems using the overhead projector, reads each aloud, and asks if the poem is good. First, she rereads "Snow Rhyme," by Christine Crow (Yolen, 1993), and a student points out that it rhymes. Next, she rereads "Dad," by Janet Wong (Kennedy & Kennedy, 1999), and a student says that he likes the way the poet compared a dad to a turtle. Then, she rereads "A Pizza the Size of the Sun," by Jack Prelutsky (1996), and several students volunteer that the exaggeration is funny and the poet uses both rhyme and repetition. Finally, Darren blurts out: "I get it. You want us to think about the five kinds of poetic devices."

3. Provide information

"I agree that poets do many things to make their poems good," Ms. Cook says, "but you are right, Darren. I want to review poetic devices." Ms. Cook reviews the five posters. Then she reads aloud several new poems and asks students to identify the poetic devices used in them.

4. Guide practice

Ms. Cook divides the class into small groups and gives each group copies of five poems to read and examine. She asks them to identify one or two poetic devices that the poet used effectively. Afterward, the students share their ideas with the class.

5. Assess learning

Ms. Cook asks students to examine one of the poems they read this week to see which poetic devices have been used and to write their reflections in their writers' notebooks.

Figure 12–9 Shared writing: Two pages from a fourth-grade class book, *The Z Was Zipped*

Sixth-grade Amanda uses a combination of traditional and unexpected similes in this poem, "People":

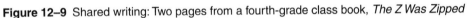 People are like birds
who are constantly getting their feathers ruffled.
People are like alligators
who find pleasure in evil cleverness.
People are like bees
who are always busy.
People are like penguins
who want to have fun.
People are like platypuses—
unexplainable!

Alliteration. Alliteration is the repetition of the same initial consonant sound in consecutive words or in words in close proximity. Repeating the same initial sound makes poetry fun to read, and children enjoy reading and reciting alliterative books such as Jane Bayer's *A My Name Is Alice* (1984) and Chris Van Allsburg's *The Z Was Zapped* (1987). After reading one of these books, children can create their own versions. A fourth-grade class created their own version of Van Allsburg's book, which they called "The Z Was Zipped." Students divided into pairs, and each pair composed a page for the class book. On the front of the sheet of paper, students illustrated their letter, and on the back, they wrote a sentence to describe their illustration, following Van Allsburg's pattern. Two pages from the book are presented in Figure 12–9. For the D page, the alliterative sentence is "The D got dunked by the duck," and for the T page, it is "The T was terrified."

Tongue twisters are an exaggerated form of alliteration in which almost every word in the twister begins with the same letter. Dr. Seuss's *Oh Say Can You Say?* (1979) is an easy-to-read collection of tongue twisters for primary-grade students. Alvin Schwartz's *A Twister of Twists, a Tangler of Tongues* (1972) and Steven Kellogg's *Aster Aardvark's Alphabet Adventures* (1987) are two good books of tongue twisters for older students. Through practice with tongue twisters and alliterative books, children's awareness of alliteration is increased, and they are more likely to use alliteration in the poems they read and write.

Onomatopoeia.   Onomatopoeia is a device in which poets use sound words to make their writing more sensory and more vivid. These sound words, such as *crash, slurp, varoom,* and *me-e-e-ow,* sound like their meanings. Children can compile a list of sound words found in stories and poems they read. The list can be displayed on a classroom chart or entered in their writing notebooks for children to refer to when they write.

Peter Spier has compiled two books of sound words. *Gobble Growl Grunt* (1971) is about animal sounds, and *Crash! Bang! Boom!* (1972) is about the sounds people and machines make. Children can use these books in selecting sound words to use in their writing. Comic strips are another good source of sound words. Children collect frames from comic strips with sound words and add them to a classroom chart. Collecting these words naturally leads to a discussion of the spelling of sound words. Sounds can be stretched out by repeating letters in words, such as *g-r-r-r.*

In *Wishes, Lies, and Dreams* (2000), Kenneth Koch recommends having children write noise poems in which they include a noise or sound word in each line. These first poems may sound contrived (e.g., "A dog barks bow-wow"), but through these experiences, children learn to use onomatopoeia effectively. This poem, "Greyhound," written by seventh grader Brian, illustrates onomatopoeia:

> Fast and slick
> Out of the dogbox—
> ZOOM, ZOOM, ZOOM
> Burst into the air
> Then they smoothly touch the ground.

Repetition.   Repetition of words and phrases is another device that writers of stories and poems can use effectively to structure their writing and add interest. Edgar Allan Poe's effective use of the fearful word *nevermore* in "The Raven" is one poetic example, as is the gingerbread boy's boastful refrain in *The Gingerbread Boy.* An easy way to introduce repetition of words in poetry is through a class collaboration poem. In this collaborative poem, "Wishing

Time," a first grader's comment "Gee, it's fun wishing!" is repeated after every three wishes:

> I wish I could go to the moon.
> I wish I had a pony.
> I wish I was a professional baseball player,
> Gee, it's fun wishing!
>
> I wish I had a million dollars.
> I wish I could go to Disneyland.
> I wish I could be a movie star.
> Gee, it's fun wishing!
>
> I wish I owned a toy store.
> I wish I was the smartest kid in the world.
> I wish I could never stop wishing.
> Gee, it's fun wishing!

This repetition adds structure and enjoyment. As students read the poem aloud, the teacher reads each stanza and the students chant the refrain. In the following poem, "Chocolate," a fifth grader writes about a piece of chocolate, using the refrain "Here it comes" to heighten anticipation and to structure the poem:

> I drool.
>   Here it comes.
> The golden brown covering never looked
> so scrumptious, so tempting, so addicting.
>   Here it comes.
> I don't know anything that's going on around me.
> All I can concentrate on is chocolate.
>   Here it comes.
> I can feel the sweet, rich, thick chocolate
> on the roof of my mouth. A-a-a-ah-h!
>   And the chocolate is gone.

One way to encourage improvement in a child's poem is to suggest that the child repeat a particularly effective phrase throughout the poem.

Rhyme. It is unfortunate that rhyme has been considered synonymous with poetry. Although rhyme is an important part of many types of poetry, it can dominate children's poems. When rhyme comes naturally, it adds a delightful quality, but it can interfere with wordplay and vivid images. In the following Halloween poem, a fifth grader describes a witch's brew using rhyming words and an invented magical word, *allakaboo*:

> Bats, spiders, and lizards, too
> Rats, snakes—Allakaboo!
> Eggs and spiderwebs, a-choo
> Wings of a bug—Allakaboo—
>   a witch's brew!

Teaching Children to Write Poems

Children learn to write poems through minilessons about wordplay, poetic forms, and poetic devices; through reading poems; and through writing poems. It is not enough to simply invite children to read or write poetry; they need instruction and structured writing experiences in order to develop their concept of poetry. In the vignette at the beginning of the chapter, Miss Clark incorporated all three components in her poetry workshop, and her sixth graders were very successful.

Children learn poetic forms and write poems in connection with a literature focus unit on poetry, in response to literature they have read, and in writing workshop. They also write poetry in connection with social studies and science thematic units. For example, they might write an "If I Were in Charge of the World" poem from Paul Revere's point of view or from the viewpoint of a favorite book character. Students might also write five-senses poems in connection with a theme on the four seasons, or "If I were . . . " poems or concrete poems about animals as part of a theme on animals.

Introducing Children to Poetry

Many children have misconceptions about what poetry is and how to write it. Too often they think poetry must rhyme or they are unsure about what it should look like on a page. Children need to have a concept of poetry before beginning to write poems. One way to expand children's knowledge of poetry is to share a variety of poems written by children and adults. Choose from poems included in this chapter as well as poems written by well-known poets who write for children, such as Karla Kuskin (1975, 1980), David McCord (1962, 1967, 1977), Jack Prelutsky (1976, 1977, 1983), and Shel Silverstein (1974, 1981). Include poems that do not rhyme, as well as concrete poems with creative arrangements on the page.

Another way to introduce poetry is to read excerpts from the first chapter of Lois Lowry's *Anastasia Krupnik* (1979). In this book, 10-year-old Anastasia, the main character of the story, is excited when her teacher, Mrs. Westvessel, announces that the class will write poems. Anastasia works at home for eight nights to write a poem. Lowry does an excellent job of describing how writers search long and hard for words to express their meaning and the delight that comes when writers realize their poems are finished. On the appointed day, Anastasia and her classmates bring their poems to class to read aloud. One student reads his four-line rhymed verse aloud:

> I have a dog whose name is Spot.
> He likes to eat and drink a lot.
> When I put water in his dish,
> He laps it up just like a fish. (p. 10)

Anastasia is not impressed. She knows that the child who wrote the poem has a dog named Sputnik, not Spot! But Mrs. Westvessel gives it an A and hangs it

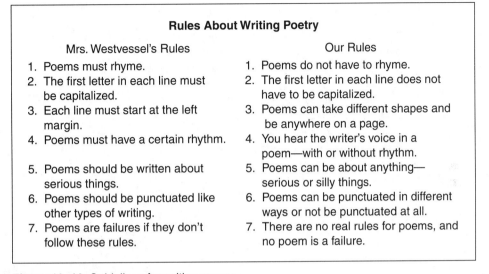

Figure 12–10 Guidelines for writing poems

on the bulletin board. Soon it is Anastasia's turn. She is nervous because her poem is very different. She reads her poem about tiny creatures that move about in tidepools at night:

> hush   hush   the sea-soft night is aswim
> with wrinklesquirm creatures
> listen(!)
> to them   move   smooth   in the moistly dark
> here in the   whisperwarm   wet. (pp. 11–12)

In this free-form poem without rhyme or capital letters, Anastasia has created a marvelous word picture with invented words such as *whisperwarm* and *wrinklesquirm*. Regrettably, Mrs. Westvessel has an antiquated view that poems should focus on serious subjects, use rhyme, and incorporate conventional capitalization and punctuation. Mrs. Westvessel doesn't understand Anastasia's poem and gives Anastasia an F because she didn't follow directions.

Although this episode from the book presents a depressing picture of elementary teachers and their lack of knowledge about poetry, it is a dramatic introduction to what poetry is and what it is not. After reading excerpts from this first chapter of *Anastasia Krupnik,* teachers develop a chart with their students comparing what poetry is in Mrs. Westvessel's class and what poetry is in their class. A class of upper-grade students developed the chart in Figure 12–10. Expanding children's understanding of poetry is a crucial first step because although most children have some knowledge about poetry, many of their notions are more like Mrs. Westvessel's than like Anastasia's.

Teaching Children to Write Poems Using a Poetic Form

After being introduced to an enlightened view of poetry, children are ready to write poetry. Beginning with formula poems (e.g., "I wish . . ." poems and color poems) will probably make the writing easier for young children or for older students who have had little or no experience with poetry. The steps for writing any type of poetry are presented in the step-by-step feature on page 417.

Children in a fourth- and fifth-grade remedial reading class composed the class collaboration poem "If I Were a Tornado" presented in Figure 12–11. The class began by clustering ideas about tornadoes, and then students used the

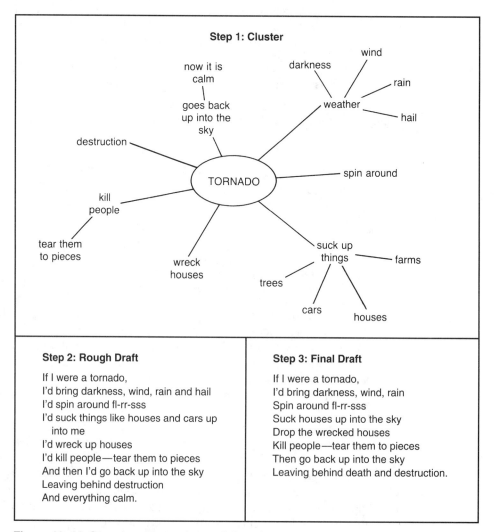

Figure 12–11 Steps in writing a class collaboration poem, "If I Were a Tornado"

Step by Step: Writing Poems

1. **Explain the poetic form.** Teachers describe the poetic form and explain what is incorporated in each line or stanza. Displaying a chart that describes the form or having students write a brief description of the poetic form in their writing notebooks will help them remember the information.

2. **Share examples written by children and adults.** Teachers read poems adhering to the poetic form. Poems included in this chapter can be shared, as well as poems published in books of poetry and poems written by students. They also point out how the writer of each poem used the form.

3. **Review the poetic form.** Teachers review the pattern or formula and share another poem that follows the form. Next, teachers ask children to explain how the poem fits the form. Or children can quickwrite about the poetic form to check their understanding.

4. **Write class collaboration poems.** Teachers have children compose a class collaboration poem before writing individual poems. It is guided writing when students each contribute a line for a class collaboration "I wish . . ." poem or a couplet for an "I used to . . . /But now . . ." poem. It is shared writing when children work together to suggest ideas and words for other types of poems, such as apology or concrete poems. They dictate the poem to the teacher, who records it on the chalkboard or on chart paper. Older students often work in small groups to create their poems. Through writing a class collaboration poem, children review the form and gather ideas that they might later use in writing their own poems.

5. **Write individual poems using the writing process.** With the background of experiences gained through learning about a poetic form and writing a collaborative poem, children are prepared to write their own poems. They prewrite to gather and organize ideas, write rough drafts, meet in writing groups to receive feedback, make revisions based on this feedback, and then edit their poems with a classmate and with the teacher. Then children share their poems in any of a variety of ways. Often they keep their poems in a poetry notebook.

words in the cluster in dictating a rough draft of the poem. After reading the draft aloud, one child commented that the poem looked "too full of words" and counted 52 words in the poem. The children decided to "unwrite" some of the unnecessary words (e.g., the repetitious "I'd" at the beginning of four lines) and reduced the number of words in the poem to 41. After making the changes and reading the revised poem aloud, the children declared the poem finished. It was then copied on a sheet of paper, and copies were made for each student.

Too often, teachers will simply explain several poetic forms and then allow students to choose any form they like and write poems. This approach ignores the teaching component; it's back to the "assign and do" syndrome. Instead, students need to learn and experiment with each poetic form. After these preliminary experiences, they can apply what they have learned and write poems adhering to any of the poetic forms they have studied. Class collaborations are a crucial component because they provide a practice run for children who are not sure what to do. The 5 minutes it takes to write a class collaboration poem may make the difference between success and failure for many would-be poets.

Assessing Children's Poems

A variety of poetic formulas have been presented in this chapter. These formulas allow children to experiment with different ways to express their thoughts. Although children should experiment with a variety of forms during the elementary grades, they should not be tested on their knowledge of particular forms. Knowing that a haiku is a Japanese form composed of 17 syllables arranged in three lines will not make a child a poet. Instead, information about the forms should be available in the classroom.

Assessing the quality of children's poems is especially difficult because poems are creative combinations of wordplay, poetic form, and poetic devices. Instead of trying to give a grade for quality, children's writing can be assessed on these three criteria:

- Has the child written the poem following the formula presented in class?
- Has the child used the process approach in writing, revising, and editing the poem?
- Has the child used wordplay or a poetic device in the poem?

Teachers might also ask children to assess their own progress in writing poems. Children should keep copies of the poems they write in their writing folders or in poetry booklets so they can review and assess their work. If a grade for quality is absolutely necessary, children should be permitted to choose several of the poems in their writing folders to be evaluated.

ANSWERING TEACHERS' QUESTIONS ABOUT . . .

Poetry Writing

1. Isn't it true that children either have poetic ability or they don't?

Perhaps it is true that great poets are born, not made, but every child can write poems and enjoy the experience. Children benefit from experiences with poems; they develop a sensitivity to language and learn to play with words and evoke fresh images. The poetic forms presented in this chapter have been field-tested with students in kindergarten through eighth grade, and both teachers and students find these poetry-writing activities to be valuable learning experiences.

2. My students think that poems must rhyme. How can I convince them that poems don't have to rhyme?

Many children think that poems must rhyme. Reading the excerpt from Lowry's *Anastasia Krupnik* (1979) and developing a list of poetry rules for your class like the one described in Figure 12–10 will introduce the concept that poems are more than strings of rhyming words. Teaching students about concrete poems, haiku, and other forms that don't use rhyme will help them understand that they have options other than rhyming in poetry. Also, read aloud to students some poetry that does not rhyme.

3. My students' poems look more like paragraphs than poems. What can I do?

Have students examine the poems written in books to see how they are arranged on the page. Also, write class poems and discuss with students the various options that poets have for arranging their poems on the page. To demonstrate some of the options, have small groups of students each design a different arrangement for a class collaboration poem. If you have access to a word processor, have students type their poems on the computer and arrange the poem in various ways. For example:

> Words
> written
> up and down
> and
> centered
> SMACK
> in the middle
> of the page—
> That's a poem to me!

If the poems also sound like a paragraph, some "unwriting," in which children delete unnecessary and repetitive function words, might be necessary. For example, the following paragraph was unwritten to create the poem just mentioned:

> In a poem you can write words up and down on a page. They are centered right in the middle of the page. They are fun to write. That's what a poem is to me.

4. How can I teach poetry when I've never liked it or been any good at writing poetry myself?

Teachers often ask this question. Note that this book offers a new way of writing poetry, in which the emphasis has changed from rhyming verse to wordplay, expressing feelings, and word pictures. Children's enthusiasm for this type of poetry is contagious; even the most skeptical teacher quickly becomes a convert.

CHAPTER **13**

Persuasive Writing

Preview

 **Purpose** Students use persuasive writing to argue logically with reasons, to present other viewpoints, to sway opinions, and to persuade someone to do something.

 Audience The audience may be known or unknown. When students write to family members, friends, or a state legislator, the audience is known, but when they write to the editor of a newspaper, the audience is unknown. It is crucial that writers have a clear sense of audience and that they adapt their writing and the reasoning they use to their audience.

Forms Forms include posters, letters, letters to the editor, essays, advertisements, and commercials.

Instructional Preview: Persuasive Writing	
Grades	**Goals and Activities**
Kindergarten–Grade 2	**Goal 1:** Create persuasive posters that offer an opinion • Students make posters about favorite books. • Students make posters about nutrition, patriotism, ecology, and other issues.
	Goal 2: Write persuasive letters and books that present a position and provide some reasons or examples • Students write letters to persuade family members about a particular concern or issue. • Students use *The Important Book* (M. Brown, 1997) format to write persuasive cards and books.
Grades 3–5	**Goal 1:** Write persuasive letters that express opinions, arguments, and feelings • Students write letters to persuade friends or family members about a particular issue.
	Goal 2: Write persuasive essays that state the argument logically and with conviction • Students write book and movie reviews. • Students write essays comparing book and film versions of a story and choose the version they prefer. • Students write persuasive essays about a health or contemporary issue. • Students write persuasive essays in response to a newspaper article.
	Goal 3: Create other persuasive materials • Students make persuasive posters. • Students design brochures and pamphlets that persuade the reader to a course of action or to a particular position.
Grades 6–8	**Goal 1:** Present counterarguments • Students create graphic organizers to consider counterarguments that could be used to refute their arguments. • Students add counterarguments to strengthen their arguments in letters and essays.
	Goal 2: Recognizing propaganda devices • Teachers compare and contrast persuasion and propaganda. • Teachers explain the eight propaganda devices. • Students examine print advertisements and television commercials for propaganda devices. • Students write advertisements using these devices.

Writing Mother's Day Cards

It is a week before Mother's Day, and a group of second graders in Mrs. Carson's classroom is meeting to talk about the Mother's Day cards they want to make. Earlier that morning at the whole-class meeting that she uses to begin each writing workshop session, Mrs. Carson had mentioned Mother's Day and encouraged the children to think about making Mother's Day cards or some other writing for their mothers. Now Mrs. Carson is meeting with a group to talk about their Mother's Day projects.

Five children are in the writing group: Maria, Bobby, Elizabeth, Teri, and John. John is a leader in the group, and as soon as Mrs. Carson asks the children what ideas they have for Mother's Day projects, he explains, "I want to make a card to tell my mom that she's the best mom in the world. I know she is and I want to tell her." Mrs. Carson follows his lead. "John, what does she do that makes you think she's the best mom?" John thinks for a minute and then begins to list her attributes: "My mom cooks me the best meals . . . she taught me to read when I was a little kid . . . you know, she takes care of me." Teri, Bobby, and the other children in the writing group join in the discussion, talking about their moms and what makes them special.

Four of the five students in the group decide to write letters to their moms telling why they are the best moms in the world. The fifth child chooses to write a poem instead, and she gets to work on her project. Mrs. Carson continues to meet with the other four students to talk about persuasive writing. Mrs. Carson says, "I think you are telling me that you want to convince your mom and everyone else who reads your Mother's Day card that your mom is the best. You will want to have lots of reasons or examples to make your point. John told us several reasons why his mom is the best. Can you think of some reasons why your mom is the best, too?"

The students share ideas, and then Mrs. Carson reviews the writing process and the steps they will follow in writing their cards. She asks them to draw a cluster and to include at least three reasons why their moms are the best, and she remains with the group while they get started. Then she moves off to another writing group.

Over the next 2 days, these four students write rough drafts of their cards. They all begin their cards by saying that their moms are the best and then incorporate the reasons and examples from their clusters into their writing. This group of four second graders is a very supportive group. As they write, they share their drafts with each other and get compliments and feedback on their writing. They also get ideas from each other. One child writes "I love you 100 times" on her rough draft, and soon others are writing "I love you 10,000 times" and another "I love you 1,000,000 times." Students aren't sure how to write such large numbers, so when Mrs. Carson checks on the group, she takes a moment to explain how to write large numbers.

On Wednesday, Mrs. Carson meets with the writing group about revising their cards. As each child reads his or her card aloud, Mrs. Carson and group members offer compliments and make suggestions for improvement. Mrs. Carson notices that John is the only student to have an ending for his card. Taking a moment to talk about writing, she reminds the group that many kinds of writing have a beginning, middle, and end. She uses a sandwich model made of two pieces of light-brown sponge cut into the shape of slices of bread, slices of meat and cheese cut from felt, rubber pickles, and mesh lettuce. She reminds them, "The beginning is the statement that your moms are the best," and she points to the top slice of bread. "The middle is where your reasons and examples go," and she points to the meat, cheese, and other ingredients. Then she points to the bottom slice of bread and asks, "Do your cards have an end?" John announces that his did, and he reads it aloud: "See I told you that you are the best mom on the Earth." No one else had an ending, so Mrs. Carson and John help the students write endings, such as "And that's why you are the bestest" and "Thank you for loving me so much."

After students make their revisions, Mrs. Carson meets with the writing group again to help them edit their writing. The three editing skills that she focuses on are spelling, capitalization, and punctuation. For some writing assignments, Mrs. Carson focuses on punctuation marks or capital letters and ignores many of their invented spellings other than high-frequency words; however, this is an important writing project, and the children want their cards to be as adultlike as possible. Mrs. Carson reads over each paper and points out corrections. She explains some of the changes, and for others she simply says, "We usually put a comma here, so is it OK if I add it?"

After editing, students copy their letters on "good" paper and glue the paper to the construction-paper cards they have decorated. On Thursday and Friday afternoons, the class meets to share their cards before they take them home. Mrs. Carson always makes time for students to share their writing to help them develop a sense of authorship and feel that they are members of a community of writers.

John's cluster and Mother's Day message are presented in Figure 13–1. This message, written by a second grader, includes the same three parts that older students who write more complex persuasive essays and letters use: a beginning, in which the position is stated; the middle, which provides at least three supporting reasons; and the end, in which the position is restated.

Figure 13–1 Guided writing: A second grader's cluster and Mother's Day message

PARENTS HAVE LITTLE DOUBT that children are effective persuaders as they argue to stay up beyond their bedtimes or plead to keep as a pet the stray puppy they have found. John's letter to his mother shows that primary-grade students can write persuasively, even though researchers have found that children's persuasive writing abilities develop more slowly than their abilities in any other genre (Applebee, Langer, & Mullis, 1986; Hidi & Hildyard, 1983).

A sense of audience and the ability to tailor writing to fit that audience are perhaps most important in persuasive writing because the writer can judge how effective the persuasion is by readers' reactions. Although an audience's enjoyment of a story or poem or the information learned from a research report can be hard to gauge, the effect of persuasion on others is not. Researchers examining audience adaptation (Crowhurst & Piche, 1979; Kroll, 1978; Rubin & Piche, 1979) have found that upper-grade students were unable to decenter their writing and focus on the needs of their audience. But Barry Kroll (1984) found that sixth graders could adapt to their audience in writing persuasive letters. He concluded that when students have a clear purpose and a plausible reason for writing, they can adapt their writing to meet the needs of their readers.

Persuasive arguments can be drawn on posters or written as essays or letters. Students write essays arguing against the use of drugs or make posters to recommend a book they have read. They present a point of view and then defend the position by citing several supporting reasons or examples. Students also write letters to legislators or to the editor of the local newspaper to express their opinions about community, state, or national issues and to try to persuade others to support their viewpoint. Persuasive writing can take the form of advertisements: through print advertisements and scripted video commercials, students use both persuasion and propaganda to influence people to "buy" ideas, products, and services.

In this chapter, you will learn about the types of persuasive writing that elementary students can use effectively and how to teach children to write persuasively. The key points presented about persuasive writing are:

- Elementary students, even young children, use persuasion to influence people.
- Arguments include a beginning, middle, and end.
- Children can write persuasive posters, letters, essays, and advertisements.
- Teachers can show students how to write persuasively.
- Checklists and rubrics are used to assess children's persuasive writing.

Persuasion

To persuade is to win someone over to your viewpoint or cause. In contrast to propaganda, which has a more sinister connotation, persuasion involves a reasoned or logical appeal. Propaganda can be deceptive, hyped, emotion-laden, or one-sided. Although the purpose of both is to influence, there are ethical differences.

Three Ways to Persuade

People can be persuaded in three basic ways. The first appeal a writer can make is based on reason. People seek to make logical generalizations and draw cause-and-effect conclusions, whether from absolute facts or from strong possibilities. For example, people can be persuaded to practice more healthful living if told about the results of medical research. It is necessary, of course, to distinguish between reasonable and unreasonable appeals. For example, urging people to stand on their head every day for 30 minutes based on the claim that it will increase their intelligence is an unreasonable appeal.

A second way to persuade is through an appeal to character. Other people are important to us, and we can be persuaded by what another person recommends if we trust that person. Trust comes from personal knowledge of the person or the reputation of the person who is trying to persuade. Does the persuader have the expertise or personal experience necessary to endorse a product or a cause? For example, can we believe what scientists say about the dangers of nuclear energy? Can we believe what a sports personality says about the effectiveness of a particular sports shoe?

The third way people can be persuaded is by an appeal to their emotions. Emotional appeals can be as strong as intellectual appeals because people have a strong concern for their well-being and for the rights of others. We support or reject arguments according to our strong feelings about what is ethical and socially responsible. At the same time, fear and the need for peer acceptance are strong feelings that also influence our opinions and beliefs.

Any of the three appeals can be used to try to persuade another person. For example, when a child tries to persuade her parents that her bedtime should be delayed by 30 minutes, she might argue that neighbors allow their children to stay up later; this is an appeal to character. If the argument focuses on the amount of sleep that a 10-year-old needs, it is an appeal to reason. When the child finally announces that she has the earliest bedtime of anyone in her fourth-grade class and it makes her feel like a baby, the appeal is to the emotions.

These same three types of appeal are used for in-school persuasion. When trying to persuade classmates to read a particular book in a "book-selling" poster project, for example, students might argue that the book should be read because it is short and interesting (reason), because it is hilarious and you'll laugh (emotion), or because it is the most popular book in the second grade and everyone else is reading it (character).

Propaganda

The word *propaganda* suggests something shady or underhanded. Although propaganda, like persuasion, is designed to influence people's beliefs and actions, propagandists may use underhanded techniques to distort, conceal, and exaggerate the facts. Two of these techniques are deceptive language and propaganda devices.

People seeking to influence us often use words that evoke a variety of responses. For example, they claim something is "improved," "more natural," or "50% better." Such loaded words are deceptive because they have positive connotations but may have no basis in fact. For example, when a product is advertised as 50% better, consumers need to ask, "50% better than what?" That question is rarely answered in advertisements.

Doublespeak is another type of deceptive language; it is language that is evasive, euphemistic, confusing, and self-contradictory. For example, janitors may be called "maintenance engineers," and reruns of television shows may be termed "encore telecasts." William Lutz (1984) cites a number of kinds of doublespeak, including euphemisms and inflated language, that elementary students can easily understand. Other kinds of doublespeak, such as using jargon specific to particular groups, overwhelming an audience with words, and using language that pretends to communicate but does not, are more appropriate for teaching older students about propaganda.

Euphemisms are words or phrases, such as "passed away," used to avoid a harsh or distasteful reality. They are often used out of concern for someone's feelings rather than to deceive. Inflated language includes words designed to make the ordinary seem extraordinary. For example, car mechanics become "automotive internists," and used cars become "pre-owned." Children need to learn that people sometimes use words that only pretend to communicate; at other times, they use words to intentionally misrepresent. For instance, a wallet advertised as genuine imitation leather is a vinyl wallet, and a faux diamond ring is made of glass (the word *faux* is French for "false"). Children need to be able to interpret this deceptive language and to avoid using it themselves.

Advertisers use propaganda devices such as testimonials, snob appeal, and rewards to sell their products. Eight devices that children can identify are listed in Figure 13–2. Children can locate examples of each propaganda device in advertisements and commercials and discuss the effects the device has on them. They can also investigate how the same devices are used in advertisements directed at youngsters, teenagers, and adults. For instance, a snack food advertisement describing a sticker or toy in the package will appeal to a youngster, and an advertisement for an appliance with a factory rebate will appeal to an adult. The propaganda device for both ads is the same: a reward! These devices can be used to sell ideas as well as products. Public service announcements about quitting smoking or wearing seat belts, as well as political advertisements, endorsements, and speeches, use these same devices.

1. Glittering Generality

Generalities such as "motherhood" and "patriotism" are used to enhance the quality of a product or the character of a political figure. Propagandists use an attractive generality so that listeners do not challenge the speaker's real point.

2. Testimonial

To persuade people to purchase a product, an advertiser associates it with a popular personality such as an athlete or film star. Listeners consider whether the person offering the testimonial has the expertise to judge the quality of the product.

3. Transfer

Persuaders transfer the prestige of a person to another person or object that will then be accepted. A film star is shown using a soap, and viewers are to believe that they can have youthful skin if they use this soap. Likewise, politicians appear with famous athletes so that the luster of the stars will rub off on them.

4. Name-calling

Advertisers try to pin a bad label on something they want listeners to dislike. In a discussion of health insurance, for example, an opponent may call the sponsor of a bill a socialist. Whether or not the sponsor is a socialist does not matter to the name-caller; the purpose is to cause unpleasant associations to rub off on the victim. Listeners consider the effect the label has on the product.

5. Card Stacking

Persuaders often choose only items that favor one side of an issue; unfavorable facts are ignored. To be objective, listeners seek information about other viewpoints.

6. Bandwagon

This technique appeals to people's need to be a part of a group. Advertisers claim that everyone is using this product and you should, too. For example, "More physicians recommend this pill than any other." Listeners ask: Does everyone really use this product? What is it better than?

7. Snob Appeal

Persuaders use snob appeal to attract the attention of people who want to be part of an exclusive group. Advertisements for expensive clothes, cosmetics, and gourmet foods often use this technique. Listeners consider whether the product is of high quality or merely has an expensive nametag.

8. Rewards

Advertisers often offer rewards for buying their products. For example, cereal products offer toys, and adults are lured by this device, too. Free gifts, rebates from manufacturers, and low-cost financing are being offered with expensive items. Listeners consider the value of rewards and how they increase the product's cost.

Figure 13–2 Eight propaganda devices
Techniques 1–5 adapted from Devine, 1982, pp. 39–40.

When children locate advertisements and commercials that they believe are misleading or deceptive, they can write letters of complaint to the following watchdog agencies:

Action for Children's Television
46 Austin Street
Newtonville, MA 02160

Children's Advertising Review Unit
Council of Better Business Bureaus
845 Third Avenue
New York, NY 10022

Federal Trade Commission
Pennsylvania Avenue
  at Sixth Street NW
Washington, DC 20580

Zillions AD Complaints
256 Washington Street
Mt. Vernon, NY 10553

In their letters, children should carefully describe the advertisement and explain what bothers them about it. They should also tell where they saw the advertisement (name of magazine and issue) or where they saw or heard the commercial (date, time, and channel).

Organization of an Argument

Much like a story, an argument has a beginning, middle, and end. In the beginning, writers state their position, argument, or opinion clearly. In the middle, the opinion is developed as writers select and present three or more reasons or pieces of evidence to support their position. These reasons may appeal to logic, character, or emotions. Writers sequence the evidence in a logical order and use concrete examples whenever possible. They often use cue words such as *first, second,* and *third* to alert readers to the organization. Upper-grade students also refute counterarguments in the middle. In the end, writers lead their readers to draw the conclusion that they intend through giving a personal statement, making a prediction, or summarizing the major points. The organization of an argument is illustrated in Figure 13–3.

Marion Crowhurst (1991) has identified several problems in children's persuasive writing that this organizational scheme can help to ameliorate. First, children's persuasive compositions are typically shorter than the stories and reports that they write. In these shorter compositions, children neither develop their arguments nor provide reasons to support their claims. Second, their persuasive essays show poor organization because children are unfamiliar with how an argument should be structured. Third, children's writing style is often inappropriate; their language is informal, and they use words such as *also* to tie arguments together rather than the more sophisticated stylistic devices, such as *if*

> **Teacher's Note: Supporting Struggling Writers**
>
> Using a graphic organizer like the one illustrated in Figure 13–3 is essential for struggling writers because it provides a plan that students can use as they develop their persuasive letters and essays. It is the prewriting stage that often determines the success or failure of a writing project, and this maxim is especially true for struggling writers, who typically make fewer plans before beginning to write.

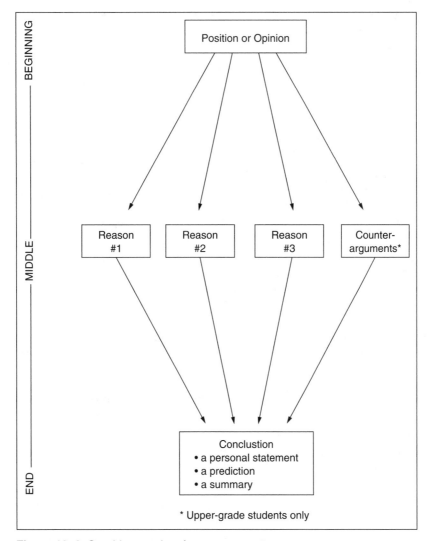

Figure 13–3 Graphic organizer for an argument

. . . *then* statements, typically used in persuasive writing. When children talk their way through the organizational scheme as a prewriting activity and listen to classmates discuss their plans, they develop more sophisticated writing styles and tighter arguments.

Although the organization of an argument typically involves a statement, the development of three (or more) reasons, and a conclusion, this scheme is not equivalent to a traditional five-paragraph theme. Persuasive writing requires a more elaborate schema than the simplistic, formulaic five-paragraph theme

(Crowhurst, 1991). In persuasive writing, children devise ways to introduce an argument, present supporting reasons, draw conclusions, and persuade the reader to accept the writer's viewpoint.

Types of Persuasive Writing

Persuasion is a part of everyday life. Children and adults frequently try to persuade others to do or believe a certain thing. Andrew Wilkinson and his colleagues (1980) investigated the ability of children (ages 7–13) to write persuasively. They found that children at all ages could state an opinion, and, not surprisingly, that as children grew older, they were better able to provide a logical justification for their opinions. Younger children were very egocentric in their reasoning and often failed to consider others' viewpoints. Furthermore, they found that children age 10 and older often wrote self-contradictory essays. In these essays, children started with a definite position, but through writing a justification for that position, they concluded with a position that was opposite of the one made in the beginning. However, it should be noted that these children wrote single-draft compositions and did not participate in writing groups to critique and revise their writing.

Topics for persuasive writing come from at-home and in-school activities as well as from literature and content-area study. At home, children might try to persuade their parents to let them go to bed later, play on a football team, go to a slumber party, buy new clothes or shoes, join the Boy or Girl Scouts, have a larger allowance, buy a new toy, or have a pet. At school, children might try to persuade their teachers to let them have less homework, go outside for recess in cold weather, change lunchroom rules, or sponsor a student council election. In the subjects they study, students can use writing to persuade others to stop smoking, avoid drugs, ban nuclear weapons, stop polluting our environment, endorse particular political candidates, read a certain book, see a certain movie, or support community, state, or national issues.

Persuasive Posters

A combination of drawing and writing is used to state a position on persuasive posters. Children are surrounded by persuasive posters, ranging from "Keep America Beautiful" billboard signs and "Don't drink and drive" bumper stickers to the motivational posters typically displayed in school hallways and cafeterias. As projects during literature focus units and theme cycles, children make similar posters.

After reading Mercer Mayer's *Liverwurst Is Missing* (1981), fourth-grade Kyle designed the

---

 Teacher's Note: Assisting English Language Learners

Even though persuasive writing is often considered the most difficult genre, don't assume that children who are learning English as a second language don't know how to use persuasion and can't be successful in persuasive writing. As a first step, try having your English learners work with partners or small groups to make persuasive posters that use a combination of drawing and writing to express a viewpoint.

Figure 13–4 Independent writing: A fourth grader's lost-and-found poster

poster illustrated in Figure 13–4 to help locate Liverwurst, the baby rhinoster-wurst that is missing from the circus. In the story, Liverwurst is finally found and saved from a terrible fate: becoming the world's first rhino-burger. Kyle's poster provides the important logical-appeal information and picture typically found on lost-and-found posters. In addition, a reward is promised. Liverwurst's tears add a tug-at-your-heart emotional appeal, too.

As part of a unit on drugs, a class of sixth graders designed posters to display in their community to warn youngsters about the dangers of drugs. In the poster presented in Figure 13–5, the student used a logical cause-and-effect

Figure 13–5 Independent writing: A sixth grader's poster about drugs

appeal to warn of the dangers of driving under the influence of alcohol or drugs. The poster is particularly powerful because the student used *gamble* and other loaded words in his caption.

Persuasive Letters

Children write letters to persuade family members and friends. As with other types of letters, these letters are written to real audiences and are mailed. As part of a unit on drugs, students in a fifth-grade class each chose a family member or a friend to write a persuasive letter to. Some children wrote to parents or grandparents, arguing that they should stop smoking; others wrote to siblings or friends, urging them not to take drugs or not to mix drinking and driving. Fifth grader Tom wrote this letter to his friend Mike:

Dear Mike,

    I think drugs are very bad. They hurt people a lot and they can cost money. Mike, I know you're 15 and you don't think drugs can hurt you, but you can get addicted to drugs just the same as everybody else.

    You can get hurt taking drugs, Mike. Some of the possible consequences are that you may get hurt dealing drugs, you may get AIDS by sharing infected needles or the pressure may become so great you just commit sui-

Figure 13–6 Independent writing: A seventh grader's letter to the editor
Source: The Norman (Okla.) *Transcript.* Reprinted with permission.

Editor, The Transcript:

I am a student at Longfellow Middle School. I am writing to express my feelings on the price teenagers pay to get into the movie theater. In most movie theaters at the age of 13, they consider you an adult, so you have to pay full price. But you pay the adult price to see a children's movie. They say we aren't old enough to see these movies, yet they consider us adult enough to pay the adult price. Why is this? I strongly urge the movie theaters to think this through and change the price, so if you are an adult you pay the adult price to see an adult movie and if you are a child you pay to see a children's movie. I am not saying that at the age of 13 you should be able to see "R" rated movies, but I'm saying don't make us pay for them. Let us pay for what we see.

REBECCA PIERCE
Norman

cide. You might hurt others, too. You could rob a bank, hurt people in an auto accident, or just get violent and hurt someone. Michael, you might lose a friend and get into fights, be unpopular, or just be sad.

Drugs are out and it's the truth. More people are saying no to drugs. It isn't worth it, so be smart, not stupid, and don't get into trouble. Don't waste your time, and it costs lots of money to do drugs and you will be depressed a lot.

Many people say drugs are only as bad as cigarettes. That is not so. See Mike, you could go from $1 a day on cigarettes to $100 a day on heroin. Money and health problems arise from drugs. Each year, 200,000 are hurt by drugs and 25,000 people die from drug-related accidents. Half a million people are arrested for drugs each year.

So, doing drugs is wrong. This evidence is that you should not take any kind of drugs, Mike. I hope you make the right decision.

Your friend, Tom

In his letter, Tom uses appeals to reason, character, and emotion. He uses statistics and cause-and-effect arguments in his rational appeal to Michael not to use drugs. He says in his appeal to character that people who take drugs are stupid, and he evokes the universal fear of contracting AIDS in his appeal to emotion. Tom tells Michael that he might die or hurt other people if he takes drugs.

Persuasive letters can also be sent to newspapers. A letter sent to the editor of a local newspaper is presented in Figure 13–6. In this letter, seventh grade

Becky argues that the adult admission prices that teens pay at movies are unfair considering that they are not allowed to see adult movies.

Children also write persuasive letters as part of literature focus units; they assume the role of a character and write simulated letters to another character. Even though these letters are not mailed, students can exchange letters and write back from the viewpoint of another character. As part of a literature focus unit on *The Giver* (Lowry, 1993), seventh graders wrote persuasive letters from one character to another, offering advice about how to make the community better. Josh writes from Jonas's viewpoint:

> Dear Giver,
>
> Gabe and I are here in Elsewhere. It is a loving community. We are safe and happy. Now it is up to you to help the community. I think you should let them deal with the memories themselves and let them make choices. You have to teach them how to make choices and try to make them use them wisely.
>
> Let them use the memories for good. The memories of war would teach them that war is bad. The memories of color would let them enjoy life more, if they could see color. The feelings of love would make them very happy. They could learn from these memories. They could learn of the past, good or bad, sad or happy. If they have memories, they could have feelings. They could have wisdom. They could have happiness. They could be free.
>
> I know what you think. You think there would be chaos if the community had the memories. Bad and evil things could happen, but Giver, life is like that. You have the memories and you know what could happen. That's why you are there to help them.
>
> Your son,
> Jonas

Josh's letter is persuasive. He argues that when people have memories, they can become wise, happy, and free. In the final paragraph, Josh refutes a counterargument, that giving the people memories will lead to chaos, by suggesting that the Giver can help the community through the difficult adjustment.

Persuasive Essays

Children write persuasive essays in which they argue on topics they have strong beliefs and opinions about. For example, sixth grader Michael wrote the following essay about drinking soft drinks during class:

> I think we, the students of Deer Creek School, should be allowed to drink refreshments during class. One reason is that it seems to speed the pass-

ing of the day. Second, I feel it is unfair and rude for teachers to drink coffee and soft drinks in front of the students. Finally, I think if the students were not worried about making trips to the water fountain, they would concentrate more on school work. Being allowed to drink refreshments would be a wonderful addition to the school day.

Michael's essay is well organized with a well-articulated beginning, middle, and end. He begins by clearly stating his position in the first sentence. Next, he lists three reasons and cues readers to the reasons using the words *one reason, second,* and *finally.* In the last sentence, Michael concludes the argument by making a prediction.

On the topic of girls' right to play any sport, sixth grader Amy writes:

> I think there should be more sports for girls. Girls are capable of playing sports such as soccer and football. Some girls dislike basketball, but they want to participate in other sports. If girls could participate in other sports, they could learn to coordinate as a team. Everyone needs exercise and alternative activities would keep all females physically fit. Girls should have the chance to participate and excel in other sports.

Amy's essay also follows the three-part organizational structure, but she does not direct attention to her reasons using cue words as Michael did. She begins with a clear statement of her position, and at the end, she uses a summary or generalization to conclude her appeal.

As part of a thematic unit on the American Revolution, a class of fifth graders wrote persuasive essays. The teacher asked students to think about whether or not the American Revolution was a good or necessary thing. Did they favor the patriot or the loyalist position? Children brainstormed a list of reasons in support of the Revolution and a list of reasons in opposition. Then students picked one side or the other and wrote an essay articulating their position. They began by stating their position, provided at least three reasons to support their view, and then concluded the essay. Fifth grader Marshall wrote:

> I am in favor of the American Revolution and here are three of my reasons. First, after the colonists won the war, they could believe in God how they wanted. Next, if we didn't win the war, we would probably be British and not American. Third, after the war, the colonists could speak their mind without being tortured or killed. That is why I am for the American Revolution.

Tim took the opposing point of view and wrote:

> I'm against the American Revolution. I think it was a bad war and unnecessary for several reasons. The first reason is that the colonists were already pretty much free, and they didn't need to have a war. The second reason is

that there was way too much suffering, fighting, and loss of life. The last reason was that it was a tremendous loss of lots of money. These are three reasons why I'm against the Revolutionary War.

Advertisements and Commercials

Children are exposed to advertising as they watch television, listen to the radio, view billboard posters, and read magazines. Because so many advertisements are directed at children, it is essential that they learn to judge their claims critically (Rudasill, 1986; Tutolo, 1981). For example, do the sports shoes being advertised actually help you to run faster or jump higher? Will eating a certain breakfast cereal make you a better football player? Will having a certain toy make you more popular? To promote products, ideas, and services, advertisers use appeals to reason, character, and emotion, just as writers of other types of persuasive language do. However, advertisers may also use propaganda as they attempt to influence our beliefs and actions.

Two types of advertisements that elementary students can examine and compose are print advertisements and commercials. Children read print advertisements in magazines, as posters on bulletin boards, and as billboards. They view commercials on television and listen to them on the radio.

A small group of fifth graders created a commercial for a dating service they created called "Dream Date." In their commercial, children used testimonials and rewards as the propaganda devices. The children portrayed young women who met their husbands through the service and were living happily ever after. The rewards were a honeymoon for one young woman and becoming pregnant for another. An excerpt from the storyboard for the "Dream Date" commercial is presented in Figure 13–7. This storyboard was developed from the script and presents camera directions in the left column, a sketch of the scene in the middle column, and the script in the right column. After completing the storyboard, children rehearsed the commercial, added music and sound effects, and then presented the skit. Children enjoyed having their commercial videotaped so they could view it themselves.

Teaching Children to Write Persuasively

Teachers model and teach children about persuasive writing much like they teach the other writing genres. They introduce children to persuasive writing and explain what persuasion and propaganda are, share examples of persuasive writing in books children are reading, and provide opportunities for students to write persuasively.

Figure 13–7 Guided writing: An excerpt from the fifth grader's "Dream Date" storyboard

Introducing Persuasive Writing

Teachers introduce children to persuasive writing by examining how persuasion is used in everyday life. They talk with students about the points of view and positions that people take on various issues. Children might brainstorm a list of examples of persuasion they notice in their family, school, and community.

Baylor, B. (1982). *The best town in the world.* New York: Aladdin. (M)
Brown, M. W. (1997). *The important book.* New York: HarperCollins. (P)
Cohen, B. (1983). *Molly's pilgrim.* New York: Morrow. (M)
Cowcher, H. (1990). *Antarctica.* New York: Farrar, Straus & Giroux. (M)
Ness, E. (1966). *Sam, Bangs and moonshine.* New York: Holt. (P)
Scieszka, J. (1989). *The true story of the 3 little pigs!* New York: Viking. (P–M)
Siebert, D. (1991). *Sierra.* New York: HarperCollins. (M–U)
Turner, A. (1987). *Nettie's trip south.* New York: Macmillan. (M–U)
Van Allsburg, C. (1981). *Jumanji.* Boston: Houghton Mifflin. (M)
Van Allsburg, C. (1990). *Just a dream.* Boston: Houghton Mifflin. (M)
Van Allsburg, C. (1991). *The wretched stone.* Boston: Houghton Mifflin. (M–U)
Van Allsburg, C. (1985). *The polar express.* Boston: Houghton Mifflin. (M)
Weir, B., & Weir, W. (1991). *Panther dream: A story of the African rainforest.* New York: Hyperion. (M)
Yolen, J. (1992). *Encounter.* Orlando: Harcourt Brace. (M)
Zolotow, C. (1972). *William's doll.* New York: HarperCollins. (P)

Figure 13–8 Books with persuasive appeals

P = primary grades (K–2), M = middle grades (3–5), U = upper grades (6–8).

They collect advertisements from magazines and newspapers or make a display of photos of billboards and posters with persuasive arguments that they notice in the community. Through a series of minilessons, teachers can explain what persuasion is and compare it with propaganda.

Kindergarten and first-grade teachers often introduce persuasive writing using Margaret Brown's classic book, *The Important Book* (1997). On each page, something is described, and the most important characteristic or attribute is identified. The same format is used on each page, and young children can use the format as a pattern for their persuasive writing. A first-grade class used this pattern to write about firefighters:

> The important thing about firefighters is that they are brave. They fight fires with hoses and axes. They save people and pets from getting burned. They wear hats, coats, gloves, and boots to stay safe. But, the important thing about firefighters is that they are brave.

Through this patterned writing activity, children learn about brainstorming ideas, identifying the most important idea, and trying to convince others of their viewpoint.

Other teachers also share examples of trade books in which persuasion is used. They might share *Molly's Pilgrim* (Cohen, 1983), *Encounter* (Yolen, 1992), or another book in which the authors try to persuade readers to adopt their viewpoint. A list of books with persuasive appeals is presented in Figure 13-8. In *Molly's Pilgrim,* for example, Barbara Cohen argues that there are modern-day Pilgrims like Molly's mother who emigrated from Russia and came to America for religious freedom. Crowhurst's (1991) research suggests that literature should be used as a model for persuasive writing.

Teachers introduce children to persuasive writing through a series of minilessons in which children investigate persuasive techniques. Then children apply what they have learned to write persuasive letters and essays as part of literature focus units and social studies and science themes. The minilessons are important because research has shown that children benefit from direct instruction on persuasive writing (Crowhurst, 1991). Suggested topics for minilessons include: three ways to persuade people, the difference between persuasion and propaganda, the eight propaganda devices, how to organize an argument, how to develop a graphic organizer, and how to refute counterarguments. Through these lessons, children's increase their awareness of the power of persuasion and its pervasiveness today. Children also learn how arguments are organized so that they will be prepared to design persuasive posters and write persuasive letters and essays. Ms. Ohashi's minilesson on writing persuasive essays is presented in the minilesson feature on page 443.

Writing Persuasive Letters and Essays

Students use a process approach to develop and refine their persuasive letters and essays. Teachers often write a class collaboration composition with students to model the process before children begin writing their own letters or essays. Figure 13–9 shows the graphic organizer and final draft of a fourth-grade class's essay about pilgrims written after reading *Molly's Pilgrim* (Cohen, 1983). Then children use the writing process to write persuasive letters and essays. The steps are listed in the step-by-step feature on pages 444–445.

Writing Advertisements

Children learn to write advertisements through a series of minilessons in which they investigate persuasive appeals and propaganda techniques. Then children apply what they have learned to create print advertisements or television commercials for an idea or for a product or service they have created. These writing projects can be connected to literature focus units and social studies and science theme cycles. The steps in the teaching strategy are described in the step-by-step feature on page 447.

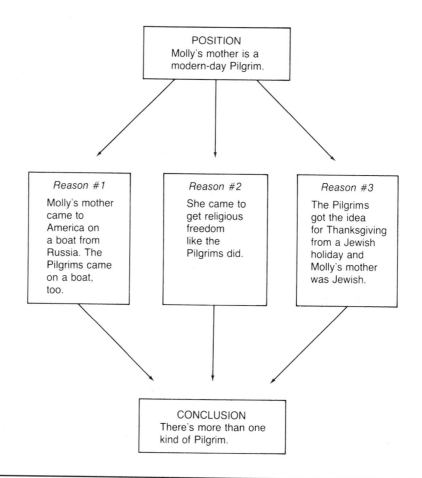

Figure 13–9 Shared writing: Fourth graders' graphic organizer and essay about *Molly's Pilgrim*

Persuasive Essays

Ms. Ohashi's fourth graders have studied persuasion, collected examples of persuasion in their community, and examined television commercials to determine the advertisers' purpose. Today the teacher is going to reread *The True Story of the 3 Little Pigs!* (Scieszka, 1989) and ask students to decide if they believe the wolf's version.

1. Introduce the topic

Ms. Ohashi quickly retells "The Three Little Pigs" to familiarize students with the traditional folktale and then introduces Scieszka's version of the story, told from the wolf's viewpoint.

2. Share examples

Ms. Ohashi reads *The True Story of the 3 Little Pigs!* aloud to students and asks them to think about the wolf's use of persuasion in the story.

3. Provide information

The students talk about the wolf's version, noting the wolf's persuasive techniques, including his friendly attitude and the repeated use of the word *true.* Next, they make a chart with three columns. In the left column, students list the wolf's bad deeds as described in the folktale; in the middle column, they list the wolf's arguments and excuses; and in the right column, they indicate whether or not they believe the wolf. For example, the pigs said that the wolf huffed and puffed and blew two houses down, and the wolf argued that he went to the pigs' houses to borrow a cup of sugar and sneezed. The children decide that they don't believe the wolf. After they finish the chart, it becomes clear that although they enjoyed the wolf's story, they believe the traditional version of the story.

4. Guide practice

"You don't believe the wolf's story, and you can explain your thinking in a persuasive essay," Ms. Ohashi explains. She quickly reviews how to complete a graphic organizer and write a persuasive essay. The children begin by identifying lines of reasoning for their arguments from the chart they developed in the previous step. They complete graphic organizers by listing three reasons for their decisions and their conclusions. Ms. Ohashi circulates around the classroom, providing assistance as needed and checking their completed graphic organizers. Then students write their essays independently.

5. Assess learning

Ms. Ohashi checks the students' graphic organizers as they complete them, and she will read their completed essays to assess their learning.

Step by Step: Writing Persuasive Letters and Essays

1. ***Identify a position and develop a list of reasons to support it.*** Children identify a position and plan their arguments using a graphic organizer. They include at least three reasons or pieces of evidence for their position, and older students also identify counterarguments that they need to refute.

2. ***Write the rough draft.*** Children write rough drafts, one or more paragraphs in length, incorporating the information listed on the graphic organizer.

3. ***Revise and edit the rough draft.*** Students revise and edit their rough drafts using feedback from classmates and the teacher. In addition, children can use a "Writer's Revision Checklist," as shown in Figure 13–10, to revise their drafts. After completing the checklist, they make any needed changes before sharing their compositions in writing groups. Children can also ask their classmates to complete a "Reader's

---

Writer's Revision Checklist

Name _____   Yes   No

1. At the beginning, did you state your position or opinion clearly?   ☐   ☐

    Write your position here:

    _____

    _____

    _____

2. In the middle, did you present three pieces of evidence to support your position?   ☐   ☐

    Write your pieces of evidence here:
    1. _____
    2. _____
    3. _____

3. At the end, did you lead your readers to the conclusion?   ☐   ☐

    How did you lead them?
    ☐ Gave a personal statement.
    ☐ Made a prediction.
    ☐ Summarized the three main points.

Figure 13–10 Revision checklists for persuasive writing

Revision Checklist," also shown in Figure 13–10. After classmates complete this form, writers compare their own responses with their classmates'. If readers' comments differ significantly from the writer's, then children should conclude that they are not communicating effectively and that additional revision is necessary. Then children proofread their essays, hunting for mechanical errors, and correct these errors.

4. ***Publish and share the composition.*** As with other types of writing, students' letters and essays should be shared with a real audience. Letters are sent to the person to whom they are addressed, and letters to the editor are submitted for possible publication in school and local newspapers. Persuasive essays can be read aloud from the author's chair or shared in some other way.

Figure 13–11 on page 446 shows the letter that fifth grader Lance wrote to his Uncle Bobby to try to persuade him to stop smoking as part of a health unit. Lance's graphic organizer is also shown in the figure.

Reader's Revision Checklist

Name _____   Yes   No

1. At the beginning, did the writer state his/her position or   ☐   ☐
   opinion clearly?

   Write the position here:

   _____

   _____

   _____

2. In the middle, did the writer present three pieces of   ☐   ☐
   evidence to support the position?

   Write the pieces of evidence here:
   1. _____
   2. _____
   3. _____

3. At the end, did the writer lead you to the conclusion?   ☐   ☐

   How did he/she lead you?
   ☐ Gave a personal statement.
   ☐ Made a prediction.
   ☐ Summarized the three main points.

Figure 13–10 *continued*

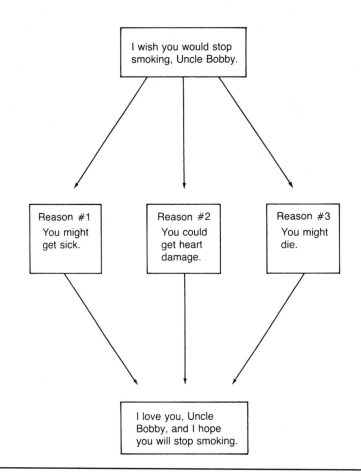

I wish you would stop
smoking, Uncle Bobby.

Reason #1
You might
get sick.

Reason #2
You could
get heart
damage.

Reason #3
You might
die.

I love you, Uncle
Bobby, and I hope
you will stop smoking.

Dear Uncle Bobby,

Please listen to me. I wish you would stop smoking. If you don't stop smoking, you will get sick
and you might die. You could get heart damage and that means you might die. I don't want you
to die.

There is a disease called emphysema. If you smoke long enough, you will get it. Then if you
try to walk a mile, it would seem like you walked fifty miles. Emphysema is a deadly disease.

When I hang around you and you smoke it is hurting my health as well as yours. You're
polluting the air in your own house. That means you are hurting your own family.

I think smoking can kill you. If I get to be president, I will take them cigarettes and burn them.
I think smoking is down right ridiculous.

If you stop smoking now, your heart will probably slow down and your lungs will be healthy
again. Your whole body will shape up.

I love you Uncle Bobby and I hope you will think about what I said and stop smoking.

Love,
Lance

Figure 13–11 Independent writing: A fifth grader's graphic organizer and persuasive letter

Step by Step: Writing Advertisements and Commercials

1. ***Examine advertisements.*** Children collect advertisements and commercials from television, radio, billboards, newspapers, magazines, and even T-shirts to examine. Working in small groups, children examine the advertisements and then decide how the writer is trying to persuade them to support the idea, use the service, or purchase the product. They can also compare the amount of text to the amount of picture space; appeals based on logic typically allocate more space to text than do appeals based on character or emotions.

2. ***Create a product or service to advertise.*** Working individually or in small groups, children create a product or service to advertise. Possible products include breakfast cereals, toys, beauty and diet products, and sports equipment. Students might create homework services and house-sitting services. They can also choose community or environmental issues to advertise.

3. ***Design the advertisement.*** Children design a print advertisement on a poster using art and text to present the message or write a script for a commercial. As they create their rough drafts, students use specific types of persuasive language and propaganda devices to sell their idea, product, or service. They choose the types of persuasion that are most effective for the audience they want to reach.

4. ***Refine and polish the advertisement.*** Children complete the writing process by meeting in writing groups to refine their advertisements. Writing group members make suggestions that deal with the most effective ways to sell the idea, product, or service. Children should take special care to edit print advertisements before making the final copy. For commercials, less attention is placed on editing because students will present the commercial as a skit. Instead, children will develop a storyboard in which they coordinate camera and stage directions with the script (as shown in Figure 13–7).

5. ***Present the advertisement.*** Children share their advertisements with an appropriate audience. The ads children develop can be shared with classmates and with children in other classes. They can display poster advertisements related to community and environmental issues around the community. Through live and videotaped presentations, children can also share commercials with classmates and students in other classes.

6. ***Critique the use of persuasion.*** Children critique their advertisements by listing the persuasive techniques and propaganda devices used in their print ads, and for commercials, they explain the techniques they used in the production.

Assessing Children's Persuasive Writing

The process that children use to plan and write persuasive compositions is at least as important as the quality of their arguments, and a process approach to assessment is recommended. The assessment instrument should include the steps that children move through as they develop their compositions, such as the following:

- Children create a plan for their writing using a scheme or cluster.
- Children write a rough draft.
- Children complete a "Writer's Revision Checklist."
- Children meet in writing groups to share their rough drafts.
- Children have classmates complete a "Reader's Revision Checklist."
- Children compare the revision checklists.
- Children make one or two revisions based on the revision checklists and suggestions made in writing groups.
- Children proofread their compositions and correct as many mechanical errors as possible.
- Children make a final copy of their compositions.
- Children share their compositions with an appropriate audience.

A checklist can be developed from these steps and used in assessing children's compositions. This checklist should be distributed to children before beginning the project so they can keep track of their progress.

When an assessment of the quality of children's writings is necessary, the three items included in the revision checklists (see Figure 13–10) can be used as criteria. It is important that the criteria children use in revising their compositions are the same ones that teachers use in judging the quality of their compositions.

Teachers assess children's advertisements according to the process that children use in creating the ads. Children should be able to identify and explain why they used particular persuasive techniques and propaganda devices. The steps in the process are subdivided into specific activities. A checklist for assessing children's advertisements is presented in Figure 13–12; this checklist can be easily adapted for commercials. Two columns are included on the right side of the checklist, one for children to track their progress and one for the teacher to use. As with other types of process assessment checklists, children should receive a copy of the checklist before beginning the advertisement project. In this way, children understand how they will be assessed and can monitor their own progress.

Assessment Checklist for Advertisements		
	Student's Check	Teacher's Check
Name _____		
1. Student examines advertisements and detects propaganda.	☐	☐
2. Student creates a product or service to advertise.	☐	☐
3. Student designs a print advertisement on a chart, using art and text to present the message.	☐	☐
4. Student meets in a writing group to share the advertisement.	☐	☐
5. Student revises the ad and makes at least one change.	☐	☐
6. Student and a partner edit the advertisement.	☐	☐
7. Student meets with the teacher for a final editing.	☐	☐
8. Student prepares a final copy of the advertisement.	☐	☐
9. Student shares the advertisement with an appropriate audience.	☐	☐
10. Student critiques the use of persuasion and propaganda in the advertisement.	☐	☐

Figure 13–12 An assessment checklist that focuses on both process and product

Teachers and children can also make rubrics to assess the quality of the final products that children create. The checklist in Figure 13–12 addresses both the process and the product, but rubrics focus on product. A 3-point rubric for assessing advertisements that children write is shown in Figure 13–13. Both children and teachers can use the rubric. They place check marks beside the statements that best describe the advertisement; some check marks will be made in more than one level of the rubric. For example, a child may have a powerful picture ad without any text that makes three arguments. The teacher or child assessing the ad would place some check marks in the level 3 section and at least one check mark in the level 2 section. The score is determined according to the section in which most of the check marks are placed.

Advertisements Rubric

---

3   VERY PERSUASIVE ADVERTISMENT

- Focuses on a single product.
- The picture and words are arranged on the page to make a strong statement.
- Both the picture and the words are persuasive.
- Two or more arguments are shown.
- There are no spelling or other mechanical errors.

---

2   PERSUASIVE ADVERTISEMENT

- Focuses on a single product.
- The picture and words fill up the page.
- Either the picture or the words are persuasive.
- One argument is shown.
- Spelling and other errors do not get in the way of the message.

---

1   NOT PERSUASIVE ADVERTISEMENT

- The ad doesn't focus on a single product.
- The picture and words don't fill up the page.
- Neither the picture nor the words are persuasive.
- No arguments are shown.
- Spelling and other errors make the ad hard to read and understand.

Figure 13–13 A rubric for assessing advertisements that students create

ANSWERING TEACHERS' QUESTIONS ABOUT . . .

Persuasive Writing

1. You must be kidding. My primary graders can't write persuasively.

Even first and second graders use persuasion in their everyday talk. With guidance and encouragement, they can use the same kinds of persuasion in their writing. The Mother's Day letters that Mrs. Carson's second graders wrote (see Figure 13–1) are good examples of the kind of persuasive writing primary-grade students can do.

2. I'm confused. What's the difference between persuasion and propaganda?

That's a good question. People use both persuasion and propaganda to influence someone to do or believe something. In both, people use appeals to reason, character, and feelings. The difference is that propagandists may use deceptive language and propaganda devices that distort, conceal, or exaggerate. The line between persuasion and propaganda is thin. Because it is so easy to cross back and forth between the two, children must learn to detect propaganda in order not to be swayed by it. One of the best ways for children to learn this is through writing persuasive essays and advertisements themselves.

3. Writing advertisements seems awfully time-consuming.

Yes, it does take time to teach children about persuasive language and propaganda devices. It also takes time for children to invent products or services and write ads or commercials. However, these activities teach children so much about oral and written language and consumer issues that it is worth the time. As children are examining ads, they use critical-thinking skills and learn to be more careful consumers as well as to read and write.

4. Can I tie persuasive writing to content areas?

Yes, children can write persuasively about topics they are learning in science and social studies. For example, they can argue about historical events and even about contributions of various historical figures. They can investigate current issues about immigration quotas, English as the official language of the United States, or the rights of Native Americans. They can clarify positions on scientific concepts and consider topical issues such as nuclear energy, global warming, pollution, and conservation efforts.

References

Professional References

Akroyd, S. (1995). Forming a parent reading-writing class: Connecting cultures, one pen at a time. *The Reading Teacher, 48,* 580–585.

Allen, C. A. (2001). *The multigenre research paper: Voice, passion, and discovery in grades 4–6.* Portsmouth, NH: Heinemann.

Anderson, K. F. (1985). The development of spelling ability and linguistic strategies. *The Reading Teacher, 39,* 140–147.

Applebee, A. N. (1978). *The child's concept of story: Ages 2 to 17.* Chicago: University of Chicago Press.

Applebee, A. N. (1980). Children's narratives: New directions. *The Reading Teacher, 34,* 137–142.

Applebee, A. N., & Langer, J. A. (1983). Instructional scaffolding: Reading and writing and natural language activities. *Language Arts, 60,* 168–175.

Applebee, A. N., Langer, J. A., & Mullis, I. V. (1986). *The writing report card: Writing achievement in American schools.* Princeton, NJ: Educational Testing Service.

Ashton-Warner, S. (1965). *Teacher.* New York: Simon & Schuster.

Atwell, N. (1987). *In the middle: Writing, reading, and learning with adolescents.* Portsmouth, NH: Heinemann.

Atwell, N. (1998). *In the middle: New understandings about writing, reading, and learning* (2nd ed.). Portsmouth, NH: Heinemann.

Au, K. H. (1992). Constructing the theme of a story. *Language Arts, 69,* 106–111.

Baker, E. C. (1994). Writing and reading in a first-grade writers' workshop: A parent's perspective. *The Reading Teacher, 47,* 372–377.

Bangert-Drowns, R. L. (1993). The word processor as an instructional tool: A meta-analysis of word processing in writing instruction. *Review of Educational Research, 63,* 69–93.

Barbe, W. B., Wasylyk, T. M., Hackney, C. S., & Braun, L. A. (1984). *Zaner-Bloser creative growth in handwriting (grades K–8).* Columbus, OH: Zaner-Bloser.

Barnes, D., Morgan, K., & Weinhold, K. (Eds.). (1997). *Writing process revisited: Sharing our stories.* Urbana, IL: National Council of Teachers of English.

Barone, D. (1990). The written responses of young children: Beyond comprehension to story understanding. *The New Advocate, 3,* 49–56.

Bear, D. R., Invernizzi, M., Templeton, S., & Johnston, F. (2003). *Words their way: Word study for phonics, vocabulary, and spelling instruction.* Upper Saddle River, NJ: Merrill/Prentice Hall.

Beers, J. W., & Henderson, E. H. (1977). A study of developing orthographic concepts among first graders. *Research in the Teaching of English, 11,* 133–148.

Bereiter, C., & Scardamalia, M. (1982). From conversation to composition: The role of instruction in the developmental process. In R. Glaser (Ed.), *Advances in instructional psychology* (Vol. 2, pp. 1–64). Hillsdale, NJ: Erlbaum.

Bergman, J. L. (1992). SAIL—A way to success and independence for low-achieving readers. *The Reading Teacher, 45,* 598–602.

Berrill, D. P., & Gall, M. (2000). *Penpal programs in primary classrooms.* Markham, Ontario, Canada: Pembroke.

Berthoff, A. (1981). *The making of meaning.* Upper Montclair, NJ: Boynton/Cook.

Betza, R. E. (1987). Online: Computerized spelling checkers: Friends or foes? *Language Arts, 64,* 438–443.

Bingham, A. (1988). Using writing folders to document student progress. In T. Newkirk & N. Atwell (Eds.), *Understanding writing: Ways of observing, learning, and teaching K–8* (2nd ed.) (pp. 216–225). Portsmouth, NH: Heinemann.

Bode, B. A. (1989). Dialogue journal writing. *The Reading Teacher, 42,* 568–571.

Bonin, S. (1988). Beyond storyland: Young writers can tell it other ways. In T. Newkirk & N. Atwell (Eds.), *Understanding writing* (2nd ed.). (pp. 47–51). Portsmouth, NH: Heinemann.

Bottomley, D. M., Henk, W. A., & Melnick, S. A. (1998/1999). Assessing children's views about themselves as writers using the Writer Self-Perception Scale. *The Reading Teacher, 51,* 286–296.

Boyd, R. (1985). The message board: Language comes alive. In J. M. Newman (Ed.), *Whole language: Theory in use* (pp. 91–98). Portsmouth, NH: Heinemann.

Bratcher, S. (1994). *Evaluating children's writing: A handbook of communication choices for classroom teachers.* New York: St. Martin's Press.

Britton, J. (1970a). *Language and learning.* New York: Penguin Books.

Britton, J. (1970b). *Language and thought.* Harmondsworth: Penguin Books.

Britton, J., Burgess, T., Martin, N., McLeod, A., & Rosen, H. (1975). *The development of writing abilities* (11–18). London: Macmillan.

Bromley, K. D. (1996). *Webbing with literature: Creating story maps with children's books* (2nd ed.). Boston: Allyn & Bacon.

Bruce, B., Michaels, S., & Watson-Gegeo, K. (1985). How computers can change the writing process. *Language Arts, 62,* 143–149.

Butler, S., & Cox, B. (1992). DISKovery: Writing with a computer in grade one: A study in collaboration. *Language Arts, 69,* 633–640.

Button, K., Johnson, M. J., & Furgerson, P. (1996). Interactive writing in a primary classroom. *The Reading Teacher, 49,* 446–454.

Cairney, T. (1990). Intertextuality: Infectious echoes from the past. *The Reading Teacher, 43,* 478–484.

Cairney, T. (1992). Fostering and building students' intertextual histories. *Language Arts, 69,* 502–507.

Calkins, L. M. (1980). When children want to punctuate: Basic skills belong in context. *Language Arts, 57,* 567–573.

Calkins, L. M. (1983). *Lessons from a child: On the teaching and learning of writing.* Portsmouth, NH: Heinemann.

Calkins, L. M. (1986). *The art of teaching writing.* Portsmouth, NH: Heinemann.

Calkins, L. M. (1991). *Living between the lines.* Portsmouth, NH: Heinemann.

Calkins, L. M. (1996). *The art of teaching writing* (2nd ed.). Portsmouth, NH: Heinemann.

Cambourne, B., & Turbill, J. (1994). *Responsive evaluation: Making valid judgments about student literacy.* Portsmouth, NH: Heinemann.

Cecil, N. L. (1994). *For the love of poetry: Poetry for every learner.* Winnipeg, Canada: Peguis.

Clay, M. M. (1975). *What did I write?* Portsmouth, NH: Heinemann.

Clay, M. M. (1991). *Becoming literate: The construction of inner control.* Portsmouth, NH: Heinemann.

Cochran-Smith, M. (1991). Word processing and writing in elementary classrooms: A critical review of related literature. *Review of Educational Research, 61,* 107–155.

Cochran-Smith, M., Kahan, J., & Pares, C. L. (1988). When word processors come into the classroom. In J. L. Hoot and S. B. Silvern (Eds.), *Writing with computers in the early grades* (pp. 43–74). New York: Teachers College Press.

Cohle, D. M., & Towle, W. (2001). *Connecting reading and writing in the intermediate grades.* Newark, DE: International Reading Association.

Collins, J. L. (1998). *Strategies for struggling writers.* New York: Guilford.

Cordeiro, P., Giacobbe, M. E., & Cazden, C. (1983). Apostrophes, quotation marks, and periods: Learning punctuation in the first grade. *Language Arts, 60,* 323–332.

Coughlan, M. (1988). Let the students show us what they know. *Language Arts, 65,* 375–378.

Crowhurst, M. (1991). Interrelationships between reading and writing persuasive discourse. *Research in the Teaching of English, 25,* 314–338.

Crowhurst, M. (1992). Some effects of corresponding with an older audience. *Language Arts, 69,* 268–273.

Crowhurst, M., & Piche, G. L. (1979). Audience and mode of discourse effects on syntactic complexity in writing at two grade levels. *Research in the Teaching of English, 13,* 101–109.

Cunningham, P. M. (1995). *Phonics they use: Words for reading and writing* (2nd ed.). New York: HarperCollins.

Cunningham, P. M., & Cunningham, J. W. (1992). Making words: Enhancing the invented spelling-decoding connection. *The Reading Teacher, 46,* 106–115.

Cunningham, P. M., & Hall, D. P. (1994). *Making words: Multilevel, hands-on, developmentally appropriate spelling and phonics activities.* Parsippany, NJ: Good Apple.

Dahl, K. L., & Freppon, P. A. (1995). A comparison of inner-city children's interpretations of reading and writing instruction in the early grades in skills-based and whole language classrooms. *Reading Research Quarterly, 30,* 50–74.

Daiute, C. (1992). Multimedia composing: Extending the resources of kindergarten to writers across the grades. *Language Arts, 69,* 250–260.

D'Aoust, C. (1992). Portfolios: Process for students and teachers. In K. B. Yancey (Ed.), *Portfolios in the writing classroom: An introduction* (pp. 39–48). Urbana, IL: National Council of Teachers of English.

daSilva, K. E. (2001). Drawing on experience: Connecting art and language. *Primary Voices K–6, 10* (2), 2–8.

de Beaugrande, R. (1980). *Text, discourse, and process.* Norwood, NJ: Ablex.

de Fina, A. A. (1992). *Portfolio assessment: Getting started.* New York: Scholastic.

DeGroff, L. (1990). Is there a place for computers in whole language classrooms? *The Reading Teacher, 43,* 568–572.

Dekker, M. M. (1991). Books, reading, and response: A teacher-researcher tells a story. *The New Advocate, 4,* 37–46.

Delpit, L. (1987). The silenced dialogue: Power and pedagogy in educating other people's children. *Harvard Educational Review, 58,* 280–298.

Delpit, L. (1991). A conversation with Lisa Delpit. *Language Arts, 68,* 541–547.

Devine, T. G. (1982). *Listening skills schoolwide: Activities and programs.* Urbana, IL: ERIC Clearinghouse on Reading and Communication Skills and the National Council of Teachers of English.

Diederich, P. B. (1974). *Measuring growth in English.* Urbana, IL: National Council of Teachers of English.

Dorotik, M., & Betzold, M. R. (1992). Expanding literacy for all. *The Reading Teacher, 45,* 574–578.

Dressel, J. H. (1990). The effects of listening to and discussing different qualities of children's literature on the narrative writing of fifth graders. *Research in the Teaching of English, 24,* 397–414.

Dudley-Marling, C. (1996). Explicit instruction within a whole language framework: Teaching struggling readers and writers. In E. McIntyre & M. Pressley (Eds.), *Balanced instruction: Strategies and skills in whole language* (pp. 23–38). Norwood, MA: Christopher-Gordon.

Dudley-Marling, C., & Dippo, D. (1991). The language of whole language. *Language Arts, 68,* 548–554.

Duffy, G. G., & Roehler, L. R. (1987). Improving reading instruction through the use of responsible elaboration. *The Reading Teacher, 20,* 548–554.

Duffy, G. G., & Roehler, L. R. (1991). Teachers' instructional actions. In R. Barr, M. Kamil, P. Mosenthal, & P. Pearson (Eds.), *Handbook of reading research* (Vol. 2, pp. 861–884). White Plains, NY: Longman.

Duffy, G. G., Roehler, L. R., Sivan, E., Rackliffe, G., Book, C, Meloth, M. S., Vavrus, L. G., Wesselman, R., Putnam, J., & Bassiri, D. (1987). Effects of explaining the reasoning associated with using reading strategies. *Reading Research Quarterly, 22,* 347–368.

Dweck, C. S. (1986). Motivational processes affecting learning. *American Psychologist, 41,* 1040–1048.

Dyson, A. H. (1993). *Social worlds of children learning to write in an urban primary school.* New York: Teachers College Press.

Edelsky, C. (1983). Segmentation and punctuation: Developmental data from young writers in a bilingual program. *Research in the Teaching of English, 17,* 135–136.

Elbow, P. (1973). *Writing without teachers.* London: Oxford University Press.

Elbow, P. (2002). Writing to publish is for every student. In C. Weber (Ed.), *Publishing with students: A comprehensive guide* (pp. 1–8). Portsmouth, NH: Heinemann.

Elley, W., & Mangubhai, F. (1983). The impact of reading on second language learning. *Reading Research Quarterly, 19,* 53–67.

Emig, J. (1971). *The composing processes of twelfth graders.* Champaign, IL: National Council of Teachers of English.

Faigley, L., Cherry, R. D., Jolliffe, D. A., & Skinner, A. M. (1985). *Assessing writers' knowledge and processes of composing.* Norwood, NJ: Ablex.

Faigley, L., & Witte, S. (1981). Analyzing revision. *College Composition and Communication, 32,* 400–410.

Farr, R., & Tone, B. (1994). *Portfolio and performance assessment: Helping students evaluate their progress as readers and writers.* Fort Worth, TX: Harcourt Brace.

Farris, P. J. (1991). Handwriting instruction should not become extinct. *Language Arts, 68,* 312–314.

Fearn, L., & Farnan, N. (1998). *Writing effectively: Helping children master the conventions of writing.* Boston: Allyn & Bacon.

Ferreiro, E., & Teberosky, A. (1982). *Literacy before schooling.* Portsmouth, NH: Heinemann.

Fine, E. S. (1987). Marbles lost, marbles found: Collaborative production of text. *Language Arts, 64,* 474–487.

Five, C. L. (1986). Fifth graders respond to a changed reading program. *Harvard Educational Review, 56,* 395–405.

Fleming, M. (1985). Writing assignments focusing on autobiographical and biographical topics. In Fleming, M., & McGinnis, J. (Eds.), *Portraits: Biography and autobiography in the secondary school* (pp. 95–97). Urbana, IL: National Council of Teachers of English.

Fleming, M., & McGinnis, J. (Eds.). (1985). *Portraits: Biography and autobiography in the secondary school.* Urbana, IL: National Council of Teachers of English.

Fletcher, R., & Portalupi, J. (2001). *Writing workshop: The essential guide.* Portsmouth, NH; Heinemann.

Flood, J., Lapp, D., & Farnan, N. (1986). A reading-writing procedure that teaches expository paragraph structure. *The Reading Teacher, 39,* 556–562.

Flower, L. S., & Hayes, J. R. (1977). Problem-solving strategies and the writing process. *College English, 39,* 449–461.

Flower, L. S., & Hayes, J. R. (1981). A cognitive process theory of writing. *College Composition and Communication, 32,* 365–387.

Fountas, I. C., & Pinnell, G. S. (1996). *Guided reading: Good first teaching for all children.* Portsmouth, NH: Heinemann.

Freppon, P. A. (1991). Children's concepts of the nature and purpose of reading in different instructional settings. *Journal of Reading Behavior, 23,* 139–163.

Freppon, P. A., & Headings, L. (1996). Keeping it whole in whole language: A first grade teacher's phonics instruction in an urban whole language classroom. In E. McIntyre & M. Pressley (Eds.), *Balanced instruction: Strategies and skills in whole language* (pp. 65–80). Norwood, MA: Christopher-Gordon.

Frith, U. (1980). Unexpected spelling problems. In U. Frith (Ed.), *Cognitive processes in learning to spell.* London: Academic Press.

Fulwiler, T. (1985). Research writing. In M. Schwartz (Ed.), *Writing for many roles* (pp. 207–230). Upper Montclair, NJ: Boynton/Cook.

Fulwiler, T. (1987). *The journal book.* Portsmouth, NH: Boynton/Cook.

Gambrell, L. B. (1985). Dialogue journals: Reading-writing interaction. *The Reading Teacher, 38,* 512–515.

Garner, R. (1987). *Metacognition and reading comprehension.* Norwood, NJ: Ablex.

Gee, T. C. (1971). *The effects of written comment on exposition composition* (Doctoral dissertation, North Texas State University). Dissertation Abstracts International, 31, 3412A.

Geller, L. G. (1981). Riddling: A playful way to explore language. *Language Arts, 58,* 669–674.

Geller, L. G. (1985). *Wordplay and language learning for children.* Urbana, IL: National Council of Teachers of English.

Gentry, J. R. (1982). An Analysis of developmental spellings in *Gyns at wrk. The Reading Teacher, 36,* 192–200.

Gentry, J. R., & Gillet, J. W. (1993). *Teaching kids to spell.* Portsmouth, NH: Heinemann.

Gibbons, P. (2002). *Scaffolding language, scaffolding learning.* Portsmouth, NH: Heinemann.

Glasser, W. (1968). *Schools without failure.* New York: Harper & Row.

Golden, J. M. (1984). Children's concept of story in reading and writing. *The Reading Teacher, 37,* 578–584.

Goodman, K. S. (1973). Windows on the reading process. In K. S. Goodman and O. S. Niles (Eds.), *Miscue analysis.* Urbana, IL: National Council of Teachers of English.

Graves, D. H. (1975). An examination of the writing processes of seven-year-old children. *Research in the Teaching of English, 9,* 227–241.

Graves, D. H. (1976). Let's get rid of the welfare mess in the teaching of writing. *Language Arts, 53,* 645–651.

Graves, D. H. (1983). *Writing: Teachers and children at work.* Portsmouth, NH: Heinemann.

Graves, D. H. (1994). *A fresh look at writing.* Portsmouth, NH: Heinemann.

Graves, D. H., & Hansen, J. (1983). The author's chair. *Language Arts, 60,* 176–183.

Graves, D. H., & Sunstein, B. S. (Eds.). (1992). *Portfolio portraits.* Portsmouth, NH: Heinemann.

Greenlee, M. E., Hiebert, E. H., Bridge, C. A., & Winograd, P. N. (1986). The effects of different audiences on young writers' letter writing. In J. A. Niles & R. V. Lalik (Eds.), *Solving problems in literacy: Learners, teachers, and researchers* (pp. 281–289). Rochester, NY: National Reading Conference.

Greesen, W. E. (1977). Using writing about mathematics as a teaching technique. *Mathematics Teacher, 70,* 112–115.

Halliday, M. A. K. (1973). *Explorations in the functions of language.* London: Edward Arnold.

Halliday, M. A. K. (1975). *Learning how to mean: Explorations in the development of language.* London: Edward Arnold.

Halliday, M. A. K. (1980). Three aspects of children's language development: Learning language, learning through language, learning about language. In Y. M. Goodman, M. M. Haussler, & D. S. Strickland (Eds.), *Oral and written language development research: Impact on the schools* (pp. 7–19). Proceedings from the 1979–1980 IMPACT Conferences sponsored by the International Reading Association and the National Council of Teachers of English.

Hancock, M. R. (1992). Literature response journals: Insights beyond the printed page. *Language Arts, 69,* 36–42.

Hancock, M. R. (1993). Exploring and extending personal response through literature journals. *The Reading Teacher, 46,* 466–474.

Hansen, J. (1994). Literacy portfolios: Windows on potential. In S. Valencia, E. Hiebert, & P. Afflerbach (Eds.), *Authentic reading assessment: Practices and possibilities* (pp. 26–40). Newark, DE: International Reading Association.

Harrison, S. (1981). Open letter from a left-handed teacher: Some sinistral ideas on the teaching of handwriting. *Teaching Exceptional Children, 13,* 116–120.

Hayes, J. R., & Flower, L. S. (1986). Writing research and the writer. *American Psychologist, 41,* 1106–1113.

Heard, G. (2002). *The revision toolbox: Teaching techniques that work.* Portsmouth, NH: Heinemann.

Henderson, E. H. (1980). Word knowledge and reading disability. In E. H. Henderson & J. W. Beers (Eds.), *Developmental and cognitive aspects of learning to spell: A reflection of word knowledge* (pp. 138–148). Newark, DE: International Reading Association.

Henderson, E. H. (1990). *Teaching spelling* (2nd ed.). Boston: Houghton Mifflin.

Hidi, S., & Hildyard, A. (1983). The comparison of oral and written productions in two discourse modes. *Discourse Processes, 6,* 91–105.

Hillerich, R. L. (1977). Let's teach spelling—not phonetic misspelling. *Language Arts, 54,* 301–307.

Hipple, M. L. (1985). Journal writing in kindergarten. *Language Arts, 62,* 255–261.

Hoot, J. L., & Silvern, S. B. (Eds.). (1988). *Writing with computers in the early grades.* New York: Teachers College Press.

Horn, E. (1926). *A basic writing vocabulary.* Iowa City: University of Iowa Press.

Horn, E. (1957). Phonetics and spelling. *Elementary School Journal, 57,* 424–432.

Howell, H. (1978). Write on, you sinistrals! *Language Arts, 55,* 852–856.

Jenkins, C. B. (1996). *Inside the writing portfolio: What we need to know to assess children's writing.* Portsmouth, NH: Heinemann.

Johnson, T. D., Langford, K. G., & Quorn, K. C. (1981). Characteristics of an effective spelling program. *Language Arts, 58,* 581–588.

Kahn, J., & Freyd, P. (1990). Online: A whole language perspective on keyboarding. *Language Arts, 67,* 84–90.

Karelitz, E. B. (1988). Notewriting: A neglected genre. In T. Newkirk & N. Atwell (Eds.), *Understanding writing* (2nd ed.) (pp. 88–113). Portsmouth, NH: Heinemann.

Killgallon, D. (1997). *Sentence composing for middle school.* Portsmouth, NH: Heinemann.

Killgallon, D. (1998). Sentence composing: Notes on a new rhetoric. In C. Weaver (Ed.), *Lessons to share: On teaching grammar in context* (pp. 169–183). Portsmouth, NH: Heinemann.

King, M. (1985). Proofreading is not reading. *Teaching English in the Two-Year College, 12,* 108–112.

Koch, K. (1990). *Rose, where did you get that red?* New York: Vintage.

Koch, K. (2000). *Wishes, lies, and dreams: Teaching children to write poetry.* New York: HarperPerennial.

Krashen, S. (1989). We acquire vocabulary and spelling by reading: Additional evidence for the input hypothesis. *Modern Language Journal, 73,* 440–464.

Krogness, M. M. (1987). Folklore: A matter of the heart and the heart of the matter. *Language Arts, 64,* 808–818.

Kroll, B. M. (1978). Cognitive egocentrism and the problem of audience awareness in written discourse. *Research in the Teaching of English, 12,* 269–281.

Kroll, B. M. (1984). Audience adaptation in children's persuasive letters. *Written Communication, 1,* 407–427.

Kucer, S. B. (1991). Authenticity as the basis for instruction. *Language Arts, 68,* 532–540.

Laminack, L. L., & Wood, K. (1996). *Spelling in use: Looking closely at spelling in whole language classrooms.* Urbana, IL: National Council of Teachers of English.

Lamme, L. L., & Ayris, B. M. (1983). Is the handwriting of beginning writers influenced by writing tools? *Journal of Research and Development in Education, 17,* 32–38.

Lane, B. (1999). *Reviser's toolbox*. Shoreham, VT: Discover Writing Press.

Langer, J. A. (1985). Children's sense of genre. *Written Communication, 2,* 157–187.

Lehr, S. S. (1991). *The child's developing sense of theme: Responses to literature.* New York: Teachers College Press.

Lewin, L. (1992). Integrating reading and writing strategies using an alternating teacher-led, student-selected instructional pattern. *The Reading Teacher, 45,* 586–591.

Lindsay, G. A., & McLennan, D. (1983). Lined paper: Its effects on the legibility and creativity of young children's writings. *British Journal of Educational Psychology, 53,* 364–368.

Lucas, C. (1992). Introduction: Writing portfolios— changes and challenges. In K. B. Yancey (Ed.), *Portfolios in the writing classroom: An introduction* (pp. 1–11). Urbana, IL: National Council of Teachers of English.

Lukens, R. J. (1999). *A critical handbook of children's literature* (6th ed.). New York: Longman.

Lutz, W. (1984). Notes toward a description of doublespeak. *Quarterly Review of Doublespeak, 10,* 1–2.

Macon, J. M., Bewell, D., & Vogt, M. E. (1991). *Responses to literature, grades K–8.* Newark, DE: International Reading Association.

Mandler, J. M., & Johnson, N. S. (1977). Remembrance of things parsed: Story structure and recall. *Cognitive Psychology, 9,* 111–115.

Markham, L. R. (1976). Influences of handwriting quality on teacher evaluation of written work. *American Educational Research Journal, 13,* 277–283.

Martinelli, S. (1996). Integrated spelling in the classroom. *Primary Voices K–6, 4,* 11–15.

McGee, L. M., & Richgels, D. J. (1985). Teaching expository text structure to elementary students. *The Reading Teacher, 38,* 739–748.

McGee, L. M., & Richgels, D. J. (1996). *Literacy's beginnings: Supporting young readers and writers* (2nd ed.). Boston: Allyn & Bacon.

McGinley, W., & Madigan, D. (1990). The research "story": A forum for integrating reading, writing, and learning. *Language Arts, 67,* 474–483.

McGonegal, P. (1987). Fifth-grade journals: Results and surprises. In T. Fulwiler (Ed.), *The journal book* (pp. 201–209). Portsmouth, NH: Boynton/Cook.

McIntyre, E. (1996). Strategies and skills in whole language: An introduction to balanced teaching. In E. McIntyre & M. Pressley (Eds.), *Balanced instruction: Strategies and skills in whole language* (pp. 23–38). Norwood, MA: Christopher-Gordon.

McIntyre, E., & Pressley, M. (Eds.). (1996). *Balanced instruction: Strategies and skills in whole language.* Norwood, MA: Christopher-Gordon.

McKenzie, G. R. (1979). Data charts: A crutch for helping pupils organize reports. *Language Arts, 56,* 784–788.

McKenzie, L., & Tompkins, G. E. (1984). Evaluating students' writing: A process approach. *Journal of Teaching Writing, 3,* 201–212.

Meyer, B. J., & Freedle, R. O. (1984). Effects of discourse type on recall. *American Educational Research Journal, 21,* 121–143.

Mohr, M. M. (1984). *Revision: The rhythm of meaning.* Upper Montclair, NJ: Boynton/Cook.

Moore, M. A. (1989). Computers can enhance transactions between readers and writers. *The Reading Teacher, 42,* 608–611.

Moore, M. A. (1991). Electronic dialoguing: An avenue to literacy. *The Reading Teacher, 45,* 280–286.

Morrow, L. M. (1992). The impact of a literature-based program on literacy achievement, use of literature, and attitudes of children from minority backgrounds. *Reading Research Quarterly, 27,* 251–275.

Morrow, L. M. (1995). *Family literacy: Connections in schools and communities.* Newark, DE: International Reading Association.

Moss, B., Leone, S., & DiPillo, M. L. (1997). Exploring the literature of fact: Linking reading and writing through information trade books. *Language Arts, 74,* 418–429.

Murray, D. H. (1982). *Learning by teaching.* Montclair, NJ: Boynton/Cook.

Murray, D. H. (1985). *A writer teaches writing* (2nd ed.). Boston: Houghton Mifflin.

Murray, D. H. (1987). *Write to learn* (2nd ed.). Boston: Houghton Mifflin.

Murray, D. M. (1990). *Shoptalk: Learning to write with writers.* Portsmouth, NH: Heinemann.

Nathan, R. (1987). I have a loose tooth and other unphotographic events: Tales from a first-grade journal. In T. Fulwiler (Ed.), *The journal book* (pp. 187–192). Portsmouth, NH: Boynton/Cook.

Newby, T. J., Stepich, D. A., Lehman, J. D., & Russell, J. D. (1996). *Instructional technology for teaching and learning: Designing instruction, integrating computers, and using media.* Upper Saddle River, NJ: Merrill/Prentice Hall.

Newman, J. (1984). *The craft of children's writing.* Portsmouth, NH: Heinemann.

Newman, J. (1986). Online: Electronic mail and newspapers. *Language Arts, 63,* 736–741.

Newman, J. (1989). Online: From far away. *Language Arts, 66,* 791–797.

Niles, O. S. (1974). Organization perceived. In H. L. Herber (Ed.), *Perspectives in reading: Developing study skills in secondary schools* (pp. 57–76). Newark, DE: International Reading Association.

O'Donnell, R. C., Griffin, W. J., & Norris, R. C. (1967). *Syntax of kindergarten and elementary school children: A transformational analysis* (Research Report No. 8). Urbana, IL: National Council of Teachers of English.

Ogle, D. M. (1986). K-W-L: A teaching model that develops active reading of expository text. *The Reading Teacher, 39,* 564–570.

O'Hagan, L. K. (1997). It's broken—fix it! In S. Tchudi (Ed.), *Alternatives to grading student writing* (pp. 3–13). Urbana, IL: National Council of Teachers of English.

Oldfather, P. (1995). Commentary: What's needed to maintain and extend motivation for literacy in the middle grades. *Journal of Reading, 38,* 420–422.

Opie, I., & Opie, P. (1959). *The lore and language of school children.* Oxford: Oxford University Press.

Opitz, M. F., & Cooper, D. (1993). Adapting the spelling basal for spelling workshop. *The Reading Teacher, 47,* 106–113.

Pappas, C. C. (1991). Fostering full access to literacy by including information books. *Language Arts, 68,* 449–462.

Pappas, C. C. (1993). Is narrative "primary"? Some insights from kindergartners' pretend readings of stories and information books. *Journal of Reading Behavior, 25,* 97–129.

Paris, S. G., & Jacobs, J. E. (1984). The benefits of informed instruction for children's reading awareness and comprehension skills. *Child Development, 55,* 2083–2093.

Paris, S. G., Wasik, B. A., & Turner, J. C. (1991). The development of strategic readers. In R. Barr, M. L. Kamil, P. B. Mosenthal, & P. D. Pearson (Eds.), *Handbook of reading research* (Vol. 2, pp. 609–640). New York: Longman.

Parsons, L. (2001). *Revising and editing.* Markham, Ontario, Canada: Pembroke.

Pearson, P. D., & Gallagher, M. C. (1983). The instruction of reading comprehension. *Contemporary Educational Psychology, 8,* 317–344.

Perl, S. (1994). The composing processes of unskilled college writers. In S. Perl (Ed.), *Landmark essays on the writing process* (pp. 39–62). Davis, CA: Hermagoras Press.

Peyton, J. K., & Seyoum, M. (1989). The effect of teacher strategies on students' interactive writing: The case of dialogue journals. *Research in the Teaching of English, 23,* 310–334.

Piccolo, J. A. (1987). Expository text structures: Teaching and learning strategies. *The Reading Teacher, 40,* 838–847.

Pitcher, E. G., & Prelinger, E. (1963). *Children tell stories: An analysis of fantasy.* New York: International Universities Press.

Potter, G. (1989). Parent participation in the language arts program. *Language Arts, 66,* 21–28.

Pressley, M., & Harris, K. R. (1990). What we really know about strategy instruction. *Educational Leadership, 48,* 31–34.

Queenan, M. (1986). Finding grain in the marble. *Language Arts, 63,* 666–673.

Rafoth, B. A., & Rubin, D. L. (1984). The impact of content and mechanics on judgments of writing quality. *Written Communication, 1,* 446–458.

Ray, K. W. (2002). *What you know by heart: How to develop curriculum for your writing workshop.* Portsmouth, NH: Heinemann.

Read, C. (1975). *Children's categorization of speech sounds in English* (NCTE Research Report No. 17). Urbana, IL: National Council of Teachers of English.

Read, C. (1986). *Children's creative spelling.* London: Routledge & Kegan Paul.

Readence, J. E., Baldwin, R. S., & Head, M. H. (1987). Teaching young readers to interpret metaphors. *The Reading Teacher, 40,* 430–443.

Reutzel, D. H., & Hollingsworth, P. M. (1991). Reading comprehension skills: Testing the skills distinctiveness hypothesis. *Reading Research and Instruction, 30,* 32–46.

Reyes, M. de la L. (1991). A process approach to literacy using dialogue journals and literature logs with second language learners. *Research in the Teaching of English, 25,* 291–313.

Rhodes, L. K., & Nathenson-Mejia, S. (1992). Anecdotal records: A powerful tool for ongoing literacy assessment. *The Reading Teacher, 45,* 502–509.

Rico, G. L. (1983). *Writing the natural way.* Los Angeles: Tarcher.

Rief, L. (1992). *Seeking diversity: Language arts with adolescents.* Portsmouth, NH: Heinemann.

Roblyer, M. D., Edwards, J., & Havriluk, M. A. (1997). *Integrating educational technology into teaching.* Upper Saddle River, NJ: Merrill/Prentice Hall.

Rogovin, P. (2001). *The research workshop: Bringing the world into your classroom*. Portsmouth, NH: Heinemann.

Romano, T. (1987). *Clearing the way: Working with teenage writers*. Portsmouth, NH: Heinemann.

Romano, T. (1995). *Writing with passion: Life stories, multiple genres*. Portsmouth, NH: Heinemann/Boynton/Cook.

Romano, T. (2000). *Blending genre, altering style: Writing multigenre papers*. Portsmouth, NH: Heinemann/Boynton/Cook.

Rosen, H. (1986). The importance of story. *Language Arts, 63,* 226–237.

Rubenstein, S. (1998). *Go public: Encouraging student writers to publish*. Urbana, IL: National Council of Teachers of English.

Rubin, D. L., & Piche, G. L. (1979). Development in syntactic and strategic aspects of audience adaption skills in written persuasive communication. *Research in the Teaching of English, 13,* 293–316.

Rudasill, L. (1986). Advertising gimmicks: Teaching critical thinking. In J. Golub (Ed.), *Activities to promote critical thinking* (pp. 127–129). Urbana, IL: National Council of Teachers of English.

Rumelhart, D. (1975). Notes on a schema for stories. In D. G. Bobrow (Ed.), *Representation and understanding: Studies in cognitive science*. New York: Academic Press.

Ryder, R. J., & Hughes, T. (1997). *Internet for educators*. Upper Saddle River, NJ: Merrill/Prentice Hall.

Rynkofs, J. T. (1988). Send your writing folders home. In T. Newkirk & N. Atwell (Eds.), *Understanding writing: Ways of observing, learning, and teaching K–8* (2nd ed.) (pp. 226–235). Portsmouth, NH: Heinemann.

Salem, J. (1982). Using writing in teaching mathematics. In M. Barr, P. D'Arcy, & M. K. Healy (Eds.), *What's going on? Language/learning episodes in British and American classrooms, grades 4–13* (pp. 123–134). Montclair, NJ: Boynton/Cook.

Scardamalia, M., & Bereiter, C. (1986). Written composition. In M. Wittrock (Ed.), *Handbook of research on teaching* (3rd ed., pp. 778–803). New York: Macmillan.

Schmitt, M. C. (1990). A questionnaire to measure children's awareness of strategic reading processes. *The Reading Teacher, 43,* 454–461.

Schneider, J. J. (2001). No blood, guns, or gays allowed: The silencing of the elementary writer. *Language Arts, 78,* 415–425.

Schubert, B. (1987). Mathematics journals: Fourth grade. In T. Fulwiler (Ed.), *The journal book* (pp. 348–358). Portsmouth, NH: Boynton/Cook.

Searle, D., & Dillon, D. (1980). Responding to student writing: What is said or how it is said. *Language Arts, 57,* 773–781.

Serafini, F. (2001). *The reading workshop: Creating space for readers*. Portsmouth, NH: Heinemann.

Shaughnessy, M. P. (1977). *Errors and expectations: A guide for teachers of basic writing*. New York: Oxford University Press.

Shuy, R. W. (1987). Research currents: Dialogue as the heart of learning. *Language Arts, 64,* 890–897.

Smith, F. (1982). *Writing and the writer*. New York: Holt.

Smith, F. (1988). *Joining the literacy club: Further essays in education*. Portsmouth, NH: Heinemann.

Smith, J. (1991). DISKcovery: Goin' wild in HyperCard. *Language Arts, 68,* 674–680.

Smith, P. L., & Tompkins, G. E. (1988). Structured notetaking: A new strategy for content area readers. *Journal of Reading, 32,* 46–53.

Sommers, N. (1982). Responding to student writing. *College Composition and Communication, 33,* 148–156.

Sommers, N. (1994). Revision strategies of student writers and experienced writers. In S. Perl (Ed.), *Landmark essays on the writing process* (pp. 75–84). Davis, CA: Hermagoras Press.

Sowers, S. (1985). The story and the "all about" book. In J. Hansen, T. Newkirk, & D. Graves (Eds.), *Breaking ground: Teachers relate reading and writing in the elementary school* (pp. 73–82). Portsmouth, NH: Heinemann.

Stanford, B. (1988). Writing reflectively. *Language Arts, 65,* 652–658.

Staton, J. (1980). Writing and counseling: Using a dialogue journal. *Language Arts, 57,* 514–518.

Staton, J. (1987). The power of responding in dialogue journals. In Toby Fulwiler (Ed.), *The journal book* (pp. 47–63). Portsmouth, NH: Boynton/Cook.

Stauffer, R. G. (1970). *Directing the reading-thinking process*. New York: Harper & Row.

Stein, N. L., & Glenn, C. G. (1979). An analysis of story comprehension in elementary school children. In R. O. Freedle (Ed.), *New directions in discourse processing*. Norwood, NJ: Ablex.

Steinberg, M. (1991). Personal narratives: Teaching and learning writing from the inside out. In R. Nathan (Ed.), *Writers in the classroom* (pp. 1–13). Norwood, MA: Christopher-Gordon.

Stires, S. (1991). Thinking throughout the process: Self-evaluation in writing. In B. M. Power & R.

Hubbard (Eds.), *The Heinemann reader: Literacy in process* (pp. 295–310). Portsmouth, NH: Heinemann.

Strickland, J. (1997). From disk to hard copy: Teaching writing with computers. Portsmouth, NH: Boynton/Cook/Heinemann.

Tchudi, S. (Ed.). (1997). *Alternatives to grading student writing.* Urbana, IL: National Council of Teachers of English.

Temple, C., Nathan, R., Burris, N., & Temple, F. (1988). *The beginnings of writing* (2nd ed.). Boston: Allyn & Bacon.

Templeton, S. (1979). Spelling first, sound later: The relationship between orthography and higher order phonological knowledge in older students. *Research in the Teaching of English, 13,* 255–265.

Templeton, S. (1983). Using the spelling/meaning connection to develop word knowledge in older students. *Journal of Reading, 27,* 8–14.

Tiedt, I. (1970). Exploring poetry patterns. *Elementary English, 45,* 1082–1084.

Tierney, R., Carter, M., & Desal, L. (1991). *Portfolio assessment in the reading-writing classroom.* Norwood, MA: Christopher-Gordon.

Tompkins, G. E. (1992). Assessing the processes students use as writers. *Journal of Reading, 36,* 244–246.

Tompkins, G. E. (2002). *Language arts: Content and teaching strategies* (5th ed.). Upper Saddle River, NJ: Merrill/Prentice Hall.

Tompkins, G. E. (2003). *Literacy for the 21st century* (3rd ed.). Upper Saddle River, NJ: Merrill/Prentice Hall.

Tompkins, G. E., & Camp, D. E. (1988). Rx for writer's block. *Childhood Education, 64,* 209–214.

Tompkins, G. E., & Yaden, D. B., Jr. (1986). *Answering students' questions about words.* Urbana, IL: National Council of Teachers of English and the ERIC Clearinghouse on Reading and Communication Skills.

Tutolo, D. (1981). Critical listening/reading of advertisements. *Language Arts, 58,* 679–683.

Tway, E. (1980a). How to find and encourage the nuggets in children's writing. *Language Arts, 57,* 299–304.

Tway, E. (1980b). Teacher responses to children's writing. *Language Arts, 57,* 763–772.

Van DeWeghe, R. (1982). Spelling and grammar logs. In C. Carter (Ed.), *Nonnative and nonstandard dialect students: Classroom practices in teaching English, 1982–1983* (pp. 101–105). Urbana, IL: National Council of Teachers of English.

Wagner, B. J. (1986). *The effects of role-playing on written persuasion: An age and channel comparison of fourth and eighth graders.* Unpublished doctoral dissertation, University of Illinois at Chicago (University Microfilms No. 8705196).

Watson, J. J. (1991). An integral setting tells more than when and where. *The Reading Teacher, 44,* 638–646.

Weaver, C. (1996). *Teaching grammar in context.* Portsmouth, NH: Heinemann.

Weaver, C. (Ed.). (1998). *Lessons to share: On teaching grammar in context.* Portsmouth, NH: Heinemann.

White, E. M. (1985). *Teaching and assessing writing.* San Francisco: Jossey-Bass.

Wilde, J. (1988). The written report: Old wine in new bottles. In T. Newkirk & N. Atwell (Eds.), *Understanding writing* (2nd ed., pp. 179–190). Portsmouth, NH: Heinemann.

Wilde, J. (1993). *A door opens: Writing in fifth grade.* Portsmouth, NH: Heinemann.

Wilde, S. (1992). *You kan red this! Spelling and punctuation for whole language classrooms, K–6.* Portsmouth, NH: Heinemann.

Wilde, S. (1996). A speller's bill of rights. *Primary Voices K–6, 4,* 7–10.

Wilkinson, A., Barnsley, G., Hanna, P., & Swan, M. (1980). *Assessing language development.* Oxford: Oxford University Press.

Wilson, L. (1994). *Write me a poem: Reading, writing, and performing poetry.* Portsmouth, NH: Heinemann.

Winograd, P., & Hare, V. C. (1988). Direct instruction of reading comprehension strategies: The nature of teacher explanation. In C. Weinstein, E. Goetz, & P. Alexander (Eds.), *Learning and study strategies: Issues in assessment, instruction, and evaluation* (pp. 121–139). San Diego: Academic Press.

Wollman-Bonilla, J. E. (1989). Reading journals: Invitations to participate in literature. *The Reading Teacher, 43,* 112–120.

Wood, A. J. (1974). Some effects of involving parents in the curriculum. *Trends in Education, 35,* 39–45.

Zarnowski, M. (1988). The middle school student as biographer. *Middle School Journal, 19,* 25–27.

Children's Books

Adler, D. A. (1990). *A picture book of Helen Keller.* New York: Holiday House.

Ahlberg, J., & Ahlberg, G. (1986). *The jolly postman; or, other people's letters.* Boston: Little, Brown.

Aliki. (1988). *A weed is a flower: The life of George Washington Carver.* New York: Simon & Schuster.

Andersen, H. C. (1979). *The ugly duckling.* New York: Harcourt Brace Jovanovich.

Avi. (1991). *Nothing but the truth: A documentary novel*. New York: Orchard.

Babbitt, N. (1975). *Tuck everlasting*. New York: Farrar, Straus & Giroux.

Barrett, J. (1978). *Cloudy with a chance of meatballs*. New York: Macmillan.

Barrett, J. (1983). *A snake is totally tail*. New York: Atheneum.

Bayer, J. (1984). *A my name is Alice*. New York: Dial.

Baylor, B. (1982). *The best town in the world*. New York: Aladdin Books.

Bernstein, J. E. (1979). *Fiddle with a riddle: Write your own riddles*. New York: Dutton.

Bing, C. (2000). *Ernest Lawrence Thayer's Casey at the bat: A ballad of the republic sung in the year 1888*. Brooklyn, NY: Handprint Books.

Blos, J. (1979). *A gathering of days: A New England girl's journal, 1830–1832*. New York: Scribner.

Blume, J. (1972). *Tales of a fourth grade nothing*. New York: Dutton.

Blume, J. (1974). *The pain and the great one*. New York: Bradbury.

Bowen, G. (1994). *Stranded at Plimoth Plantation, 1626*. New York: HarperCollins.

Brown, M. (1954). *Cinderella*. New York: Scribner.

Brown, M. (1983). *What do you call a dumb bunny? And other rabbit riddles, games, jokes, and cartoons*. Boston: Little, Brown.

Brown, M. W. (1997). *The important book*. New York: HarperCollins.

Brown, R. (1996). *Toad*. New York: Puffin.

Bunting, E. (1991). *Fly away home*. New York: Clarion.

Burch, R. (1966). *Queenie Peavy*. New York: Viking.

Burch, R. (1980). *Ida Early comes over the mountain*. New York: Viking.

Burns, M. (1981). *The hink pink book*. Boston: Little, Brown.

Byars, B. (1970). *Summer of the swans*. New York: Viking.

Byars, B. (1977). *The pinballs*. New York: Harper.

Carle, E. (1969). *The very hungry caterpillar*. New York: Philomel.

Cleary, B. (1981). *Ramona Quimby, age 8*. New York: Morrow.

Cleary, B. (1983). *Dear Mr. Henshaw*. New York: Morrow.

Cleary, B. (1985). Dear author, answer this letter now . . . . *Instructor, 95*, 22–23, 25.

Cohen, B. (1983). *Molly's pilgrim*. New York: Lothrop, Lee & Shepard.

Cole, J. (1981). *A snake's body*. New York: Morrow.

Cole, J. (1992). *The magic school bus on the ocean floor*. New York: Scholastic.

Cowcher, H. (1990). *Antarctica*. New York: Farrar, Straus & Giroux.

Cox, J. A. (1980). *Put your foot in your mouth and other silly sayings*. New York: Random House.

Cushman, K. (1994). *Catherine, called Birdy*. New York: HarperCollins.

Dahl, R. (1961). *James and the giant peach*. New York: Knopf.

Dahl, R. (1978). *The enormous crocodile*. New York: Knopf.

de Gasztold, C. B. (1992). *Prayers from the ark*. New York: Viking.

Denenberg, B. (1996). *When will this cruel war be over? The Civil War diary of Emma Simpson*. New York: Scholastic.

de Paola, T. (1975). *The cloud book*. New York: Holiday House.

Draper, S. (1994). *Tears of a tiger*. New York: Atheneum.

Edwards, P. D. (2001). *Slop goes the soup: A noisy warthog word book*. New York: Hyperion.

Ehlert, L. (1995). *Snowballs*. San Diego: Harcourt Brace.

Fitzhugh, L. (1964). *Harriet the spy*. New York: Harper & Row.

Fleischman, P. (1985). *I am phoenix: Poems for two voices*. New York: HarperCollins.

Fleischman, P. (1988). *Joyful noise: Poems for two voices*. New York: HarperCollins.

Fleischman, P. (1991). *Bull Run*. New York: HarperCollins.

Forbes, E. (1970). *Johnny Tremain*. Boston: Houghton Mifflin.

Fox, P. (1973). *The slave dancer*. New York: Bradbury.

Fritz, J. (1973). *And then what happened, Paul Revere?* New York: Putnam.

Fritz, J. (1981). *Traitor: The case of Benedict Arnold*. New York: Viking.

Fritz, J. (1983). *The double life of Pocahontas*. New York: Putnam.

Funk, C. E. (1984). *A hog on ice and other curious expressions*. New York: Harper & Row.

Galdone, P. (1974). *Little Red Riding Hood*. New York: Seabury.

Galdone, P. (1984). *The teeny-tiny woman*. New York: Clarion.

George, J. C. (1972). *Julie of the wolves*. New York: Harper & Row.

Gibbons, G. (1987). *Weather forecasting*. New York: Four Winds Press.

Goble, P. (1989). *Iktomi and the berries*. New York: Orchard.

Gregory, K. (1996). *The winter of red snow: The Revolutionary War diary of Abigail Jane Stewart.* New York: Scholastic.

Gregory, K. (1999). *Cleopatra VII: Daughter of the Nile.* New York: Scholastic.

Gwynne, F. (1970). *The king who rained.* New York: Windmill Books.

Gwynne, F. (1976). *A chocolate moose for dinner.* New York: Windmill Books.

Gwynne, F. (1980). *The sixteen hand horse.* New York: Prentice Hall.

Gwynne, F. (1988). *A little pigeon toad.* New York: Simon & Schuster.

Harter, P. (1994). *Shadow play: Night haiku.* New York: Simon & Schuster.

Hawes, J. (1997). *Lady bug, lady bug, fly away home.* New York: Ty Crowell Co.

Hines, A. G. (1996). *When we married Gary.* New York: Greenwillow.

Hoban, L. (1982). *Arthur's pen pal.* New York: Harper & Row.

Howe, D., & Howe, J. (1979). *Bunnicula: A rabbit-tale of mystery.* New York: Atheneum.

Hunt, J. (1989). *Illuminations.* New York: Bradbury Press.

Hutchins, P. (1968). *Rosie's walk.* New York: Macmillan.

Janeczko, P. B. (1994). *Poetry from A to Z: A guide for young writers.* New York: Bradbury.

Kellogg, S. (1987). *Aster Aardvark's alphabet adventures.* New York: Morrow.

Kennedy, X. J., & Kennedy, D. M. (1999). *Knock at a star: A child's introduction to poetry* (rev. ed.). Boston: Little, Brown.

Kimmel, E. A. (2000). *The runaway tortilla.* Delray Beach, FL: Winslow Press.

King-Smith, D. (1995). *Babe the gallant pig.* New York: Random House.

Konigsburg, E. L. (1983). *From the mixed-up files of Mrs. Basil E. Frankweiler.* New York: Atheneum.

Kuskin, K. (1975). *Near the window tree.* New York: Harper & Row.

Kuskin, K. (1980). *Dogs and dragons, trees and dreams.* New York: Harper & Row.

Langstaff, J. (1974). *Oh, a-hunting we will go.* New York: Atheneum.

Lasky, K. (1983). *Beyond the divide.* New York: Macmillan.

Lasky, K. (1996). *A journey to the new world: The diary of Remember Patience Whipple.* New York: Scholastic.

Lasky, K. (2000). *The journal of Augustus Pelletier: The Lewis and Clark expedition, 1804.* New York: Scholastic.

Lasky, K. (2002a). *Elizabeth I: Red rose of the House of Tudor.* New York: Scholastic.

Lasky, K. (2002b). *A time for courage: The suffragette diary of Kathleen Bowen.* New York: Scholastic.

Lear, E. (1995). *Daffy down dilly: Silly limericks by Edward Lear.* Honesdale, PA: Wordsong.

L'Engle, M. (1962). *A wrinkle in time.* New York: Farrar, Straus & Giroux.

Lester, J. (1998). *To be a slave.* New York: Dial Books.

Lewis, C. S. (1950). *The lion, the witch and the wardrobe.* New York: Macmillan.

Lewis, J. P. (1995). *Black swan/white crow.* New York: Atheneum.

Lewis, R. (1968). *Of this world: A poet's life in poetry.* New York: Dial.

Lewis, R. (1970). *The way of silence: The prose and poetry of Basho.* New York: Dial.

Livingston, M. C. (Sel.). (1991). *Lots of limericks.* New York: McElderry Books.

Lobel, A. (1983). *Pigericks: A book of pig limericks.* New York: Harper & Row.

Lowry, L. (1979). *Anastasia Krupnik.* Boston: Houghton Mifflin.

Lowry, L. (1989). *Number the stars.* Boston: Houghton Mifflin.

Lowry, L. (1993). *The giver.* Boston: Houghton Mifflin.

MacLachlan, P. (1985). *Sarah, plain and tall.* New York: Harper & Row.

Macrorie, K. (1985). *Telling writing* (4th ed.). Upper Montclair, NJ: Boynton/Cook.

Maiorano, R. (1980). *Worlds apart: The autobiography of a dancer from Brooklyn.* New York: Coward.

Mammano, J. (1996). *Rhinos who surf.* San Francisco: Chronicle Books.

Mammano, J. (1999). *Rhinos who skateboard.* San Francisco: Chronicle Books.

Martin, B., Jr., & Archambault, J. (1985). *The ghost-eye tree.* New York: Holt, Rinehart and Winston.

Mayer, M. (1974). *Frog goes to dinner.* New York: Dial.

Mayer, M. (1981). *Liverwurst is missing.* New York: Four Winds Press.

Mayer, M. (1987). *The Pied Piper of Hamelin.* New York: Macmillan.

McCloskey, R. (1969). *Make way for ducklings.* New York: Viking.

McCord, D. (1962). *Take sky.* Boston: Little, Brown.

McCord, D. (1967). *Everytime I climb a tree.* Boston: Little, Brown.

McCord, D. (1977). *One at a time: Collected poems for the young.* Boston: Little, Brown.

McGill, A. (1999). *Molly Bannaky.* Boston: Houghton Mifflin.

McKissack, P. C. (1997). *A picture of freedom: The diary of Clotee, a slave girl*. New York: Scholastic.

McMillan, B. (1991). *Play day: A book of terse verse*. New York: Holiday House.

Most, B. (1991). *A dinosaur named after me*. San Diego: Harcourt Brace.

Musgrove, M. (1976). *Ashanti to Zulu: African traditions*. New York: Dial.

Myers, W. D. (2001). *The journal of Biddy Owens: The Negro leagues*. New York: Scholastic.

Naylor, P. R. (1991). *Shiloh*. New York: Atheneum.

Ness, E. (1966). *Sam, Bangs and moonshine*. New York: Holt.

Noyes, A. (1983). *The highwayman* (C. Mikolaycak, Illus.). New York: Lothrop, Lee & Shepard.

O'Dell, S. (1960). *Island of the blue dolphins*. Boston: Houghton Mifflin.

O'Neill, M. (1989). *Hailstones and halibut bones: Adventures in color*. Garden City, NJ: Doubleday.

The Oregon Trail (CD-ROM simulation game). (1997). Cambridge, MA: The Learning Company.

Paterson, K. (1977). *Bridge to Terabithia*. New York: Crowell.

Paul, A. W. (1991). *Eight hands round: A patchwork alphabet*. New York: HarperCollins.

Podendorf, I. (1981). *Insects*. New York: Children's Press.

Polacco, P. (1990). *Thunder cake*. New York: Philomel.

Prelutsky, J. (1976). *Nightmares: Poems to trouble your sleep*. New York: Greenwillow.

Prelutsky, J. (1977). *The snoop on the sidewalk and other poems*. New York: Greenwillow.

Prelutsky, J. (1980). *The headless horseman rides tonight: More poems to trouble your sleep*. New York: Greenwillow.

Prelutsky, J. (1982). *The baby uggs are hatching*. New York: Mulberry.

Prelutsky, J. (1983). *The Random House book of poetry for children*. New York: Random House.

Prelutsky, J. (1984). *The new kid on the block*. New York: Greenwillow.

Prelutsky, J. (1985). *My parents think I'm sleeping*. New York: Greenwillow.

Prelutsky, J. (1996). *A pizza the size of the sun: Poems by Jack Prelutsky*. New York: Greenwillow.

Provensen, A. (1995). *My fellow Americans: A family album*. San Diego, CA: Browndeer.

Rathmann, P. (1995). *Officer Buckle and Gloria*. New York: Putnam.

Russo, M. (1996). *Grandpa Abe*. New York: Greenwillow.

Rylant, C. (1985). *The relatives came*. New York: Bradbury Press.

Schwartz, A. (1972). *A twister of twists, a tangler of tongues*. New York: Harper & Row.

Scieszka, J. (1989). *The true story of the 3 little pigs!* New York: Viking.

Sendak, M. (1963). *Where the wild things are*. New York: Harper & Row.

Seuss, Dr. (1979). *Oh say can you say?* New York: Random House.

Shannon, C. (1996). *Spring: A haiku story*. New York: Greenwillow.

Siebert, D. (1991). *Sierra*. New York: HarperCollins.

Silverstein, S. (1974). *Where the sidewalk ends*. New York: Harper & Row.

Silverstein, S. (1981). *The light in the attic*. New York: Harper & Row.

Snyder, Z. K. (1967). *The Egypt game*. Boston: Atheneum.

Soto, G. (1995). *Chato's kitchen*. New York: Putnam.

Speare, E. G. (1958). *The witch of Blackbird Pond*. Boston: Houghton Mifflin.

Speare, E. G. (1983). *The sign of the beaver*. Boston: Houghton Mifflin.

Spier, P. (1971). *Gobble growl grunt*. New York: Doubleday.

Spier, P. (1972). *Crash! Bang! Boom!: A book of sounds*. New York: Doubleday.

Stanley, D. (2000). *Michelangelo*. New York: HarperCollins.

Steig, W. (1982). *Doctor De Soto*. New York: Farrar, Straus & Giroux.

Sterne, N. (1979). *Tyrannosaurus wrecks: A book of dinosaur riddles*. New York: Crowell.

Stevens, J. (1987). *The three billy goats Gruff*. San Diego: Harcourt Brace Jovanovich.

Taylor, M. C. (1976). *Roll of thunder, hear my cry*. New York: Dial.

Terban, M. (1982). *Eight ate: A feast of homonym riddles*. New York: Clarion.

Terban, M. (1983). *In a pickle and other funny idioms*. New York: Clarion.

Terban, M. (1987). *Mad as a wet hen! and other funny idioms*. New York: Clarion.

Terban, M. (1990). *Punching the clock: Funny action idioms*. New York: Clarion.

Terban, M. (1991). *Hey, hay: A wagonful of funny homonym riddles*. New York: Clarion.

Turner, A. (1987). *Nellie's trip south*. New York: Macmillan.

Van Allsburg, C. (1981). *Jumanji*. Boston: Houghton Mifflin.

Van Allsburg, C. (1984). *The mysteries of Harris Burdick*. Boston: Houghton Mifflin.

Van Allsburg, C. (1987). *The Z was zapped*. Boston: Houghton Mifflin.

Van Allsburg, C. (1991). *The wretched stone*. Boston: Houghton Mifflin.

Ventura, P., & Cesarani, G. P. (1985). *In search of Tutankhamun*. Morristown, NJ: Silver Burdett.

Viorst, J. (1977). *Alexander and the terrible, horrible, no good, very bad day*. New York: Atheneum.

Viorst, J. (1981). *If I were in charge of the world and other worries*. New York: Atheneum.

Waber, B. (1972). *Ira sleeps over*. Boston: Houghton Mifflin.

White, E. B. (1980). *Charlotte's web*. New York: Harper & Row.

White, E. E. (2002). *The journal of Patrick Seamus Flaherty: United States Marine Corps, Khe Sanh, Vietnam, 1968*. New York: Scholastic.

Williams, V. B. (1982). *A chair for my mother*. New York: Mulberry.

Wood, A. (1982). *Quick as a cricket*. London: Child's Play.

Wyeth, S. D. (2001). *Freedom's wings: Corey's Underground Railroad diary* (Book 1). New York: Scholastic.

Wyeth, S. D. (2002). *Flying free: Corey's Underground Railroad diary* (Book 2). New York: Scholastic.

Yolen, J. (1987). *Owl moon*. New York: Philomel.

Yolen, J. (1992). *Encounter*. Orlando: Harcourt Brace.

Yolen, J. (1993). *Weather report: Poems selected by Jane Yolen*. Wordsong/Honesdale, PA: Boyds Mills Press.

Zemach, M. (1983). *The little red hen*. New York: Farrar, Straus & Giroux.

Zolotow, C. (1972). *William's doll*. New York: Harper & Row.

Author Index

Subject Index